THE PRAISE OF FOLLY
AND OTHER WRITINGS

A NEW TRANSLATION
WITH
CRITICAL COMMENTARY

Norton Critical Editions in the History of Ideas

A NORTON CRITICAL EDITION

Desiderius Erasmus

THE PRAISE OF FOLLY AND OTHER WRITINGS

A NEW TRANSLATION
WITH
CRITICAL COMMENTARY

Chosen, translated, and edited by

ROBERT M. ADAMS

PROFESSOR EMERITUS OF ENGLISH
UNIVERSITY OF CALIFORNIA AT LOS ANGELES

W · W · NORTON & COMPANY · *New York* · *London*

From Huizinga, *Erasmus of Rotterdam* (New York, 1924; reissued London, Phaidon Press, 1952), 101–116. Reprinted by permission of Phaidon Press Limited.

From H. R. Trevor Roper, *Men and Events: Historical Essays* (New York: Hippocrene Books, 1977), 35–60 (Chapter VII). Reprinted by permission of Octagon Books, A Division of Hippocrence Books, Inc.

From *Renaissance Quarterly* 23 [1970] 1–14, reprinted by permission of the Renaissance Society of America.

From P. S. Allen, *The Age of Erasmus* (England: Clarendon Press, 1914, 1963), 252–275 (Chapter X).

From Mikhail Bakhtin, *Rabelais and His World*, translated by Helene Iswolsky. Reprinted by permission of The MIT Press.

Hans Holbein, from LeClerc's 1703 edition of *Erasmi Opera Omnia*, Vol. IV. This and other Holbein pictures which appear throughout the text are reprinted by permission of Cornell University Library.

Printed in the United States of America.

The text of this book is composed in Electra, with display type set in Bernhard Modern. Composition by Vail-Ballou Manufacturing by Maple-Vail Book Group Book design by Antonina Krass

First Edition

Library of Congress Cataloging in Publication Data

ISBN 0-393-95749-7

W. W. Norton & Company, Inc., 500 Fifth Avenue, New York, N.Y. 10110
W. W. Norton & Company Ltd., 10 Coptic Street, London WC1A 1PU

7 8 9 0

Contents

Editor's Preface

As modern curricula divide up the teaching of literature according to the language in which it was written, there isn't much room for a displaced person like Erasmus. He always described himself as a citizen of Rotterdam, but in fact his mother moved there only to conceal the birth of a son whom his father could never acknowledge because he was already in holy orders. Whether Erasmus could ever speak fluent Dutch is in question; he certainly never wrote in that tongue, and never resided in his native city—if it was his native city—any longer than he had to. Before he was out of his teens, his guardians had stuffed him into a monastery, where Latin became as much of a native tongue as he ever had. But Latin was not a language that came naturally to anyone in the fifteenth century. It amounted to a composite tongue, based on the literary Latin of Horace, Virgil, and Cicero, but twisted into new shapes by centuries of theological discussion and dispute, enriched and perhaps vulgarized by its use in the law courts and marketplaces of Europe. Erasmus used it brilliantly and taught others to use it; in the early sixteenth century, before most of the vernacular languages had established themselves as capable of varied literary effects, Erasmus's sort of Latin really was the lingua franca of Europe, his best means of reaching an international audience. But the future lay with the vernacular tongues; and it's been a permanent hobble on Erasmus's reputation that he must be reached, everywhere, through the second-best medium of translation.

His prestige, if irregular, and always more learned than popular, has been persistent. If no country can claim him as a true native son (for he lived in Belgium, Switzerland, Italy, England, and Germany, as well as Holland, and rarely for long in any one place), his real home has always been in the republic of letters. Wherever the values of literary scholarship are prized, Erasmus has found a welcome. No doubt the world holds values deeper than those of literary scholarship, and for periods of time these deeper currents have drowned out the clear, quiet, intelligent voice of the first and greatest humanist. But after almost half a millennium, Erasmus's power of survival has defined itself in its own distinctive way. The keenness of his intelligence, the gaiety of his wit, and the independence of his judgment have not faded with time, and don't seem likely to. That Erasmus can continue to accomplish this in a language completely alien to most of his readers suggests how much more deeply "style" is settled in the mind than a mere knack for verbal arrangement could be.

It would be an idle, artificial exercise to arrange the works of Erasmus in some formal, predetermined scheme, even something as arbitrary as a chronological sequence. He did not write his books in any clearly developing order, but settled on topics as they suggested themselves or were suggested to him by bishops, potentates, or friends. He never hesitated to repeat himself, or to work his convictions about one matter into his arguments about another. He was, with kaleidoscopic, quick-change virtuosity, now a scholar, now a journalist, now a moral instructor, now a political adviser, now a malicious satirist, now a devoted friend and (sometimes simultaneously) a reptilian enemy—but always and everywhere an entertainer. To read through the entire body of his writings from beginning to end would be a fearful chore; but from selected facets of his different works the imaginative reader can assemble a vivid picture of the man in his full, fallible, but often inspiring humanity. That is the purpose of this collection. But, not wishing to scorn formal arrangements entirely, I include on pp. 339–40 a chronology of Erasmus's life, which enables the various writings of this collection, as well as numerous others and some related historical events, to be placed in the context of the author's biography.

The illustrations peppered through the *Praise of Folly* text are very early work done by Hans Holbein the younger shortly after his arrival at Basle in 1515. Holbein went on to become a polished painter of important portraits in the courts of Europe; but his little sketches for *Folly* are in a more popular vein. In their very crudeness, they capture the rowdy jocosity of Erasmus's free-spirited carnivalesque caper.

The critiques of Erasmus which follow his writings were chosen not only for their own sake and as illuminations of Erasmus, but to introduce the reader to some major currents of modern thought about this still-vital figure. Though many times written off as a dead letter, neither Erasmus nor his creed of humanism has succumbed over the centuries to dusty obsolescence. The past is most exciting to investigate as it reveals not only its authentic pastness (in which we too will all too shortly participate) but imaginative resources for dealing with problems vital to us that in the past took very different forms. For the thoughtful reader this book of selections, critical as well as textual, may serve as the start of many further intellectual explorations; and I hope it will do so.

ROBERT M. ADAMS

Selections from
THE WRITINGS

The Praise of Folly

Author's Preface

Desiderius Erasmus of Rotterdam to his friend Thomas More[1] Greetings

Recently when I was on my way from Italy to England, instead of wasting all the time I had to spend on horseback in idle chatter and empty gossip, I tried occasionally to think over some of the things we have studied together, and to call to mind the conversation of my most learned and agreeable friends from whom I was then separated. Among those friends, you, my dear More, were the first whose name occurred to me, since I find just as much pleasure in thinking of you when we are apart as I do in your company when we are together. And, upon my soul, nothing in life has ever brought me more pleasure than your friendship. Well, since I felt I must be doing something, and the circumstances were hardly proper for serious study, I thought I might occupy myself with the praise of folly. What put such a notion in my mind? you may ask. My first hint came from your family name of More, which is just as close to Moria, the Greek word for folly, as you are remote from the thing itself. In fact, everyone agrees that you're as far removed from it as possible. Besides, I had a suspicion that this joke would be agreeable to you because you particularly enjoy jests of this sort—that is, if I don't flatter myself, jests seasoned with a touch of learning and a dash of wit. ←
For that matter, you enjoy playing the role of Democritus in all the common business of life.[2] Though as a result of your searching and original mind you're bound to hold opinions very different from those of common men, yet by virtue of your warm and sincere manner you

---

1. The son of a London judge and a practicing attorney himself, More in 1510 was about thirty-three years old, thus some ten years younger than Erasmus. In sharp contrast to his older friend, who remained celibate all his life, More had committed himself to a secular career and had married; he was already the father of three children. Intellectually and socially, More and Erasmus were immediately and deeply sympathetic. Both were scholars in the humanist tradition with a special interest in Greek, both were witty ironists, both recognized the need for liberal reforms in church and state. Their first meeting was in 1499, when Erasmus visited England at the invitation of a former pupil, Lord Mountjoy, whom he had known in Paris; it was therefore inevitable that when Erasmus came north again in 1509, he should stay with More.
2. Though primarily significant as a physicist and mathematician, Democritus (of the fifth century B.C.) was popularly known as the "laughing philosopher" in contrast to Heraclitus, the "weeping philosopher."

can get along with all sorts of people at any time of day,[3] and actually enjoy doing so. Will you then accept this little declamationlet of mine as the keepsake of a friend, and take it under your protection? For now that it is dedicated to you, it is properly yours, not mine. I don't doubt that there will be busybodies to condemn the book, some saying that it's composed of trifles too silly to befit a theologian's dignity, others declaring that it's too sharp of tooth[4] to accord with the modest behavior of a Christian—they will thunder out comparisons with the Old Comedy and the satires of Lucian,[5] they will say I snap and slash at everyone like a mad dog.

Well, will the people who are offended by the frivolity of the argument and the absurdity of the jokes kindly reflect that I'm not setting the style here? The same thing has been done before, again and again, by famous authors of the past.[6] It was centuries ago that Homer toyed with his "War Between the Frogs and the Mice," Virgil with his "Gnat" and his "Garlic Salad," Ovid with his "Nut." Polycrates wrote in praise of Busiris the tyrant, and Isocrates, though no friend to Polycrates, did the same thing; Glaucon spoke up for injustice. Favorinus praised Thersites and the quartan ague, Synesius had words to say in favor of baldness, and Lucian wrote panegyrics on a fly and a parasite. Seneca ridiculed Claudius in his *Pumpkinification*, Plutarch wrote a dialogue in which Ulysses disputed with a hog, Gryllus, both Lucian and Apuleius wrote about life as seen by an ass, and some anonymous author wrote the last will and testament of a hog named Grunnius Corocotta, of which Saint Jerome preserved a recollection.[7]

If it makes them any happier, let the complainers imagine that I spent my travel-time playing chess or riding on a hobby-horse. Every other profession is entitled to a bit of leisure—what's so terrible if scholars take a little time off for play, especially if their foolery leads to something slightly more serious? Some jokes can be managed in such a way that a↙

3. The Latin is *omnium horarum hominem agere*, and it is adapted from the "Life of Tiberius" (42) by Suetonius. Its meaning there is distinctly disreputable; it implies a man who can drink night and day. Erasmus applies it with a very different meaning to More, and a man named Whittinton translated it in 1520 as "a man for all seasons"—hence the title of a popular play by Robert Bolt (1966) where the implications are not only laudatory but saintly.

4. More is concerned that his jest not be thought excessively cynical in spirit; the cynical philosophers got their name from the Greek word for dog, *kune*. The talk about sharp teeth and snapping at people all plays on the basic metaphor of a vicious dog.

5. Old Comedy (as in Aristophanes) attacked people by name; New Comedy (as in Menander) represented general types. Erasmus's *Praise of Folly* could not possibly be compared with Old Comedy; but it does come very close to the dialogues of Lucian, known as "the scoffer," and sometimes as "the atheist." By joining an absurd charge with one

that might have some substance, Erasmus is able to dismiss them both.

6. Among his predecessors Erasmus mingles examples of the mock-epic with those of the mock-panegyric. The examples attributed to Homer, Virgil, and Ovid were in fact by later parodists of the great poets. Busiris was a semimythical tyrant (i.e., Pharaoh) of Egypt, Isocrates the greatest Greek orator of his day. Glaucon was the brother of Plato, who in Republic 2 makes him speak for injustice in order to set up Socrates' rebuttal.

7. Thersites was the ugliest and least heroic of all the Greeks at Troy; Aulus Gellius (Noctes Atticae 17.12.2) tells how Favorinus wrote mock-orations praising both Thersites and the quartan fever, which we now call malaria. Seneca's piece mocking the deification of Claudius is really quite funny. The fantasies of Plutarch, Lucian, and Apuleius, all involving metamorphosis, have only this in common with the other works cited, that they are written in a "low" comic style. The will of Grunnius Corocotta the swine is a real oddity of the subliterature, a third-century joke for school children.

reader who isn't altogether thick of nose can profit by them—more, perhaps, than from the pompous formal arguments of certain people we know. I have in mind some paltry fellow who patches up an oration in praise of rhetoric or philosophy, or another supple rascal who's set on flattering his prince, or some agitator who wants to rouse up everyone to go off and fight the Turk. There are fools who pretend to predict the future and others who strain to settle some subtle and difficult point that doesn't matter a fraction of a trifle either way. Just as it's the height of triviality to treat serious matters in a trivial way, so there's nothing more delightful than finding that some trifles have been managed so that they turn out far from trivial. About my own performance it's not for me to judge; but unless I'm completely misled by 'self-love,' my praise of folly hasn't been performed altogether foolishly.

Now let me answer those cavillers who object to what they call biting satire. Good wits have always been allowed the liberty to exercise their high spirits on the common life of men, and without rebuke, as long as their sport doesn't become savagery. That's why I'm so impressed by the delicacy of modern ears which can scarcely endure anything but formal titles of honor. You can even find some religious men so topsy-turvy in their values that they listen more complacently to real blasphemies against Christ than to the mildest of jokes about the pope or the local prince, especially if the joke might 'touch them in the pocketbook.' But if someone attacks the vices of human kind without mentioning any individual by name, is he harming people or rather teaching them, admonishing them? Consider in addition on how many scores I attack my own self. Besides, when men of every different sort are censured, it's clear that vice in general is the target, not a particular person. So if anyone complains that he's been harmed, it's either his conscience that accuses him or his guilt. Saint Jerome wrote in this vein much more freely and bitterly, sometimes not even suppressing personal names.[8] I have not only avoided naming people, but have softened my style so that any intelligent reader will understand my intention was to divert, not to insult. Unlike Juvenal, I made no effort to rake in the sewer of hidden crimes;[9] my aim was to ridicule absurdities, not to catalogue sins. And if there's someone who can't be calmed by these reflections, let him recall that it's a kind of compliment to be attacked by Folly; when I chose her as my spokesperson, I was bound to observe the proprieties of her character. But why do I say all these things to you, who are so skilled an advocate that even in causes that aren't the best, you can put up the best defence? Farewell, most learned More, and defend your Folly faithfully. From the country, June 9, 1510.[1]

8. Saint Jerome, most erudite and least saintly of the early church fathers, was noted, if not always admired, for his strident polemical tone.
9. Juvenal, of the first century A.D., bore the reputation of a harsh and biting satirist of ancient Rome, by contrast with his predecessor Horace, who wrote more light and amusing verses.
1. Early editions give the date as 1508, which is impossible, since Erasmus could not have described his sojourn in More's house before he arrived there in the second half of 1509. The date may be an accident, a joke, or a deliberate misstatement; but if the preface was written under the circumstances it describes, 1510 is the first possible date. Nobody knows where "in the country" was.

The Praise of Folly

FOLLY SPEAKS:[1]
However people commonly talk about me—and I know perfectly well what a bad name folly has, even among the biggest fools—I'm the one, the one and only, let me tell you, who have the power to bring joy both to gods and to men; in proof of which, you can see for yourselves that as soon as I stood up to speak in this crowded hall, all your faces lit up with a sudden and quite unaccustomed hilarity, your brows cleared, and you expanded in such smiles, chuckles, and applause that I suddenly felt myself in the presence of so many Homeric divinities well laced with nectar, and nepenthe too—whereas before you sat solemn and grum-

[Folly Presents Herself]

1. *Note on the annotations:* For some years before the writing of *Folly* (1509), Erasmus had been compiling, augmenting, and publishing in successive editions (1500 and 1508) a collection of adages or pithy sayings, mostly from classical sources. He had over three thousand of them, and scattered them through *The Praise of Folly* with a liberal hand. I have indicated their presence, and the presence of certain other catchwords not taken directly from the *Adages*, by single quotation marks in the text. But it has not seemed worth the clutter to trace every verbal tag down to its source, or more

frequently, its sources. More scholarly editions, like that of Professor Clarence Miller (Yale, 1979) can be consulted if specific details are needed.

With regard to biblical citations, Erasmus quotes largely from memory, and by allusion to the Latin Vulgate, which differs frequently both in verbal details and in its numbering of verses from most modern Bibles. To make things easier for the modern student, I have modified most quotations and some citations to conform to the King James version. Obviously the anachronism is gross; I hope the added convenience justifies it.

faced as if you had just been let out of Trophonius's cave.[2] But as it happens when the sun first shows his radiant golden face over the land, or when the fresh south wind wafts a breath of spring after a bitter winter so that all things put on a new face and a fresh color, and youth itself seems to return—so, when you laid eyes on me, you were quite transfigured. And thus what various mighty orators could hardly accomplish with their long and laborious speechifying—that is, to dispel the gloomy shadows of the soul—I brought about instantly just by my appearance.

As for why I come forth today in this unusual costume, you will soon learn if you'll just lend me your ears—not those, to be sure, that you bend toward preachers of the holy word, but the kind that you commonly bring to street-performers, comedians, and buffoons, the style of ears that my friend Midas once displayed to the god Pan.[3] For it's now my pleasure to act the sophist for a while in your company—not the sort whose daily bread is cramming the minds of schoolboys with painful trivialities or who teach the tricks of quibbling with more than female

[Midas with Ears]

2. Nectar, nepenthe, and (not mentioned here) ambrosia are food and drink for the classical gods. After descending into the legendary cave of Trophonius in search of truth, an ancient Greek traditionally emerged with a bad case of the blues.

3. Because he had the bad taste to prefer the pipe music of the rural goat-god Pan to the majestic melodies of the solar deity Apollo, King Midas (unfortunate as well in the matter of his "golden touch") was fitted with ass's ears.

stubbornness—rather I want to imitate those men of old who in order to avoid the odious designation of "Sages" (Sophi, wise men) preferred to be known as "Sophists."[4] Their function was to crown with highest praises the gods and the noblest of men. Praises you shall hear, therefore, but not of Hercules or Solon,[5] but my own praise of myself, that is, of Folly. Nor do I care a rap for those wise fellows who say it's the height of stupidity and insolence for a person to praise himself. Let it be as stupid as they like, they will have to admit it's in my character. Indeed, what's more appropriate than for Folly to sing her own praises, and, as they say, "blow her own horn"? Who can explain me better than I can myself—unless, perhaps, someone who knows me better than I do? Actually, I think what I am doing here is more decent than what the common ruck of pundits and patricians do when, under cover of a certain perverse mock-modesty, they hire some servile rhetorician or limber-tongued poet, and bribe him literally to pour forth their praises, praises that are nothing but flat-out lies. While the recipient of all this adulation spreads his borrowed plumes and raises his crest aloft like a peacock, the barefaced orator expatiates, comparing his good-for-nothing subject to some god or other, and proposing him as the absolute model of all the virtues, especially those of which they both know he doesn't possess 'a single grain.' Still, the speaker doesn't hesitate to deck his crow in borrowed plumes, to 'whitewash his Ethiopian,' or finally to 'puff up his gnat to the size of an elephant.' In any case, I'm following the advice of that trite old proverb that says a man is entitled to praise himself when there's nobody else to do it.[6]

And here let me pause a moment to wonder at the ingratitude—or is it, perhaps, the laziness?—of mankind, since of all those who have followed in my path and partaken of my generosity, not one over all these centuries has undertaken to speak up in public praise of folly. Yet there was no lack of people to burn the midnight oil and rack their brains composing elaborate disquisitions in praise of Busiris and Phalaris, of quartan agues, flies, baldness, and other misfortunes of that sort.[7] From me you can expect only an extempore and unlabored—but for that reason a more truthful—oration. I know you won't suppose I made it up to show off my wit, as the common herd of orators do. For, as you well know, after they've been sitting on a speech for thirty years or so—and sometimes it's not even their own work—they will tell you it's a mere trifle, tossed off in the last three days, not written down at all, just dictated. But I've always preferred just to say 'whatever pops into my head.'

4. Sophists, who taught the way to make the worse appear the better cause, had an ill repute as pseudo-wise men; but from Folly's point of view, they are better every way than the truly wise.
5. Hercules as demigod and Solon as one of the earliest and best legislators would be worthy subjects of true encomia.
6. Folly scatters proverbs and proverbial expressions through her discourse in the same way that she sprinkles scraps of Greek; both are devices to tease a reader with the resemblance between Erasmus and his puppet.
7. Mock-encomia on these and similar topics, many written in classical times, no doubt had something to do with suggesting to Erasmus a mock-praise of Folly. Busiris was another name for the Egyptian pharaoh, and Phalaris, who roasted his victims alive in a brazen bull, was the subject of a mock-encomium by Lucian.

But now don't let anyone expect that, like the common lot of speech-makers, I'm going to begin with a definition and then go on to divide up my topic—that least of all. Either procedure would be inappropriate; circumscribing a power whose genius extends everywhere is as absurd as dividing up a force in whose service all the orders of being agree together. Besides, what's the point of setting before you by verbal definition what can only be the copy or shadow of me, when you have me, in person, here present before you? I am, as you can plainly see, that true and proper 'giver of divine gifts' whom the Latins know as STULTITIA and the Greeks as MORIA.

Of course there was no real need for me to tell you this, as if it wasn't written large across my features and in my very bearing who I am. A single good look would be enough to convince anyone who had supposed I might be Minerva or the goddess Sophia,[8] even without hearing me talk, though speech is the least deceptive mirror of the mind. I use no makeup, I don't wear one expression on my face and hide another in my heart. I'm always exactly like myself, so that even those who most aspire to the name and reputation of wisdom cannot hide my presence even though they strut about 'like apes in scarlet robes or asses in lions' skins.' However carefully they disguise themselves, somehow those protruding asses' ears will give away the Midas in them.[9] An ungrateful lot of men, these rascals, who though they're entirely of my faction, yet in public are so ashamed of my proper name that they hurl it against others as a term of ultimate insult. Don't you think we could best call these people, who are actually superfools but want to look like wise men, by the title of 'foolosophers'?[1]

For in this respect too I've thought best to imitate the rhetoricians of our day who consider themselves as good as gods if like horse-leeches they can seem to have two tongues; in their view it's a mighty accomplishment to work a few Greek vocables into the texture of their Latinity, like chips stuck in a mosaic, whether they're appropriate or not.[2] Then if they still don't have enough foreign terms, they dig out of their moldy old manuscripts four or five obsolete expressions with which to thicken the darkness of the listener's mind. If anybody understands, he's impressed with his own erudition; those who don't understand are impressed even more. We fools have a particular trick of liking best whatever comes to us from farthest away. But if they are a little more pretentious than the rest, they will smile wisely and applaud, 'waggling their ears' in true asslike fashion so that everybody else can see that they understand. 'And so much for that.'[3]

8. Sophia: wisdom (Gr.). Minerva (known to the Greeks as Athene) was Olympic goddess of intelligence.
9. See above, p. 7, n. 3.
1. Sir Thomas Chaloner in 1549 first found this fine equivalent for *morosophos*, an inversion of which is the common word *sophomore*, a wise fool.
2. In making fun of Greek phrases, Folly takes care to use a lot of them. Greek was not just a flashy cultural possession in Erasmus's day, but a highly prized key to the interpretation of the New Testament.
3. Two Greek tags terminate the attack on Greek tags. For all the snowstorm of Greek snippets, it's worth knowing that Erasmus, when alluding to the text of Plato, consulted the Latin trot of Marsilio Ficino.

Now let me get back to my main point. You know my proper name, then, you gentlemen most—let's see, what epithet should I apply to you?—gentlemen most asinine. For what more fitting and forthright title could the goddess Folly use to rally her followers? But since not many people know the stock from which I spring, with the help of the Muses I will now try to set the matter straight. My father was not Chaos, nor Orcus, nor Saturn, nor Iapetos, nor any one of that set of obsolete and moth-eaten deities. Rather, he was Plutus himself, god of riches, who, in spite of what Hesiod and Homer say, and in spite of Jove himself, was 'father of gods and men.'[4] At the mere nod of his head, all institutions both sacred and profane are turned upside down—so it always was and is nowadays. His decision controls wars, truces, conquests, projects, programs, legal decisions, marriage contracts, political alliances, international treaties, edicts, the arts, matters serious and silly—my breath is giving out—in short, all the public and private business of mortal men is under his control. Without his help the entire populace of poetic divinities—or let me put it more strongly—even those twelve loftiest gods who live atop Olympus would either not exist at all or would live in meager retirement and 'eat in the kitchen.'[5] If anyone has Plutus for an enemy, not even Pallas Athene will be able to help him; and, on the other hand, if Plutus favors him, he can tell Jove himself, thunderbolt and all, to go hang. "I'm proud to be the child of such a father."[6] And he did not give birth to me out of his brain, as Jupiter did with that sullen sourpuss Pallas, but begot me on Neotes [Youth], the most beautiful of all the nymphs and the lustiest as well. What's more, they weren't cramped into the dreary bonds of matrimony, such as produced that limping blacksmith,[7] but in a manner more agreeable by far, "entwined in ardent love," as our Homer likes to say. But don't get the wrong impression, the Plutus who begot me was not that decrepit person who appears in Aristophanes, half-blind and completely senile,[8] but a young man flushed with youth, and not just with youth but with several draughts of nectar that he had drunk off at a recent banquet of the gods, in goodly quantities and quite unmixed. If you want to know where I was born— since nowadays people think it's a major point in making up your pedigree to know where you uttered your first infant mews and squalls— well, I was not born on wandering Delos or rocked on the bosom of the restless ocean nor yet raised in any hollow-resounding caves,[9] but rather I was born on the Fortunate Isles, where all things grow 'unsown and uncultivated.' In that part of the world nobody works, grows old, or

---

4. Traditional progenitors of the pagan gods were Chaos, Orcus (or Pluto), and Saturn (or Cronos); Iapetos was a Titan who begot sundry giants, and Plutus is the money-god. Hesiod wrote a very early poem on the genealogy of the gods, the *Theogony*.
5. Satirists like Lucian had made the point that without burnt offerings from humans, the gods would have only lean fare.
6. The phrase is Homeric. Pallas Athene is goddess of wisdom.
7. Lame Vulcan was the legitimate but deformed

offspring of Juno and Jupiter, not the most congenial of couples.
8. Probably the last of Aristophanes' eleven surviving plays, *Plutus* puts on stage a very decrepit deity.
9. Apollo and Diana were born on Delos, Venus from the ocean itself, and Jove was reared in a cave on Mount Ida in Crete. The Fortunate Isles, though a very old concept (mentioned by Hesiod and Pindar), are not Homeric.

suffers from sickness; the fields bear no day-lilies, mallows, leeks, beans, or vulgar vegetables of that sort. But everywhere eyes and noses are gratified with moly, heal-all, nepenthe, marjoram, ambrosia, lotus, roses, violets, and hyacinths, as in the garden of Adonis.[1] And being born amid these delights, I didn't enter life bawling and screaming, but from the first smiled on my mother happily.

Neither do I have any reason to envy 'Jove himself,' who was suckled by a goat,[2] since I nursed at the breasts of two dainty nymphs, Methe [Tipsy] the daughter of Bacchus, and Apaedia [Ninny] the child of Pan. You can see them here and now in the company of my other companions and followers. But if you want to know the names of the others, by heaven, you won't get them from me except in Greek. This lady whom you recognize by her supercilious air is evidently Philautia [Self-Love].[3] The one you see next to her, with laughing eyes and clapping hands, is Kolakia [Flattery]. This one, with eyes half shut, who seems about to doze off, is Lethe [Forgetfulness]. The one leaning on her elbows with her hands folded is called Misoponia [Lieabout]. This one, wearing a rosy garland and drenched with perfumes, is known as Hedone [Pleasure]. The one with restless eyes that roll every which way is Anoia [Imbecility]. The girl with the fair complexion and the voluptuous figure is called Tryphe [Fascination]. You can also see a couple of male deities among the ladies, one of whom is called Comus [Festivity], and the other Negretos Hypnos [Sound Sleep]. These then are the members of my family, with whose faithful help I maintain dominion over all things, and rule even emperors themselves.

So now you have heard of my birth, my bringing up, and my companions. And lest you imagine I have no reason to assume the title of goddess, prick up your ears and I'll tell you how many benefits I bestow on both men and gods, how widely my sacred powers extend. For as somebody shrewdly remarked, this is the true quality of a god, to bring joy to mortals; and as those persons are rightly included in the assembly of the gods who showed men the uses of wine, grain, or some other commodity of the sort,[4] why shouldn't I be decreed and designated 'Number One' among all the gods, since I alone confer all benefits on all men?

Just for starters, what could be sweeter or more precious than life itself? And to whom does life owe its very beginnings, if not to me? It isn't the spear of 'potent-fathered Pallas' or the aegis of Jove the 'cloud-compeller' that begets human beings or propagates the race. In fact the father of gods and king of men whose nod makes all Olympus tremble must set aside his three-pronged lightning bolt and put off that majestic expression with which he can terrify the other gods at will, and, just like

1. As part of the worship of Adonis, Venus's lover, women throughout the Middle East used to plant little pots with spring flowers; they flourished and died, mirroring in their brief life that of the deity slain in his lovely prime.

2. Jove, hidden from his devouring father Saturn, was nursed by a goat—perhaps a nymph—named Amalthea.

3. Most of these figures are personified abstractions coined by Erasmus; Lethe had a little reality as an underground river, and Comus as a festive son of Bacchus.

4. Bacchus was god of wine, for example, Ceres goddess of grain. Pliny in his *Natural History* (2.5) said it was the function of gods to help men.

[The Amorous Stoic]

an actor, he must put on another character entirely when he wants to do, what he never tires of doing, that is, 'make babies.'

Now the stoics[5] consider themselves next thing in this world to deities. But give me a triple or a quadruple stoic, or if you choose a six-hundred-fold stoic, yet in this matter, just think if he won't have to shave off that beard which is his special badge of wisdom (though in fact he shares it with a billygoat), lower his lofty expression, smooth out his forehead, set aside his hard and fast dogmas, and talk a bit of nonsense, verging even on madness. In short, it's to me, to me I say, that the wise man will have to have recourse if he wants to become a father. And why shouldn't I speak to you even more openly, as my manner is? Let me ask you if the head or the face or the breast or the hands or the ear, all of which are reputed the more seemly parts of the body, actually beget either gods or men? Not as I see it; it's that other part, so stupid and even ridiculous that it can't be named without raising a snicker, that propa-

5. The stoics (so called because their original gathering place was a porch [stoa] or colonnade) were a philosophical sect who held that man by using his reason could and should subdue the lower nature that renders him subject to pleasure and pain. Though fully systematic stoics were comparatively rare, many writers of antiquity, like Cicero, were tinged with stoicism; major elements of the philosophy were adapted into Christianity, and it enjoyed a strong revival during the Renaissance. To this day a good many people practice if they do not preach a sort of diluted stoicism.

gates the human race. That is the sacred fount from which all things draw their existence—from that more truly than from the quaternion of Pythagoras,[6] if you please.

Come now, let me ask you, what man would put his neck into the yoke of matrimony if, as the learned philosophers advise, he first counted over in his own mind the inconveniences of the estate; or what woman would let a man approach her if she had fully calculated the pains and perils of childbirth, to be followed by all the troubles of rearing a child? If you owe your life to a marriage and that marriage to my follower 'Imbecility,' then you see just how deeply you're indebted to me. And would a woman who has gone through this procedure once ever want to do it again unless my servant 'Forgetfulness' were at hand to help her? Nor would Venus herself deny, whatever Lucretius may say to the contrary,[7] that without the help of my influence, her powers would be limp and unavailing. And so it is that from that pixilated and ridiculous little game of mine come forth, first the supercilious philosophers whose place has now been taken by the so-called 'monks,'[8] and purple-robed kings and godly priests and the thrice-sacred pontiffs—in addition to the whole crowd of poetic gods, so numerous that Olympus can hardly harbor the whole crew, spacious though it is.

But don't let it count to my credit that life owes to me its seedbed and origin, if I can't show that everything good in life is also a gift from me. For what is this life, should it even be called life at all, if you remove pleasure from it? You applaud. Well, I know none of you is so wise, or so silly rather—but perhaps I'd better say so wise—as not to agree with me on that point. Not even the stoics really despise pleasure, though they try hard to pretend they do, and attack it publicly with a thousand insults—but only so that, when they've scared everyone else away, they may enjoy it more freely themselves. But let them tell me, in God's name, what part of life is not gloomy, not sullen, not drab, not dull and dreary, unless you add a dash of pleasure, the condiment of folly? Convincing authority for this view is to be found in Sophocles, a man far above all praise, who wrote an elegant line in my honor: "The happiest life is to know nothing at all."[9]

But come now, let me look into the matter more closely. First of all, who doesn't know that the earliest age of man is by all odds the happiest, the most agreeable by a long shot to everyone? What is the quality in infants for which we kiss them, coo over them, cuddle them—as even an enemy would do at that age—what is it but the charm of foolishness, which prudent nature purposely bestows on the newborn so that by this pleasure, as a sort of compensation, they may mollify the exasperations of bringing them up and win the favor of their guardians? After that

6. Pythagoras, whose thought was interwoven with numerology, considered four a particularly powerful and significant number.
7. Lucretius, in the opening verses of his poem *On the Nature of Things*, attributes supreme power to Venus.
8. Monks "replace" philosophers because both are anchorites or recluses, or are supposed to be.
9. Sophocles' play *Ajax*, l. 554.

succeeds adolescence; how welcome it is to everyone, how warmly accepted, how gladly encouraged, how liberally offered the helping hand! And where does this youthful grace come from? Why, it comes from no one but me, by whose special favor the young have so little knowledge and by the same token are so ingratiating. But when they have grown a little older, learned a little of the way of the world, and started to acquire the disciplines of men, call me a liar if their bright and shining faces don't get duller, their quick minds don't slow down, their wit doesn't grow cold, their energy doesn't start to flag. The further they depart from me, the less they really live, until they are overtaken by 'hateful old age'—hateful not only to others but to themselves as well.[1] And old age would really be unendurable to everyone, were it not that I am once again at hand to take pity on its troubles. As the gods of the poets always save the perishing with a timely metamorphosis, so I come to the aid of those with one foot in the grave, and return them, if only for a brief moment, to their infancy. These are the oldsters who are said, quite rightly, to be in their 'second childhood.' As for how the transformation is worked, I won't conceal it. I lead them to the fountain of my hand-maid Lethe, which rises in the Fortunate Isles though a little trickle of it gets diverted to the underworld, and there they drink long draughts of forgetfulness. Before long their anxieties relax and they become like children again. People say they are silly and inconsequent, and of course they are: that's what second childhood means. Is first childhood anything else than being silly and inconsequent? Isn't that the most delightful part of infancy, not to know a single thing? Who wouldn't shrink from a boy with grown-up wisdom, as if he were some sort of freak? There's a common proverb, "I hate a child who's wise beyond his years."[2] Just imagine doing business with an old man who in addition to years of experience had the sharp and vigorous mind of a youngster. So, with my help, this old man goes a bit soft in the head.

But now this dotard of mine is free from all the miseries and anxieties by which a wise man is tormented. As a pot-companion he can still be quite amusing. He doesn't feel the tedium of life, which even for a man in his health can be almost unendurable. Sometimes he reverts to the state of the graybeard in Plautus[3] who knew only three letters, A*M*O; if he had any sense, he would be wretched, but meanwhile, with my help, he lives happily, keeps his old friends, and occasionally cuts up as the life of the party. You'll note that in Homer the speech of Nestor is sweet as honey, while that of Achilles is bitter;[4] and in the same author the old men sitting by the wall are said to speak with 'lily-sweet voices.' On this one score alone old men have the better of children, whose voices, though sweet, are often obliged to be silent; and thus they lack the supreme pleasure of life, which is chit-chat. Besides, old people

1. The phrase is Homeric: *Iliad* 8.103.
2. The dictum is from the so-called *Apology* of Apuleius.

3. Plautus, *Mercator* (The Merchant), l. 304; the three letters AMO spell "I love."
4. *Iliad* 1.249, 223.

enjoy the company of the young, as the very young are drawn to the society of the old, 'like naturally consorting with like.'[5] For what is the difference between them, apart from the fact that the elders have more wrinkles and more birthdays? Otherwise, in their whitish hair, toothless gums, frail bodies, love of milk, stammering, babbling, foolishness, forgetfulness, thoughtlessness, and a host of other qualities, they are quite alike. The older men get, the more childish they become, until, like veritable children, without any weariness of life or fear of death, they depart this existence.

Now let anyone who cares compare these benefits of mine with the metamorphoses worked by the other gods. What they do in a rage I don't want even to think about; but at the height of their benevolence they may turn a human being into a tree, a bird, a cricket, or even a snake—as if one were not, in effect, killed by being transformed into another creature entirely.[6] But I restore the selfsame man to the best and happiest period of his life. So that if men would refrain completely from any sort of commerce with wisdom, but spend their time entirely in my company, they would never grow old, but instead would live happily in the enjoyment of perpetual youth.

Only look at those heavy, solemn fellows who've devoted themselves to philosophic studies or to serious and difficult business—they have started to grow old even before their youth, their vital spirits and animal juices all dried up as a result of constant worry and the pressure of painful, intensive cogitation. But my morons are all plump, with sleek and glistening skins, like the 'hogs of Acarnania' (as people say),[7] 'never feeling any of the sorrows of old age unless by chance they pick up some trouble by contagion from the wise. So true it is, that into each life some rain must fall.

Add to this the popular saying very much to the point, that 'folly is the one and only one thing that delays youth in her flight and keeps sour old age at a distance.' There's still another popular saying about the Brabanters that while advancing years bring increasing prudence to other men, the Brabanters as they grow older get dumber.[8] No other people bring so much joviality to their everyday get-togethers, none are less troubled by the miseries of declining age. Near neighbors to them, alike in temperament and close geographically, are my Hollanders—I call them mine because they are so addicted to folly that they've made quite a name for themselves. They're not in the least ashamed of it, and bandy it around freely among themselves.

Mortals in their craze for perpetual youth run off every which way— let them go!—in search of Medeas and Circes and Venuses and Auroras,

---

5. *Odyssey* 17.218.
6. An anthology of these and similar tranformations is Ovid's famous book titled *Metamorphoses*.
7. In Acarnania, a remote district of Greece, pigs grew proverbially fat. Horace, when describing

himself as "a pig from Epicurus's sty," used words like "plump" and "sleek."
8. Brabant is a distinct area of what is now northern Belgium and southern Holland. The proverb has not been traced.

and that fabulous fountain to be found I can't imagine where.[9] But all the time, I'm the only person who can and does perform that miracle. I alone possess that miraculous juice with which Aurora the daughter of Memnon prolonged the youth of her ancestor Tithonus; I am the same Venus by whose favor Phaon renewed his youth so he could be loved so passionately by Sappho.[1] Mine are the herbs, if there are any, mine the enchantments, mine the bubbling waters which not only renew lost youth but (better still) preserve it forever. So if you agree with this sentiment that nothing is better than youth, nothing more detestable than old age, I think you will see how much you owe me, since I preserve the one and delay or prevent the other.

But why do I talk only of mortal men? Cast your eye across the heavens, and you can call me foolish indeed if you find any one of the gods who isn't ugly and despicable except so far as he is made agreeable by my influence. Why, for example, is Bacchus always boyish and curly-haired? No doubt because he is always frolic and tipsy, spending his whole life in parties, high-jinks, and games, and never having a moment's truck with Pallas. He doesn't want to be thought wise; in fact, he prefers that his worship take the form of games and jokes, and he's not at all offended by the proverb that assigns him the epithet of 'fool,' as in the saying "Dumber than Morychus." For in olden times the farmers gave that name to the statue of Bacchus sitting before his temple, when they had smeared it with fresh wine and new figs in the course of their revels. And then what insults used to be heaped on this god by the Old Comedy! Oh, an absurd god, they used to say; about the sort you'd expect to be born out of someone's thigh![2] Well, wouldn't you rather be silly and ridiculous like him, always joyful, always young, always ready for a frolic or a feast—than like Jove with his 'deep-laid plans' who terrifies everybody, or Pan who with his routs and riots turns everything upside down,[3] or Vulcan always busy about his fires and black with the smoke of his forge, or Pallas herself with her Gorgon shield and terrible spear, 'always grimly glaring'?[4] Why is Cupid always a little boy? Why indeed, except that he's a mischief-maker who never does or says 'a single sensible thing?' Why does the loveliness of Venus bring with it a perpetual springtime? No doubt about it, because she is a close relation of mine, sharing with me the complexion of our father and thus known to Homer as 'golden Aphrodite.' Besides, she is always laughing and smiling, if we are to believe the poets or the sculptors who follow in their footsteps. What

9. Medea (who provided a youth-giving bath for Jason's father, Aeson), Circe (who kept Ulysses young), Venus (who returned Phaon to his youth), and Aurora (who could have helped Tithonus remain young, but didn't) are all associated with the fantasy of eternal youth. Ponce de Leon is famous for seeking the fountain of youth (1509), but many legends preceded his trip to Florida.
1. In her vehemence, Folly repeats one of her examples (Phaon and Sappho) and gets another wrong (Tithonus and Aurora). But what else should

one expect of Folly?
2. After Semele was struck dead by Jupiter's awesome presence, her unborn child Bacchus was introduced into Jupiter's thigh and born again; see Ovid, *Metamorphoses* 3.
3. From Pan's penchant for scaring people, we get the word "panic."
4. Pallas, though generally armed, is not invariably ferocious; but Folly sees her so because wisdom is always a threat to folly.

deity did the Romans worship more devotedly than Flora the giver of all pleasures? Actually, if you look carefully into the behavior of the solemn gods as reported by Homer and the other poets, you will find their lives to be full of foolishness from beginning to end. No reason for me to tell tales about all the others when you know perfectly well all the scandalous escapades of Jove himself, the thunderer. Or take Diana, heedless of the modesty fitting her sex and devoted to hunting, who in her spare time dies for love of Endymion. Stories like these they ought to be hearing from Momus,[5] and in fact they used to hear them regularly from him until lately they got angry and threw him along with Ate [Discord] down to earth because he interrupted the bliss of the gods with his illtimed truth-telling. Nor did any mortal offer shelter to this exile, least of all anyone in the courts of princes, where my follower Kolakia [Flattery] reigns supreme; she and Momus would get along together about as well as a wolf and a lamb. And so, in the absence of Momus, the gods revel much more freely and carelessly, 'taking all things lightly,' as Homer says,[6] now that they have no censor. What an array of japes they get from that blockhead Pan! Think of the thievish games played by deceitful Mercury.[7] Then they have Vulcan to 'act the buffoon' at the banquet of the gods and liven the feast with his ungainly limp, his foolish quibbles, and his ridiculous stories. Or there is Silenus, that dirty old man, who likes to do the 'belly-dance' while Polyphemus 'jangles his lyre' and a chorus-line of 'barefoot nymphs' caper about. Goatfoot satyrs perform their obscene frolics, and brainless Pan raises a general laugh with some silly limerick which the gods would rather hear than the Muses themselves. Especially when they're liquored up with nectar, they have no taste or discretion. But why should I go on to describe what the drunken gods do after their banquet?—things so stupid, by God, that Folly herself, as I am, can hardly keep from laughing at them. Yet perhaps at this point I'd better take counsel of Harpocrates [god of silence], lest some snoopy god overhear me telling about matters that weren't safe even for Momus to mention.[8]

But now it's time that I follow Homer's example, and turn from the heavenly sphere to matters down here on earth, where we'll find nothing either joyous or pleasant which doesn't owe a debt to me. And we'll notice first how providentially nature, the mother and creator of the human race, has arranged that men shall never be without a good seasoning of folly. For if, as the stoics define the matter, wisdom consists of being guided by reason, while folly is being moved by the emotions, Jupiter, to prevent our life from being gloomy and sad, mixed into our

---

5. Diana, among the Olympian gods, was a virgin huntress; her love for the shepherd Endymion was a story widely diffused through classical antiquity; Ovid and Cicero are among the authors touching on it. Momus was a patron of mockery and satire; Hesiod calls him a son of Night. Ate (pronounced Ah-tay, with two syllables) was goddess of discord.

6. *Odyssey* 4.805.
7. Mercury, or Hermes, who started stealing practically the moment he was born, became the patron of thieves and protector of liars.
8. Harpocrates was originally the Egyptian god Horus. Because he was represented with his finger on his lips, the Romans made him god of silence.

[Polyphemus Capering with Satyrs]

composition far more feeling than reason. How much more? Well, I
would say about ten pounds of feeling to a half-ounce of reason. Besides,
he cramped the reason into one narrow corner of the head, but distributed the feelings through all the rest of the body. Then he set up two
furious tyrants to war on solitary reason: anger, which occupies the fortress of the breast, and therefore the very fountain of life, which is the
heart; and lust, which maintains its mighty empire further down, around
the area of the groin.[9] What reason can do against these twin powers,
the common life of man makes sufficiently clear; she does all she can,
scolds herself hoarse, and repeats all the platitudes of proper behavior.
But the passions just tell their so-called ruler to go hang, and bluster on
more offensively than ever until reason submits out of sheet exhaustion
and throws up her hands.

Since the male was born to be in charge of things, he has been given
a tiny scruple more of reason, which he consults as best he can; and
when, as has happened before, Jupiter came to me, I gave him some
advice worthy of myself. I told him, that is, to join man with woman—
a stupid animal and a clumsy one, but funny and endearing—so that
through constant association her foolishness might temper and mollify
his sullen male intelligence. For when Plato seems to make a question
whether he should class women among rational beings or with brutes,
all he meant to say was that their sex rejoices in unusual foolishness.
And if a woman wants to be thought wise, that just shows that she's
doubly stupid, as if one should lead a bull, kicking and bellowing, into
a beauty parlor. It's the height of idiocy for anyone to deny nature,
assume an artificial virtue, and throw one's talent out of its proper orbit.
Just as, according to the Greek proverb, 'a monkey is always a monkey
even if dressed in purple,' so a woman is always a woman, that is, foolish, whatever mask she puts on.

Still, I don't think that women as a class are so stupid that they would
be offended if I, who am a woman myself and Folly in person, attribute
folly to them. For if they think the matter over, they are bound to feel
real gratitude because, thanks to folly, they are on so many scores better
off than men. First, they have the gift of beauty, which they rightly
prefer to anything else, by means of which they can exercise tyranny
over tyrants themselves. Where else do men get their ugly features, crusty
skin, and shaggy beard—incipient marks of senility—than from being
infected with prudence? Whereas the cheeks of women are always smooth,
their voices gentle, their skin soft, as if they were blessed with eternal
youth. What else do they ask of life except to be as attractive to men as
possible? Isn't that the purpose of all their primping and makeup, their
special rinses, hairdos, creams, perfumes, all their arts of adorning,
painting, and arranging their faces, eyes, and skin? Now what counts
more in attracting men than folly? What indulgence is there that men
will not allow to women, and what do they expect to get from it but

9. This view of reason's warfare with the unruly passions is essentially Platonic; cf. the *Phaedrus*.

pleasure? Women have no other way of giving pleasure than through folly. Nobody will deny the truth of this who recalls what nonsense a man talks to a woman, what follies he performs as soon as he seeks the pleasures of female society.

Here, then, you've seen the first and chief delight of life, the fountain from which everything else flows. Some people think, to be sure—they are chiefly old men who are more fond of wine-bibbing than skirt-chasing—that the prime pleasure of life lies in drink. Whether there can be a really festive gathering without any women present, it's not for me to say. One thing is for sure, without a dash of folly there'd be no fun in it at all. If there's nothing to raise a laugh, in the form of real or simulated foolishness, the revellers will send out to hire a 'comedian' or call for some ridiculous buffoon who by cracking a few jokes and tickling a few funnybones will lift the company out of their morose and dumpish silence. What good does it do to load the belly with dainty pastries, rich desserts, and rare liqueurs unless the eyes, the ears, yes, and the whole soul is equally delighted with laughter, jokes, and witty remarks? But I am the only deviser of these *hors d'oeuvres*. As for those other traditional banquet amusements such as naming the king of the feast, dicing for drinks, singing comic songs, 'drinking round the table,' and acting out ridiculous stories—those were not invented by the seven sages of Greece,[1] you can be sure, but by me, for the benefit of the human race. And it's the nature of all such things that the more foolish they are, the more they benefit human life, which without them would be so gloomy it wouldn't deserve to be called living. But gloomy it is bound to be unless with amusements of this sort you expel boredom, the first cousin of gloom.

Perhaps some people will dismiss this sort of pleasure, preferring instead the love and companionship of friends, which they place before all other things—declaring it indeed no less necessary to life than air, fire, and water.[2] Besides, they say, friendship is so joyous that anyone who would expel it from society might as well pull the sun out of the sky; and it is so honorable, if that enters into the case, that grave philosophers have not hesitated to number it among the prime good things of life. But what if I show that in the makeup of this lofty virtue I myself supply both the first and last ingredients? It's a point that I'll make, not by logical syllogisms, dilemmas, and other thorny devices of the dialectic, but by demonstrating it, as they say, in the broad light of day, to the eye of common sense. Look here now, when you condone your friend's vices, when you overlook them, blind yourself to them, deceive yourself about them, even convince yourself that his vices are virtues and worthy of admiration—isn't that the next thing to folly? When a man kisses his girlfriend on her mole, when another is delighted with his mistress's misshapen

---

1. The seven sages of Greece (not always assigned the same names) flourished around the seventh and sixth centuries B.C. Some were historical, others legendary.

2. Cicero wrote a book on friendship, praising it very highly indeed; friendship was a common theme for declamation in the Renaissance.

nose, when a father says his cross-eyed son has a lively expression—
what, I ask you, is that if not pure folly? People may call it folly as much
as they like, and folly it is; but this one quality provides the tie that binds
friends together. I'm talking here about ordinary men, none of whom is
born without faults and the best of whom is simply the least bad. But
among those stoics of godlike wisdom,[3] there is either no friendship at
all, or a certain sour and reluctant liking that they extend to very few —
I won't say to none at all, since most men are silly on occasion, there's
nobody who doesn't have his weak point, and like dispositions are naturally drawn together. Even if a certain mutual benevolence does grow
up between these severe devotees of virtue, it can never be securely
grounded or long lasting when men are so morose of temper and sharp
of sight that they study the vices of their friends like eagles or the serpent
of Epidaurus.[4] Of course they shut their eyes to their own vices, and
never realize what a sack of faults and follies is hanging from their own
shoulders. It's the nature of human life that no individual can be found
who's not subject to great vices and faults. Add to that the great and
many differences of age and interest, all the mistakes, slips, and errors
that men make, and all the common misunderstandings of everyday
existence—how can you expect these Argus-eyed men to be capable even
for an hour of the pleasures of friendship, unless you add to it what the
Greeks used to call *eueitheia*, which can be translated either as foolishness or as good-nature? But, after all, isn't Cupid, creator and begetter
of all intimacy, so myopic that for him 'even ugliness looks beautiful'?[5]
Thus he plays on you humans so that each finds beauty in his own,
Darby sticks to Joan and Jack to his Jill. These things happen all the
time, and people laugh at them, but absurdities like these are what binds
society together in mutual pleasure.

What I've said about friendship applies even better to marriage, which
is nothing but the inseparable joining together of two lives. By the immortal
gods! how many divorces or catastrophes worse than divorce would take
place if the domestic adjustments of men and women weren't sustained
and eased by flattery, jokes, yielding dispositions, mutual misunderstandings, dissimulations—all of them assistants to me. Lord, how few
marriages would ever come off if the groom looked suspiciously into the
various tricks his delicate little flower, as she seems to him, his blushing
virgin bride, had pulled off before her marriage! And how many fewer
would hold together, once begun, if the ignorance or indifference of
husbands didn't allow the doings of most wives to pass unnoticed. And
these triumphs are properly credited to folly, because she brings it about
that the wife pleases her husband, the husband his wife, the house is

3. Stoics who pretend that by reason they can attain
a state of indifference to pain and pleasure are particular objects of Folly's satire.
4. Aesculapius, god of medicine, had a shrine at
Epidaurus in southern Greece, where he appeared

in the form of a serpent—keen-sighted because his
business was diagnosis. The serpent survives in the
medical caduceus.
5. Cupid's poor eyesight is a medieval addition to
classical fable.

[Cuckold and Cuckoo]

tranquil, the marriage holds together. The husband is mocked, called cuckoo or cuckold or whatever, when he kisses away the tears of his whorish little wife. And how much happier he is in his errors than if he ate his heart out with jealousy, and turned the whole comic performance into a tragedy!

Briefly, no society, no association of people in this world can be happy or last long without my help; no people would put up with their prince, no master endure his servant, no maid stand her mistress, no teacher his pupil, no friend his friend, no wife her husband, no landlord his tenant, no soldier his drinking buddy, no lodger his fellow-lodger—unless they were mistaken, both at the same time or turn and turn about, in each other. Now they flatter one another, now they wisely overlook failings, now they exchange blandishments, foolish but sweeter than honey.

I suppose you think this is the most that can be said; but I have more. For let me ask you if a man will love anyone else when he hates himself? Will he ingratiate himself with another person if he's his own enemy? How can a person who's severe and disagreeable to himself bring pleasure to another? Nobody, I expect, would say such a thing unless he were more foolish than Folly herself. But, leaving me out of it, a man who despised himself would have no tolerance of anyone else; he would stink in his own nostrils, disdain his own possessions, hate everything about him. For nature, more like a stepmother in many matters than a true mother, has planted this evil in the minds of men, especially men of some discrimination, that they are discontented with their own possessions, but envy the possessions of others. And through this cast of mind all the talents, all the graces and accomplishments of life wither away and perish. What good is beauty, pre-eminent gift of the immortal gods, if tarnished by the breath of decay? What does youth amount to if corrupted by the sour ferment of approaching old age? In short, what proper style[6] can you maintain in any part of life, whether you act alone or with others (and in life, as in art, one wants to perform even minor tasks in high style)—what can you hope to accomplish, I ask, if my Philautia [Self-Love] is not at hand, she who is closest of kin to me, and warmly seconds my every action?

Face it, nothing is more foolish than to be pleased with yourself or to look on yourself with admiration. Yet if you really dislike yourself, what can you hope to do that is agreeable, gracious, not in bad taste? Take this savor out of life, and at once the orator will freeze in the middle of his speech, music with all its many effects will fail to please, the actor with all his gestures will be booed from the stage, the poet and his muses will be laughed to scorn, the painter will be dismissed with his pictures, the doctor will starve with his box of pills in his hand. Without self-love, instead of Nireus you will resemble Thersites, instead of Phaon Nestor, and instead of Minerva a sow;[7] you will be mute as a post instead of eloquent, and a lout instead of a man of the world. That's how necessary it is that everyone flatter himself and gain a measure of esteem in his own eyes before he can expect to be commended by others. Finally, since it's the highest peak of felicity to want to be what you actually are, my Philautia [Self-Love] achieves that end in short order, since by her ministrations nobody is dissatisfied with his appearance, his intelligence, his family tree, his education, or his position in the world. Because nobody regrets his nationality, an Irishman would never dream of changing places with an Italian, a Thracian with an Athenian, or a Scythian with a man from the Fortunate Isles. And oh, the singular dexterity of nature that, with such a great variety of gifts to bestow, she made all equal! Wherever she scanted her gifts a trifle, Philautia compensated with an extra helping of self-esteem—but I've got things all backward here because really self-satisfaction is the greatest gift of all.

Had I not better say straight out that no great project is undertaken without my support, no great discoveries made in the arts of which I am not at the bottom? For instance, isn't war the prototype of all honorable and heroic enterprises? But what is more stupid than to start a conflict

---

6. The Latin of this sentence turns on the concept of *decorum*, which implies behaving in a seemly and decent manner. It can be a literary as well as a social standard.
7. Nireus was the most handsome of the Greeks at Troy, Thersites the ugliest; Phaon was a youth

beloved by Sappho, Nestor a hero who lived three generations. A sow teaching Minerva is proverbial for a blockhead pedant explaining a subject he doesn't understand to a student who already knows it.

for reasons uncertain at best, from which both sides are bound to reap a harvest more of evil than of good? About those who perish, as about the Megarenses, there's 'nothing more to be said.'[8] But when the armed ranks are drawn up on both sides and the trumpets bray, what, I ask you, is then the value of those wise men who have worn themselves out on their studies till they hardly have any life left in their chilly veins? Lusty and thick-thewed men are called for, with as much courage as may be, and as few brains. An exception might be made for a soldier like Demosthenes, who followed the precept of the poet Archilochus, and at the first sight of the enemy threw down his shield and took to his heels—as pitiful a soldier as he was a far-sighted orator.[9] But, they say, wise strategy is very important to the art of war. In a general I don't doubt it is; but even in him it is military, not philosophical wisdom, and in the ranks, war is the work of parasites, panders, pickpockets, highway robbers, plowboys, sots, beggars, and similar riffraff. It's no work for philosophers carrying the lighted tapers of wisdom.

The career of Socrates shows clearly how little philosophers are worth in the common business of life. Though he was called wise by the oracle of Apollo—and that wasn't the wisest of its judgments—he tried only once to bring up a matter of public business, and then he was hooted out of the assembly.[1] In fact, he wasn't altogether silly, for he declined the epithet of "wise," saying it belonged only to god; and he also said a sensible man should keep clear of public business. But he would have done better to warn anyone aspiring to be included in the human race to avoid wisdom altogether. After all, what was it but his wisdom that led Socrates to drink the hemlock when he was under accusation?[2] While he was philosophizing about clouds and abstractions, measuring the foot of a flea and marvelling at the voice of a gnat, he failed completely to study those matters that pertain to the common life of men.[3] But here to help out this teacher under sentence of death comes his pupil Plato, a doughty supporter, no doubt, who was so upset by the buzz of a crowd that he was hardly able to pronounce the first half of his opening sentence.[4] That reminds me of Theophrastus, who started a speech and abruptly fell silent, as if a wolf had glared at him. Isocrates was so faint of heart that he could barely speak above a whisper in public. When Cicero started his orations he was generally all of a tremble, like a timorous schoolboy. Quintilian explains his weakness as natural to a con-

8. Halfway between Corinth and Athens, Megara was caught up in the great Peloponnesian war; the city's anticlimactic disappearance from that war is described in chapter 13 of Thucydides' history; after that, he has nothing to say of them.
9. Plutarch tells us that the Spartans expelled Archilochus the poet as soon as they learned he had written a line saying it was better to quit than fight. Plutarch's life of Demosthenes tells the story of his deserting on the field of battle.
1. The story of Socrates' debacle in the assembly is Folly's invention.
2. Socrates, accused of impiety by bigots, was forced

to drink the poison hemlock.
3. Folly's impressions of Socrates' intellectual pursuits are largely taken from Aristophanes' satiric play The Clouds.
4. Plato's failure as a public speaker is recorded by the biographer of philosophers, Diogenes Laertius 2.41. The story about Theophrastus is told by Aulus Gellius, Noctes Atticae 8.9. That a wolf's glare could freeze the words in a person's throat was a popular superstition formalized in a folk saying. Isocrates was a famous Greek orator of the third century B.C.

scious orator measuring the difficulty of his task;[5] but isn't that excuse actually an admission that wisdom interferes with performance? What would these men do in a battle to be fought with cold steel if they're so frightened of a mock engagement with mere words?

After all this, Lord help us, we're bound to be served up with that famous saying of Plato's that 'societies will be happy only if philosophers are kings or kings philosophers.'[6] But if you look into the historians you will find beyond question that states were never worse off than when the kingship fell to some philosophaster or bookworm. I expect the example of the two Catos will prove the point: the first continually vexed the smooth flow of state business with his idiot accusations, and the second, while defending the liberties of the Roman people with all the wisdom in the world, effectually subverted them.[7] You can add to them your Brutuses, Cassiuses, Gracchuses, and even Cicero himself, who did just as much damage to the Roman republic as Demosthenes did to the Athenian.[8] Marcus Aurelius—if we concede he was a good emperor, for I could challenge his title to that distinction, since he was burdensome to his subjects and much hated just because he was such a philosopher[9]— even though he was a good man himself, did more harm to the state through the son he left behind than he did good through his administration. And this is the way of these learned men, they are unlucky in general and particularly in their children. I think nature arranges this on purpose, to keep the infection of wisdom from spreading too widely through humankind. And so, as everyone knows, the son of Cicero was a degenerate, and the children of Socrates resembled their mother more than their father,[1] as some fellow delicately put the matter: the blunt of it is that they were fools.

If it were just in public business that your wise men were about as deft as 'an ass with a lyre,' that would be tolerable; but they're not a tad better on any other of life's occasions. Bring a sage to a banquet and he'll either sit in gloomy silence or confound the company by turning the occasion into a doctor's oral. Ask him to a dance, and you'll get an idea of how a camel waltzes. Take him to the theater and his sour puss will curdle everyone else's enjoyment, so that your learned Cato will be asked to vacate the premises if he can't alter his contemptuous expression.[2] Let him drop in on a friendly conversation; suddenly it's a case of the wolf

---

5. Quintilian's book on oratory mentions this trait of Cicero 11.1.
6. Plato said it in *The Republic*.
7. The two Catos are the Censor (234–149 B.C.) and his great-grandson, Cato of Utica (95–46 B.C.); Plutarch wrote biographies of both.
8. Brutus and Cassius are faulted for their conspiracy against Caesar; Gaius and Tiberius Gracchus (of the second century B.C.) for their support of plebeians against patricians; Cicero as a leader, with Antony, of the unsuccessful war against Octavius (Augustus), and Demosthenes for having incited the Athenians to a fatal war against Philip of Macedon.

9. Marcus Aurelius was not an unpopular emperor, and his *Meditations*, written in Greek and for private occasions, could not have made him so. Folly in her mock-encomium sometimes assumes the privilege of Momus, to put the worst construction on everything.
1. Seneca the elder reports the worthlessness of Cicero's son, and Aristotle in his *Rhetoric* says the sons of Socrates were dullards. *Suasoriae*, 7.13; *Rhetoric* 2.16.
2. Cato the Censor, most severe of moralists, was naturally outraged by the shows of the Floralia, most licentious of Roman festivals.

in the fable.[3] If something is to be bought, or a contract is to be negoti-
ated, or, in a word, if any of those arrangements are to be made without
which daily life would not go on, you'll find your wise man more like a
wooden post than a human being. So in fact he is completely useless to
himself, his family, or his country because he knows nothing of everyday
matters and exists on a completely different plane from that of common
opinion and popular customs. Naturally people dislike him; his way of
life and habit of thinking are completely different from theirs. For what
goes on among the common people that isn't full of foolishness, contrived by fools for fools? If anyone wants to stand apart from all this
foolishness, let him imitate Timon, seek out a desert, and there live
alone revelling in his wisdom.[4]

But let me go back to a topic on which I barely started: what force do
you suppose brought into civil concord those primitive men, savage as
their native rocks and forests—what force if not mutual flattery? The
lyres of Amphion and Orpheus can signify nothing else.[5] What impulse
recalled the Roman plebeians, on the brink of mutiny, to their civic
allegiance? Was it a philosophic discourse? Scarcely. Rather, it was a
ridiculous and puerile fable about the belly making its apology to the
other members of the body. Hardly any better was the tale told by Themistocles about the fox and the hedgehog.[6] What learned oration could
have worked as well as the silly story recited by Sertorius to the Spaniards
about a fantastic white deer? or the equally ridiculous Spartan stories
about trained and untrained puppies? or that other one about pulling
hairs from a horse's tail one strand at a time?[7] I hardly need mention
Minos and Numa, both of whom reigned over their stupid subjects on
the strength of fabulous stories.[8] It is trifles like this that stir to action
that great beast the people. What city ever accepted the laws devised by
Plato and Aristotle, or undertook to guide itself by the precepts of Socrates? On the other hand, what impulse led the Decii to devote themselves to death? what force drew Quintus Curtius into the abyss,[9] unless
it was thirst for glory, a most alluring siren, but marvellously unpopular
with the men of wisdom. What sight could be more stupid, they ask,

---

3. See above, p. 24, n. 4.
4. Lucian wrote a dialogue on Timon the misan-
thrope, and in 1506 Erasmus had translated it.
5. Amphion with his charmed lyre built the stone
walls of Thebes; Orpheus with his music charmed
beasts, trees, and rocks into a circle of concord.
6. The fable about the belly and the rest of the
body, originally told in Livy 2, is best known from
its recital in Shakespeare's *Coriolanus* 1.1. The fox,
though covered with bloodsucking flies, forbade the
hedgehog to remove them because they would just
be replaced by other, hungrier flies. The story,
which Erasmus assigns to Themistocles, comes from
Plutarch's *Moralia* 10.115.
7. Sertorius used the white deer, supposedly of
divine origin, to impose on some credulous Spaniards; he also showed his army that hard tasks are
better accomplished gradually by having one man
pull hairs singly from a horse's tail, while another

man tugged vainly at another horse's tail, grasping
all the hairs at once (Plutarch, *Life of Sertorius*).
Lycurgus, the Spartan lawgiver, showed the
importance of training by putting a bowl of food
and a live rabbit between two dogs, only one of
whom had been taught to hunt (Plutarch, *On the
Education of Children*).
8. Minos on Crete and Numa in Italy both claimed
they had supernatural guidance and imposed that
belief on their people.
9. The Decii (father and son) both sought death
on the field of battle to ensure Roman victories
(Livy 8 and 10). The story of Marcus Curtius is
told in Livy 7; an abyss opened in the Roman
forum, and the oracle declared it could not be closed
till Rome's most precious jewel was cast into it;
Curtius mounted his horse, leaped in, and was
swallowed up.

than a candidate begging humbly for votes, flattering the dregs of the populace, buying their favor with handouts, basking in the applause of all those idiots, lapping up their applause, and allowing himself to be carried like a dummy in parades before the people, only to stand in the forum finally, a piece of brass?[1] The hero must put up, as well, with special names and epithets, divine honors (often granted to very sorry predecessors), and public ceremonies associating him, as part of the pantheon, with a set of very scoundrelly tyrants indeed. These carryings-on are utterly ridiculous, you'd need more than one Democritus to laugh at them properly.[2] Who denies it? And yet from these sources spring the deeds of mighty heroes, trumpeted to the heavens by the literary works of innumerable scribblers. This same foolish desire of praise gave rise to cities, held together empires, built legal and religious systems, erected political and religious structures; in fact, human life as a whole is nothing but a kind of fool's game.

Now, to turn to the arts and sciences, what rouses men to invent and exploit such extraordinary (as they suppose) exercises, if it isn't desire of reputation? They put long hours and agonized efforts into the pursuit of fame—I can't imagine how they conceive of it, but nothing could be more inane. Now aren't these the most foolish of mortal men? To be sure, you can enjoy, thanks to their folly, all the good things they produce, and you don't even have to be as crazy as they are—which is the best thing of all.

And now that I've established my titles to valor and industry, suppose I prove that I am also the champion of prudence. Somebody is bound to say that I might just as well try to mix fire with water. But I think I can do this too, if you'll favor me, as you've done so far, with attentive ears and minds. To begin, if prudence rises from experience of things, who is more likely to deserve the honor of this attribute, the wise man who (partly from modesty and partly from fearfulness) never takes a chance, or the fool, who is quite undeterred by modesty, which he lacks entirely, or by danger, which he never recognizes? The man of learning hides behind the volumes of the ancients, and derives nothing from them but empty verbal formulas. The fool, approaching the problem directly and venturing upon it boldly, acquires true prudence from his experience, if I'm not mistaken. Even blind Homer seems to have seen this, when he says, "once a thing is done, a fool sees it."[3] Two obstacles chiefly prevent us from acquiring knowledge of things: diffidence, which beclouds the mind, and fearfulness, which prevents us from trying anything that looks hazardous. But how gloriously folly liberates us from these two

1. Bronze statues were erected in the forum to honor dead heroes. Horace, Satires 2.3, may be responsible for the sardonic turn of phrase, but censorious old Cato also disdained the practice.
2. Democritus, "the laughing philosopher," ridiculed everything.
3. Iliad 17.32. The Homeric context shows clearly

that some fools do not draw wisdom from an event. Menelaus speaks the line as a threat to Euphorbus; he foolishly disregards it and is promptly killed. The proverb "Don't be a fool and learn from experience" is also cited in Plato's Symposium, by Alcibiades.

encumbrances! Few men realize how many different benefits can come from not being ashamed or afraid of anything.

But if they prefer to limit prudence to good judgment, let me beg you to note how far they are from the thing itself when they lay claim to the name. For it's clear that all human affairs, like the Silenus-figures described by Alcibiades,[4] have two faces quite different from one another. So that what at first glance (so to speak) appears death, is really, if you look under the surface, life; on the contrary, what looks like life is really death. What seems beautiful is really ugly; riches are poverty; the contemptible is glorious, the erudite is ignorant, the strong feeble, the noble vulgar, the joyful melancholy, the promising fatal, the friendly hostile, the healthy diseased—in short, if you open up the Silenus, you will find everything the opposite of what the exterior promised. If you find this notion a little abstract and philosophical, take heart, I'll make it clear as day—'plain as a pikestaff,' to use the old expression. It's generally admitted that a king is both wealthy and powerful. But if he possesses none of the goods of the mind, if nothing gives him any satisfaction, then he is poor indeed. And if his mind is afflicted with many vices, then he is a most abject slave. I could multiply examples, but this one instance will suffice. Well, someone will ask, So what? What's the point? Let me make my case. If someone in a theater should try to strip the masks off the actors in the middle of the play, and show the actors' actual faces, wouldn't he be destroying the entire illusion, and wouldn't he deserve to be pitched out of the theater by the entire audience as a troublesome lunatic? For what he had revealed would be seen as a whole new order of things; the actor who before had appeared a woman would now be seen as a man, the juvenile would be revealed as a gaffer, the mighty king of a minute ago would be a mere milksop, a god would shrink to a dwarf. In short, if you take away the illusions, you ruin the whole fable. It's the makeup and the scenery that catch the eyes of the spectators. Now what else is the life of mortal men but a kind of fable in which the actors appear on stage under the disguise of different masks?[5] Each plays his assigned part till the stage manager comes forth and takes them off stage. Indeed, he often assigns one actor several roles, so the performer who just now acted a king in purple majesty presently comes back a humble servant in rags. They are all but shadows of real persons, yet there's no other way to put on the show.

But here some wise man might well drop out of the sky to confront the audience and cry out that this nobleman whom everyone hails as lord and master is not even a proper man because he is driven by his emotions like a beast, that he is the lowest of slaves because subjected through his own choice to so many and such shameful masters. Or again, suppose our lofty moralist takes after someone grieving for the death of a parent and tells him to be merry because now at last his beloved parent

4. In Plato's *Symposium*, Alcibiades praises Socrates as resembling the little jewel boxes shaped like Silenus—ugly on the outside, precious within.

5. The comparison of life to a stage play was a common theme long before Shakespeare wrote "All the world's a stage," etc. (*As You Like It*, 2.7).

is starting to live in heaven, whereas on this earth he had nothing to anticipate but death. Suppose he came up to a man very proud of his ancestry, and called him a baseborn bastard because he was a stranger to virtue, which is the only source of true nobility. And then suppose he treated all other people the same way. What would he get by this behavior except to be considered by everyone a raving lunatic? As wisdom out of place is the height of the ridiculous, so prudence perversely misapplied is the height of imprudence. The perverse man fails to adjust his actions to the present state of things, he disdains the give-and-take of the intellectual marketplace, he won't even acknowledge the common rule of the barroom, drink up or get out—all of which amounts to demanding that the play should no longer be a play. On the other hand, the truly prudent man reflects that since he is mortal himself, he shouldn't want to be wiser than befits a mortal, but should cast his lot in with the rest of the human race and blunder along in good company. But this, they say, is folly. I can hardly deny it, but let them confess also that this is the way the play of life is staged.

But now, oh ye immortal gods, shall I bring up this new topic or leave it concealed? Why be quiet, though, when the point is truer than true? Perhaps in such a momentous matter I'd better call down the muses from Helicon,[6] ladies whom the poets commonly invoke on smaller occasions than this. Approach, then, a little closer, ye daughters of Jove, while I show that there is no access to that marvellous wisdom, the fortress of felicity as the wise themselves call it, without taking folly for a guide.

And first of all, it's confessed on all sides that the emotions are the province of folly. Indeed, this is the way we distinguish the wise man from the fool, that the one is governed by his reason, the other by his emotions. Thus the stoics banish all emotions from the wise man's life, as so many diseases. Yet these emotions not only serve as guides for those who press toward the gates of wisdom, they also act as spurs and incitements to the practice of every virtue, and stimulate men to the performance of good deeds. No doubt that double-dyed stoic Seneca strongly rejects this idea, denying that the wise man is entitled to any emotion whatever;[7] but in so doing he doesn't leave him a shred of humanity, converting him instead into some sort of new god or *demiurgos*, such as never existed or will exist anywhere on earth. Or rather, to put it more accurately, what he produces is a marble statue of a man, insensitive and without a trace of human feeling.

Well, if that's what they want, let them rejoice in their wise man, love him without fear of any rivals, and carry him off to live in Plato's *Republic* or, if they prefer, in the realm of abstract ideas or in the gardens of Tantalus.[8] Who, catching sight of such a man, would not stand aghast,

6. Myth declares that the muses live atop Mount Helicon in Greece.
7. Seneca, epistles 71 and 85—though they don't properly represent his full position.

8. The gardens of Tantalus, who was tortured by the gods with perpetual thirst and hunger, are exactly nowhere.

and run away from him as from a spook or a monster?—a man so hard-
ened to all the feelings of nature, so indifferent to love or pity, that he
might as well be made of flint or Parian marble. Nothing escapes him,
he never makes a mistake; as if he were gifted with the eyes of Lynceus,[9]
there's nothing he doesn't see, nothing about which his judgment isn't
absolutely correct, nothing of which he's ignorant. He's absolutely satisfied with himself, rich in himself, healthy in mind and body without
help, king over himself, absolutely free—in short, completely self-suffi-
cient and utterly complacent. He welcomes no friend, and is nobody
else's friend, he wouldn't hesitate to tell the gods themselves to go hang,
he despises and ridicules as madness whatever life has to offer. And an
animal of this sort is your man of ideal wisdom. I ask you, if it came to
a vote, what city would wish itself a magistrate of that ilk, what army
would impose on itself such a general? What woman would choose for
herself a husband of that sort, what host would want that sort of guest,
what servant would hire out to such a master or continue long in his
service? Who wouldn't prefer any random fellow from the crowd of common fools, who being foolish himself could give orders to other fools or
take orders from them, who would please his fellow-fools (that is, practically everyone), who would be loving to his wife, a boon companion
to his friends, a jolly good fellow in the tavern, an entertaining dinner-
guest—in short, a man who thinks nothing human alien to him?[1] But I
confess this wise man has already become a bore; let's turn the topic in
some other direction.

Well, then, if someone could look down from a lofty point of vantage,
as the poets say Jove does, he would see the endless array of calamities
that beset human life. How painful and squalid is the act of birth, how
troublesome the process of education, what perils surround infancy, what
labors are imposed on young manhood, what weariness fills old age,
how bitter is the approach of death, what legions of diseases lie in wait,
how many accidents threaten, what troubles pile up—there's nothing
that isn't dipped in gall. And I can't even number all those evils that
men inflict on one another, such as poverty, imprisonment, shame,
torture, treachery, libel, slander, litigation, and fraud. But, it's obvious,
I've just started to 'number the sands of the sea.' What crimes men have
committed to deserve such punishment, or what angry god forced them
to be born into such misery, it's no part of my business to say here. But
if anyone thinks over the matter seriously, won't he be inclined to approve
the example, wretched though it is, of the Milesian maidens?[2] Yet who
were those who most often shortened their own lives? Who but the near
neighbors and associates of wisdom? Among whom, though I might dwell
on Diogenes, Xenocrates, Cato, Cassius, and Brutus, there was Chiron,

9. Parian marble was traditionally the hardest, used
for the best sculpture. Lynceus, pilot of Jason's
adventurous ship the Argo, could see through a
wall; hence the modern name for a sharpsighted
wildcat, "lynx."

1. The phrase is from Terence's play *Heautonti-
morumenos* (The Self-Torturer).
2. The virgins of Miletus were reported to hang
themselves in unusual numbers for no particular
reason.

who had immortality in his grasp but preferred death.[3] You see, I don't
doubt, what would happen if all men were wise: we would need a fresh
supply of clay and another potter to replace Prometheus.

But I make such good use of human ignorance and imbecility, playing sometimes on forgetfulness of evils and other times on hope of good,
sprinkling in a bit of pleasure here and there, that I bring mankind some
relief from their accumulated woes. Indeed, they don't generally want
to quit life even when the thread of the Fates has run out, and life has
all but left them. The less reason they have for holding to existence, the
more avidly they cling to it with blind tenacity. Thanks to my help you
see everywhere men as old as Nestor, in whom even the appearance of
a human being barely survives—babblers, mindless, toothless wrecks,
white-haired or bald entirely; or, let me put it in the better words of
Aristophanes,[4] "slovenly, stooped, wrinkled, bald, toothless, impo-
tent"—yet they cling to life so fiercely, and try so hard to 'seem young,'
that one old codger will dye his last gray hairs, while another will stick a
wig on his pate, and still another will fill his gums with false teeth,
borrowed perhaps from a pig's jaw, and a fourth will languish for love of
a girl, performing more amorous antics than any young man you want
to name. And then for an old dotard like this, with one foot in the grave,
to marry some tender young bud of a girl, without a dowry of course,
and destined quickly to become someone else's peaches and cream—
that's so common nowadays that it's almost considered the height of
good form.

But it's even more macabre to think of the old women in the last stages
of senility and so cadaverous that you'd think they'd been pulled out of
the grave; yet they never cease repeating "life is good," while they're
constantly in heat, or, as the Greeks put it, 'rutting like a goat'[5]—hiring
a young gigolo for scads of money, smearing their faces with makeup,
hovering over the mirror, plucking hairs out of their crotch, showing off
their withered and pendulous breasts. They quaver out love-songs in the
hope of rousing a lover's languishing desire, they drink deep and try to
join the company of younger women, they scribble billets-doux. Everyone laughs at these idiocies, and considers them ridiculous, as they are;
but the old crones are delighted with themselves, they float in an ocean
of pleasure and swim up to the chin in honey. With blessings from me,
they are happy. People who find this spectacle just too ridiculous ought
to stop and ask themselves if it's better to live this sort of enjoyable life
with the aid of folly, or to 'look around for a beam,' as they say, 'from
which to hang oneself.' Indeed, they may draw popular contempt on
themselves, but that's nothing to my fools, who either don't recognize
the disgrace or if they do, easily disregard it. If a rock falls on your head,

3. Except for Xenocrates, who died in an accident, all these classical figures deliberately shortened their own lives. Chiron, wisest and gentlest
of the centaurs, was accidentally wounded by Hercules' poisoned arrow; being immortal, he could
have recovered, but bestowed his immortality on
Prometheus. Some say he can still be seen in the
nighttime heavens as Sagittarius.
4. Aristophanes, Plutus.
5. Ibid.

[Lustful Old Lady]

that's definitely painful. But shame, infamy, scorn, and ill words do harm only so far as they are felt; if one isn't aware of them, they do no damage at all. "What matter if the whole community hisses you, so long as you can applaud yourself?"[6] And for that to take place, just leave it to folly.

But I think I hear the philosophers raising objections. It's utter misery, they say, to be in the clutches of folly, to be bewildered, to blunder, never to know anything for sure. On the contrary, I say, that's what it is to be a man. I don't see why they should call that condition miserable into which we were born, in which we were bred, in which we have grown up—which is the common fate of every one of us. There's nothing miserable about what conforms with one's basic nature—unless someone wants to argue that man should be considered wretched because he can't fly like the birds, gallop around like the quadrupeds, or threaten his foes with horns like a bull. Such a fellow might equally well deplore the fate of a thoroughbred horse because he has never learned grammar and doesn't eat pasty pies, or think a bull must be wretched because he cuts such an ill figure as a gymnast. In fact, a horse ignorant of grammar is not wretched for that reason, and no more is a foolish man automatically unhappy, because these conditions belong to their natures.

6. Horace, *Satires* 1.1.

But the quibbleweavers have something else to say. A special talent for the learned disciplines has been granted to man, so they say, in order that by using them he may compensate for the deficiencies that nature has imposed on him. As if this notion had the least face of truth, that nature, who lavished so many pains on perfecting gnats, grasses, and flowers, nodded off to sleep while making man, so the sciences would be needed to perfect him—the sciences, which Thoth,[7] that demonic enemy of the human race, invented for man's ultimate destruction, and which are so far from serving human happiness that they actually hinder it. That is the real reason they were invented, as the ingenious king described by Plato argues concerning the invention of letters.[8] That is how the arts and sciences crept into human life, along with other banes of our existence; the same creators devised them all—that is to say, the demons, sources of all evil, whose very name [daemones = scientes] means "those who know."

In the golden age, simple men flourished, without all that armor-plate of the sciences, under the leadership of nature and natural instincts alone. What need was there of grammar when everyone spoke the same language, and nobody demanded anything of speech except that one man should understand another? What was the use of legal rhetoric when no man brought suit against his neighbor? Why was special wisdom required to draw up laws when men had not yet developed the bad habits from which, it's generally admitted, the need for good laws arose? Men were too religious in those days to go poking with profane curiosity into the hidden aspects of nature, such as the dimensions, motions, and influences of the stars, or the occult causes of phenomena; they thought it wicked for mortal man to seek more knowledge than befitted his destiny. The madness of asking what lay behind the highest heavens never so much as entered their minds. But as the purity of the golden age faded with time,[9] first the arts were discovered (by evil geniuses, as I said). At first there were not many of them, and those few were known to only a few people. Afterwards, the superstitious Chaldeans added six hundred more,[1] and the idle ingenuity of the Greeks contributed an overflow of purely verbal ingenuities, so that by now study of a single grammar can provide a lifetime of torture.

Still, among these many different disciplines, those are most highly prized which come closest to common sense, that is, to popular folly. Theologians starve, natural scientists are cold-shouldered, astrologers are ridiculed, and dialecticians neglected. "The doctor of medicine alone is worth all the others put together."[2] And within this profession itself, the

---

7. Thoth is the Egyptian god who invented letters and the art of writing; his sacred bird is the ibis.
8. In the *Phaedrus* Plato has a Theban king, Thamus, argue that writing struck a fatal blow at man's powers of memory.
9. Ducking the problem of original sin, as Folly does here by invoking the myth of the golden age,

makes Folly's argument, semi-serious at best, a lot easier.
1. The Chaldeans, who lived in Persia, were thought to have inherited the occult wisdom of the Babylonian astrologers. "Six hundred" is a deliberately impressionistic number.
2. Homer, *Iliad* 11.

closer a man comes to an ignorant, arrogant, inconsiderate quack, the more highly he will be esteemed even by princes seated in lordly state. For medicine, especially as it is now practiced by most doctors, is nothing but a branch of flattery, like rhetoric itself.

After doctors, next place must be given to shyster lawyers—indeed, I'm not sure they shouldn't occupy the first position, since—setting my own opinion aside—the philosophers have agreed in overwhelming numbers to ridicule their profession as asinine. Yet, asses though they are, great matters and small alike are settled by the judgments of these men. By their means and for their benefit great fortunes are amassed, while the theologian, having struggled through all his volumes of divinity, dines on beans and wages war on bugs and black beetles. Thus it appears those arts are most blessed which have the closest affinity with stupidity, and those people are happiest who have been able to avoid contact with the arts and sciences altogether, simply following nature, which never fails them except when they try to reach beyond the proper bounds of their human nature. False faces are odious to nature, and a man gets ahead much faster if he does without artifice.

For, look you, isn't it clear that among the other creatures those enjoy most happiness who are most remote from formal learning and are instructed by no tutor other than nature herself? What community is more happy or more remarkable than that of the bees? Though they don't seem even to have all the bodily senses, what has architecture discovered to equal their structures? What philosopher ever devised a better republic than theirs?[3] On the other hand, the horse, whose bodily senses are like those of humans and who has learned to live in close association with men, has had to share in human misfortunes. The competitive spirit that makes him strain to win races often leaves him broken-winded, and when he carries his rider into battle, both often fall before the pikemen and bite the dust together. I needn't detail the other tortures, such as cruel bits and sharp spurs, the prison of the stable, the whips, cudgels, hobbles, and saddles—in brief, all the apparatus of his slavery—to which he submits when, following the men of war, he trudges off blindly to do battle with the enemy. How much to be preferred is the life of flies and birds, who live for the moment and are subject only to the laws of nature—so long, that is, as they avoid the snares of men. When birds are shut up in cages and taught to imitate human voices, it's amazing how far they degenerate from their natural brilliance: clear evidence that what nature teaches is better for creatures of every sort than the contrived devices of art.

Let me recall to you that never-sufficiently-to-be-praised Pythagorean cock,[4] who in his own person had occupied many shapes, as of a philos-

---

3. The bees do not, as it happens, have a republic. They are a gynocratic monarchy, ruled by a queen. But Folly is following Virgil (*Georgic* 4), not nature.

4. Lucian's dialogue *The Cock* details the adventures of a talkative chicken who, in the course of his metamorphoses, as imagined by Pythagoras, had been many different creatures.

opher, a man, a woman, a king, a lowly subject, a fish, a horse, a frog, even I think a sponge—after which he concluded that no animal was more wretched than man because all the others were content with the limits imposed by nature, but only man tried to go beyond those limits. The same learned bird greatly preferred blockheads to learned and important men; and the hog Gryllus was a great deal smarter than Ulysses, that man of many schemes, when he preferred to grunt in a sty rather than take part with the hero in his numerous misfortunes.[5] Homer too, though the father of many fables, seems to have been much of this mind because, while he calls mortal men 'wretched and miserable' and repeatedly refers to Ulysses, his model of a wise man, as 'ill-fated,' he never applies such a word to Paris, Ajax, or Achilles. Why so? Why plainly because the wily trickster never acted without consulting Pallas, he knew too much for his own good, and removed himself too far from nature's guidance. So it is among all men, those are farthest from felicity who strive most earnestly for wisdom, showing themselves double fools, first as they are born men, and then because they have forgotten that basic condition, and like the giants make war on nature with the machinery of their learning.[6] By contrast, those men seem least wretched who come closest to the condition and intelligence of beasts, and never try to rise above their human status.

I'm going to make this clear, not with the enthymemes of the stoics, but by a plain and obvious example. Tell me, by all the gods, is anyone happier than that class of men whom we commonly call fools, idiots, morons, and simpletons—names, in my opinion, of exquisite beauty? On the face of it, you may think what I am saying is eccentric or even absurd, but I assure you it's absolutely true. In the first place, they are free from the fear of death—not the least of evils, by heaven! They suffer no remorse of conscience, they are not haunted by ghost stories or frightened by bogies and banshees; they endure no agonies of fear over impending punishments, nor are they tantalized with expectations of future rewards. In short, they are exempt from a thousand ills to which this life is subject. They know neither shame nor fear, neither hope, nor hate, nor love. If they could approach a little closer to the condition of beasts, they would even be incapable of sin, from what the theologians tell us.[7] Think it over some time, you ape of wisdom, add up the troubles that distress your mind night and day, make a single heap out of all the discontents of your existence, and then you'll have some idea of all the troubles from which I've liberated my fools. Add to this that they are not only perpetually joyful themselves, playing, singing, and laughing, but they are also a source of delight to others, spreading smiles, jokes,

5. Plutarch's dialogue *Gryllus* stimulated much semi-jocose reflection on whether it's better to be a man or a pig.
6. In classical mythology, the giants tried to revolt against Jove, but were crushed and thrown out of heaven. The idea of the "over-reacher" who tries

to overstep his prescribed limits recurs frequently in Renaissance morality and fable.
7. That animals could not be damned (because they had no free will) was bothering men as late as the seventeenth century; see John Donne, "Holy Sonnets" 9 and 12.

[Fool with Coxcomb]

quips, and giggles wherever they turn, as if they had been created by
God expressly to enliven the melancholy of human life.

And this is why, though other men cherish different feelings toward
one another, everyone feels the same possessive warmth toward my fools.
People seek out their company, feed them liberally, protect and embrace
them, rush to their aid if any evil befalls them. They can say or do just
what they like. Nobody tries to harm them, even wild beasts refrain from
attacking them as if aware on instinct of their innocence. They are in
fact sacred to the gods, and especially to me, and this is why everyone
holds them in the very highest esteem. Loftiest monarchs are so delighted
with them that without their presence some cannot eat a meal, undertake any business, or pass an idle hour.[8] Indeed, kings sometimes show
a striking preference for these imbeciles of mine before those grim men
of wisdom—whom, neverthless, for appearance's sake, they are obliged
to patronize. And the reason for this preference is not hard to find, or
very surprising. The men of widom set before monarchs nothing but bad
news; out of confidence in their own wisdom, they don't hesitate to grate
the tender ear with gritty truths. But my fools provide something that
kings are always glad to get from any quarter, in any form—that is, jokes,
jollity, a good laugh, fun.

8. On the history of privileged fools, see Barbara Swain, *Fools and Folly during The Middle Ages and the
Renaissance* (New York, 1932).

[A King and His Fool]

And notice also this other talent, far from contemptible, that is the special gift of fools they and they alone are always direct and truthful. No doubt that saying of Alcibiades reported by Plato attributes truth to wine and boys,[9] but all that praise should really be directed to me, as Euripides bears witness in a famous proverb he made about me, "The fool speaks out his folly,"[1] Whatever a real fathead has in his heart, he shows it in his face, and promptly pours it forth. But wise men carry in their mouths a double tongue (as the same Euripides has said), of which one speaks the truth and the other what is expedient at the moment.[2] The wise men can turn black to white, blow hot and cold, and say one thing while thinking something entirely different. Princes, though their state is doubtless happy in general, seem to me utterly wretched in this respect, that there's nobody who will tell them the truth, and they are constrained to take flatterers for friends.

But, someone will say, princes hate to hear the truth, and that's why they avoid the company of the wise, one of whom might be more outspoken than the others, and say what's really right instead of what he thinks will please. That's how it actually is, princes do hate the truth. But a strange thing happens with my fools, that when they speak truths,

9. Alcibiades (in Plato's *Symposium*) doesn't quite say that drunks, like children, tell the truth, but he comes close.

1. Euripides, *The Bacchae*.
2. The play titled *Rhesus*, alluded to here, is not certainly by Euripides, at least in its known form.

even unwelcome truths, they are received with uproarious laughter. In fact, the very same words which, spoken by a wise man, would cost him his life are accepted with incredible pleasure when spoken by a fool. For truth has genuine power to please, if not accompanied by anything offensive; and this gift god has granted only to fools. For the same reason, or almost so, women delight in the company of fools, the sex being naturally more inclined to pleasure and trifling. Then whatever comes of their dallying in this way, even if it sometimes gets a little too serious, they pass off as a joke and a game, women being naturally clever that way, especially in covering up their own follies.

Let me return, then, to the felicity of the foolish, who, when they have completed the term of their life in perfect pleasure, without any fear of death or even awareness of it, depart for the Elysian fields,[3] there to entertain the pious, peaceful souls of the dead with their japes. And now compare if you will the lot of any wise man you want to name with a fool of this description. Imagine that you oppose to him some paragon of wisdom, a man who has devoted his entire youth and early manhood to acquiring the arts and sciences, who has lost the best part of his existence in perpetual study, pain, and anxiety, who has not enjoyed in all the rest of his life so much as a scintilla of pleasure, always sparing, saving, sad, solemn, severe, and strict on himself, morose and melancholy with others, afflicted with a pallid complexion, a gaunt figure, a stooped posture, premature senility and white hairs, departing life before his time. Though in fact what does it matter when a man of this sort dies, since he can't properly be said ever to have lived? There's the portrait of your wise man.

But now the 'chorus of stoic frogs' starts croaking at me again, saying that "nothing is more wretched than madness," and folly of the highest order is either madness or next thing to it. What else, they ask, is insanity but mental aberration? But they have it all wrong, and with the help of the Muses I can rip up this syllogism of theirs like the others. Their point seems, on the surface of things, well taken. But just as Socrates taught in Plato's dialogue[4] that we should make two Venuses by cutting the one apart, and two Cupids by dividing the solitary figure, so I think it behooves these dialecticians to distinguish one madness from another, at least if they want to pass for sane men themselves. For not all madness is a calamity, otherwise Horace would hardly have written, "Does a welcome madness now come over me?"[5] Nor would Plato have assigned the madness of poets, prophets, and lovers a conspicuous place among the good things of life; nor would the priestess have referred to the great undertaking of Aeneas as a sort of madness.[6] In fact, madness takes two different shapes, one which the fearful Furies call forth from the underworld when, with snaky locks flying, they stir the passions of men to

3. In classical mythology, the Elysian fields are the place where those favored by the gods enjoy after death a blissful existence.
4. Plato, Symposium.

5. Odes 3.4.
6. Plato, Phaedrus; Aeneid 6.135. The great undertaking of Aeneas was the founding of Rome.

warlike hatred or rouse them to insatiable thirst for gold, to illicit and forbidden lust, to parricide, incest, sacrilege, and other such hateful actions. Again, they sometimes haunt the soul conscious of its own guilt with ghastly apparitions and fiery premonitions of revenge. But there's another sort of madness, far different from this, for which I am responsible, and which is above all things to be desired. It comes about whenever some genial aberration of the mind frees it from anxiety and worry while at the same time imbuing it with the many fragrances of pleasure. And this sort of mental error is what Cicero, writing to Atticus, wishes for his friend as a special bounty of the gods, a delusion that will relieve his distress over the evils of the age.[7] Neither was that Greek in Horace very far astray, whose mania took the form of going to the theater every day by himself, to laugh, applaud and cry "Bravo!" because he thought wonderful plays were being performed, though in fact nobody was there at all. In every other respect, he was perfectly normal—'jovial with his friends, devoted to his wife, and indulgent with his servants, to the point of overlooking an occasional bottle missing from the cellar.' A course of medical treatments cured the man of his delusions, and restored him to perfect health, but he complained bitterly: "By God, you haven't helped me, friends, you've destroyed me by taking away my greatest pleasure and rooting out the folly that gave my life its richest savor."[8] And I think he was right, that they were more in need than he of a dose of hellbore when they treated such a merry and harmless folly as some sort of disease, to be expelled by medication.

As a matter of fact, I haven't yet decided whether every error of the senses or of the mind ought to go by the name of madness. If a nearsighted man takes a mule for a donkey or an uneducated man takes a snatch of doggerel for great poetry, neither will be thought really crazy. But if someone is deceived, not so much in his senses as in his mind—preternaturally and permanently deluded—he may be thought close to madness. Thus a man hearing an ass bray might think he was hearing a marvellous symphony, or a pauper from a backwoods hamlet might fancy himself Croesus king of Lydia.[9] But this sort of madness, if (as generally happens) it involves an agreeable delusion, brings no little amusement both to the person who experiences it and to those who can recognize the madman's folly because their own happens to be of a different sort. For this variety of insanity is more widespread than the average man realizes. Sometimes one madman laughs at another, and each gets pleasure from the other's absurdities; indeed, you will often find that the one who is more crazy laughs harder than the one who is less so.

Still, if Folly may venture to judge, I think the more different ways a man runs mad, the happier he is, provided he sticks with that variety of madness which is my specialty. But that leaves a wide field. I hardly

---

7. *Letters to Atticus* 3.13, but inaccurately cited.
8. *Epistles* 2.2. Hellbore was a potent purgative, supposedly good for addled brains.
9. "Rich as Croesus" was a proverbial expression in antiquity, and still is.

know whether anyone can be found in the entire human race who is wise twenty-four hours a day, and who is not subject to madness in one form or another. One sort of difference is clear. The man who, when he sees a pumpkin, supposes it's a woman, will be called crazy because not many people take part in that particular delusion of his. But when another man swears that his wife, whom he shares with half the neighborhood, is more chaste than Penelope,[1] and so flatters himself to the top of his bent, nobody calls him mad, because it's recognized as the common fate of husbands. The same sort of idiocy afflicts those who prefer before everything else the chase of wild beasts, and say they get indescribable delight from the blast of hunting horns and the howling of hounds. I expect such people think even dog-turds smell like cinnamon. But what pleasure is there in slaughtering animals, in whatever numbers? Killing bulls and sheep is a job for common butchers, but cutting up a wild animal, forsooth, is permitted only to a man of noble birth. Baring his head, on bended knee, using a special knife (for it would be sacrilege to use any other), he makes the ritual gestures, and then cuts off certain prescribed pieces in an exactly prescribed order. Meanwhile a hushed circle stands around, watching the ceremony as if it were a brand-new discovery, though they've seen it a hundred times before. If one of them happens to be given a little scrap of meat, he feels himself exalted as by a new accession of nobility. And so when they have finished dissecting and devouring the dead beast, what have they accomplished except to degrade themselves into beasts while imagining that they are living the life of kings?

Very similar to these is the class of men who are devoured by an insatiable passion for building, remodeling round structures into square ones and vice versa, knowing no limit or moderation, till they have reduced themselves to the last stages of poverty, without a place to set a table or lay their heads. But what of that? They have spent the intervening years in a dream of delight.

Beside these builders I think we can range those who strive by means of new, exotic skills to alter the substance of things, and who ransack heaven and earth for a certain fifth element, or quintessence.[2] These men are so besotted with the milk and honey of hope that they spare neither labor nor expense but go to enormous pains to delude themselves, persisting in their happy delusions till, having spent all their money, they can no longer afford to set up another furnace. Yet they don't cease to dream dreams, but try as hard as they can to involve others in pursuit of the same glittering mirage. And then when their last hope is gone, they have one fine phrase left—a great solace, no doubt—that "in great enterprises to have tried hard is enough."[3] At last, they cry out against

---

1. Ulysses was absent from Ithaca for twenty years, during which Penelope had to discourage suitors every day.
2. Erasmus took a dim view of alchemy and wrote

two colloquies satirizing it.
3. The phrase—though not the context—is from Propertius 2.10.

the brevity of life as inadequate for the accomplishment of great projects.

As for dicers, I'm in grave doubt whether they should be admitted to our college. Still, they provide a completely ridiculous spectacle, especially when we see some gamesters so addicted that no sooner do they hear the dice rattling than their hearts leap up and start to pound. Then when they've been drawn in deeper and deeper by the hope of winning, and have exhausted their resources, their ship finally goes smash on Dice-Box rock, more dangerous than the point of Malea.[4] Even if they struggle dripping ashore in their bare shirts, they would rather defraud anyone else but the man who took their money, lest that give them the reputation of welshers. What a spectacle are those old, half-blind players who have to peer through their glasses to see the dice! And in the last stages, when a well-deserved case of the gout has crippled their hands, they hire an assistant to put the dice in the box for them. A comic spectacle indeed, if it weren't that the game usually ends in a brutal brawl, and that concerns the Furies, not me.

Here's another lot of men who definitely belong to my sect, men who like to hear or tell tall tales about miracles and other prodigious lies. They never weary of these fables as long as something weird is involved, whether ghosts, demons, goblins, or vampires, and they can tell you thousands of stories about apparitions of that sort. The more far-fetched the tales, the more eagerly they are accepted, and the more they tickle the ears of the devotee. For they serve not only to pass the time but also to coin money, especially when recited by pardoners and preachers.[5] Near neighbors of these are the folk who nourish the comfortable if stupid illusion that if they have looked on some wooden image or painting of Polyphemus-Christopher,[6] their lives will be safe that day; or that a man who has recited a prayer to Saint Barbara in set form will return unscathed from battle; or that if one repeats a prayer to Saint Erasmus on a particular day, lighting special candles and using precise formulas, riches cannot fail to follow immediately. To go with their new Hippolytus, they have lately found in Saint George another Hercules;[7] they devotedly worship his very horse, tricking it out with harness and studs and even offering it gifts—while swearing by the rider's brazen helmet is an oath worthy of kings.

---

4. Point Malea at the southernmost tip of the Peloponnesus is a dangerous headland, for sure, but Folly is more interested in the pun on *malea*, a bad throw of the dice.

5. In attacking current abuses within the Christian church, Folly heightens the tension of her discourse; she must, accordingly, choose her words carefully.

6. Christopher as a Christian giant is equated with Polyphemus (of *Odyssey* 9). (It is perhaps worth remarking that Christopher and George, with several other historically dubious saints, have now been desanctified.) Saint Barbara was patroness against lightning and gunpowder explosions; Saint Erasmus (whose name became corrupted to Saint Elmo)

was patron of sailors. His career in the church was full of accidents and misunderstandings, and Folly may be jokingly perpetrating another when she says that through his favor one becomes rich. Erasmus himself certainly didn't.

7. Saint Hippolytus, like the classical Hippolytus (of whom he may have been just a linguistic double), was killed by wild horses. Folly says Saint George in killing the dragon was copying Hercules, who, as his second labor, killed the hydra of Lerna; in fact he is more likely to have been a double of Perseus, who rescued Andromeda from the Orc not far from George's field of operations in Asia Minor.

What's to be said of those who happily delude themselves with forged pardons for real sins, measuring out time to be spent in purgatory as if on a chronometer, calculating the centuries, years, months, days, and hours as if on a mathematical table, so as not to make the slightest error?[8] Or of those who promise themselves, as a result of certain magic formulas and prayers (dreamed up by a sanctimonious impostor and imparted out of mischief or for money), nothing less than everything—wealth, honor, pleasure, abundance, unbroken good health, long life, a green old age, and then a seat in Heaven itself right next to Christ's—but that they don't want too soon, only when the pleasures of this life have been exhausted (and they will hang onto them tooth and nail), only then will they be ready for the joys of heaven to follow.

Here I think I see some businessman or soldier or judge putting down one solitary coin out of the great pile that he has successfully stolen, and expecting that that will atone for the whole pestilent swamp of his life; all his perjuries, lusts, drunken brawls, murders, deceits, treacheries, and double crossings will, he thinks, be redeemed as if by purchase, and so thoroughly redeemed that he will now be entitled to embark on a new world of crime as a new man. What can be more stupid or more comforting than the notion that reciting seven verses of the psalms every day will admit one to the realm of ultimate felicity? I think they are the verses that some joking devil, more talkative than intelligent, told Saint Bernard he knew about—though the saint foiled him in the end.[9] These things are so stupid that I myself am almost ashamed of them, yet they are accepted and approved, not just by the uneducated, but even by the teachers of religion. And isn't it almost as bad when different districts lay claim each to its own special deity, and divide saints up according to function, assigning to each his own special observances and occasions? Thus one is good for the toothache, another helps women in labor, still another restores stolen goods, there's a special saint in case of shipwreck, another who watches over livestock, and so forth—for to run over the whole list would take a long time. Some religious figures serve a number of different functions, like the Virgin Mary, whom the common people reverence almost more than her Son.

And what do men beg of their saints, except things pertaining to folly? Among all the votive offerings that you see covering the walls of churches right up to the ceiling, did you ever see one put up to commemorate a close escape from folly or an unexpected access of wisdom—even a tiny bit of it? One man escaped drowning, another was run through by his enemy's sword, but survived. Still another, while his comrades were still fighting the battle, was able by good luck to turn tail and boldly run

8. Folly is careful here to attack only forged pardons or indulgences, which (however misunderstood by simpleminded purchasers) related only to remission of temporal punishments, not to punishment in purgatory. Still, Erasmus here runs very close to what would be the Protestant line.

9. A devil told Saint Bernard that he knew seven verses of the psalms that if recited daily assured one's salvation; unable to find out which verses they were, Bernard said he would recite the whole psalter every day. That would have been too much piety for the devil, so he revealed the verses; but the fable does not tell whether Bernard then made them public.

[Saint Bernard and the Devil]

away. Though already strung up on the gallows, someone slipped safely
from the noose through the favor of a saint friendly to thieves, and so
was able to relieve numerous people of the heavy burden of their money.
This fellow broke out of jail and made his getaway; that one recovered
from a fever, much to his doctor's surprise; another one swallowed poison, but it purged him instead of killing him, leaving his wife in despair
at the failure of her plan and the loss of her money. Here's a man whose
wagon upset, but who drove his horses home unhurt; another survived
when his house fell down around him; another was caught in the act by
an enraged husband, but got away.[1] Not one gives thanks for an escape
from folly. It's so agreeable to know nothing, that mortals pray for anything else rather than release from folly. But why have I launched into
this ocean of superstitions?

> Not with a hundred tongues, as many mouths,
> And with a voice of brass could I begin
> To list the forms of folly and their names.[2]

For the whole life of Christians everywhere is infected with idiocies of
this sort; yet priests tolerate them without misgivings, and even encour-

---

1. In the colloquy *The Alchemy Scam*, an adulterer who has escaped from an enraged husband
gives thanks to the Virgin.

2. The verses are adapted from *Aeneid* 6, which
in turn imitates a passage in *Iliad* 2.

age them, being well aware how much money can be coined out of them. In this state of affairs, suppose some hateful wise man were to get up and sing a counter-melody rather like the following, all of which is perfectly true: "You won't die badly if you live well; your sins will be forgiven if, to your bit of money, you add hatred of evildoers, tears of true repentance, vigils, prayers, fasts, and a complete change in the pattern of your life. Your favorite saint will bless your endeavors if you live up to his example." Imagine these words and a few others like them to be murmured by the wise man, and you see at once how much peace of mind the human soul will be deprived of, what dismay men will be thrown into.

In the same class of fools belong those who during their lifetime made elaborate arrangements for their funerals, going so far as to stipulate how many torches, how many mourners, how many singers, and how many silent attendants they want in the procession—as if they expected their senses to come back to them, so that they could appreciate the spectacle—or as if they imagined the corpse blushing for shame if the burial were less than magnificent. They are as eager in the whole matter as if they had been appointed to public office and made responsible for providing a public banquet and circus games.[3]

I have to hurry on, but I can't omit those who, though they differ not at all from the commonest drudge, yet flatter themselves with incredible complacency on an empty title of nobility. One man derives his family tree from Aeneas, another from Brutus, still another from King Arthur—and each has busts and family portraits to prove the connection.[4] They rattle off the names of their grandfathers and great-grandfathers, and recite all the ancient titles, showing themselves to be no less blockish than dumb statues and worse no doubt than the ones they show off. Yet thanks to my lovely handmaid Philautia [Self-Love], they lead the happiest of lives. And there is no lack of fools, just as stupid, who look up to this breed of beast as if it were of divine origin. But why should I talk of one class of men more than another, as if my girl Philautia did not with her marvellous skill make everyone everywhere supremely content with himself? Though he's uglier than an ape, this man clearly thinks himself as handsome as Nireus.[5] Another succeeds in drawing three lines with a compass, and promptly fancies himself a Euclid; still another, whose musical talents are those of an 'ass with a lyre' and who 'sings worse than a cock who's just finished treading his hen,' imagines himself another Hermogenes.[6] Still another variety of madness, surely the most delightful of all, is that which leads some men to credit themselves for whatever talent is displayed by any of their servants. Such was that fellow described by Seneca, as happy as he was rich, who when he started an anecdote always had servants nearby to supply him with proper names.[7]

---

3. Men elected to the post of aedile at Rome were expected to provide enormous sums of money for lavish public entertainments.
4. Antique genealogies, without exception fantastic, were all the rage during the Renaissance; how seriously they were taken is another matter.

5. For Nireus, see above, p. 23, n. 7.
6. Hermogenes sang for the emperor Augustus, and is several times mentioned by Horace (*Satires* 1, 3, and 9). Euclid is of course the geometer.
7. Seneca, *Epistles* 27.

Though so weak physically that he could scarcely be said to live, he wouldn't have hesitated to get into a fist-fight because he could always summon up a pack of muscular servants.

As for artistic performers, what a spectacle they offer! since self-love is the special mark of them all. You will sooner find one of them ready to surrender his patrimony than one who will admit he is not at the pinnacle of his profession. This is especially true of actors, singers, orators, and poets; the more ignorant one of them is, the better pleased he will be with himself, the more he will preen and show off. And as like is attracted to like, the more incompetent the performer, the more admirers he will attract, so that the worst art delights most people—the greater part of mankind being, as I said before, given over to folly. If then the incompetent man pleases himself best and gains the admiration of most people, why should he bother with real skills which will cost him a lot to acquire, yield little, afflict him with doubts and misgivings, and in the end please many fewer people?

And now I see that Philautia has attached herself not only to individuals, but to nations and cities, sinking the roots of self-love in all these communities. That is why the British pride themselves on their good looks, their good music, and their good food, among other things. The Scots preen themselves on their noble descent and royal connections, as well as their skill at the dialectic; the French brag about their genteel manners, though the Parisians, dismissing the claims of everyone else, make a special point of their skill in theology. The Italians lay claim to literary culture and eloquence and on that basis flatter themselves that they alone of all the human race are not barbarians. The Romans enjoy this folly most, lost as they are in fantasies about the old Roman empire. The Venetians have a high opinion of their own nobility, the Greeks boast they they invented the arts, and besides they claim descent from the vaunted heroes of antiquity; while the Turks and that whole horde of barbarians pride themselves on their religion and ridicule Christians as superstitious. The Jews are even more happily deluded between constant expectation of their Messiah and a tenacious hold on their Moses; the Spaniards yield to none in military prowess, the Germans boast of their muscular frames and their skill in magic. And, not to go into all the details, I think you see how Philautia breeds pleasure everywhere, in groups as well as in individuals, almost in the same degree as her sister Flattery.

For in fact self-love is the same thing as flattery, only performed on yourself instead of someone else. Nowadays flattery has a bad name, but only among those who are more impressed by the names of things than by the things themselves. People think flattery is the enemy of good faith; how wrong this is they could learn from the examples even of the brute beasts. For who fawns on his master more than a dog, and yet is more faithful? What creature is more gentle than the squirrel, and more friendly to man? Perhaps you imagine that savage lions, cruel tigers, or fierce leopards are somehow better disposed toward human beings. I concede there is a sort of unhealthy adulation, of which unscrupulous hypocrites make use to destroy their miserable victims. But this flattery of mine rises from a gracious and candid mind; it comes much closer to virtue than its opposite, which is a sharpness of disposition and what Horace calls a 'sullen, surly morosity.'[8] My flattery lifts dejected spirits, raises people out of the dumps, enlivens the languishing, animates the dull, heartens the sick, placates the angry, brings lovers together, and keeps them together. It attracts young people to the study of literature, livens the existence of old folk, and under the guise of praise it warns and instructs princes without any offence in the world. In short, it causes every man to have a better and more sanguine opinion of himself, which is in fact the chief component of happiness. What sight is more gratifying than a pair of mules rubbing necks? I need not emphasize that this flattery forms a major part of that much admired art, eloquence; it's just as important to medicine, and supremely valuable for the poet; in fact, it is the honey and spice of all human intercourse.

But, they say, to be deceived is to be miserable; not so, I answer, it is truly miserable *not* to be deceived. How wrong men are when they suppose that human happiness lies in things themselves. It depends on opinion. For such is the obscurity and variety of human affairs that nothing can be certainly known, as my friends the Academics[9] used to say, the least insolent of all the philosophers. Or if anything can be known, it rarely makes for the cheerfulness of human life. For the mind of man has been so formed that it is much more attracted to appearances than to realities. Anyone who wants proof of that point can find it by attending church sermons, where, if anything serious is proposed, the auditory all sleep or yawn or give signs of distaste. But if the tub-thumper (beg pardon, I meant to say elocutionist) begins some old wive's tale, as often happens, look how the members of the congregation will open their eyes, sit up straight, and pay eager attention. Also if there is a particularly fabulous or romantic saint—you may imagine George, or Christopher, or Barbara to belong to this class—you'll find that saint attracts more devotion than Peter or Paul or Christ himself. But this is not the place for topics of this sort.

Now consider how little you pay for the increase in satisfaction wrought by self-love. Substantial things are apt to cost a great deal, even the lightest of them, such as the acquisition of grammar. But opinion is easily picked up, and it contributes just as much, if not more, to happiness. Look, suppose a man is eating some rotten salt fish, so offensive that his neighbor can't even stand the smell of it; but if to him it seems like ambrosia, what, I ask you, does the other man's opinion matter in point of happiness? Again, if caviar makes a man sick to his stomach, what does it matter to him that it's supposed to be a gourmet dish? Though

8. Horace, *Epistles* 1. 18.
9. The Academy, where Plato taught in Athens, long continued to give its name to thinkers in his tradition; their views, however, were steadily modified and rendered more popular, till, by a series of stages, they eventuated in the practical eclecticism of Cicero. Folly's judgment of them (as "least insolent") was probably in large part that of Erasmus as well.

a man has an outstandingly ugly wife, if her husband thinks she's in a class with Venus, isn't that just as good as if she were really beautiful? Say that a man sees a picture smeared over with red lead and mud, admires it, and persuades himself that it is by Apelles or Zeuxis[1]—wouldn't he be happier than another man who paid a high price for the genuine article but perhaps enjoyed it less? I know a man of my name[2] who gave his new bride some artificial gems, telling her—for he was a great practical joker—that they were not only genuine stones, but extraordinarily, incalculably valuable. I ask you now, what difference did it make to the girl if her eyes were delighted and her mind gratified by the glass? She kept her trifles, as if they were some immense treasure, hidden near her person; the husband saved expense and was amused by his wife's error; while she was no less devoted to him than if he'd given her real gemstones. What do you think is the difference between those who lurk in Plato's cave admiring the shadows and appearances of things[3] but never desiring the actual objects, and perfectly pleased with what they have —and your wise man who comes out of the cave to look at the things themselves? If Mycillus in Lucian's dialogue[4] had been allowed to continue forever in that golden dream of his, there was no reason why he should have wished for any other sort of pleasure.

Between delusion and reality, there's either no difference at all, or if there is a difference it's all in favor of the deluded fool. In the first place, his bliss costs him practically nothing, only a bit of self-persuasion. And then he enjoys it in common with many other fools—and nothing is truly enjoyable unless it's shared. Now everybody knows how few men are wise, if in fact you can even find one. In the course of seven centuries the Greeks were able to muster only seven sages, among whom, for sure, if you looked them over closely, I doubt if you'd find even half a wise man—no, by God, not even the third part of one.

Among the many praises of Bacchus this is one of the first, that he lightens the troubles of the mind, though only for the time being—for as soon as you've slept it off, back they come, all your troubles in a rush, 'riding six white horses,' as they say. Now how much more prompt, powerful, and permanent is my assistance since I freely fill the mind with a continual intoxicating diet of delights, frolics, and caperings. Besides, I don't refuse my presents to any mortal, unlike the other gods, who reserve their gifts for a chosen few. You can't grow in just any vacant lot the rich and generous wine that dispels gloom and dances attendance on bountiful hope. Physical beauty, the gift of Venus, is granted to very few, and eloquence, Mercury's gift, to even fewer. Not many people get rich with the help of Hercules; Homer's Jupiter doesn't

1. Two famous Greek painters.
2. Probably Thomas More. The anecdote is not out of character, and More's first wife, whom he married in 1505, died in 1511, so she could not have been embarrassed by this story, which shows her as a bit of a fool.
3. In book 7 of The Republic, Plato compares men

to cave-dwellers who see only the shadows of real things on the walls of their caves and so cannot know or desire the realities themselves.
4. Lucian, The Dream, or The Cock. At the start of this dialogue, Mycillus complains that his glorious dream has been broken by the cock's crowing.

bestow on many the right to rule.[5] Very often the god of war favors neither combatant; many who approach the tripod of Apollo depart from it in deepest gloom. The son of Saturn [Jove] speaks often in thunder, and Apollo showers down the arrows of pestilence; Neptune swallows up more mariners than he preserves. As for the underworld gods, Pluto, Ate, Poena, Febris, and evil spirits of that sort,[6] I don't consider them gods at all, but butchers. I, Folly, am the only divinity who embrace all men equally and include them all within the scope of my generosity. What's more, I don't demand offerings or sulk and insist on special expiatory gifts if some ceremony has been overlooked. Neither do I throw heaven and earth into an uproar if someone invites all the other gods to a celebration, but leaves me out so I don't get even a sniff of the smoke of their sacrifices. As for those other gods, they are so peevish that one is better off neglecting than worshipping them. In the same way there are men so irritable and touchy that it's better not to know them at all than to have them as friends.

But it's well known that nobody sacrifices to Folly, or has ever put up a temple to her; and, as I said before, I'm a bit surprised at this ingratitude. I suppose, though, it's a consequence of my good nature; and, at bottom, they are attentions that I don't really want. Why should I care for a donative of incense or grain, a slaughtered goat or hog, when all men already worship me in the way that theologians most approve of? Maybe I ought to envy Diana because she is placated with human blood;[7] but I consider myself to be most devoutly worshipped when all men everywhere bind me to their souls, express me in their manners, objectify me in their lives—exactly as they do now. Even among Christians, such heartfelt devotion is uncommon. What a crowd of them can be seen lighting candles to the Virgin Mary, and in broad daylight, when there's no need for them! Yet how few of the same crowd try to imitate her in the chastity and modesty of her life, in her love for celestial things! For that after all is true worship and by all odds most welcome in heaven. Besides, why should I want a special temple of my own when the whole globe is a temple for me, and, if I'm not mistaken, a very beautiful one. I lack for worshippers only where there are no men at all. And you needn't suppose I'm such a fool that I want sculptured or painted images of myself; they would just get in the way, as they always do when dull clods worship the figures instead of the divinities themselves. And that leaves all us gods in the position of those who are pushed out of their jobs by their substitutes. I consider that I have as many statues erected to me as there are mortals bearing my image in their face—even if they would rather not.

5. Folly's list of the pagan gods and the special gifts they are supposed to bring seems too slight a target to be worth her satire, but it reflects on the earlier list of special-purpose Christian saints (p. 42 ff.). Erasmus often has Folly attack pagan vices when he's really glancing at "Christian" practices.
6. Pluto was god of the underworld, Ate (above, p. 17, n. 5) goddess of discord, Poena goddess of punishment, Febris god of fever; only Pluto, of the lot, was a proper god in good standing; the others are convenient abstractions.
7. The people of Tauris in the Crimea sacrificed strangers shipwrecked on their shores to a virgin goddess identified with Diana. Plays by Euripides and (much later) Goethe turn on the practice.

And so there's no reason at all for me to envy the other gods if some of them are worshipped with special zeal in special corners of the earth on special days. Let Apollo have his shrine on Rhodes, Venus on Cyprus, Juno at Argos, Minerva at Athens, Jupiter at Olympus, Neptune at Tarentum, Priapus at Lampsacus—[8]as long as I have the whole world offering far greater sacrifices to me.

And if you think I'm saying this more out of brashness than regard for truth, just look for a moment at the actual ways men live and see from that how much they owe me and how much regard they have for me, the men of position no less than the rabble. But to save space, I won't look over the lives of ordinary people; if I concentrate on the more prominent, it will be easy to judge from them what the rest are like. Besides, what would be the point of reminding you of the common herd, all of whom without any controversy belong to my camp? They riot in so many different forms of folly, and every day bring forth so many new ones, that not even a thousand Democrituses would suffice to laugh at them; and then you'd need one extra Democritus to laugh at the thousand laughers.

It's absolutely incredible what a show the human race puts on for the gods, what new japes and jokes they dream up every day.[9] For the gods spend their sober morning hours settling squabbles and listening to prayers. But when they're well liquored up with nectar and unfit for serious business, then they adjourn to a convenient promontory of heaven and sit there with faces bent downward to see what humans are up to. You can't imagine a performance they would enjoy more. Lord almighty, what a theater is this, what a wild storm of follies! I myself sometimes enjoy sitting down among the poetic gods to watch. Here's a fellow dying for love of a pretty filly, and the less she can stand him, the more desperately he adores her. Here's one who married a dowry, not a wife; another who prostitutes his own wife; and a third so jealous he watches over his lady like Argus with a hundred eyes. Over there is a man in mourning, but, good lord! look at the foolish things he says and does! hiring mummers like a troupe of actors to put on a show of grief for him. There's another sobbing over the grave of his mother-in-law.[1] Whatever food this next fellow can scrape together he stuffs into his belly, but in a few minutes he'll be ravenous again. This man exists only to sleep and loaf, and with that he's happy. Some people are so busy minding everybody else's business, they have no time for their own. There's a broker who fancies himself rich on his client's money, but soon he'll go bankrupt. Another believes in starving himself so that his heir can be rich. The dubious lure of a little gold entices men to cross oceans one after the other, risking amid winds and waves a life for which no amount of

8. These are all local cults, of which only the last two need comment. Tarentum as a major port of embarkation for Greece and the Near East was naturally interested in Neptune, god of the sea; Lampsacus on the Asian side of the Hellespont was the center of a wine-growing district, and so devoted to the worship of Pan.
9. Hints for the following passage came from Lucian's dialogue *Icaromenippus*.
1. I.e., a hypocrite.

money can compensate them. Others go off looking for loot in a military campaign, when they could live quietly and comfortably at home. Some seek out childless old men, hoping to pick up a painless inheritance; others make up to rich old women for the same reason. It's a cause of particular delight to the watching gods when these schemers are betrayed by the very victims they had hoped to snare.[2]

Businessmen are not only the most foolish of fools but the most sordid, since they spend their whole life grubbing for money and resort to the meanest tricks to get it: they lie, they perjure themselves, they steal, defraud, and mislead the public; and then, as proof of what sterling fellows they are, they flaunt fat fingers covered with gold rings. Nor do they lack an attendant band of flattering friars, who make much of them and openly address them as 'Right Worthy,' obviously in the hope that a little overflow from the sewer of ill-gotten gains will be diverted their way. Over there you will find some practical Pythagoreans[3] who hold that all things should be held in common, so whatever they find that isn't nailed down they blithely take to themselves, as if it were their particular inheritance. Some are rich only in their great expectations, live their lives in a rosy glow of pipe-dreams, and consider that happiness enough. Others make a point of seeming rich to their neighbors but live a meager, hungry life at home. One man rushes headlong to spend every last penny he possesses, another hoards his coppers like a miser. Here's a candidate for public office who canvasses high and low for votes; his counterpart dozes by the fireside. Many people occupy themselves with interminable litigation and carry their battle from courtroom to courtroom, each party trying to best the other—to the great profit of the judge, who puts off his decision indefinitely, and the collusive lawyers, who urge the suit ever onwards. This man dreams of the revolution to come, and that one cherishes a vast, vague project. The pilgrim departs for Jerusalem, Rome, or Compostela,[4] where he has no business being— meanwhile leaving his wife and children to shift for themselves. In short, if you could see the innumerable activities of men from a perch in the moon, as Menippus once did,[5] you would think you were looking at a swarm of flies or gnats, all struggling, fighting, and betraying one another, robbing, playing, lusting, birthing, sickening, and dying. You'd never be able to believe what tumults and tragedies could be set in motion by this puny homunculus who is destined to disappear so quickly. For again and again a war over some trifling occasion, or an epidemic of disease, will wipe out the species by the thousands.

But here I'd outdo my own stupidity and would deserve all the ridicule of which Democritus is capable if I tried to list all the shapes taken by

2. The passage looks back to Horace, Satires 2.5, but forward to Ben Jonson's play on the same theme, Volpone.
3. Pythagoras taught community of goods; a thief systematically confounds yours with mine.

4. Three major destinations of religious pilgrimages—of which Erasmus had, in general, no high opinion. A famous colloquy exposes satirically the follies of devotional journeys.
5. Lucian, Icaromenippus.

[A Fool on Pilgrimage]

popular foolishness and insanity. Let me come closer to those men who maintain some pretence to wisdom and try at least to grasp the golden bough, as men say.[6] Among these the teachers of grammar are the most wretched of men, the most miserable, the most forsaken of God—or so they would be unless I mitigated the awfulness of their profession by dabbling them with the sweet dew of my madness. For they are subject not just to 'the five miseries' of the Greek epigram[7] but to six hundred more, being penned up, grubby and half-starved in their classrooms—or 'beating-mills,' should I say, or shambles—amid herds of boys, growing old at their labors, deaf with the constant racket, and sick because of the constant stench and squalor. Yet, thanks to my efforts, they consider themselves the happiest of men, particularly when they can terrify their flock of trembling schoolboys with glowering expressions and thunderous voices. Yet when they savage the wretched infants with canings, floggings, and the strap, they are simply emulating the ass of Cumae described by Aesop.[8] Meanwhile all this beastliness seems to them the height of elegance, the stuffy classroom smells of wildflowers, and their

6. The golden bough given by the sibyl to Aeneas (Aeneid 6) was commonly allegorized as wisdom.
7. The first five lines of the Iliad mention five different calamities; a Greek epigram commented on the fact.
8. The ass dressed in a lion's skin played the bully till someone stripped off his disguise.

[The Happy Tutor]

own miserable drudgery seems a royal kingdom, such as they wouldn't exchange for the supreme sway of Phalaris or Dionysus.[9] But what raises them to the heights of ecstasy is if they discover some new point of interpretation. What they teach their students is utter gibberish, but they think their own critical discernment is far beyond that of the greatest grammarians, like Palaemon or Donatus.[1] And, though I don't know by what flim-flam they do it, they are able to persuade the mothers and fathers of their pupils that they themselves are just as great as they make out. Another special delight they take is to dig out of some moldy old manuscript some exotic fact, like the name of Anchises' mother,[2] or some completely obsolete word such as 'cuhyrde,' 'eperotesis,' or 'cuttle-bung;' sometimes one of them comes up with a fragment of old rock carved with a few broken letters. And then, oh Lord, what elation, what cries of triumph, what tributes of praise, as if Africa had been conquered or Babylon put to sack.

As for those frigid and clumsy verses they display everywhere (and some people may even be found to admire them), the authors of them act as if Virgil's soul had been infused into their breasts. But what they

---

9. Absolute tyrants at different periods of Sicilian history.
1. Both were famous early grammarians.

2. Anchises' mother would be Aeneas's grand-mother, her name lost in the mists of antiquity.

enjoy most of all is getting together for a session of reciprocal back-scratching and mutual admiration combined with mutual malice. If one fellow blunders over a single syllable and some sharper-eared fellow catches him, then, 'oh thunder and lightning,' what tragic declamations we get, what caterwaulings, word-wars, and bitter invectives! May I have the whole academic world about my ears if I exaggerate. I once knew a certain 'polymath' who had studied Greek, Latin, mathematics, philosophy, and medicine, and was 'skilled in all of them;' at sixty years of age he set everything else aside, and spent more than twenty years torturing his mind with the problem of deciding (if he should be happy enough to live so long) how the eight parts of speech should be distinguished.[3] Hitherto, he felt, none of the Greek or Latin authors had made the matter sufficiently clear; and it would practically be a cause for war if somebody made a conjunction out of a word that really belonged among the adverbs. Doubtless for this reason, there are as many grammar books as there are grammarians, or even more; for my friend Aldus[4] alone has produced more than five of them, overlooking none, however barbarically or badly written; but he corrects and prints them all, keeping a jealous eye on everything that's done in this line, however incompetent it may be—so fearful is he that someone else will grab the glory and rob him of his many years of labor. Would you rather call this madness or folly? Personally, I don't care, so long as you concede that I'm the animating spirit and that an animal, otherwise the most miserable of all, can be raised with my help to such a peak of felicity that he wouldn't change state with the kings of Persia.

The poets owe less to my favor, though by their own admission they are of my faction, for they are 'a tribe of free spirits' (as the proverb has it) who devote themselves entirely to tickling the ears of fools with pretty nothings and absurd stories. And yet, strange to say, they devote all their time to these things, promising themselves on the basis of them immortality and a life equal to that of the gods; what's more, they promise the same gifts to other people. 'Self-love and flattery' are the special cronies of the poetic tribe, and I myself am worshipped by no other breed of men more devotedly or faithfully. As for the rhetoricians, though they quibble a lot and pretend to line up with the philosophers, there are many reasons to show that they belong in my camp, and this above all, that among other frivolities, they have written so much and so sharply on the art of cracking jokes. And that folly itself is one of the classes of wit is declared by the man, whoever he was, who wrote *Ad Herennium* on the art of eloquence; moreover, in the works of Quintilian, who was one of the best to write on this topic, there's a chapter on laughter that's even more long-winded than the *Iliad*.[5] Everyone concedes this point in

3. It's generally supposed that Folly alludes to Thomas Linacre, physician to Henry VIII.
4. Aldus Manutius, the Venetian printer, to whose establishment Erasmus paid an extended visit early in his career.
5. Though it passed for a while as Cicero's, the rhetorical treatise *Ad Herennium* was already questioned in the sixteenth century, and we still don't know who wrote it. Quintilian's chapter on being funny is not much worse than most treatises on the topic.

wit's favor that arguments which can't be refuted logically can often be eluded with a jest—though somebody may object that this is not really Folly's job to raise a laugh with ridiculous sayings, especially when they're produced on purpose.

Baked in the same oven are the halfwits who expect to achieve immortal fame by writing books. The whole tribe of them are deeply in my debt, most obviously those who blacken reams of paper with pure piffle. But there's not much to be said, either, for those who write learned books for the judgment of a few other learned men and expect to be studied even by Persius and Laelius.[6] These erudites seem to me more pitiable than happy, since they are assiduous self-torturers. They change, they interline, they erase something and put it back in, they rewrite the whole thing, after rephrasing a passage they show it to their friends and after all they closet up the manuscript for nine years[7] but without ever satisfying themselves—and this for an empty reward of praise from a mere handful of critics. And this idle end they pursue despite vast expense of midnight oil, frequent loss of sleep (of all things the most precious), and endless waste of life's good things on unprofitable or insoluble riddles. Add to this the loss of health, the crumbling away of good looks, bleared eyes or even blindness, poverty, envious colleagues, rejection of pleasures, sudden senility, untimely death, and anything else of the sort that you can think of. All this grief they gladly accept as the price of having their work appreciated by a couple of blear-eyed "experts." But a writer of my school cultivates a much happier vein of craziness, since he takes no care over his work, but just writes down whatever pops into his head or slips off his pen, even his dreams. No waste of paper here! He knows perfectly well that the sillier the nonsense he puts down, the better it will appeal to a mass audience, who are almost all fools and blockheads. What does it matter if three men of judgment—even supposing they read his work in the first place—despise it? What weight will their minority opinion carry in such an overwhelming crowd of admirers?

Smarter yet are those who adopt the writings of others as their own, easily transforming another man's hard work to their own account and cheered with the pleasant thought that even if they're ultimately convicted of plagiarism, they will have been able to coin plenty of money in the meantime. It's really a joy to watch these people preening themselves on their popularity when they're pointed out in a crowd ("this is the famous writer") or when their works are displayed in the bookstores with three names on the title page,[8] especially if they're exotic names like those used by conjurers. What are they, in the name of God, but empty names? Taking into account the vastness of the world, how few people will recognize the names of even the best-known authors? and of that few, what a trifling number can be expected to like a particular

---

6. An allusion to Cicero's book *De oratore*, 2.7, the names implying ultra-scrupulous and perhaps nitpicking critics.

7. Horace's advice to fledgling poets: keep your poems to yourself for nine years.

8. To the Romans, possession of three names denoted nobility.

book, since even among the ignorant many different independent tastes exist? Many authors write under pen-names which they invent or adapt from books of the ancients; and then what does their fame amount to? One man calls himself Telemachus, another is Stelenus or Laertes; here we have Polycrates, while there someone prefers Thrasymachus. They might just as well sign their books Chameleon or Pumpkin, or else, like the philosophers, distinguish them as Alpha, Beta, and so forth.

Most enchanting of all is the spectacle when they start flattering one another back and forth with epistles dedicatory, commendatory verses, and mutual complimentary allusions. A fool puffs the work of other fools, an ignoramus cries up the accomplishments of other blockheads. For one fellow his friend is a better poet than Alcaeus; the friend says the first fellow outsoars Callimachus.[9] In the opinion of his friend B, A is far superior to Cicero; A returns the favor, his friend B is more learned than Plato. Or else two of them gang up against a third, by contrast with whom their reputations are, or should be, far more brilliant. Thus literary wars arise, to the great confusion of the vulgar, until finally both party leaders declare themselves triumphant and march off the field to celebrate the victory. Wise men laugh at all this play-acting, considering it, as it really is, the height of the ridiculous. But meanwhile, with my help, the actors lead lives of utmost complacency, and wouldn't change places with either of the Scipios.[1]

The scholars have all sorts of fun deriding others and ridiculing their madness, but they themselves owe no small debt to me, and they can't deny it without appearing altogether ungrateful. The lawyers are just as well pleased with themselves. Laborious as Sisyphus heaving aloft his boulder,[2] they are constantly stitching together six hundred different precedents to make a single ruling, and couldn't care less which side they're engaged on. Glosses must be written on glosses, opinions piled on opinions. Thus their discipline appears the most difficult of all; and just because it's tedious, they think it distinguished to the n'th degree. Near relatives of theirs are the dialecticians and sophists, a race of men more noisy than crashing Dodonian brass,[3] any one of whom could outshout twenty specially selected women. They would be happier, though, if they were just babblers and not quarrelsome as well; they will squabble interminably over a goat's hair and in the end, by dint of all their bawling, lose track of the truth. Yet their self-conceit keeps them happy; armed with three syllogisms, they will challenge anyone to debate anything and thanks to their obstinacy bear it out, even if Stentor were opposed to them.[4]

Come next the natural philosophers, long of beard and furry of gown,

---

9. Alcaeus and Callimachus, famous Greek lyric poets.
1. The two Scipios, both surnamed Africanus, were national heroes, men of ultimate distinction.
2. Sisyphus, condemned to hell for fraud and avarice, had to roll up a hill a huge boulder that immediately rolled down again.

3. The woods of Dodona were sacred to Jupiter, who spoke his oracles through the crashing of brass kettles, hung from the oak branches and stirred by the wind.
4. Stentor, one of the Greek host at Troy, had a voice as loud as fifty ordinary men.

who declare that they alone possess wisdom, the rest of mankind being capable of nothing more than fleeting impressions. How agreeably they hallucinate when they construct innumerable worlds, measuring sun, moon, stars, and heavenly orbits as if with thumb and tape-rule. Never at a loss to explain thunder, wind, eclipses, and other incomprehensible events, and never even hesitating over their explanations, they act as if they were in on all the secrets of nature who created the universe, as if they came down to us bearing the word direct from on high. Yet all the time nature derides both them and their conjectures. For that nothing is settled among them is perfectly evident from the fact that they are always fighting with one another over inexplicable phenomena. Though they know nothing specific, they lay claim to know everything in general. Not only are they ignorant of themselves, they cannot avoid falling into a ditch or stumbling over a rock in the path (perhaps they are bleareyed from study or just absent-minded);[5] yet they claim to know all about abstract ideas, universals, separate forms, primary matter, quiddities, and different modes of being—objects so phantasmal I doubt if Lynceus himself could make them out. They particularly set themselves

[Natural Philosopher/Natural Fool]

5. The story of Thales, who stumbled into a ditch while watching the stars, tickled the anti-intellectuals of antiquity.

above the profane mob when they bring forth their triangles, circles, and such-like mathematical shapes, scribbling one atop the other to make a labyrinth and then sprinkling letters over them as if in battle-formations designed to submerge the plain man in waves of confusion.[6] Some of this breed venture to make predictions by consulting the stars; they promise more than magical miracles, and sometimes, when they are extra lucky, find people to believe them.

Perhaps I ought to pass over the theologians in silence and 'just not go near that open sewer' or touch that stink-weed. They are a class of men so arrogant and irritable that they're likely to attack me by squadrons with their six hundred conclusions and force me into a recantation; then if I refuse it, they'd promptly have me up for a 'heretic.' This is the thunderbolt with which they terrify anyone who for some reason has got in their black books. No other people are less ready to acknowledge my services to them; yet they're obliged to me on several important scores. For they cocker up their own self-esteem, as if raising themselves to a seventh heaven, and from that vantage look down on the rest of the human race as so many dumb beasts crawling the ground—so lowly as to be almost pitiful. Meanwhile, they protect themselves with a hedge full of academic definitions, logical argumentations, inferential corollaries, explicit and implicit propositions; they blossom out with so many 'subterfuges' that the net of Vulcan couldn't hold them down; they devise so many sharp distinctions for cutting through legal ligatures that a double-bladed axe from Tenedos couldn't do better,[7] they rattle off so many newly coined words and bawl aloud in such prodigious voices that there's no standing against them. Besides, they can explain to their own satisfaction all sorts of inexplicable matters, such as how the world was created and ordered; what channels carried original sin down to posterity; by what means, in what measure, and how long the perfected Christ lay in the Virgin's womb; and how accidents manage to subsist in the eucharist without a substance.[8]

But these are old and tired questions. Here are some others, considered worthy of distinguished and illuminate (as they're called) theologians, sufficient to stir the blood if and when they encounter them. Whether divine generation occurred at a particular point in time? Whether several filiations co-existed in Christ? Is it thinkable that God the Father hated Christ? Could God assume the shape of a woman, of the devil, of an ass, of a pumpkin, or a piece of flint? Suppose him transformed to a pumpkin, how could he have preached, performed miracles, been crucified? What act of consecration would Peter have performed if he had performed it while Christ was hanging on the cross? Whether Christ

6. A modern reader automatically thinks of algebra, but anachronistically; Folly is thinking of astrological and geometrical diagrams.
7. The king of Tenedos kept an axe handy, for prompt execution of legal sentences; hence the proverbial expression for cutting legal knots. The net of Vulcan, in which he caught his wife, Venus, bedded down with Mars, was unbreakable and inescapable.
8. The questions cited—unanswerable and indeed inexplicable—all appear in Peter Lombard's book *Sentences*, a popular theological textbook.

while on the cross, could properly be defined as a man? Whether, after the general resurrection, it will be permissible to eat and drink? (Just in case it isn't, they take aboard a good supply in the here and now.) These 'worthless quibbles' are innumerable, and there are others subtler still, involving instants of time, abstract conceptions, analogous relations, formalities, quiddities, ecceities and things so vague that nobody could possibly see them unless he could not only look through a solid wall like Lynceus, but see behind it things that never existed.[9]

And then they have their favorite hard cases of conscience, paradoxes indeed, compared with which the stoic paradoxes were lumpish and obvious platitudes.[1] For example, they will maintain that it's less criminal to cut a thousand throats than to take a stitch in the sole of a poor man's shoe on Sunday. Or that it is better for the whole world to perish, lock, stock, and barrel (as they say), than for one individual to tell a little white lie on a trivial occasion.[2] The various devices of our schoolmen only render these subtlest of subtleties more subtle yet, so you'd have a better chance of getting out of a labyrinth than out of all the equivocations devised by the Realists, Nominalists, Thomists, Albertists, Occamists, Scotists, and I can't give all their names but you have the main ones. They all boast such mighty erudition and write such tortured prose that I should think the apostles themselves must have had a very different spirit if they were to discuss topics like these with our new breed of theologians. Paul could display faith; but when he said, "Faith is the substance of things hoped for, the evidence of things not seen,"[3] that was a very un-academic definition. In I Corinthians 13, he wrote a wonderful exhortation to charity, but he altogether failed to divide charity into its component parts or define it in the proper dialectical way. No doubt the apostles consecrated the host with proper piety, but if you asked them about the *terminus a quo* [starting point] and the *terminus ad quem* [destination], or asked them to discourse on transubstantiation with an explanation of how the same body can exist simultaneously in several places; if they were called on to distinguish between Christ's bodily existence in heaven, on the cross, and in the sacrament; or if they were put to define the exact moment when transubstantiation occurs (since the prayer effecting it occupies a measurable period of time), I very much doubt if they would have responded with all the subtlety that our sons of Scotus display in laying out their questions and picking them apart.[4] The apostles all knew the mother of Jesus, but which of them could have equalled our theologians in deploying a demonstration of the

9. Some though not all of the questions ridiculed above had actually been discussed by medieval theologians. Formalities, quiddities, and ecceities were terms used to define the mode of existence of concrete things and general concepts.

1. Cicero wrote a little book, more like a letter, on the paradoxes of the Stoics; Erasmus may be alluding to it.

2. The two instances oppose apparently minor sins against God (or the truth) to apparently major benefits to the human race.

3. Hebrews 11.1. Objections were in fact raised that Paul's account of faith made it indistinguishable from hope.

4. Here again some of the hairsplitting problems that Folly mocks had actually been debated by medieval theologians. "Sons of Scotus" were followers of Duns Scotus, a thirteenth-century Scottish philosopher legendary for the subtlety of his thought.

means by which she was protected, immaculate, from the sin of Adam? Peter received the keys, and received them from one who would never have bestowed them on an unworthy person, but I doubt if he ever understood—for he never was distinguished for his subtlety—how a man can possess the keys to knowledge without having knowledge itself.[5] The apostles baptized far and wide, but never taught what are the formal, material, efficient, and final causes of baptism; they never so much as mentioned its double nature, delible and indelible. They worshipped indeed, but in the spirit, following no other guide than the evangelist who wrote, "God is a spirit, and they that worship him ought to do so in spirit and truth."[6] But it doesn't seem to have been revealed to them that they should worship an image scrawled on a wall in exactly the same way as Christ himself—so long as the image portrays him with two fingers extended, with long hair, and with three rays in the halo on his head. To gain a true understanding of these fine points you have to have wasted thirty-six years studying the physics and metaphysics of Aristotle and the Scotists.

The apostles constantly preached grace, but they never distinguished between actual grace and sanctifying grace.[7] They exhort us to good works, but without discriminating between the work as such, the work of the worker, and the work worked. Again and again they incite us to charity but never divide infused from acquired charity, or explain whether it is an accident or a substance, a created or an uncreated thing. They detest sin, but I'll be blessed if they could define sin with truly scientific precision, unless they had been enlightened by the wisdom of the Scotists.

You can't make me believe that Paul, who in point of erudition was probably about on a level with the other apostles, would have dismissed as worthless all those questions, disputations, genealogies, and "word-squabbles" (his very expression), if he had himself been expert in that sort of logic-chopping—especially since the arguments of those days were crude wrangles between uncouth bumpkins compared with the ultra-Chrysippean subtleties of our magisterial contemporaries.[8] Yet our doctors carry modesty to the point of not condemning out of hand what the apostles wrote in their untutored, unacademic dialect; no, they simply interpret it into the form and sense that they prefer. This they do out of respect partly for antiquity, partly for the apostolic name. Of course it would be unfair to expect academic correctness of the apostles, because they never heard so much as a word on the matter from their master.

5. The fundamental question was whether an ignorant, though legally ordained, priest had the power to administer the sacrament. Formally he had the keys, but not the knowledge to use them properly.

6. John 4. The exact way in which one should worship images without committing idolatry was obviously a matter for delicate definition.

7. Sanctifying grace is a permanent gift of God,

enabling us to convert others; actual grace purifies our will and enables us to achieve by specific deeds individual justification. The special mode by which grace and charity exist in sinful human beings provoked endless scholastic discussion.

8. Chrysippus was the subtlest of the stoic philosophers. The "doctors" of the next sentence are doctors of theology.

But if the same ineptitudes were to appear in Chrysostom, Basil, or Jerome,[9] our scholars would have no hesitation in writing them down, "not acceptable."

Indeed, the apostles did confute both pagan philosophers and Jews, who are by nature the most stubborn of men, but they did so more by the example of their lives and their miracles than by logical syllogisms; and they dealt with men not one of whom was fit to follow intelligently even a single one of the 'topics' propounded by Scotus. Nowadays, what ethnic or heretic could hold out an instant against the concentrated, interwoven subtleties of our theologians—unless he was so dull he didn't understand them, so impudent that he simply hissed them down, or else so skilled in the same tricks that he could fight on equal terms—like one necromancer hurling curses at another, or one warrior with a magic sword fighting another also with a magic sword. This is nothing but weaving and unweaving the web of Penelope.[1] But I think Christians would be well advised if, instead of building up all those cumbersome armies with which they've been fighting indecisive wars for some time now, they sent against the Turks and Saracens some of our most vociferous Scotists, our most pig-headed Occamists, our most invincible Albertists. Then I think the world would behold a most hilarious battle and a victory such as was never seen before. Who is so cold-blooded that the clash of these mighty intellects would not excite him? who so stupid as not to be stirred by these keen sarcasms? who so piercing of visage as not to be overwhelmed by the smoke-screens of verbiage?

Perhaps you think I'm saying all this by way of a joke, and that's not surprising, since even among the theologians there are some better trained in letters than others who are nauseated by these theological ingenuities, which they consider grotesque. They despise as a form of sacrilege this talking with unclean mouths about the deepest mysteries of religion, which we should adore, not explain; they reject as the worst form of impiety these disputes carried on with the profane cleverness of the pagans, these arrogant definitions, and this befouling of theology's divine majesty with such frigid, not to say dirty, words and sentiments. Meanwhile the interpreters are mightily pleased with their own little circle; they bask in each others' praises, so absorbed in these delicious cats'-cradles of theirs that they can't spare so much as a moment to read over a book of the gospels or look into an epistle of Paul's. And even as they quibble over their footnotes, they imagine they are supporting on the pillars of their syllogisms a church which would otherwise collapse in an instant—just as the poets say Atlas once held up the heavens on his shoulders.[2]

Now imagine how much pleasure they get from shaping and reshaping the holy scripture at will, as if it were made of wax, while they demand that their own decrees shall be observed, as soon as a few schoolmen have subscribed to them, more strictly than the laws of Solon,[3] and shall even be placed above papal edicts. As censors of the whole world, they demand retraction of all ideas that don't exactly square with their explicit and implicit conclusions. And then they speak with the authority of an oracle: this proposition is scandalousy, this needs a tad more reverence, this reeks of heresy, this rings off key.[4] So that now it's not baptism or the gospel, not Peter, Paul, Jerome, or Augustine, not Thomas himself, most Aristotelian of Aristotelians, can make a Christian; the one essential is that these learned bachelors give their consent. Who ever would have thought, if these wise owls hadn't told us, that a man can't be a Christian who thinks both these expressions, 'chamber pot, you stink,' and 'the chamber pot stinks,' are acceptable? So too with the two expressions 'that the pot is boiling' and 'the pots are boiling'— it's of the greatest importance to know that the first is less perfect than the second.[5] And who would have saved the church from the dark cave of such grievous errors if our learned men had not publicly refuted them under the seal of their great universities? And now don't you suppose that these scholars have been enjoying themselves every bit of the time?

They are particularly in their element when describing hell down to the last detail, as if they had spent many years in that part of the world. They also like to invent new worlds, just as the fancy suits them, and adding when they choose another one of their own, the largest and finest of all, so the happy inhabitants won't lack space to take a stroll, arrange a picnic, or play a game of ball. With these freaks and thousands of others their heads are stuffed so full and packed so tight that I expect Jove's brain was just as cramped when he was about to give birth to Pallas and had to borrow the use of Vulcan's axe to get her out.[6] So don't be surprised if at public disputations you see the heads of the scholars swathed in bands; it's necessary, or their brains would pop out. I often get a good laugh myself at the way they think the more eminent they are as theologians, the more coarsely and crudely they are entitled to speak. Mostly they mumble so only another mumbler can understand them, and then they swank about their 'acumen,' which is high understanding, far beyond the grasp of the vulgar. They even say it doesn't agree with the dignity of sacred letters that they should be subject to laws made by grammarians. Oh, wonderful privilege of the theologians, that they alone are entitled to speak incorrectly—though in fact it's a trait they share with a good many cobblers. They actually consider themselves near neighbors

---

3. See above, p. 8, n. 5.

4. Folly distorts the usual formulas of theological disapproval to suggest the illiteracy of the censorious doctors.

5. These fine grammatical points—though the specific examples are saturated with Folly's contempt—were actually discussed by medieval philosophers in what were called "speculative grammars."

6. Pallas was born directly out of Jove's brain; Lucian contributed the idea of Vulcan's axe as the obstetrical tool used to deliver her: *Dialogues of the Gods* 13.8. Doctors of divinity wore special caps in Erasmus's day, but hardly to keep their brains from overflowing.

to the gods when they are addressed, as in a religious formula, with the title "Magistri Nostri"—it is a phrase that they think conceals some lofty, secret allusion, like the Jewish tetragrammaton.[7] And so they say it is wicked to write MAGISTER NOSTER except in capital letters, and if anyone presumes to invert the order of things by saying "Noster Magister," he is judged to have destroyed at a stroke all the majesty of the theologian's title.

Next to them in bliss come those who are popularly called "men of religion" and "monks." Both names are completely false, since most of them avoid religion as much as they can, and wherever you go you can't help running into these men who've 'withdrawn' from the world.[8] I simply can't imagine what would be more wretched than their condition, unless I helped them out in all sorts of ways. For everyone loathes them so much that simply for one of them to show his face is considered bad luck; yet they flatter themselves gloriously. First, they think it a main point of piety to be ignorant of good letters, preferably not to be able to read at all. Then when like donkeys in church they bray out their psalms (memorized indeed, but not understood) they can imagine they are ravishing the ears of the saints with infinite delight. A good many of them make an excellent living out of their beggars' rags, bellowing for bread from door to door, and shoving into inns, carriages, and boats to the great prejudice of other beggars. And thus these delightful fellows represent themselves to us as apostles—by virtue of their filth, stupidity, grossness, and impudence, forsooth!

What can be funnier than their habit of doing everything by the book, as if following mathematical rules that it would be a sin to break? So many knots are required in the shoelace, a cloak can have only so many colors and must be of a certain material, the girdle must also be of a certain material and so many straws wide, the cowl can be cut only one way and capable of holding only so many pecks, the hair must be trimmed to the length of so many fingers, sleep is permitted for only so many hours. This rigid equality, imposed on people so very different in body and mind, is most unequal in its effects, as who can help seeing? And yet by these tricks they succeed in feeling superior not only to ordinary laymen but to one another—so that these men dedicated to apostolic charity will make frightful scenes over a habit worn with the wrong girdle or a bit too dark in color. Some you can find so severely religious that they use only rough Cilician cloth for their outer robe, though the undergarment is of fine Milesian wool; a variation of this trick is to wear linen on the outside, wool inside.[9] Still others reject mere contact with money as if it were a most contagious poison, though they are less scrupulous about wine-bibbing or intimate relations with women.

7. The satirical *Letters of Obscure Men* by Ulrich von Hutten (1515) pokes a lot of fun at pompous theologians who insist on the exact formula MAGISTRI NOSTRI. The Jewish tetragrammaton IHWH abbreviates Jehovah or Jahweh, which it would be taboo to spell or pronounce in full.
8. See the note on monks, above, p. 13, no. 8.
9. All these tricks of dress aim to give the impression of austerity while preserving the reality of comfort, even indulgence.

Finally, they all try as hard as possible not to agree with each other in their way of life; they are far less interested in resembling Christ than in differing among themselves. Thus they take special delight in their various names, some calling themselves "Cordeliers" but then subdividing their order into "Coletans," "Friars Minor," "Minims," and "Bullists." Again we have the "Benedictines" and the "Bernardines," the "Brigetines" and the "Augustinians," the "Williamites" and the "Jacobites"—[1] as if it was their last concern to be known as Christians.

The greater number of them insist so vehemently on their own ceremonies and petty traditions that they think a single heaven will hardly be adequate reward for such outstanding merit—never imagining that Christ, despising all these observances, will judge by his own standard, which is that of charity. One monk will point to his paunch, distended by eating every conceivable variety of fish; another will pour forth psalms by the bushel. Another will number up his myriads of fasts, and account for his bursting belly by the fact that he eats only one meal at midday. Another points to his huge pile of ceremonies performed, so many they couldn't be laden on seven naval transports. Another brags that for sixty years he has never touched money except with fingers protected by two pairs of gloves. Still another wears a cowl so dirty and slimy that no sailor would let it touch his body. Another boasts that for more than half a century he has led the life of a sponge, always fixed to the same spot; his neighbor claims credit for a voice hoarsened by constant singing; another for a lethargy contracted during years of solitude; and still another for a tongue atrophied during years of silence. But Christ, interrupting their boasts (which otherwise would never end), will ask, "Where did this new race of Jews come from? I recognize no law but my own, and about it I hear nothing whatever. Long ago, speaking openly and using no intricate parables, I promised that my father's kingdom would be granted, not to cowls, prayers, or fasts, but to works of faith and charity. Nor do I recognize those who make too much of their own merits and want to seem more sanctified than me; let them go live in the heavens of Abraxa[2] or, if they want, get a new heaven built for them outside mine by the men whose foolish traditions they have preferred before my commandments." When they hear these words, and see sailors and coachmen preferred before them, with what expressions do you suppose they will stare at each other? But meanwhile they cherish their own comfortable illusions, not without help from me.

Even though they have no political power, nobody dares to scorn the monks, least of all the mendicants, because they hold the keys of everyone's secret life under the seal of the confessional, as they call it. Revealing such secrets they consider very wrong, unless when they're drunk,

1. The Cordeliers were Franciscans, further divided into the four groups of the first sentence. Of the other orders, Williamites were followers of Saint William of Medaval, and Jacobites were Dominicans who got their second name because their house in Paris occupied a hospice dedicated to Saint James (Jacobus). The point of these obscure groups and semi-private names is clearly derisive.

2. A sect of Greek gnostics believed in 365 different heavens; they became known as Abraxians because the numerical equivalents of the Greek letters in "Abraxa" add up to 365.

and want to please the company with spicy stories; then they sketch the outlines of the tale, but allusively, leaving out all the names. But if anyone stirs up these hornets, then they defend themselves in public sermons, alluding indirectly and subtly to their enemy, so that only a complete dummy will fail to get the point. And there'll be no end to their yapping till you stop their mouths with a bone.[3]

Tell me, now, what comic actor or street-corner charlatan would you rather watch in action than these fellows making their sermons? Though they can't avoid ridiculous blunders, they try to imitate everything the old rhetoricians have handed down on the art of discourse. Good lord, how they gesticulate, how they change pitch, how they crow and strut and fling themselves wildly about, putting on special expressions from time to time, and getting everything mixed up in their outcries. And this art of oratory they hand down as a secret tradition from brother to brother; though I'm not permitted to know what it is,[4] still I can make a guess.

First they make an invocation, a trick borrowed from the poets. Then if their theme is going to be charity, the exordium will be all about the river Nile in Egypt; or if the theme is to be the mystery of the cross, they will find a happy starting place in Bel the dragon of Babylon; if it's to be about fasting, they will begin with the twelve signs of the zodiac, and if they're going to preach on faith, they talk a good long time on the squaring of the circle.[5] I myself once heard a distinguished fool—beg pardon, I meant to say "doctor"—who in a much publicized sermon that was to explain the mystery of the Holy Trinity tried to show that his approach was not the conventional one, but fit for the most theological ears in his audience. His new approach was to begin with letters, syllables, and sentences and so work up to the agreement of subject with verb and adjective with noun. Meanwhile everyone was amazed, and some people whispered to one another that phrase from Horace, "What does all this stink amount to?"[6] But finally he worked around to his main idea, that he could show an emblem of the Trinity so clearly indicated in the rules of grammar that no geometrician could demonstrate it better by drawing a diagram. And over this one sermon our 'ultra-theologian' had sweated eight whole months, so that today he's stone-blind, the discernment of his eyesight having been sacrificed to the sharpness of his wit. But the man does not regret his blindness, and thinks his glory was cheaply purchased at such a price. I've also heard of another man fully eighty years old who was so much a theologian that you'd have thought him Scotus incarnate. To clarify the mystery of the name JESU he demonstrated with marvellous subtlety that whatever can be expressed on this subject lies hidden in the letters themselves. For the fact that the word can be declined in three and only three different cases is a manifest

---

3. The way to get past Cerberus, three-headed dog guarding the gates of hell, was to throw him a bone.
4. As a woman, Folly is not supposed to know the trade secrets of monks.
5. The overflowing Nile leads into overflowing

charity; Bel the Dragon (Daniel 14) is a deep mystery; the zodiac can be used to measure the season of Lent; squaring the circle, like faith, is an exercise above the reach of reason.
6. Horace, *Satires* 2.7.

symbol of the Holy Trinity. Then because the first form *Jesus* ends in *s*, the second *Jesum* in *m*, and the third *Jesu* in *u*, this deep observation must be understood to enclose an 'ineffable' mystery, for the three letters indicate Christ is the *sum*, the *middle*, and the *ultimate*. Then within this mystery, he found one even more abstruse, involving the mathematics. Dividing the word *Jesus* in two equal parts leaves the letter *s* in the middle. Now that letter in Hebrew is pronounced *Shin*, which is not far from the word that the Scots use for *peccatum*, that is, *sin*; and this is a plain demonstration that Jesus takes away the sins of the world. This novel exordium left the audience open-mouthed in admiration, especially the theologians who were nearly petrified with astonishment, as Niobe was with grief.[7] As for me, I nearly suffered the same fate, from splitting my sides, as befell that rascally figwood Priapus when he spied on the secret rites of Canidia and Sagana.[8] And no wonder; for when did Demosthenes in Greek or Cicero in Latin ever dream up any such complicated roundabout? They considered any prefatory remarks faulty that wandered away from the main point. Not even a swineherd, with nothing but nature to instruct him, would ever start a speech that way. But the preachers all think their preamble, as they call it, is a great piece of rhetoric when it has nothing to do with the rest of the argument because it leaves the listener amazed and muttering to himself, "Now where's he going from here?"[9]

After the exordium, they offer by way of a narration, a perfunctory interpretation of a gospel passage, but hastily and as if incidentally, though in fact that should be the main order of their business. Then finally, putting on a whole new face, they propose some question of theology 'never heard of before on earth or in heaven,' and this they take for an occasion to show off the higher reaches of their art. This is where they attain the peak of theological pomposity, battering our ears with majestic titles and citing Distinguished Doctors, Subtle Doctors, Supersubtle Doctors, Seraphic Doctors, Divine Doctors, and Irrefutable Doctors. Then they scatter over the unlearned audience their syllogistic majors and minors, their conclusions, corollaries, ridiculous hypotheses, and hair-splitting distinctions. The fifth act of the comedy comes next, and for that they've reserved their best fireworks. Here they dredge up some stupid and inane story out of *The Mirror of History* or *The Deeds of the Romans*,[1] and proceed to interpret it allegorically, tropologically, and anagogically. And this is how they assemble their Chimera, a monster such as Horace never imagined when he wrote, "Stick on a human head," etc.[2]

But they've heard, I don't know where, that in its first stages a speech should be soothing and easy on the ears; at the beginning, then, they

---

7. From grief at the death of her many children, Niobe turned to stone.
8. Priapus, eavesdropping on some witches, was so scared at what he heard that his figwood buttock split, and he farted loudly. Horace, *Satires* 1.8.
9. Virgil, *Eclogue* 3.

1. Both these books are compendia of brief ancient narratives often mined to get snappy illustrative material for sermons.
2. Illustrating the necessity of decorum, Horace begins his *Art of Poetry* by imagining a creature assembled from many incongruous pieces.

speak so softly that they can't hear themselves—as if there were any point in saying what nobody can undertand. But they've also heard somewhere that exclamations are just the thing for stirring up the emotions, so after mumbling along for a while they suddenly break out in a wild clamor, though there's absolutely no occasion for it. You would swear the man needed a dose of hellbore[3] for bellowing like that without any reason. Besides, since they've been told that a speech ought to warm up gradually, they limp painfully through the first part, break out in a wild clamor even though they're in the dullest part of their subject, and then fall silent so abruptly you'd think they were out of breath. Finally, they've learned from the rhetoricians that it's a good idea to indulge a little humor now and then, so they try to mix a few jokes in with their talk; 'Lord help us all,' how gracefully they do it, and how à propos—you'd say it was a clear case of 'an ass with a lyre.' From time to time, they give a little satirical nip, too, but they take care to tickle rather than wound. And in fact they never flatter more than when they pretend to be 'speaking most sharply.' In short, the whole performance is such that you'd swear the preachers must have studied with street-corner charlatans, who are better performers, indeed, but follow the same procedures so closely that it's obvious one group must have learned its rhetorical tricks from the other.

And yet these preachers find that, thanks to my assistance, their audiences imagine that they're hearing a modern Demosthenes or a Cicero. Shopkeepers and women are the hearers they like best, and they try hardest to please them, because the former if stroked the right way may be coaxed into untying their moneybags, and the ladies, among many other reasons for liking the clergy, know they can always find there an understanding ear in which to pour out their grievances against their husbands.

You see now, I guess, how much men of the cloth owe to me, since with their petty little ceremonies, their trifling formulas, and loud mouths, they can wield a practical tyranny over the laity, and pass themselves off as actual Saint Pauls or Saint Anthonys.[4] But I'm happy to be rid of these shoddy play-actors, who are as good at taking my gifts without showing gratitude as they are at putting up a show of piety for the public. For now I'd like to say something about princes and courtiers who, like the free and liberal-minded men they are, seek my favors quite openly and unabashedly. These noblemen, if they have just half an ounce of good heart, must surely lead the most wretched lives in the world, and the most to be avoided. For what man would ever dream of trying to seize royal power by perjury or parricide if he reflected what a heavy burden falls on the shoulders of anyone who assumes the part of a true prince? If he wants to guide the ship of state, he must think continually

3. A strong purgative used to clear (among other things) cobwebs from the brain.
4. These would more likely be the Apostle Paul and Saint Anthony of Padua than the hermits Paul and Anthony of the fourth century, neither of whom was renowned as a preacher.

of the public welfare, not his own; indeed, he can consider nothing but the public good. He must not depart by a finger's breadth from the laws he has designed and promulgated; he must see to the integrity of all his officers and magistrates. His own life is exposed to public scrutiny; thus, if his manners are virtuous, he can be a star to steer by, and of the utmost benefit in all human affairs—or if, on the contrary, he is like a deadly comet, he can bring total destruction in his wake.[5] Other men's vices are not so obvious, nor are they so far-reaching in their effects. A prince stands on such an eminence that if something turns him ever so slightly from the path of honesty, a moral pestilence spreads through thousands of his subjects. Then because a ruler's position brings with it many things to distract him from virtue, such as pleasure, leisure, flattery, and luxury, he must be vigilant and keen to avoid disgracing his office. Finally, passing over all the plots, jealousies, and other perils that threaten, he is subject to the judgment of that one true King who will exact retribution for his least failing, and the more strictly, the greater has been his authority. If a prince would reflect on these and similar matters—and he would if he were wise—I doubt if he would enjoy either his evening dinner or a good night's sleep.

But now, thanks to my bounty, princes dismiss all these problems and send them to Jericho;[6] they look out for their own sweet selves and won't even admit anyone to their presence who can't keep the conversation light, and far away from disagreeable subjects. They suppose they're performing all the duties of a prince if they ride regularly to hounds, keep a stable full of fine horses, sell government offices for their own profit, and think every day of a new way to squeeze money out of the citizens and funnel it into the royal treasury. But these tricks are always performed under cover of precedent, so that even if the proceedings are iniquitous, they can at least make a pretence of equity; and they're always accompanied by a few words of flattery, to keep on the good side of public opinion.

Picture to yourself a man, like quite a few existing nowadays, who is ignorant of the law, almost an open enemy of the public good, concerned only with his own private advantage, a hater of liberty, learning, and truth, thinking of nothing less than the welfare of his country, but judging everything by his own pleasures, his own profit. Now hang a golden chain on his neck to symbolize the linkage of all the virtues, and set on his head a crown studded with gems to remind him that he should excel everyone else in heroic qualities. Put a scepter in his hand to symbolize justice and a heart free from corruption, and give him a purple robe to show his outstanding devotion to the welfare of his country. If a prince were to compare these symbols with his actual behavior, I think he might be ashamed of his trappings, and fear lest some satiric commentator might turn all his fine apparel into a ridiculous joke.

5. All "advice to princes" books, of which Machiavelli's *Prince* is a culminating example, begin with a statement along these lines.

6. Horace, *Odes* 1.9. The Latin is *Diis permittunt*, i.e., leave it to the gods.

Courtiers are another story. Though generally they're the most meeching, slavish, stupid, abject creatures conceivable, they fancy themselves the most distinguished of men. In one respect, they take the prize for modesty, because they content themselves with the gold, gems, purple robes, and other insignia of virtue while relinquishing to others all concern for the virtues themselves. One thing makes them perfectly happy, if they can address the king as 'Sire,' if they can speak three words of greeting to him, and then fill out the rest of their speech with formulas like 'Serene Majesty,' 'Your Lordship,' and 'Your Imperial Highness.' The rest of their talent is just barefaced flattery. And these are the proper skills of a noble courtier. But if you look more closely at their way of life, you'll find they are nothing but Phaeacians, or Penelope's suitors— you know the rest of the poem,[7] which Echo can give you better than I. They sleep till noon, when some miserable, mercenary little priest comes to their bedside and runs through mass for them almost before they're awake. Next to breakfast, which is hardly finished before it's lunchtime. Then on to dicing, draughts, betting, comedians, fools, drabs, games, and dirty stories, with a goodie to nibble on every so often between these activities. Dinner time now, followed by drinks, more than one, you can be sure. And in this way, without a moment's boredom, hours, days, months, years, and ages glide away. I myself get thoroughly sick of them, and take off, when I see them 'putting on the dog,' their ladies preening themselves on their long trains as if that made them superior beings, the men elbowing one another out of the way so they can be seen standing next to the prince, or when they string heavy gold chains around their necks, as if trying to show off their muscles at the same time as their money.

For a long time now, this courtly manner of life has been eagerly imitated by the loftiest Popes, Cardinals, and Bishops, some of whom have even surpassed their originals. But does anyone think what the priest's linen vestment means by its snow-white color, that it is the sign of a spotless life? Or what is the meaning of that two-horned mitre, with each point rising to a tight knot, if not to indicate absolute knowledge of the Old and New Testaments? Or why his hands are covered with gloves, if not to keep them clean of all contact with human affairs, and free to administer the sacraments? Why does he carry a crozier, if not to take vigilant care of the flock entrusted to him? Why the cross carried before him if not to signify victory over all human appetites? If any one of the clergy were to reflect on these and many other similar matters, I ask you, wouldn't he live a pretty sorry and wretched life? But now they're perfectly content, as long as they've stuffed themselves. As for watching over the flock, they either let Christ take care of that chore or put it off on curates and the 'Brethren,' as they call them. They never even think of

---

7. The Phaeacians, with whom Ulysses spent his last days before returning to Ithaca, were a care-free, pleasure-loving people, as were Penelope's less genial suitors. The poem Folly alludes to so coyly is Horace, *Epistles* 1.2; it characterizes the suitors as good-for-nothings (*nebulones*) absorbed in manicures and massages (*in cute curanda*). But Echo's part is not very clear.

the meaning of their title 'Bishop,' which means "overseer," and implies work, caring, taking pains. Yet when it comes to raking in the revenues, they're sharp-sighted enough; no 'careless oversight' there.

Likewise the Cardinals, if they reflected that they are successors to the Apostles, and that the same things are required of them as of their predecessors, might consider that they are not masters but administrators of spiritual gifts, for which an exact accounting will have to be rendered. They might even philosophize for a moment over their vestments, and ask themselves a few questions. For example: what is the meaning of this white outer garment, if not supreme, spotless innocence of life? Why the purple beneath, if not to show an ardent love of God? And again, that capacious cloak spreading out to envelop not only the Most Reverend Father but his mule as well—and sufficient to cover even a camel—does it not signify universal charity, extending to every person everywhere, in the form of teaching, exhorting, correcting, admonishing, pacifying quarrels, resisting wicked princes, and freely expending for the benefit of the Christian community not only his money but his blood? And why do they need money at all if they stand in the place of the Apostles, who were all poor men? If they thought over these matters, as I say, they wouldn't be so ambitious for the post, might even resign it— or at least live lives as strenuous and devoted as those of the original Apostles.

[Cardinal Asinino]

And the Popes themselves, vicars of Christ, if they tried to imitate his life—his poverty, his toil, his teaching, his suffering on the cross, his contempt of life—if they ever thought of the name 'Pope,' which means Father, or their title 'Your Holiness,' what soul on earth would be more downcast? Who would purchase that position at the expense of all his belongings, or would defend it, once bought, with sword, poison, and violence of every sort? Think how many comforts would be lost to them if they ever admitted a gleam of reason! Reason, did I say? Rather, just a grain of the salt Christ spoke of.[8] Off they would go, all those riches, honors, powers, triumphs, appointments, dispensations, special levies and indulgences; away with the troops of horses, mules, flunkies, and all the pleasures that go with them! (You'll note what a marketplace, what a harvest, what an ocean of pleasures I've crammed into a few words.) Instead of which, wisdom would bring wakeful nights, long fasts, tears, prayers, sermons, hours of study, sighs, and a thousand other griefs of that sort. And let's not forget the other circumstances, all those scribes, copyists, notaries, advocates, prosecutors, and secretaries, all those mule-drivers, stable hands, money-changers, pimps, and—I almost added something gentler, but I'm afraid it would grate on certain ears.[9] In short, this whole gang of people which battens on the Holy See—sorry, I meant to say, "which distinguishes it"—would be reduced to want. What a crime! abominable and inhuman; and to make it worse, the highest princes of the church and true lights of the world would be reduced to taking up scrip and staff.[1]

But as things stand now, whatever work may be called for in the church is passed along to Peter and Paul, who have ample free time; if there's any splendor or pleasure being given out, that our church leaders are willing to take on. And so it happens that, thanks to my efforts, no class of men live more comfortably or with less trouble. They think they've amply fulfilled Christ's commandments if they play the part of bishop with mystical and almost theatrical pomp, with formulas of Your Beatitude, Your Reverence, and Your Holiness, salted with some blessings and anathemas. Performing miracles is, for them, old-fashioned and obsolete, not at all in tune with modern times; teaching the people is hard work, prayer is boring, tears are weak and womanish, poverty is degrading, and meekness is disgraceful, quite unworthy of one who barely admits even the greatest kings to kiss his feet.[2] Death is a most unattractive prospect, and the idea of dying on a cross is quite out of the question.

All that's left to them in the way of weapons are those good words and fair speeches described by Paul[3] (and of those things they are sufficiently

---

8. Matthew 5.13.
9. Folly, who often insinuates sexual misconduct by clerics, may be hinting in this passage at pederasty.
1. I.e., begging for their bread.
2. More than four hundred years had passed since Gregory VII compelled Emperor Henry IV to a

humiliating act of self-abasement at Canossa (1076); but the memory of that scene still lingered.
3. Paul, in Romans 14.18, warns against those who cause dissensions and divisions, and who "by good words and fair speeches deceive the hearts of the simple."

generous)—along with interdicts, suspensions, warnings many times
repeated, anathemas, fearful images, and that horrifying thunderbolt with
which, by a mere nod of the head, they dispatch the souls of mortal men
to the depths of Tartarus.[4] It's a weapon that the most holy fathers in
God and vicars of Christ on earth launch at no one more fiercely than
at those who, instigated by the Devil, try to whittle away the patrimony
of Peter to a mere morsel. This patrimony, though the Evangelist says,
"We have left all and followed you,"[5] is understood to include farm-
lands, taxes, tithes, and judicial privileges. Ablaze with Christian zeal,
they fight with fire and sword to defend these belongings, at no small
expense of Christian blood—and all the time they declare that this is the
apostolic way to defend the church, the bride of Christ, by putting to
flight her enemies, as they call them. As if, indeed, there were any
enemies of the church more pernicious than impious popes, who by
their silence allow Christ to be forgotten, lock him up behind their money-
making laws, contaminate his teachings with their interpretations, and
murder him with their atrocious manner of life.

Moreover, though the Christian church was founded, confirmed, and

[Devils Despoiling Peter]

4. I.e., excommunication.   5. Matthew 19.27.

spread by the blood of sacrifice,[6] they try to get their own way with the sword, just as if Christ had perished completely, who protects his own people in his own way. War is such a monstrous pursuit that it's proper only for beasts, not men; so crazy that even the poets suppose Furies bring it upon us; so infectious that it spreads moral corruption far and near; so unjust that it's most effectively waged by the most cruel of thieves; so impious that it is utterly detestable to Christ. Yet, setting everything else aside, church leaders devote themselves to war and war alone. Here you see doddering old men who display the audacity of youth, indifferent to expense, undaunted by difficulties, and not caring a rap if laws, religion, and all the decencies of human society are turned upside down by their passions.[7] Nor is there any shortage of learned flatterers to call this midday madness by the names of zeal, piety, and fighting spirit—having contrived a formula by which a man can draw a yard of cold steel and plunge it into his brother's guts while still preserving that supreme charity which, by Christ's own precepts, every Christian should maintain toward his neighbor.

I still can't decide whether certain bishops in Germany have taken example from the popes or given it, when they act plainly and simply as secular lords, doing without ecclesiastical dress, benedictions, and other ceremonies of the sort, to the extent that they consider it cowardly and unworthy of a bishop to die anywhere but on the battlefield. Naturally, the lower priests are ashamed to fall below the standard set by their superior, so, behold, off they go like good soldiers to fight for their tithes, using swords, spears, rocks, and all manner of military gear. Meanwhile, the more sharp-witted among them rummage through ancient documents for precedents to terrify the poor people and extort from them even more tithes.[8] Yet all the while they deliberately ignore the many passages in those documents emphasizing the duties that the clergy owe the people in return. They never reflect on what their tonsure means, that a priest should be free from all the desires of this world and reflect only on heavenly matters. But these fine fellows feel they've performed all their priestly functions when they've mumbled over their office one way or another—though, Lord knows, I'd be amazed if any god either heard or understood such prayers, which they themselves neither hear nor understand, even when they're bawling them aloud. But priests have this in common with laymen, that they're all alert to glean every grain of money that's due them; on that point, not one of them is ignorant of the law. Of course if there's a job to be done, that they prudently pass on to the next fellow, and so down the line. Just as lay princes delegate parts of their administrative power to assistants who pass it around from

6. The Latin text does not specify "of sacrifice" as the kind of blood on which the church was founded, etc.; but sense demands it.
7. Warlike Julius II is clearly glanced at in this passage.
8. Collection of tithes was for a long time justified by the example of Melchizedek the high priest who (Genesis 14.20) received tithe after Abram's victory. But when this slender precedent came to be questioned, and the clergy began looking for positive laws requiring tithes, few could be found.

one to the other, so they put off onto common people the exercise of piety. The people push it back on those whom they call 'ecclesiastics,' just as if the church were none of their concern—as if, in fact, the vows made at their baptism were null and void. Then the priests who call themselves 'secular,' as if they'd devoted themselves to the world, rather than Christ, push the burden toward the canons regular; the canons regular[9] put it on the monks; the less strict monks put it on the more strict, everybody lays it on the mendicants, and the mendicants shunt it off to the Carthusians, where indeed some piety lies hidden, but so deeply buried that it's hardly ever visible. In the same way those popes who are busiest getting in the money harvest delegate their properly apostolic labors to the bishops, the bishops to the priests, the priests to their vicars, the vicars to the mendicant friars, who finally pass the job along to those who will be shearing the sheep.[1]

But it's no part of my present business to arraign the lives of popes and priests, lest I seem to be composing a satire rather than an encomium; and I don't want anyone to suppose I'm casting blame on good princes when I praise bad ones.[2] I raised the whole matter only in passing, to make clear that no mortal can possibly live happily unless he is initiated into my rites and enjoys my favor.

How could it be otherwise when even Nemesis the glory of Rhamnus,[3] who controls the fortunes of human beings, has always agreed warmly with me in hostility to the wise, while granting all her favors to fools, even in their sleep? You doubtless recall that Timotheus whose very name means 'favored by God,' and the proverb applied to him, "Even in sleep his net catches fish for him."[4] There's another that goes "The owl flies by night." Quite different are the sayings applied to the wise man: he is said to be "born on the fourth day," or else "has got Sejanus's horse," or else he "has found the lost gold of Toulouse."[5] But I won't 'proverbialize' any more, or you'll think I've been pillaging the notebooks of my friend Erasmus.

To get back to the point: fortune favors the dimwits and the brash, the people who are fond of saying "the die is cast." But wisdom makes men weak and timid, and that's why you'll generally find wise men living in the smoky corners of the world, neglected, rejected, and despised, in poverty and hunger, while fools are rolling in money, governing the state, and, in a word, flourishing like weeds. If anyone thinks it's a good life to be on intimate terms with princes and move in the gaudy, glitter-

9. Canons (from Latin *canon* = list) are clergy-men of a large church or cathedral enrolled on a special roster; canons regular follow the rule *(regula)* of Saint Augustine. Carthusians are the strict-est of the monastic orders.
1. Who the sheep-shearers could be in this alle-gory is hard to guess, since everyone else in the church seems accounted for already.
2. As Folly hasn't at all been praising bad princes (or "pontiffs," as the text reads before 1514), her point here is unclear.

3. Nemesis (who had a shrine at Rhamnus) pur-sues *everyone* with retribution; it is Fortune who favors fools. Here again Folly seems confused.
4. Timotheus was an Athenian general of the fourth century B.C. The proverb about the owl plays on the bird's reputation for wisdom and its nocturnal activity.
5. All these sayings mark the person born to mis-fortune. Fulfilling Folly's promise not to prover-bialize any more, the next paragraph opens with a proverbial saying, Caesar's "The die is cast."

ing circles of the court, nothing can be of less value to him than wisdom, because nothing is more offensive to the great. Suppose you want to make a pile of money, how will wisdom help you do that? The wise man will shrink from perjury, blush if caught in a lie, and worry himself sick over the scruples thought up by moralists regarding theft and usury. How can anyone make money that way? Again, if he aspires to honors and wealth through a career in the church, any donkey or ox will reach the goal sooner than a wise man. If it's pleasure you're after, well, girls (who are the best part of that game) adore fools and avoid a wise man with as much loathing as if he were a scorpion. In fact, everyone who wants a little fun in life will shut his doors on the wise man and sooner let in any other creature whatever. Wherever you turn, then, among popes, princes, judges, magistrates, friends, enemies, from the top of the ladder to the bottom, everything is to be had for ready cash; and since the wise man despises money, it generally takes care to keep away from him.

But though there's no end or limit to my praises, still an oration has to find an ending somewhere, it's a necessity. And so I will conclude, but not without a few words to show that many important authors have spread my fame abroad, in deeds as well as words. I wouldn't want anyone to suppose I'm alone in thinking well of myself, and I wouldn't want some knavish lawyer to complain that I brought in no supporting witnesses. So I'll cite my authorities just as they do theirs, that is, 'completely off the point.'

To begin, then, everyone knows the proverb that tells us, "Where the thing itself can't be had, a good imitation is best." And in line with this, schoolboys learn the lesson early that "playing the fool can sometimes be the height of wisdom."[6] You can see for yourselves what a good thing folly must be when the mere illusion of it wins such praises from men of learning. Even more direct is that plump, sleek hog of Epicurus's herd[7] who urges us to "mingle folly with our serious counsel," though he's not so smart when he qualifies it, "just for a while." Likewise elsewhere, "It's pleasant to play the fool now and then," he says; and in another passage, "I'd rather seem silly and worthless than smart and crabby." Besides, in Homer's poem, Telemachus, whom the poet praises to the skies, is sometimes described as 'childish,' and the tragic poets freely apply that word to boys and young men to indicate a promising disposition. Anyhow, what is the subject of that revered poem the *Iliad* if not 'the squabbles of foolish kings and their foolish subjects'?[8] What could be more explicit than Cicero's words in my praise: "Everything is full of folly"; and who can't see that if a thing is good in the first place, the more widely it's distributed, the better?

But perhaps pagan writers like these carry little weight with Christian

---

6. The saying is in the *Distiches* of Cato, a Latin primer.
7. Horace refers to himself this way, *Epistles* 1.4. The next two quotations are from *Odes* 4.12, and the third from *Epistles* 2.2. Telemachus is the son

of Odysseus in the *Odyssey*.
8. Horace, *Epistles* 1.2. Cicero's remark occurs in his *Familiar Letters* 9.22; the context is a discussion of obscene meanings in familiar words.

readers, so if you like I'll find support for my praises in the Holy Scriptures, or, as scholars like to say, I'll ground my demonstration on that foundation. And first I must excuse myself to the theologians and beg pardon for trespassing on their territory. And since it's a hard job I'm undertaking, and calling on the Muses to come down again would probably be presumptuous—since it's a long trip from Mount Helicon, especially when the subject isn't really in their line—perhaps I'd better act the part of the theologian, and to help me along my thorny path invoke the spirit of Scotus, which is more prickly than any hedgehog or porcupine. So let him leave his beloved Sorbonne and live for a while in my breast, after which he can go where he will, 'to Tophet' for all I care.[9] I only wish I could put on a fresh face for this part, and dress up in a theologian's robe. But if I played the part too well, I'm afraid someone might charge me with theft, as if I'd been secretly going through the desks of our 'Master Doctors,' just because I know so much theology. But it's not to worry; I've been associating long and intimately with theologians, and it's only natural that I've picked up their jargon. Even that rascally figwood god Priapus collected and remembered some Greek words just from listening to his master read aloud. And after some time in the society of men, Lucian's cock learned to speak quite acceptably.[1]

But now, if the coast is clear, let's get down to the matter. In his first chapter Ecclesiastes wrote, "The number of fools is infinite,"[2] and in making the number infinite doesn't he seem to include the entire human race except for a few poor specimens on whom I doubt if anyone ever laid eyes? Jeremiah makes the same point even more directly in his tenth chapter when he writes: "Every man is rendered foolish by his own wisdom." To God alone he attributes wisdom, leaving folly to mankind at large. And again, a little earlier, he says, "Man should not glory in his wisdom." And why shouldn't he glory in his wisdom, most excellent Jeremiah? For this simple reason, he would answer, that he has no wisdom to glory in. But let me come back to Ecclesiastes. When he cries, "Vanity of vanities, all is vanity,"[3] what do you suppose he meant, if not, as I was saying before, that human life is a puppet show containing nothing but folly? Thus he confirms that celebrated vote cast by Cicero in my favor, and which I've already quoted, to the effect that "The world is full of fools." So too with that wise man Ecclesiasticus, who said "The fool changes like the moon, the wise man endures unchanged like the sun";[4] what can he have meant, if not that the entire human race is foolish, but the word "wise" belongs to God alone? By "moon" we understand human nature, by "sun" the source of all light, God. The idea is confirmed when Christ in the Gospel says no one is to be called "good" except God alone.[5] Thus, if anyone who is not wise is foolish,

9. Duns Scotus spent as much time in Oxford as in Paris, but for Folly he is a Parisian because of all the followers he left there.
1. Horace, Satires 1.8; Lucian, The Dream, or The Cock.
2. Ecclesiastes 1.15. The King James version

translates, "What is lacking cannot be numbered." The quotations from Jeremiah are from 10 and 9.
3. Ecclesiastes 1.2.
4. Ecclesiasticus 27.12.
5. Matthew 19.17.

[Folly with Scotus's Soul on her Tongue]

and if, as the Stoics claim, whoever is wise must also be good, then it necessarily follows that the entire human race must be given over to foolishness. Again, Solomon in his fifteenth chapter says, "Folly is joy to him that is destitute of wisdom,"[6] thereby making abundantly clear that without folly there is no joy in life. In the same vein is that other text, "He who increases knowledge increases grief, and in much understanding is much vexation."[7] And the same thing is said quite explicitly by the Preacher in his seventh chapter, "The heart of the wise is in the house of mourning, but the heart of the fool is in the house of mirth."[8] That makes it clear that he thought mere knowledge of wisdom insufficient without knowledge of me as well. And if you don't believe me, here are his very words, as written in his first chapter: "I gave my mind to know wisdom and to madness and folly."[9] In this passage you must particularly note that folly is given the highest praise because she is placed last in the sentence. Ecclesiastes wrote it, and you know that the ecclesiastical ordering always places the person of highest dignity in last place—folllowing in this respect at least the precept of the evangelist. In addition, Ecclesiasticus, whoever he was, makes the superiority of folly to

6. Proverbs 15.21.   8. Ecclesiastes 7.4.
7. Ecclesiastes 1.18.   9. Ecclesiastes 1.17.

wisdom abundantly clear in his forty-fourth chapter,[1] though I'm not going to cite his words unless you help me compose my 'preliminary induction' by answering my questions as meekly as Socrates' interlocutors do in the dialogues of Plato. Well, then, which is it better to conceal, things rare and precious, or those which are common and cheap? What, no answer? Even if you play dumb, there's a Greek proverb to answer for you, "The waterjug is left on the doorstep." (Just in case someone is lacking in respect for these words of wisdom, they come to us from Aristotle, the god of our theological masters.) But are any of you foolish enough to leave gold and jewels in the open street? Not you, I'm sure. You hide them away in the innermost chambers of your house, you put them in the secret compartments of your strong box, while you leave trash lying out in the open. So if the precious thing is hidden away while the less valuable thing is left out, isn't it obvious that wisdom, which we're forbidden to hide away, must be less valuable than folly, which we're advised to conceal? Here it is in the very words of Ecclesiasticus: "Better the man who conceals his folly than the one who conceals his wisdom."[2]

Now consider this: the scriptures attribute to the foolish a candid and generous mind, while the wise man thinks himself superior to everyone else. That at least is the way I interpret what Ecclesiastes wrote in his tenth chapter: "When he that is a fool walketh by the way, his wisdom faileth him, and he saith to everyone that he is a fool."[3] Now don't you think that a mark of exceptional candor, to think everyone your equal, and instead of puffing yourself up, to share your merits with everybody else? And so even King Solomon the Great was not ashamed of this epithet when he said in his thirtieth chapter, "I am the most foolish of men."[4] Even Paul, the teacher of the gentiles, was not ashamed to call himself a fool when writing to the Corinthians. "I speak as a fool," he says; "I am more"—as if it were a disgrace to be outdone in stupidity.[5]

But now I hear an outcry from certain Greeklings,[6] eager to put down all the modern theologians by throwing dust in their eyes—that is, a smokescreen of annotations. The second place in this gang, if not the first, belongs to my friend Erasmus, whom I mention from time to time by way of compliment. A really foolish allusion, people will say, and worthy of Folly herself! The apostle actually meant something different from what you suppose. For he didn't use these words in order to be thought more foolish than others; but when he asked, "Are they servants of Christ?" and answered himself, "So am I," then, having equated himself with the other apostles, he added by way of correction, "and even more so," feeling that he was not just the equal of the others but in some degree their superior. And though he meant this as the real truth, yet to

1. In fact, Erasmus seems to be alluding to Ecclesiasticus 41.18.
2. Ibid.
3. Ecclesiastes 10.3.
4. Proverbs 30.

5. 2 Corinthians 11.
6. I.e., men who upheld the value of Greek in interpreting the Bible; Folly puts on the contemptuous manner of the theological establishment in referring to the new learning.

keep his words from seeming too arrogant or offensive, he added a little cover phrase about folly. "I speak as a fool"—as if to say, it's the special privilege of fools to speak the truth without giving offense.

But what Paul really meant when he wrote these words, I leave to the arguments of scholars. For my part, I prefer to follow the most pompous, fat, thick, and popular theologians, in whose company most of the learned would rather go astray, 'by Jove,' than be in the right with those triple-tongued newcomers.[7] Not one of them considers these Greeklings any better than a flock of grackles, especially since a certain glorified theologian (whose name I carefully suppress lest the grackles descend on him with that Greek saying about 'an ass with a lyre')[8] has expounded this passage with a full panoply of theological rigmarole. Starting with the text "I speak as a fool: I am more," he gives the whole passage a new twist (which, without the full force of the dialectic would have been quite impossible); I will present it in his own words, not only formal but material. "I speak as a fool" is now understood to say, "If you thought me a fool before for equating myself with the pseudo-Apostles, you'll think me even more foolish now for placing myself above them." To be sure, a little later he seems to forget this reading entirely, and relapses into another interpretation.

But why should I exercise myself so much over a single example, when it's the acknowledged privilege of theologians to stretch the heavens—that is, the Holy Scriptures—as wide as a tanner stretches a piece of leather? Even in Saint Paul, some words are conscripted to do battle for the Holy Scriptures which in their original context do no such thing—at least that's the opinion of 'five-languaged' Saint Jerome.[9] When Paul once happened on an altar in Athens, he twisted the inscription on it into an argument for the Christian faith by leaving out all the words on it that didn't serve his purpose, and fastening on just two, *ignoto deo*, to the unknown god[1]—and even those he changed. For the complete inscription read, "To the Gods of Asia, Europe, and Africa, to the Unknown and Foreign Gods." I expect it's this example that our modern 'sons of theology' follow when they pick out four or five words from different passages—distorting them, if necessary—and apply them to their purposes, even if the passages that come before or after are on an entirely different topic, or directly contradict what they say. And all this they carry off with such confident assurance that pettifogging lawyers frequently express envy of the theologians.

Is there anything they can't do, now that the great man—I almost let slip his name, but that Greek proverb stuck in my throat—has twisted the words of Luke into a doctrine about as compatible with the thought

7. The three languages are Greek, Latin, and Hebrew.
8. Folly alludes, not very subtly, to the fourteenth-century theologian Nicholas de Lyra, whose interpretations of scripture were considered authoritative by conservatives.
9. Saint Jerome, who prepared the Latin translation of the Bible that eventually became the Vulgate, knew five languages: Greek, Latin, Hebrew, Chaldee, and his native Dalmatic. (He was, as we would say, a Yugoslav.)
1. Acts 17.23. Jerome's commentary explains what the inscription really said.

of Christ as fire is with water? For when the final peril threatened, and the disciples gathered around their teacher, ready to defend him 'fighting shoulder to shoulder,' Christ deliberately set out to persuade his disciples not to rely on defences of this sort. So he asked them whether they had lacked anything when he sent them forth without provisions for their journey—without shoes to protect them from rocks or thorns, without a well-stocked pack to keep them from hunger. When they said they had lacked for nothing, he went on. "But no," he said, "whoever has a purse should take it, and likewise his pack; and he that hath no sword, let him sell his garment and buy one."[2] Since the whole teaching of Christ inculcates nothing but gentleness, tolerance, and readiness to give up one's own life, how can anyone misunderstand what is meant by this passage? Namely, that the disciples should be disarmed even further, that they should not just do without shoes and pack, but should throw their cloaks on the pile in order to begin preaching the gospel naked and unencumbered, taking along nothing but a sword—not the sword wielded by highwaymen and murderers, but the sword of the spirit, which pierces to the recesses of the heart, cutting off all worldly attachments, leaving nothing in the breast but piety.

But note, if you please, how that celebrated theologian twists the passage out of shape. He reads the sword as defense against persecution, the pack as a plentiful supply of provisions, just as if Christ had completely changed his previous position, and was now recanting instructions which seemed to send forth his spokesmen 'in not very regal style.' Perhaps the interpreter thinks he had actually forgotten what he said before, that they would be blessed when afflicted with insults, scorns, and torments, that he forbade them to resist evil because the meek, not the fierce, shall be blessed; perhaps he forgot that he had previously compared them to sparrows and lilies.[3] But now, forsooth, he doesn't want them to set off without a sword, he actually tells them to sell their garments to get swords, as if they'd be better off going naked than swordless. In addition, he thinks the word "sword" includes everything that can serve to repel force, and likewise "pack" includes all the necessities of life. And thus this interpreter of the divine word mobilizes the apostles to preach the crucified Christ in an array bristling with lances, slings, siege-machines and heavy artillery. He also loads them down with trunks, suitcases, and bundles, lest sometime they might have to leave the inn without proper breakfast. He isn't even disturbed that the sword which Christ urgently ordered to be bought, he shortly thereafter ordered to be sheathed;[4] nor is there any record that the apostles used swords and shields to fight the gentiles, as they certainly would have done if Christ had meant what this fellow says he did.

There's another of these fellows whose name I withhold out of respect, though he's well thought of; discussing the tents mentioned by Habba-

---

2. Luke 22.35–36. Folly is not quite fair to the position of Nicholas de Lyra.
3. Repeated passages in Matthew 5, 6, and 10 make use of these similitudes.
4. Matthew 26.52 and John 18.11.

kuk when he says "the curtains of the land of Midian did tremble," he fancies an allusion to the flayed skin of Saint Bartholomew.[5] The other day I attended a theological disputation, as I very often do. When someone asked about the scriptural authority for burning heretics rather than refuting them logically, a certain fierce old man, whose arrogance alone identified him as a theologian, answered angrily that Saint Paul had made the rule when he said, "A man that is a heretic, after the first and second warning, reject *(devita)*." And when he kept shouting these words over and over, till people started to wonder what ailed the man, he finally explained that the heretic should be removed from life *(de vita)*.[6] Some people laughed at him, but there were a few who thought the argument thoroughly theological. Then when disagreement persisted, an 'ultimate authority,' as they say, a supreme arbiter, undertook to cut the knot. "Here's the truth of the matter," he said. "It is written, 'You shall not suffer an evildoer to live,'[7] every heretic is an evildoer, therefore, etc." Everyone was amazed at the man's mighty intellect, and stampeded to line up behind his judgment. And it never occurred to anyone that the rule applies only to sorcerers, magicians, and fortunetellers, who in Hebrew are called *mekaschephim*. Otherwise, we should be obliged to inflict the death penalty on fornicaters and drunkards.

But it's foolish for me to multiply examples when there are so many of them that they couldn't all fit into the volumes of Chrysippus and Didymus.[8] I only want you to be aware that our saintly scholars are pardoned for these slips, and some of the same allowances should be made for me, who am only a 'bumbler in theology,' if some of my allusions are a bit off the point. Now I return to Paul. "You suffer fools gladly," he says, speaking of himself; and he goes on, "yet as a fool receive me"; and again, "I speak not after the Lord, but as it were foolishly."[9] And elsewhere, "We are fools for Christ's sake."[1] This is high praise for folly from a high authority. And what if the same authority openly praises folly as a valuable and necessary quality of mind? "If any man among you seems to be wise in this world, let him become a fool, that he may be wise."[2] And in Luke, Jesus called the two disciples who joined him on the road "fools." I don't suppose that should be considered surprising, since Saint Paul attributes a measure of foolishness even to God himself: "the foolishness of God is wiser than men" he says.[3] and Origen in his commentary makes clear that this folly of God's cannot be explained as simply the opinion of men, as is possible with that other passage, "The preaching of the cross is to them that perish, foolishness."[4] But why should I worry all these texts when Christ himself

---

5. Habakkuk 3. Stretching the allusion to these tents into an analogy with Saint Bartholomew's flayed skin is obviously ridiculous.
6. Titus 3.10. the word *devita* can mean "reject" or "avoid"; it cannot mean "kill."
7. Exodus 22.18.
8. Chrysippus and Didymus between them wrote nearly five thousand books. Few survive.

9. 2 Corinthians 11.
1. 1 Corinthians 4.10.
2. 1 Corinthians 3.18; Luke 24.25.
3. 1 Corinthians 1.25. Origen, of the second and third centuries, was one of the most prolific and influential of the early church fathers.
4. 1 Corinthians 1.18.

in the mystic psalms directly says to the Father, "O God, thou knowest my foolishness"?[5]

Indeed, it is no accident that fools are most pleasing to God; and I think this is the reason, that just as princes suspect and dislike men who think too much—as Caesar suspected Brutus and Cassius but had no fear of drunken Anthony; or as Nero mistrusted Seneca and Dionysus Plato—so they are well pleased with men of dull and simple wits. And in the same way, Christ always scorns and condemns those opinion-mongers who put all their trust in their own wisdom. Paul bears witness to this idea in no uncertain words when he says, "God has chosen the foolish things of the world to confound the wise," and "God chose to preserve the world through foolishness," since by wisdom it could not be preserved.[6] God himself speaks to the same effect through his prophet: "I will destroy the wisdom of the wise and bring to nothing the understanding of the prudent."[7] And again, Christ gives thanks that the mystery of salvation has been hidden from the wise but revealed to little children, that is, fools. (For the Greek word for child [nepios] means foolish and is used to contrast with wise [sophos].) Relevant too are all those passages in the Gospels where Christ attacks scribes, pharisees, and doctors of the law, while carefully reserving his favor for the unlearned populace. What else is meant by that phrase, "Woe to you, Scribes and Pharisees"[8] but "woe to you, men of wisdom"? But he seems to have taken the greatest delight in children, women, and simple fishermen; even among brute beasts, those that pleased him best were least like the crafty fox. Thus he preferred to ride a donkey, though if he had wanted to he could safely have mounted a lion. His holy spirit descended in the form of a dove, not an eagle or hawk. Throughout Scripture there's frequent mention of deer, young mules, and lambs. Consider too that he uses the term "sheep" to describe those who are destined to immortal life. No animal is more stupid, as is plain from Aristotle's phrase, "dumb as a sheep,"[9] which he says was derived from the imbecility of the beast, and is often used to insult stupid and blockish minds. And this is the flock of which Christ declared himself the shepherd; indeed, he delighted in the title of "lamb," as when John hailed him with the words "Behold the lamb of God," a term repeatedly used in the Apocalypse.[1]

All these witnesses point to a single conclusion, that all men are fools, even the pious ones. Christ himself, though he was the wisdom of the Father,[2] took on the foolishness of humanity in order to relieve the folly of mortals, just as he became sin in order to redeem sinners. Nor did he choose to redeem them in any other way but through the folly of the cross and through ignorant, sottish disciples. His lesson to them was nothing but folly and avoidance of wisdom, as when he set before them

---

5. Psalms 69.5; interpretation must strain several points to make this Christ's speech.
6. 1 Corinthians 1.21 and 27.
7. 1 Corinthians 1.19.
8. Matthew 23.

9. Aristotle, History of Animals 9.3.
1. John 1; Revelation 5–7.
2. This paragraph is a solid texture of biblical phrases and paraphrases of them.

such examples as children, lilies, mustard-seeds, and sparrows—senseless creatures all, devoid of intelligence, and leading their lives under the promptings of nature, artless and carefree. Then he told them not to be concerned what they would say before magistrates, and forbade them to care about times and seasons [3]—what did he mean by that, except that they shouldn't rely on their own prudence but be wholly dependent on him? In the same way, God, the maker of the whole world, prohibited the eating of the tree of knowledge, as if knowledge was poisonous to happiness. Likewise Paul directly opposes knowledge as pernicious because it puffs man up; and I think Saint Bernard was following in the apostle's footsteps when he interpreted the mountain on which Lucifer set his throne as the hill of knowledge. [4]

Perhaps I shouldn't omit the argument that folly seems to be pleasing to the higher powers because it is accepted as an excuse for errors, whereas the knowing man receives no pardon. This is why, even when they have sinned knowingly, men use ignorance as their excuse. If I remember rightly, that is how Aaron in the book of Numbers begs pardon for his sister: "Alas, my lord, I beseech thee, lay not the sin upon us wherein we have done foolishly." [5] So too Saul begged forgiveness of David, "Behold, I have played the fool and have erred exceedingly," and David in turn placates the Lord by saying, "I beseech thee, O Lord, take away the iniquity of thy servant; for I have done very foolishly" [6]—implying that he would receive no pardon unless he pleaded ignorance and foolishness. Even more cogent is the example of Christ on the cross when he prayed for his enemies: "Father, forgive them"—he made no other excuse for them than their ignorance—"for they know not what they do." [7] In the same vein, Paul writing to Timothy says, "I obtained mercy because I did it ignorantly, in unbelief." [8] What does he mean by "I did it ignorantly," if not, 'I did it out of foolishness, not in malice'? And what is the force of "because" if not that he wouldn't have obtained mercy if he hadn't pleaded the excuse of folly? The mystic psalmist, whom I forgot to mention in his proper place, also strengthens my case when he writes, "Remember not the sins of my youth, nor my stupidities." [9] You see the two excuses he makes, namely youth (on whom I'm a constant attendant) and stupidities, which are put in the plural to make us understand the full force of folly.

And now to sum up (lest I go on with these citations to infinity), the entire Christian religion seems to bear a certain natural affinity to folly, and to relate far less clearly to wisdom. If you want evidence of this, consider first that children, old folk, women, and simpletons are, of all people, most attracted to the services of our holy religion and are always found in closest proximity to the altar—drawn there solely by their nat-

3. Acts 1.7.
4. 1 Corinthians 8.1; Saint Bernard's comments are from one of his sermons.
5. Numbers 12.11.
6. Samuel to David in 1 Samuel 26.21; David to the Lord in 2 Samuel 24.10.
7. Luke 23.34.
8. 1 Timothy 1.13.
9. Psalms 25.7.

ural instincts. Then you see that the first founders of this religion were great admirers of simplicity and equally bitter enemies of learning. Finally, you see that no fools are more distracted than those whose ardent zeal for Christian piety has wholly eaten them up. They discard their belongings, swallow insults, put up with trickery, treat friends and enemies alike, avoid pleasure, and subsist on fasts, vigils, tears, toils, and humiliations. They shun life, seek death, and seem completely numb to all human feeling as if their souls existed somewhere else, not in their bodies. What other name can we give this condition than "insanity"? We shouldn't be surprised, either, if the apostles were thought to be drunk on new wine, or if Paul seemed insane to his judge Festus.[1]

But now that I've 'got on my high horse' I want to take the next step, and argue that the happiness after which Christians strive so passionately is nothing but a certain kind of folly amounting to madness. Don't startle at the words, but look at the realities. First of all, Christians come close to agreeing with the Platonists that the mind is buried deep in the body and bound to it by chains so thick and heavy that they prevent it from seeing and enjoying things as they really are. Next, Plato defines philosophy as a 'meditation on death' because it leads the mind away from visible, bodily things, just as death does.[2] And so, as long as the mind makes use of the body's organs, it is called 'sane'; but when, breaking these bodily shackles, it tries to achieve its own liberty, as if meditating flight from a prison, then people call it 'insane.' If this happens as a result of sickness or some bodily defect, then everyone unhesitatingly agrees in calling it 'madness.' And yet we see men in such dire straits predict the future and speak in tongues they were never taught—thus giving clear evidence of some divine presence. And I don't doubt that this happens because the mind at this juncture is a little freer of the contamination of the body, and now starts to resume its native powers. For the same reason I think something similar happens to people hovering in the shades of death, so that they utter astounding things, as if they were inspired.

Now if such a thing should happen as a result of the pursuit of piety, it might not be madness of exactly the same sort, but it would be so close that most men would consider it madness pure and simple, especially since the number of really earnest devotees is so small compared with the grand total of the human race. Thus the majority find themselves in the position of those described in Plato's myth of the cave, who are chained up in darkness, knowing only the shadows of things.[3] But then one man escaped and came back to tell them that he had seen things as they really are, and that they were much mistaken in thinking nothing existed but those paltry shadows. The man who has achieved understanding pities his comrades who are in the grip of such a fundamental error; he deplores their insanity. But they in turn ridicule him as a raving

1. Acts 2.13; 26.24.
2. Plato, *Phaedo*.

3. On the myth of the cave, see above, p. 47, n. 3.

lunatic, and throw him out. Just so, the run of common men keep their
eyes fixed on corporeal things, and think that is all that properly exists.
But pious persons, on the other hand, judge more poorly of things the
closer they approach to the corporeal, and devote themselves entirely to
the contemplation of things invisible; in that contemplation they are
absorbed. The common man gives first place in his thoughts to money,
next to bodily comforts, and last place to things of the mind, which he
doesn't generally believe in anyway, because he can't see them with his
eyes. Quite otherwise, the pious devote themselves entirely to apprehending God who is purity itself; after him, and yet as part of him, they
concern themselves with the soul; as for pampering the body, they neglect
it completely, and they scorn wealth, deliberately avoiding it as so much
garbage. And if they are forced to deal with such worldly matters, they
do so reluctantly and with distaste, having as if they did not have, pos-
sessing as if they did not possess.[4]

Even in small matters, they take quite different lines. First, though
all the senses have some relation to the body, yet some are more gross
than others, as touch, hearing, sight, smell, and taste, while others are
more remote from the body, as memory, intellect, will. Wherever the
spirit directs its energies, there it becomes strong. And since pious men
direct their minds to those matters that are most remote from the gross
senses, those senses in them become torpid and atrophied. In common
men, the lower senses are highly developed, the higher ones hardly at
all. This is the reason behind those stories we've heard of godly men
who drank oil by mistake for wine.[5]

Then consider the affections of the soul. Some men have more traffic
with impulses of the sluggish body, such as sexual passion, hunger, and
desire for sleep, as well as wrath, pride, and envy; the pious wage ceaseless war on these impulses, while the common people can't imagine life
without them. Then there are certain intermediate affections which could
be called natural, such as honoring one's father, loving one's children,
feeling affection for one's kinfolk and friends. Ordinary people approve
such feelings completely; but the pious try to root out even them, except
so far as they can be harmonized with the highest part of the mind. Thus
one loves one's father not simply as a father (for what did he beget except
the body, and even that we owe to God the father, as well) but as a good
man through whom shines the image of that loftiest mind which they
call 'the highest good,' and apart from which they teach that nothing is
to be loved or desired.

By this same rule they measure all the other occasions of life, so that
in every case what is visible, if not altogether to be despised, is always
subordinated to those things that cannot be seen. Even in the sacraments
and offices of piety, they say, bodily and spiritual elements can be distinguished. Thus in fasting they aren't much impressed by mere abstinence

4. 1 Corinthians 7. 29–30.   5. According to *The Golden Legend*, this hap-
                                              pened to Saint Bernard.

from food and drink—which common folk suppose is all that fasting amounts to—unless one also reduces the passions, admitting less anger than usual, and less pride, so that the spirit, shaking off the weight of the body, may succeed in tasting and relishing the joys of heaven. Similarly, in receiving the Eucharist, though the ceremonies accompanying it are not to be scorned, yet by themselves they are not very valuable and may even be harmful if a spiritual element is not also present, namely that which is represented by the visible signs. In the Eucharist is represented the death of Christ, which men should reenact by mastering, destroying, and (as it were) laying in the grave the passions of the body, so they may rise again to a new life, made one with him and with each other. This is what the pious man does, these are his thoughts. But the ordinary person thinks the service consists of nothing but standing by the altar, as close as possible, listening to the mumbling of certain formulas, and gaping at the least details of the ceremony. I cite these two actions only by way of example, for in every part of his life the pious man shrinks as far as he can from the concerns of the body, and allows himself to be lifted to the realm of eternal, invisible, and spiritual things. Thus the difference between these two groups on practically every topic is so profound that each thinks the other quite mad. As a matter of fact, I think that expression is better applied to the pious than to the ordinary people. This will be clearer if in a few words I make evident, as I promised to do, that the ultimate reward for which they strive is nothing but a kind of madness.

First, then, you should consider that Plato had some premonition of this idea when he wrote that "the madness of lovers is the height of felicity."[6] For one who loves passionately no longer lives in himself but in the object of his love, so that the farther he departs from himself and the closer he comes to the love-object, the more joyful he is. Now when the soul prepares to leave the body and no longer exercises perfect command over its organs, that state you would call madness, and rightly so. Otherwise, what would be the sense of those common expressions, 'he is beside himself,' 'he has come to,' and 'he is himself again'? Moreover, the more profound the love, the greater is the madness, and the happier. What then is that future life in heaven for which pious minds yearn so ardently? At that point the spirit, stronger and at last victorious, will absorb the body, and this it will do more easily in part because now it will be in its own kingdom, and in part because in its former life it had been purging and refining the body in preparation for this transformation. Now the spirit will be mingled with the highest mind of all, which is far greater than its infinitude of parts, so that the whole man will be outside himself, will be utterly happy at being outside himself, and will receive unspeakable bliss from that highest good which attracts everything to itself.

Now this felicity can be perfect only when the soul has re-entered its

6. Plato, *Phaedrus.*

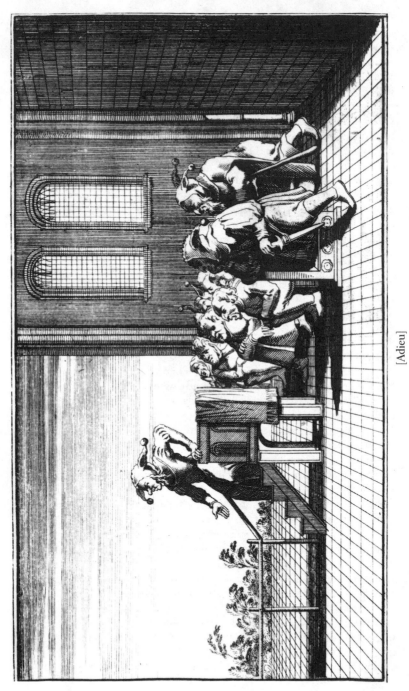

[Adieu]

former body and both are received into immortality, yet since the life of the pious is nothing but a meditation on that future life and, as it were, a shadow of it, they sometimes are able to experience a certain savor and relish of the life to come. Though it's only the tiniest drop from that fountain of eternal bliss, yet it far surpasses all the pleasures of the body, even if all the delights of all mortal men were rolled into one ball. So far do spiritual things surpass things of the body, things invisible to mortal sight the things that can be seen. This is what the Prophet promised: "Eye has not seen nor ear heard nor have entered into the heart of man the things that God has prepared for them that love him."[7] And this is the part of Folly which shall not be taken away from her by the transformation of life, but brought to perfection. Those who are lucky enough to know this experience, and it happens to very few, undergo something very similar to madness. Their talk is incoherent and not like the ordinary speech of men; they make meaningless sounds and their faces continually change expression. One minute they rejoice, the next they are dejected, now they weep and now they laugh, then they sigh; in short, they are completely and truly beside themselves. When they come to, they say they do not know where they have been, whether in the body or out of it, awake or asleep. They cannot tell what they heard, saw, said, or did, except through a mist, as in a dream. All they know is that they were supremely happy while they were out of their minds; and they regret their return to reason because their one desire is to be continually mad with this sort of insanity. And yet this is just the tiniest taste of the bliss to come.

But I've long since forgotten myself and 'overstepped my boundaries.' If you think I've been too cheeky or long-winded, remember you've been listening to Folly and a woman. You might also keep in mind the Greek proverb, "Even a foolish man sometimes says something to the point"— though you may not think this applies to women. I see you expect an epilogue, but you're out of your minds if you suppose I still remember what I said after spouting such a jumble of words. The old saying was, "I hate a drinking companion with a memory," and here's a new one to go with it, "I hate an audience that won't forget." And so I'll say Goodbye. Clap your hands, live well, and drink deep, most illustrious disciples of Folly.

---

7. 1 Corinthians 2.9. The next sentence echoes Luke 10.42, with a latent pun linking *Moriae pars*, the part of Folly, with *Mariae pars*, the part of Mary.

The Complaint of Peace

When *The Complaint of Peace* appeared in 1517, the terrible European struggles known collectively as "the wars of religion" still lay in the future. They were to smolder on, flaring up occasionally into outbreaks of communal violence and systematic devastation, through the sixteenth and seventeenth centuries. But even in 1517, Erasmus's first readers could look back on centuries of random, bloody slaughter—of countrysides overrun by predatory marauders, of cities smashed by rival cities, of states crushed by their ambitious neighbors, of systematic robbery carried out under the name of dynastic right or religious zeal. Especially with the growth of national administrations and national armies (France, England, and Spain all unified their territories in the late fifteenth and early sixteenth centuries), the powers of destruction grew more terrible, the disastrous effects of a wholesale European scrimmage more apparent. Erasmus's tirade against war could not have been more timely.

Not that immediate circumstances had much influence on Erasmus's attitude toward war. He was a pacifist on principle, opposed from his early years to war and violence in all their many forms; much of the rhetoric used in his plea for peace dates back to the *Panegyric of Philip* (1504). In the *Complaint*, he admits, faintly and cautiously enough, that some wars of self-defense may be more just than others; but his categorical summary statement emphatically declares that the worst peace is always better than the best war. It's a point of view that limits the rhetorical variety available to the *Complaint*; and it leaves one disappointed that Erasmus did not turn his thought toward a discussion of the moral equivalents of war. At the time he wrote it, Erasmus was serving momentarily as adviser to Charles, duke of Burgundy, shortly to become king of Spain as Charles I and immediately thereafter Holy Roman Emperor as Charles V. If the *Complaint* was written for Charles's eyes, Erasmus (like Raphael Hythloday, in More's *Utopia*) was offering his prince counsel of perfection. The record of Charles's many military activities shows how far Erasmus was from the disagreeable political realities of his day. But as the statement of an ideal, the *Complaint* has its own permanent authenticity, even more relevant in the age of atomic explosives and intercontinental missiles than it was at the time of broadswords and popgun artillery.

The Complaint of Peace

Discarded and Despised by the Nations Everywhere

PEACE SPEAKS:
If it was for some advantage of their own that mankind has dismissed, rejected, and disgraced me, though I've deserved no such treatment, I

might bewail my own misfortune and denounce their iniquity. But now that men have cast out me, who am the source of all human happiness, a misfortune greater than my own grief calls for lamentation. They have left themselves exposed to an endless flood of troubles, and though I ought to be angry with them, I am bound to grieve for them and commiserate with them. To drive away a lover is severity, to scorn a deserving person is ingratitude, but to visit affliction on the protector and preserver of the entire human race is villainous. Not only do they rob themselves of all the extraordinary benefits I bring with me, they rush instead into a foul swamp of the most atrocious evils: now doesn't that look like the terminal phase of total insanity? With common criminals it makes sense to be angry, but when men are possessed by the Furies, what can we do but weep? And what people are more to be pitied than those who don't realize how pitiful they are? Who are more unhappy than those who are unaware of their own misery? Who are sicker than those who can't even reach out after health because they don't recognize the enormity of their disease?

Being Peace, I am praised by all voices, both human and divine, as the fountain, source, nurse, and sponsor of all good things to be found in heaven and on earth. Without me there is no growth, no safety for life, nothing pure or holy, nothing agreeable to men or pleasing to the gods. And, on the other hand, war is like a vast ocean of all the evils combined, harmful to everything in the universe. Under its influence, sprouting buds wither, plants shrivel up, the frail collapse, the strong perish, and sweet things turn sour; indeed, war is a force so sinister that, like a violent plague, it wipes out all traces of piety and religion. Nothing is more destructive to man or more hateful to the Deity. And if all this is so, let me ask, in the name of almighty God, who can suppose these are human beings—who can think there's a speck of sanity in them— when they try to reject me, being who I am, at such enormous expense, with such strenuous efforts, with such tortured arguments, with so many tricks and dodges, so many dangers and deceits—in order to acquire at an exorbitant price an interminable morass of troubles? If wild beasts scorned me like that, I would understand their contempt as the work of nature, which formed their minds to a pattern of savagery. Even with dumb cattle, I'd pity their ignorance, because their minds have been denied the sharpness to recognize the benefits of my gifts. But oh! what a shameful and almost monstrous thing it is to say! there is just one animal that nature created with the endowment of reason, which leads to benevolence and social discourse—yet I can find my place among the wild beasts and dull cattle more readily than among human beings.

For thousands of centuries the many celestial bodies, though they don't follow the same orbits or exercise the same powers, have been living and flourishing in harmony with one another. The several elements, though they often battle with each other, generally strike a balance by which they maintain a constant peace, creating by mutual understanding and interchange a concord out of discord. Within the bodies of living creatures, how faithful is the agreement of the various limbs and organs with one another, how readily they cooperate in the common defense. Nothing could be more different in their natures than the soul and the body; yet nature has bound these two partners together by a conjunction so tight that we realize its force only when it is dissolved. Similarly, as life is nothing but the joining of soul and body, so any sort of corporation draws its health from the working together of its various parts. Even without the aid of reason, living creatures everywhere assemble in communities, and live quietly together. Elephants gather in herds, pigs and sheep feed in groups, cranes and grackles fly in flocks, storks have their societies and even their rulers, dolphins act to protect one another, and the commonwealths of the ants and bees, as well as their cooperative work habits, are well known.

But why am I so forward to speak of creatures which, though without reason, yet have the use of their senses? In trees and herbs you can recognize the elements of friendship. Some female plants are barren unless associated with a male, the vine clings to the elm, the peach tree welcomes the vine. Even objects devoid of feeling seem to be aware of the benefits of peace. They may not have the power of perception, but with such life as they have they are attracted to their neighbors. What could be less animate than a rock? Yet even in these, something like a sense of peace and concord inheres. The magnet attracts iron to itself, and holds it. Even the most ferocious animals make and keep agreements with one another. The savagery of lions isn't directed against other lions. One boar doesn't attack another with flashing tusks, the lynx lives in peace with his fellow-lynx, dragons don't destroy other dragons, and the concord of wolf with wolf has been celebrated in a proverb.[1] I will add what seems even more remarkable, that the very demons by whom the perfect concord of heaven and earth was first broken observe a truce with one another, and join in support of the tyranny, such as it is, under which they live. Only men, who above all other species should agree with one another and who need mutual understanding most of all, cannot be united in mutual love by nature (so powerful everywhere else), nor by training, nor by all the advantages to be anticipated from concord, nor even by awareness of the many evils resulting from war.

Only this one animal is capable of speech, the best reconciler of conflicting needs; he has also been granted the seeds of science and virtue, an intelligence which is gentle in itself and naturally inclines him to benevolence. He instinctively likes to make himself liked by others, and enjoys receiving the gratitude of those he has benefited—unless he is corrupted by his own depraved desires or by the poisons of Circe,[2] and turns into a beast. This is why in common speech anything that pertains to well-doing is called humane, so that the word "humanity" may not designate a mere natural difference, but a distinction of manners worthy of a man. Humans possess as well the gift of tears, evidence of a gentle

---

1. Erasmus may have in mind the catch-phrase *homo homini lupus,* "man is like a wolf to his fellow-man," which perhaps implies that wolves are not wolfish to each other.

2. Circe, in the *Odyssey,* turned Ulysses' companions into beasts by means of drugs.

disposition, by means of which, should anything have happened to offend a neighbor or anger a friend, one can easily be restored to favor.

Just look at all the ways in which nature herself persuades us toward agreement. Not content with the allurements of mutual benevolence, she makes harmonious relations not only convenient but necessary. Thus she divided up the gifts of body and mind in such a way that nobody has them all, or so many that he may not some time need help from another, however insignificant. Not everybody has the same or even equal gifts; the way to level out this inequality is through friendly collaboration. Products are grown in one country that may be wanted in another, and so commerce springs up. Among the other creatures, each carries his own weapons and sees to his own defense; only man can walk unarmed, weak in himself and protected by nothing but a pact based on mutual need. Necessity led to cities, and necessity taught the value of social agreements by which the strength of all could be used against animal and human predators. Nowhere in human life does a single man take complete care of himself. In the early stages of infancy, the babe would perish altogether if the harmony of the parents didn't help him grow up. Indeed, the child would not be born at all, or would perish before he'd even crossed the threshold of existence, if the little tyke weren't helped along by the friendly hand of the midwife and the loving care of the nurse. In the same way nature kindles in the parents those fervent fires of devotion which lead them to love what they have not even seen as yet. Then nature encourages the child to feel fondness for his parents so that he will get from them the protection that his weakness requires; and that weakness appears touching to all concerned   as the Greeks say, it's mutual flattery.[3] Then the bonds of kinship and natural affinity cement the child to its parents; very often a similar cast of mind, a likeness of temper, or a physical resemblance makes itself felt as a positive attractive force. In many families there grows up a latent sense of sympathy, marvellously congenial to everyone, which the ancients, struck with awe, ascribed to a god or a genius.[4]

In all these different ways, nature teaches us peace and concord; she has tricks to lure us, traps to snare us, a thousand devices to compel us. And yet, despite all her efforts, the hateful Fury comes, devoted on her side to destruction; she smashes down what nature has built up, rips it to rags, shakes it to the winds, and fills human hearts with a perpetual passion for fighting. If our sense of amazement hadn't been dulled by long custom, how could we suppose that men endowed with human reason could carry on such continual riots, feuds, and brawls in the prosecution of their battles, forays, and wars? Then with their rapes, murders, sieges, and devastations, they overwhelm everything that's sacred under the flood of their brutal passions. There's no treaty so sacred that

3. By contrast with the *Praise of Folly*, Erasmus in *The Complaint of Peace* used Greek tags sparingly. He was evidently intent on being widely understood. Another mark of this difference is the frequent use of repetition for emphasis.
4. The genius of the ancients was a person's special guardian angel.

it can cut short their orgies of mutual slaughter. If for no other reason, the fact that they share the name of "man" ought to be enough to make them agree better. But even if nature did nothing for man (though her law prevails with beasts), does the word of Christ have no influence on Christians? Evidently the teachings of nature are of no avail with humans, but if the teaching of Christ is more authoritative than that, why doesn't it persuade those who profess to believe it, in the one point that he emphasizes above all others, the need for peace and mutual good will? On the contrary, our worser nature successfully enforces that beastly and insane doctrine of making war.

When I hear the word "man," I am naturally attracted toward him, as a creature born to serve me; I expect that in him I will find a place of repose. When I hear the title of "Christian," I'm even more attracted, hoping that there certainly I will be honored. But I'm ashamed and disgusted to tell the truth. The streets, the courts, the churches, and the assembly halls are bursting at the seams with litigants and adversaries; there was nothing like it even in pagan days. It used to be that a very good part of human misfortune could be blamed on the crowd of busy advocates; but now they are swamped under the waves of litigation, hardly one is to be found. I see a city, and hope springs in my breast; there at least some men must have reached accord where they are all sheltered by the same walls, ruled by the same laws, and, like men crowded on shipboard, surrounded by the same dangers. But, oh my grief! when I find that here too they are eaten up by the same dissensions, so that hardly a single home can be found to shelter me.

Leaving aside the common people, who are as turbulent as a wind-whipped sea, I betake myself to the courts of princes, as if in search of a safe harbor. There, I tell myself, a resting place for peace will surely be found among people who are wiser than the vulgar crowd, the very minds and eyes of society. These are the servants of him who is the teacher and the prince of peace; though he directed everyone to cherish me, he par-ticularly recommended me to rulers. And at first all things look prom-ising. I see civil salutations, friendly embraces, a cheery exchange of drinks, and all the other signs of social accord. But, oh, the shame of it! among these people not a shadow of real sympathy is to be found. It's all fronts and frauds; the whole court is riddled with open factionalism, secret conspiracies, and buried animosities. In short, among these peo-ple I'm so far from finding a place for peace, that I recognize in them the very seedbeds and forcing-houses of war. Where can I turn, then, in my misery, now that my hopes have been crushed?

Well, I tell myself, perhaps princes are more powerful than wise, directed more often by their lusts than by good judgment. Let me take refuge, then, in the society of the learned, recalling that "Good letters make men, philosophy makes superior men, and theology makes saints." After being beset by so many traps, surely I will find a resting place among these people. But, Lord help us, what do I find here but another sort of war, less bloody perhaps, but no less lunatic. One school squabbles with another, as if truth changed her face with her residence, so the knowledge of one district won't stand travel to the next. Some truths can't pass the Alps, others can't cross the Rhine, even in the same college the rhetorician is at war with the dialectician, the law professor is at swords' points with the theologian. Even within the same discipline, Scotist is found battling Thomist, Nominalist arrayed against Realist, Platonist warring on Peripatetic.[5] They can't agree with one another on the smallest trifle, they will do battle over the tenth part of a hair till the fury of their controversy rises from a conversation to a shouting match, from a shouting match to fisticuffs—and then, though their war may not be settled with daggers and poniards, they attack each other with poison pens, ripping each other up with the keen phrases of satire and hurling lethal darts of insinuation at each others' reputations.

Where do I go now these word-warriors have disappointed me? Nothing remains except the last anchor of my hope, Religion. Though all Christians share in it, still the people known as priests make a particular profession of holiness in their titles, manner of dress, and devotion to regular ceremonies. Looking at them from the outside, everything gives me hope that here I will find safe harbor. Their robes are spotlessly white, which is my special color; I see the cross, symbol of peace; I hear that sweetest of all titles, the name of brother, which promises exemplary charity; I hear blessings exchanged in the name of peace, which can only be of good omen; I see a total community of property, a united congregation, a common church, identical rules, daily gatherings. Who wouldn't be confident that here was a proper home for peace? But oh, the shame of it! hardly ever do you find the chapter agreeing with the bishop or the members of it agreeing with one another on their factional differences. Was there ever a priest who wasn't at odds with another priest? Paul thought it a matter hardly to be endured that one Christian should go to law with another, one priest sue another, one bishop litigate with another bishop.[6] Perhaps such behavior should be overlooked nowadays, since by longstanding custom the religious have joined company with the profane, enjoying the same sort of possessions and by the same title. So let them rejoice in their lawsuits, of which they've now established possession.

There's another class of men who are so closely bound to the religious life that they can't possibly leave it, any more than a tortoise his shell. Among these people I might hope to find a resting place, if all my previous failures haven't reduced me to despair. So, rather than leave anything untried, I made the experiment. What happened? The greatest delusion of all. For what could I hope for when I found one cult at war with another? There are as many factions as there are orders, the

---

5. Platonists and Peripatetics were Christian theologians understood to be influenced (often remotely enough) by Plato and Aristotle respectively. Nominalists and realists (several different camps of the latter) differed over the degree of reality to be attributed to universal essences, i.e., abstract ideas. Scotists and Thomists are followers of Duns Scotus and Thomas Aquinas.
6. 1 Corinthians 6.1–6.

Dominicans quarrel with the Minorites, the Benedictines with the Bernardines;[7] there are so many different denominations, so many different practices, so many different ceremonies, that there's no area of agreement; every group pleases itself, despises the others, and hates everyone else. Even within the same community there are divided factions; the Observants rail at the Coletans,[8] and both of them at a third group the Conventuals, so called because there's no agreement [conventus] among them.

Having tried everything else, I tried to bury myself in some obscure little monastery, that I hoped would be perfectly quiet. I'm ashamed to say it, and I wish it weren't true, but I found nothing there that wasn't infected with theological odium and factional bitterness. I'm ashamed to describe the trivialities and absurdities over which old men, apparently venerable for their white hairs, nearly came to blows. And yet they were absolutely convinced in their own minds that they were not only scholars but saints. One last hope lingered, that I might somehow find a place in one of the many married households. It looked promising— the shared hearthside, the joint stake in life, the matrimonial couch, children in common, and the law that binds two people together to make of them one flesh. But even here that wicked spirit of discord crept in, and by corrupting the minds shattered the bonds uniting the couple. And yet among these families I thought I might find a refuge sooner than among those who proclaimed their charity amid such a profusion of titles, insignia, and ceremonies.

At last I began to hope that I might be received within the breast of a single individual. But even that failed, because the same man is often at odds with himself, his reason battling with his emotions and one emotion with its opposite, piety calling him one way and greed another, while he is tugged at, turn and turn about, by lust, anger, ambition, and avarice. And though all men are of this sort, none of them are ashamed to call themselves Christians, even though they disagree in every possible way with what Christ said most emphatically and distinctively. Looking at his life overall, what is it but one long lesson in mutual concord and brotherly love? What else is inculcated by his precepts, his parables, and his practice, but peace and mutual charity? That wonderful prophet Isaiah, when, under the inspiration of the holy spirit, he foretold the coming of Christ the conciliator of all things, did he promise a military governor? A stormer of cities, a general of the armies, a conqueror? By no means. What then? The prince of peace.[9] Isaiah wanted his prince to be understood as the best of all possible princes, so he assigned him that attribute which he understood to be the highest of all possible values. And it's no marvel that the prophet Isaiah saw things in that light, since Silius the pagan poet wrote of me in this fashion:

7. Minorites are Franciscans; Benedictines and Bernardines follow (obviously) Saint Benedict and Saint Bernard, both of whom laid down strict rules for monkish conduct.
8. After years of controversy, in 1517 (the very year of the *Complaint of Peace*), Leo X divided the Franciscans into the more strict Observants and the less strict Conventuals. Coletans were a special reformed order of Franciscans.
9. Isaiah 9.6.

Peace, best of things
That nature e'er bestowed on man. [1]

The words of the mystic psalmist agree with this: "And his place," he writes, "was made in peace." [2] In peace, he said, not in tabernacles, not in armed camps. He is the prince of peace, peace is what he loves, conflicts are hateful to him. Hear Isaiah again: "The work of justice is peace," he says, agreeing, if I'm not mistaken, with the sentiments of Paul—once turbulent Saul, but now rendered tranquil and a teacher of peace. Preferring charity before all the other gifts of the spirit, how passionately and eloquently he poured out my praises before the Corinthians! [3] Why shouldn't I be praised in this way by a man so praiseworthy? Elsewhere he speaks of "the God of peace" as well as "the peace of God," making perfectly plain that the two concepts are so intimately related that peace cannot be where God is not, and God cannot be where peace is not. [4] We sometimes read in holy scriptures about "angels of peace," who are true and obedient ministers of God—it's quite clear from that what power the angels of war are serving. Hearken, then, you furious warriors, you see under whose banner you fight, the banner of him who first sowed the seeds of dissent between God and man. Whatever calamities the human race has suffered since are due to that first division.

It's a frivolous thought that some people put forward when they say that in scriptures the hosts of the Lord are mentioned, and in the name of God vengeance is threatened. There's a tremendous difference between the God of the Jews and that of the Christians, for all that in his essential nature he is one and the same God. If the old expressions please you, let him be Lord of hosts, if by "hosts" you understand the legions of serried virtues by which good men overcome the forces of vice. Let him be the God of vengeance, but understand by vengeance the correction of vices, in the same way that you interpret the bloody battles described in the Old Testament, not as the actual butchery of men, but as the tearing of wicked impulses out of your hearts.

But to get back to the earlier point, whenever the scriptures want to refer to absolute felicity, they do so under the name of peace. Isaiah declares that "my people shall sit down in the beauty of peace," and elsewhere he says, "Peace upon Israel"; and to quote Isaiah yet again, he "marvels at the feet of those who announce peace, announce good news." [5] Whoever announces Christ announces peace. Whoever preaches war preaches service to him who is most unlike Christ. What, then, let me ask, drew down the Son of God to earth except the desire to reconcile the world to the Father? the wish to bring men together in bonds of mutual, indissoluble charity? to make humankind more devoted to him-

1. From somewhere in the fourteen thousand lines of Silius's *Punica*, one of the world's worst poems.
2. Perhaps from Psalms 55.18. Isaiah 30.17.
3. 1 Corinthians 13.

r. Romans 15.33; Colossians 3.15.
5. Approximately from Isaiah 32.18. The second quotation is from Psalms 128.6, the third from Isaiah 52.7.

self? He was, therefore, a messenger from me, it was my work that he came to do. And for that reason he chose as a type of himself, Solomon, who is known as "the peaceful." Great as David was, because he was a warrior and polluted with blood, he was not allowed to build the house of God, and he did not deserve to enact the type of Christ the peacemaker. Think it over, you man of war; if wars pollute even when begun and pursued by command of the Almighty, what of those inspired by ambition, wrath, fury? If the shedding of pagan blood polluted even a pious king, what will be the effect of shedding rivers of Christian blood? Oh Christian prince—if you really are a Christian—let me implore you to look on your pattern of a supreme prince. Consider how he entered upon his kingdom, how he advanced through it, the manner of his leaving it; then you will soon understand how he wants you to behave, that is, that your highest concern should be the establishment of peace and good will.

When Christ was born, did the angels sound the trumpets of war? Did military marches resound through the skies? Did the angels promise victories, triumphal processions, trophies? Not at all. What then? It was peace that they announced, agreeing therein with the oracles of the prophets; and they announced it, not to warriors eager for death and battle, straining after the clangor of arms, but to men of good will, naturally inclined to concord. Whatever grievances men pretend to have, they wouldn't seek out such bloody conflicts with one another if war itself weren't pleasant to them. As a grown man, what did Christ preach except peace, what else was his message? He always greeted his disciples in the name of peace, saying "Peace be with you," and that was the form he recommended to his followers as the only one worthy of Christians. And the apostles carefully observed this rule, they open all their epistles with words of peace, they wish peace to those whom they particularly favor. To wish someone health is a very proper thought, but to wish him peace is to call down on him the sum of all human happiness. When he was at the point of death, it's notable how carefully he recommended the peace that his whole life had been devoted to expounding. "You will love one another," he said, "as I have loved you."[6] You see what he leaves to his disciples? Not horses, not followers, not an army, not riches, no, none of these. What then? Peace he gives, peace is what he bequeaths: peace with friends, peace with enemies.

Reflect, if you will, what it was he begged of the Father at the last supper, when the time of his death was already near; what were his final prayers? No vulgar request was his, for he knew he could obtain whatever he asked. "Holy father," he begged, "preserve them in your name so they may be one as we two are one."[7] You see, don't you, what an extravagant measure of concord Christ demands of his followers: not that they agree on certain ideas, but that they be one entirely; and not just one in some random way, but one as we, he says, are one, identified

6. John 13.35, also 15.12.   7. John 17.21.

by an utterly perfect and ineffable principle. Thus he indicates directly that only in this way can mortal men be saved, if they preserve mutual peace with one another.

Because the princes of this world like to distribute decorations, especially in time of war, by which leaders and commanders can be distinguished from the others, note here the mark by which Christ distinguished his own; it was none other than the mark of mutual charity. "By this," he said, "men shall know that ye are my disciples"—not because they would wear special clothing, eat special food, or fast on special occasions, not because they would constantly be singing psalms, but "because ye love one another," and not just casually, but "as I have loved you." [8] The precepts of the philosophers are innumerable, the laws of Moses are numerous, the edicts of kings beyond calculation, but not so with Christ. "This is my only precept," he says, "that ye love one another." When giving his followers a form of prayer to be used, does he not in the very first words summon us to Christian brotherhood? "Our Father," he begins. It is one form of prayer for all, everyone implores the same thing, we are of the same household and live in one family, we all came of one father—how then can we justify our passion for killing one another? You cannot conceivably address a credible prayer to the father of all men when you have just driven a sword into your brother's bowels. That Christ wished peace and peace alone to be the highest concern of his people is shown by the many symbols, parables, and precepts with which he recommended it. He calls himself the shepherd and his followers sheep; [9] let me ask you now if you ever saw sheep fighting among themselves? And what will the wolf be up to while the flock is torn by faction fights? Again, when he calls himself the root of the vine, his followers the tendrils, [1] what does he imply but the unity of the organism? It would be considered a fearsome portent if the tendrils of a single vine were ever seen to be in conflict with one another; is it not equally so when one Christian fights with another? Finally, if anything whatever is sacred to Christians, the most sacred and precious things of all ought to be Christ's last commandments, which he left to us almost as a bequest, commending them to us as things he wanted never to be forgotten. [2] And what else does he teach, recommend, and implore in those final words, but mutual love among men? What else is signified by the communion of holy bread and sacred cup but a renewed, indissoluble, holy unity of spirit?

When he knew that peace could not prevail against the struggle for advantage, glory, riches, and revenge, he undertook to root up all passions of that sort from the minds of his followers; he forbade them to resist evil, urging them to do good even to the undeserving and to pray for their enemies. And do those men pretend to be Christians who because of some trifling offense drag the greater part of the world into warfare? By his orders, the man who is chosen as prince should act as a servant

---

8. See above, p. 96, n. 6.   1. John 15.
9. John 10.   2. John 14.27.

and not try to take precedence over others except in trying to do good for them. Yet some rulers are not ashamed to raise mighty tumults in order to add some tiny scrap of ground to their territories. He teaches us to live for the day, like the birds and lilies of the field. He forbids us to take care for the morrow, and wants us to rely wholly on heaven; he excludes all rich men from the kingdom of God; yet don't some men show themselves ready every day to shed blood over a bit of money not paid on time, perhaps never even owed? Nowadays these are accepted as very proper reasons for raising a war. Is this the message of Christ when he orders his followers to learn from him meekness of spirit and gentleness of conduct? When he commands that the donative be left before the altar and not placed on it till the donor is reconciled with his brother,[3] isn't he plainly teaching that as peace I am preferable to every other thing, and no sacrifice is acceptable to God, save with my blessing?

God rejected the gift of the Hebrews, perhaps a goat or a sheep, because it was offered by contentious men; can Christians engaged in bloody war with one another presume to think their offerings will be acceptable? When Christ compares himself with a mother hen folding her chicks under her wings, how aptly does the metaphor express peace! He gives his shelter, and how then does it befit us Christians to act like birds of prey? He is called the keystone because he holds together both sides of the arch; how does it agree with this that his vicars rouse the whole world to arms by pitting one kingdom against another?[4] Men brag that they have in him the supreme conciliator, yet they refuse to be reconciled to one another. Christ reconciled Pilate and Herod: can't he bring his own followers into agreement? When Peter, who was still half-Jewish, was prepared to defend with the sword his lord and master, then in deadly peril, he was ordered to put up his weapon; yet Christians draw without a moment's thought and on the most trivial occasions, even on fellow-Christians. Would he have welcomed defense by the sword who even in the moment of his death was praying for those who carried it out? All the Christian books, whether of the Old or New Testament, teach nothing but peace and agreement; what power can it be other than beastly ferocity that will not be repressed or even mitigated by religious authority? Men should either cease to claim the title of Christian, or put the Christian doctrine into practical form by living at peace. How long will daily practice give the lie to pious words? You may decorate your house and garments with the sign of the cross as much as you like, Christ recognizes no other symbol than the one he prescribed, that is, a loving heart. The apostles saw Christ ascend to heaven, and were ordered to await the holy spirit that he promised would always be present wherever his followers were gathered together.[5] Let no man anticipate, then, that the spirit will ever be present in battle. For what is that fiery spirit for whose descent we are still waiting, but the spirit of charity? Nothing is

3. Matthew 5.24.   5. Matthew 18.20.
4. Matthew 23.37; Luke 20.17.

more common than fire, and fire begets fire without further fuel being added; so shouldn't that first spark have begotten a universal peace? The answer is everywhere around us. "In all of them," Christ declared, "there was one heart and one spirit."[6] Now just as when the spirit leaves the body, all the nerves and tendons dissolve, so when the spirit of peace abandons a Christian community, it disintegrates. Hundreds of theologians affirm nowadays that the holy spirit is present in the sacraments; if it is, where is the special effect of that spirit—minds and hearts in a state of cordial unanimity? But if it's all make-believe, why is the ceremony observed so meticulously? I say this, not to detract from the sacraments, but so that Christians may be ashamed of the way they actually live.

A Christian people is commonly referred to as a church; what does that teach us, if not the lesson of mutual agreement? Does the church have anything at all in common with an armed camp? The one speaks of unity, the other of disunity; if you are proud to be part of the church, you can't possibly take part in warfare. If you've taken yourself out of the church, what do you have to do with Christ? If all men have the same home, serve a common lord, seek the same goals, share the same sacraments, rejoice in the same gifts, are nourished by the same benefits, and look forward to the same final reward, what's all the tumult about? We see among those lawless swashbucklers who in their mad rush for booty spread death and destruction across the land, that they hang together simply because they serve under the same flag; cannot good men do the same thing in the service of piety? Do the holy sacraments serve no purpose at all? Baptism is a rite common to all Christians; by it we are born again in Christ, cut off from the world, and made members of Christ's living body. What can be unified more closely than the several parts of a living body? No person is outside the communion, not slave or freeman, Greek or barbarian, not man or woman; all are in Christ who brings all into concord. The Scythians have a rite whereby a few drops of blood drunk from a shared cup render them lifelong friends, each ready to face death for the other's sake. Friendship was sacred among the pagans, and sharing a meal sanctified it. Cannot the holy wafer and divine cup bring Christians to friendship, when Christ himself blessed it, when the ceremony is every day renewed, when community is enacted in repeated acts of communion? If Christ died in vain, why do we go through all these ceremonies? If he achieved something significant, why is its real content neglected while the forms are acted out like a comic play on a stage? Does any man dare to approach that holy table which itself symbolizes unity, does anyone dare to accept the symbols of communion, who is meditating war on his fellow Christians, who anticipates shedding the blood of people for whom Christ shed the last drops of his blood? Oh hearts harder than rock! Though so many circumstances invite to concord, yet life is so full of meaningless conflict. We are all born by the same process, we all face the same necessity of growing old and

6. Acts 4.32.

dying. We are all of the same species and profess the same lord, author of our religion; we were all redeemed by the same blood, all passed through the same initiatory rites; we were nurtured by the same sacraments; whatever the rewards of our belief, they come to us all from the same wellspring, access to which is equally available to everyone. We all belong to the same church and expect the same ultimate reward. The heavenly Jerusalem to which all Christians aspire gets its name from the vision of peace, and of this vision the church here below is an earthly shadow. How does it happen, then, that our church is so far distant from its exemplar? Has nature, for all its energy, accomplished so little; has Christ himself accomplished nothing with all his teachings, mysteries, and metaphors?

Evil agrees easily with evil, whether among men or deeds, so the proverb says; neither good nor bad fortune will reconcile Christians to one another. What is more fragile than human life, what is shorter or more exposed to illness and accident? And yet, when already burdened with more trouble than they can stand, these madmen try to bring down on themselves even more misfortunes and worse. Human minds are so blind that they cannot see this; they act so impetuously that they tear through all the restraints of nature and Christianity in order to smash, crush, and destroy whatever agreements exist. They fight everywhere and with such fury that there's no limit or end to their violence. Race attacks race, city fights with city, faction with faction, and ruler with ruler; because of the stupidity or ambition of two petty mannikins who will die tomorrow like a pair of mayflies, all human arrangements are thrown topsy-turvy. Let me set aside the terrible tragedies of past wars, and mention only those of the last decade,[7] during which, by sea and by land, the nations of the world have been wading in blood—and all to no purpose. What region has not been littered with corpses? What river, what arm of the sea has not been dyed red? And oh, to our utter shame, our soldiers fight more ferociously than the ancient Jews, than the pagans, than the wild beasts themselves. Whatever wars the Jews waged against alien tribes were, as it were, figures, to teach Christians to struggle with the same zeal against their vices; but we have made a truce with our vices and now war on our fellow-men. And yet it was a divine command that incited the Jews to their battles; taking away all their specious pretexts and looking directly at the matter, what animates Christians is raw ambition, animal rage (the worst guide to conduct in the world), and insatiable greed. The Jews fought only foreign foes; Christians have made peace with Turks to prosecute more fiercely their wars with fellow-Christians. The pagan tyrants of old sought warfare for the sake of glory, but when they had subdued the barbarians and savage tribes, they took pains to soften the effects of their triumph, and even in victory to seek con-

---

7. Written in 1517, the *Complaint of Peace* came at the end of more than two decades of endemic European violence, starting with the French inva- sion of Italy in 1494; as Erasmus fortunately could not predict, the devastation would reach a climax in 1527 with the savage sacking of Rome.

ciliation with the vanquished. They did their best to ensure that the victories should, as far as possible, be bloodless—first, to win for themselves the name of magnanimous victors, and then to make life bearable for their new subjects. But I'm ashamed to recall the ridiculous and contemptible causes for which Christian princes have involved the world in conflict. This prince either finds or forges a moldy old document giving him title to a bit of new territory—as if, in heaven's name, it mattered the slightest bit which prince rules a bit of land, as long as he gives consideration to the needs of its people. That prince takes offense because he was left out of a petty treaty between his neighbors. Another is secretly furious because of a supposed slight to his wife or an off-color joke.

Most shameful of all are those who, after the frequent fashion of tyrants, deliberately foment trouble with their neighbors. They feel their power diminished by a long period of peace, and try to restore it by whipping up war fever; they hire agents for the express purpose of stirring up trouble and finding a pretext to destroy nearby states and plunder at will the common people. In these schemes they are abetted by the lowest criminals, men who thrive on the misery of the people and in time of peace can't find an honest job. What furies out of hell are they who breathe such poison into the souls of Christians? Who instructed followers of Christ in these tyrannical devices, unknown to Dionysus, Mezentius, and Phalaris?[8] Beasts rather than men, noble only in their oppressions and brave only in hurting the helpless, cooperative only in schemes against the public good. And the people who behave this way are considered Christians, they dare—even when polluted with human blood—to enter the church and approach the altar. Such plague-carriers should be exiled to the world's most remote islands.

If Christians are all members of one body, why doesn't each individual find pleasure in the happiness of another? Yet the very fact that a nearby nation is flourishing easily becomes a pretext for war. If the truth be told, what else inspired, and still today inspires, so many other nations to attack the kingdom of France? Her fault is clearly that of all nations she is in the most flourishing condition. No neighbor has more spacious boundaries, nowhere is there a more respected senate or a more famous university, nowhere is peace more firmly established and power more secure. Nowhere are the laws better observed, nowhere is religion more pure—being neither corrupted by the practice of the Jews, as in Italy, nor touched by the proximity of the Turks and Marranos as among the Hungarians and Spanish. Germany, not to speak of Bohemia, is cut up into so many little princedoms that it doesn't even resemble a kingdom. Only France stands high like an unspotted flower of the Christian community, a bulwark of safety against any storm that may break. And yet she is attacked from so many directions, and assailed by so many slanders—and for no other reason than to delight him whose pleasure it is

8. Dionysus, Mezentius, and Phalaris were all notorious tyrants of antiquity.

to inject his poison into Christian minds. And these wicked schemes are clothed under the guise of piety; this, we hear, is following the broad highway to the kingdom of Christ. A monstrous notion indeed: they think the Christian cause is not well served unless they subvert and destroy the most beautiful and flourishing part of the Christian world. Wouldn't you say that in this matter they outdo the most ferocious beasts?

Not all beasts fight one another, though different species may do so; I said this before, and repeat it here for emphasis. Vipers don't bite other vipers, the lynx doesn't attack another lynx. Even when they do fight, they do so with the teeth, horns, and claws that nature gave them. But men, though they are born weaponless, oh, by the immortal gods, what a terrific arsenal they enlist in the service of their rage! Christians assail Christians with machines out of hell. Who would ever suppose that bombs were the invention of human beings? What's more, beasts don't line up in regiments to kill each other in greater numbers and faster. Who ever saw ten lions mount an attack on ten bulls? Yet how many times do we see twenty thousand Christians lined up on the battlefield against twenty thousand other Christians!

Is it so very agreeable to mangle your fellow creature and drink his blood? Beasts harry one another only when driven by hunger or enraged by a threat to their offspring. But when Christians are concerned, the slightest offense, the most trivial episode, serves as a pretext for belligerency. If only ignorant men behaved this way, one might excuse their simplicity. If young men did it, you could put it down to inexperience; if criminals, one might blame their ingrained viciousness of spirit. But here we see the seeds of war germinating among people whose wisdom ought to be exercised in soothing the passions of others. Crude and vulgar they may be, but common folk found noble cities, administer them sensibly, and enrich them with their labors. On these cities descend the predators, and though unproductive themselves, they steal what the workers have accumulated; only a few evildoers can snatch away what the many have labored long to build well, can destroy in a minute what took years to create.

If ancient history isn't appropriate, just recall if you will how many wars have been undertaken in the last ten years, and the reasons for which they were undertaken. You will find they were all begun to gratify some prince and waged to the infinite distress of the people over matters which didn't concern them in any way whatever. Among the pagans it used to be a matter of shame for an old man to carry a shield; Christians now consider it a matter of pride. Ovid called it a disgrace for a graybeard to go soldiering,[9] yet in our day a seventy-year-old warrior is someone to brag about. Even priests aren't ashamed to take part, though formerly God—even when he spoke through that harsh and cruel law of Moses— forbade them to have any hand in the shedding of human blood. But now Christian priests, who profess to be our absolute guides through

9. Ovid, *Amores* 1.9.4.

life, the professors of an infallible church, the very cardinals of the church and vicars of Christ, are not ashamed to perform those acts, and incite others to perform them, which Christ most wholeheartedly detested. What sort of agreement can subsist between the miter and the helmet? What has the shepherd's crook to do with the sword? the Bible with a buckler? How can peace on the tongue agree with war in the hands? Can the same mouth preach Christ the bringer of peace and then cry for war, can one celebrate God and Satan at the same time? Imagine yourself standing amid the sacred conclave, wearing the robes of God, and inciting the populace to destroy one another—when they were expecting from you the doctrine of the Evangelists! Suppose yourself to be occupying the place of the apostles, will you teach men how to fight by mocking the apostolic precepts? Aren't you afraid that the phrase used about Christ, "How beautiful are the feet of those who announce peace, good tidings, and salvation," may be turned around for you: "How foul are the tongues of priests who incite to war and evil-doing, who provoke men to their perdition"?

Among the Romans, who had their own pagan pieties, it was the custom for the high priest to swear a solemn oath never to pollute his hands with blood of any sort, even to revenge a wrong received. Titus Vespasian, a pagan emperor, observed this oath so faithfully that he was praised for it by a pagan writer.[1] But oh, the changed face of human affairs! In a Christian society, not only priests hallowed to God, but monks who pretend to be even holier than priests, inflame the minds of princes and populace alike to bloody struggle. They convert the trumpet of the evangelist to the trumpet of Mars,[2] fling their own dignity to the winds, and are willing to do or suffer anything to fan the flames of war. Though princes may be personally inclined to peace and quiet, they are incited to war by firebrand priests who would be far better occupied in reconciling quarrels. Indeed—and what is much worse—priests fight among themselves over things that the pagan philosophers learned long ago to despise, and which men of the gospel should be even quicker to hold in contempt. Some years ago when an ominous epidemic was drawing the whole world into conflict, certain evangelical tub-thumpers, that is, Franciscan as well as Dominican friars, sounded the alarm from their pulpits, and began stirring to battle-frenzy people who were only too ready to listen to them. They roused British against French, French against British, and pushed both nations into war.[3] Nobody spoke up for peace except one or two people who would have been mobbed on the spot if I had ever dared to mention them by name. Neglecting their duties and their dignity, holy bishops ran hither and yon, doing their best to beat the war-drums. First they stirred up Pope Julius, and then they agitated the secular princes—as if they weren't crazy enough already;

1. Suetonius, "Life of Vespasian" 15.
2. The Roman god of war.
3. As soon as he gained influence in Henry VIII's court, Wolsey encouraged war with France (1512–13).

and all the time they camouflaged this manifest insanity behind the most specious verbiage that could be devised.

In this way we twist out of shape not only impudently but (if I may say so) impiously, the laws of our ancestors, the writings of holy men, and the text of holy scripture. Things have reached the point now that it's considered foolish and even wicked to protest against war and to praise those things that Christ was most ready to praise. The man is considered a public enemy and a traitor who urges the most beneficial policy of all, and dissuades us from the most disastrous. Priests now follow the armies around, bishops are present on the battlefield; leaving their churches unattended, they enlist under the banner of the battle-goddess. War creates its own priests, bishops, and even cardinals, for whom the title of military legate is a thoroughly honorable one, worthy of the successors of the apostles. What wonder if they speak the language of Mars, when Mars himself begot them? And this is the craziest perversion of all; they pass off this hideous impiety as the highest form of piety. Their standards are decorated with crosses; a bloodthirsty soldier, lavishly paid to cut throats, carries a cross as he goes to war, and the symbol that should prohibit war becomes a means of inciting it. What have you got to do with the cross, you scoundrel soldier? Minds and deeds like yours are more suitable to dragons, tigers, and wolves. That cross you carry is the emblem of one who lived, not by fighting, but by suffering, who saved men instead of destroying them; he could teach you, if only you were a Christian, who your real enemies are and how you can overcome them. Do you dare carry the emblem of the cross as you hasten to murder your brother, and destroy with your cross him who was saved by it? Doesn't it strike you that after taking the sacrament in camp (at one of the field-altars temporarily installed there) and observing the supreme rites of Christianity, you rush out to battle, drive the cold steel in your brother's guts, and make Christ a spectator—if indeed he deigns to be present at all—at the most horrible of all crimes?

The maddest thing is that over both camps and both lines of battle the same cross is displayed, on both sides the same prayers for victory are recited. What unnatural procedure is this? Cross fighting with cross, Christ at war with Christ? This sign of the Christian name used to terrify enemies of the faith; why do men now fight against what they worship? If they had just one cross, but worshipped it in a spirit of true devotion, that would be enough.

Let me ask, what does the soldier say when he recites his prayers? *Our Father*—bonehead, do you dare to petition our father when you're trying to cut your brother's throat? *Hallowed be thy name*—how can the name of God be more disgraced than by your constant murderous violence? *Thy kingdom come*—is that what you pray for while you wade through blood to set up a tyranny here on earth? *Thy will be done on earth as it is in heaven*—what he wills is peace, what you study is war. *Give us this day our daily bread*—so you plead to the father of all, and promptly ravage your brother's fields, preferring to go hungry yourself rather than

that he should prosper. What sort of face do you put on when you repeat
And forgive us our debts as we forgive our debtors, at the very moment
when you're on your way to commit a fratricide? *Lead us not into temptation* you pray, and then put yourself in the way of the very worst
temptations in order to entice your brother there too. *Deliver us from
evil* you ask, at the very moment you are devising the greatest possible
evil for your fellow man.

Plato says that when Greek fights Greek it shouldn't be counted as
war; *sedition* is the only word, he says.[4] How can Christians fighting
other Christians refer to their cause as a sacred war, whatever its cause,
when it's fought by lawless soldiers with inhuman weapons? Pagan laws
decreed that a man who stained his steel with the blood of a brother
should be sewed into a sack and thrown into a river. Are those whom
Christ joined together any less brothers than if they were united by blood?
The crime of killing either is fratricide. What a miserable fate for soldiers! The winner is a fratricide; the loser dies, but is no less guilty of
fratricide because he attempted it.

For all this, our warriors bluster against the Turks as miscreant enemies of Christ, as if, in their ordinary conduct, they were Christians
themselves—or as if any spectacle could be more agreeable to the Turks
than the sight of Christians engaged in mutual murder. They cry out
that the Turks offer sacrifices to demons, but the best sacrifice a demon
ever receives is when one Christian immolates another. So our soldiers
do just what theirs do, only ours give the demons a double sacrifice,
they offer up their own souls and those of their victims. If anyone is fond
of the Turks and cherishes a special friendship for the Devil, he will
make frequent sacrifices of this sort.

I'm well aware of the devious excuses men make for the evil they do
one another. They act under duress, they say; it's against their will that
they are drawn into war. But take off the costume, wipe off the grease-
paint, look in your heart; you'll find it was wrath, greed, and stupidity
that got you involved, not necessity—unless you think it a kind of necessity that your mind cannot be satisfied with less than everything. The
people may be deluded by shows, but God is not mocked. Peace gets a
lot of lip-service, cries for peace are heard, the voices rise to bellows,
peace, peace, they want, give us the peace we implore, hear our prayers.
But wouldn't God have every right to answer them: "Why do you mock
me? Aren't you asking me to protect you from something for which you
are passionately eager? You deplore events for which you yourselves are
responsible." If every slight, every trivial occasion, provides an excuse
for war, who doesn't have cause for complaint? Things happen between
husband and wife that have to be made up or the marriage will go to
ruin. Suppose something of the sort happens between princes, why must
they snatch up arms right away? There are laws, there are scholars, venerable abbots, reverend bishops, by whose prudent counsel the matter

4. *Republic* 5.16. See also Cicero, *De Re Publica* 6.1.

can be composed. Why not try these arbiters, who can hardly create more problems and are likely to cause many fewer than if recourse were had to the battlefield? Hardly any peace is so bad that it isn't preferable to the most justifiable war. Calculate how much a prospective war will cost, both directly and indirectly, and you will see what a poor investment it is.

The authority of the pope is supreme, no doubt about it. But when nations and their rulers have been carrying on riotous raids and counter-raids for years on end, what happens then to the papal authority, once second only to that of Christ himself? It might be exercised even here, if the popes were not held in the grip of the same passions. Let the pope call for war, he is obeyed at once; when he calls for peace, why isn't he obeyed the same way? If the princes were so eager for peace, why did they obey Julius in his belligerent outbursts yet pay hardly any attention to Leo when he spoke out for peace? If the pope's authority is sacred, it ought to be particularly so whenever he urges the same things as Christ originally proposed. The princes who listened to Julius when he called for that awful war but then couldn't hear Leo when he called for Christian concord were practically admitting that, while using the church as a smoke-screen, they were really serving their own appetites. I won't put it more strongly than that.

But if you princes are really sick and tired of war, I'll tell you how you can reach the peace and concord you say you want. A solid peace is hardly ever achieved through treaties and alliances; more often than not, they're the causes of war. The fountains must be cleansed from which the original evils arise, those low lusts which easily fester into conflicts. While each individual pursues his own interests, the common weal suffers, and even the individual fails to get what for selfish purposes he wanted. Princes should know, and make known to their people, not just to themselves, that their authority, happiness, wealth, and spendor are to be measured only by those things that make them truly good and excellent persons. Let them look on their people, then, as a father looks on his family. Let a king measure his greatness by the benefits of his rule, happy only as he renders his people happy, eminent only as he rules over free men, wealthy as his subjects are wealthy, and flourishing in that he keeps his cities flourishing in a continual peace. And this disposition of the prince should be imitated by officials and magistrates of his government. When the values of the community are respected, each man will be better able to consult his proper interests. Do you suppose a king who thinks this way will readily allow money to be extorted from his people and handed over to a barbarous band of soldiers? Will he reduce his people to famine in order to enrich an impious tyrant, or any number of them? Will he expose his subjects to the manifold dangers of war? Not very likely. Let him exercise his royal authority, but recall that he is a man ruling other men, a free man ruling other free men, and in short a Christian ruling other Christians.

As for the people, let them grant him as much authority as they think will be for the public good; a good prince will not expect any more. The inordinate desires of the occasional bad prince will be limited by a consensus of the citizens; on both sides, moderation will have to be imposed on personal interests. Most honor will be assigned to those who by a timely thought or a word of wise counsel maintained the peace. Finally, the highest honors would go, not to him who was best able to levy an army and equip it with machines of war, but to him who averted the need for them. What a splendid idea it was that occurred (as we read) to Diocletian alone among the emperors. He proposed that if wars could not be avoided, the entire burden of them should fall on those who gave the original provocation.[5] Nowadays princes declare war in perfect safety, and the generals get fat on it, but the heaviest burden falls on the peasants and poor artisans who stand to gain nothing from it and had nothing whatever to do with declaring it. Where is the wisdom of the prince if he does not reflect on this sort of thing; where is his courage if he doesn't do something about it?

Some means must be found for keeping kingdoms stable, so that they don't, as it were, go wandering about; because every change in their dynasties or boundaries begets disorder, and the disorder war. One good change would be a rule that the children of a royal house must marry within the kingdom, or at least within neighboring kingdoms, thereby limiting the problem of succession. And it shouldn't be legal for princes to sell or alienate any part of their kingdoms, disposing of free cities as if they were so much private property. Cities, after all, may be free when a king rules them, but are enslaved when a tyrant oppresses them. At present, royal marriages produce a chaotic situation, as if an Irishman were suddenly put in charge of India or a shah of Persia overnight appointed king of Italy. Sometimes, when a king has left one realm for another which has not yet acknowledged him, because it doesn't know him—no more than if he'd been born on another planet—neither kingdom gets a proper ruler. While the candidate is trying to establish himself in his second state, he neglects and exhausts the first one, and in trying to rule both, loses both—being unfit, more than likely, to rule either. Princes ought to agree, once for all, which one will rule which region, and once the boundaries are settled not try to enlarge or diminish them by treaty or dynastic marriage. That way, each prince will enjoy that region of the earth which he is best able to render flourishing. All his energies will go into the one place, which he will try to make as opulent as possible for the benefit of his children. General prosperity can hardly fail to result.

Among themselves princes should not rely on treaties or alliances, but join together in a pure and sincere sympathy, uniting in the greatest possible zeal for making the best of human affairs. Succession should be

5. The source has not been traced, and the idea seems uncharacteristic of Diocletian.

either directly to next of kin or to the winner of a popular election. For the rest, it's enough if they have honest deputies. It's a royal trait to rise above private emotions and judge all events in the light of the public interest. As a practical matter, a prince should avoid long trips abroad— indeed, should be reluctant to cross the boundaries of his own kingdom. There is a saying confirmed by the centuries: "The brow looks better than the backside."

Let him think himself enriched, not when he's taken a prize from someone else, but when he's rendered his own estate better. When the question of war comes up, let him not take the advice of young men, who are attracted to the idea of fighting because they have no experience of its terrible consequences, nor of those adventurers who profit by public disturbances and grow fat on the miseries of the people. Instead, let him take the advice of old men with generous hearts, honest minds, and a proven devotion to their country. Never should he declare war rashly, at the behest of one or two advisers; since wars are so easy to start but so hard to finish, they are never more dangerous than when undertaken without the enthusiastic support of the entire people. On occasion, peace may have to be bought. And if you look at the matter rationally, weighing how much a war would cost and how many souls are being saved from violent death, avoiding it will seem a real bargain, even if at the moment it seems expensive. Just think of the cost of all that artillery, and try to put a money value on human lives. Balance the matter in your mind, the evils you are avoiding, the good things you are acquiring, and the cost will not upset you.

Meanwhile, let the bishops attend to their functions, let the priests be real priests, let the monks concentrate on observing their vows, and the theologians teach what is worthy of Christ. Let everyone conspire against war, let everyone be fanatical on the point. In public and in private, let men speak out for peace, let them cry it from the housetops and teach it everywhere. If all efforts to avert violence should fail, men of good will should make perfectly clear their disapproval, refuse to take part in the bloody business, and avoid paying any respect to the authors of such a scoundrelly, or at least morally dubious, activity. It wouldn't be a bad idea to decree that those killed in battle should not be buried in consecrated ground; if there are any good men among them, and certainly they are very few, they will not be deprived of their reward by this circumstance, and the profane, who are by far the largest number, may feel less complacent if religious sanctification is denied them.

I'm speaking, be it understood, only about those wars that Christians wage against other Christians for slight causes or none at all. I don't feel the same way about those in which a pure and pious zeal summons men to defend themselves against barbarian hordes, or to defend the commonwealth, at risk of life and limb, against unprovoked attack.

Nowadays our churches are filled with the tombs and trophies of men who died killing other men for whom Christ shed his blood; these warriors intrude among the statues of martyrs and apostles, as if we believed it was just as pious to make a martyr as to be one. In earlier times, it was quite enough to set up statues of warriors in the public square or in some armory; in sacred structures, which ought to be free of all pollution, nothing should be placed which has any taint of human blood. But, someone will object, the ancients placed in their temples the trophies of their victories. True, but they were sacrificing to demons, not the true God. Priests consecrated to God should have nothing to do with war except to deplore it. If they speak against it with a single voice, if under all circumstances they always deliver the same message, there seems little doubt that their united authority will have some effect.

But if, after all, the thirst for blood is so deeply ingrained in human nature that we can't endure without slaking it, wouldn't it be better to turn these fatal energies against the Turks? Of course it would be better yet to attract them toward the Christian faith by purity of doctrine, charitable deeds, and innocence of life, instead of attacking them militarily. Still, if war can't be totally eliminated, war with the Turks would certainly be a lesser evil than internecine warfare between Christians. Since mutual charity does not bring Christians together, it's just possible that a common object of hatred may do so. It wouldn't be real reconciliation, but it might be a sort of compromise.

The greater part of peace is simply the desire for it. People who really have at heart the cause of peace always find occasions to promote it; the obstacles to it they overlook or push aside, they put up with all sorts of hardships in order to bring closer their one supreme goal. On the other side, those who promote war are just as assiduous; they deride or try to discard whatever makes for peace, while exaggerating and highlighting anything that tends toward war. I'm embarrassed to mention the ridiculous trifles out of which they construct mighty tragedies, the tiny sparks they try to fan into roaring flames. Once they get the fire started, every man finds grievances of his own to keep the blaze going, meanwhile burying in oblivion all the various benefits he has received. He feels himself surrounded by enemies, threatened on every side. Often it's nothing but the private quirk of a prince that drags the world into warfare, even though the causes for which war is declared ought to be as public as possible. When there really isn't any cause for belligerence, they invent one, calling on the vocabulary of national abuse to eke out their hatred; and this vulgar error of stupid people is encouraged by dignitaries of the regime, not to mention the clergy. The Englishman despises the Frenchman for no other reason than his being French; by the same logic, he scorns the Scot for being Scottish. The German hates the Frenchman, and the Spaniard loathes them both. What depravity when the mere names of places can divide people whom so many real considerations ought to unite! The Briton pours curses on the Frenchman; why not bless him, rather, as a fellow-man and a fellow-Christian? Why does the most paltry difference count more with these people than the many bonds of nature and links of Christianity? Geography divides bodies, not minds. The Rhine once separated Germans from Frenchmen, but never

Christians from other Christians. The Pyrenees divide Spain from France, but don't interrupt the unity of the Church. Between England and France lies the Channel, but it can't blot out the communion of religion. Saint Paul was angry to hear of special sectarian names among the Christians of Corinth: *I am of Paul, and I of Apollos, and I of Cephas;*[6] he deplored this dividing up of Christ in whom all things are reconciled. And shall we consider the common slang expressions of racial hatred as serious and solemn reasons for a round of international slaughter? Not satisfied with these pretexts, some warmongers hunt high and low for other ways to provoke quarrels; they try with linguistic tricks to tear France into pieces—France, which is not divided by seas, mountains, or the real names of her districts. They even try to convert Frenchmen into Germans, lest their close proximity develop into friendship.

If the judge in vexed lawsuits, such as those for divorce, steers clear of a premature decision, and scrutinizes the various proofs with the greatest care, why do we admit such frivolous considerations in questions of war and peace, the most vexed of all? If they would just reflect on this fact, which is true as true, that our world is the common home of everyone on it, the land of our father, our fatherland; if we all descend from the same ancestors, if blood-kinship alone should make us all friends; if our church is a single family of which everyone is an equal member; if our common habitation links us through our common necessities; then, it's only right that we adapt ourselves to the situation. You put up with certain things in your father-in-law for no other reason than that that's who he is; are you to show no tolerance for him who is your fellow-believer? No chains bind more closely than those of Christian brotherhood. Why do you dwell only on those qualities in your neighbor that you find irksome? If you really are for peace, you will think of him this way: he harmed me once, it's true, but on other occasions acted as a friend; the harm he did me may have been someone else's idea. Besides, just as the Greeks in Homer's *Iliad* who were trying to make up the quarrel between Agamemnon and Achilles blamed it on the goddess Discord,[7] just so you may attribute things that can't be otherwise excused to the fates or to some evil genius, who can assume the blame instead of actual persons. Why should men be so much quicker to suspect evil than good? Persons of prudence study, reflect, and exercise some circumspection before they enter on a piece of private business. Yet when it comes to war, men shut their eyes and fling themselves recklessly into it; not caring that, once in, it will be hard to get out, or that from a silly squabble it will quickly grow to a vast holocaust, that one battle will proliferate into a dozen, and a mere pushing-match will turn in a flash to sword-play, especially when both parties to a quarrel are equally inflamed. Even if the common people don't have this much foresight, it's the business of the prince and his counsel to look ahead. Priests

---

6. 1 Corinthians 1.12–13.

7. *Iliad* 19. Agamemnon himself blames Ate [Discord] for his quarrel with Achilles.

should use all their powers of reason to get the idea across, whether their listeners want to hear it or not. Some parts of the message may stick, even if it isn't formally agreed to.

Are you getting ready for war? Look first to see what manner of thing is peace, and what is war, what good effects flow from the one, what bad effects from the other; you can then make a rational decision between the two. If things are in good shape, the kingdom flourishing, the cities prosperous, the fields well cultivated, the laws properly observed, the arts and crafts thriving, the people well behaved; then think to yourself, If I go to war, all this will be destroyed. And on the other hand, when you see devastated cities, deserted villages, burned churches, abandoned fields—a ruined countryside—and judge this spectacle to be as wretched as it is, reflect that these are the fruits of war. If you think it a poor idea to bring into your kingdom a gang of cutthroat murderers who will batten on your subjects, enslave them, and attract their allegiance, while you must cringe and commit yourself and your safety to their tender mercies—think then that these are the conditions of war. If you abominate robbery, that's what war teaches; if you loathe parricide, that's one of war's first lessons. For how can an angry man be expected to shrink from killing a single individual when at a word from his commander he is bound to kill thousands? If neglect of the law poses an immediate threat to society, the voice of law is always drowned out by the clatter of arms. If you deplore rape, incest, and crimes even worse than these, war is the teacher of them all. If the source of all evils is impiety and neglect of religion, this rises directly out of the maelstrom of war. If you think a republic is tottering when the worst men in it have most power, in wartime it's the worst scoundrels who seize authority. The men whom in peacetime you would haul to a gallows find their chosen careers in war. Who is better at scrounging supplies out of a conquered countryside than a practiced thief? Who could rush more fiercely on an enemy and skewer his vitals more savagely than a gladiator or a holdup-man? Nobody could set a besieged town ablaze more deftly than a well-trained arsonist. A pirate with long experience of capturing ships and looting them would make an admirable naval officer. If you want to see clearly what a ruffianly exercise war is, just look at the men who carry it on.

If nothing is closer to the heart of a pious prince than the safety of his subjects, then of all things war should be the most hateful to him. If the happiness of the prince is to rule over happy subjects, peace should be the highest of his values. If it's the special ambition of the good prince to rule over the best possible subjects, he should detest war, which is the cesspool of all vice. If he likes to think he is the true owner of whatever his subjects possess, he should by all means avoid war, since even at best it erodes everyone's prosperity, and what hard work produced has to be squandered on a set of murderous butchers.

Let rulers reflect that in his own eyes every man's cause seems good while hope bends on him a flattering smile; especially when his objective is none of the best, his concern for it makes him think it flawless and so leads him astray. But suppose war is undertaken for a cause as just as can be conceived, suppose the triumph as complete as imaginable, suppose you have solved all the problems over which the war was begun, and gained all the objectives that victory could achieve. You will hardly ever gain a completely bloodless victory, so all your soldiers are now polluted with the crime of homicide. Add to that the corruption of public morals and social discipline, not to be made whole at any cost. You have exhausted your treasury and plundered your people, burdening the honest taxpayer and inciting the dishonest to underhand measures, so that even before the war is over, its consequences are upon you. The arts and crafts languish, business establishments close their doors. In order to take possession of the enemy's territories, you have shut yourself out of many more spacious regions. Before the war, all the neighboring districts were yours; through peaceful commerce, you had a share in all their possessions. Now see how much of that plenty you lack; you scarcely possess as much as what your district alone used to produce. You wanted to capture some little town of the enemy; how many different siege-engines did you need, how extensive a blockading camp! You had to make an imitation city in order to destroy a real one; but in fact it would have been cheaper to erect a second real one. To keep the enemy penned up in his city, you had to sleep yourself on the cold ground. Building new walls would have cost less than battering old ones down. I won't even pause to calculate how much money has slipped away as it passed through the hands of the tax-collectors, the quarter-masters, and the captains-general—certainly not the least part. When you have calculated all these expenses, if you don't find that peace could have been had for just one-tenth of what war cost, you can show me the door forever, and I won't protest.

Perhaps you think it's not right for a man of lofty mind, like your princely self, to overlook any sort of insult; but in fact there's no better evidence of a base, unkingly disposition than to take vengeance for trifles. Perhaps you think your royal dignity diminished if, in dealing with the prince of a nearby state (perhaps a kinsman or a close ally of yours, or someone else who has merited your generosity), you have to abate a few of your privileges. But how much lower would you sink your dignity if you were forced to pour out a stream of endless gold to some barbarous mercenaries, the very scum of the earth—or to crawl and send meeching petitions to some mean and stupid allies, while you entrust your life and your fortunes, not to speak of your family, to the faith of those who recognize neither contract nor oath. If peace seems somehow shameful to you, think of it this way: not "I'm giving this or that," but "I'm buying peace at such and such a price." Or a subtler argument might be made: "I would easily make the sacrifice if the matter pertained just to me as a private citizen. But I'm a prince, the business is public; well, like it or not, I'll act for the public."

A man will not lightly pick up the gauntlet who considers nothing but the interest of his people. On the contrary, we see that almost all wars rise from causes that don't pertain in any way to common folk. Do you want to avenge this or that faction within your country; what has that got to do with the general welfare? You might as well punish a man who insulted your daughter—it has nothing whatever to do with the public weal. Overlooking these issues and working toward their resolution is the work of a wise man and a great prince. Who ever ruled more splendidly over a greater empire than Octavius Augustus? But even he was willing to lay down his authority if he could find anyone in the empire who would make a better ruler. What he said on that occasion has been widely praised by discerning authors: "Let my children be set aside if someone else can be found who will serve the republic better."[8] Unbelievers though they were, some of these emperors devoted themselves to the service of society in a manner that would have done credit to true believers; but the Christian princes of our day think so little of their Christian subjects that they are willing to gratify their private lusts or avenge their private wrongs by throwing the whole world into turmoil.

But now I hear certain querulous quibblers who propose that they cannot live in safety unless they take decisive actions against the conspiracies of the wicked. Why, then, among the many Roman emperors, did only the two Antonines, Pius and Marcus the Philosopher, go unattacked? The reason must be that no man rules in greater safety than one who stands ready to give up his throne when the interests of the community, as distinct from his own, require it.

So now, if nothing else moves you—not the impulses of nature, nor respect for religion, nor fear of disaster, at least let respect for the Christian name direct you into harmony with one another. What proportion of the globe is now controlled by Christians? Very little. And yet this is that city placed high on a hill that it might be conspicuous to both God and man. But what can the enemies of Christ think, what can they say, what blasphemies will they spit out against Christ, when they see Christians doing battle with one another, for slighter causes even than pagans, with greater cruelty than unbelievers, and with more frightful mechanisms of war than anyone else in the world? Who was responsible for the invention of artillery? Was it not Christians? And, worst of all, they baptize their cannon with the names of the apostles and decorate them with the images of saints. Oh, brutal mockery! Must Paul, who urged men to perpetual peace, now help to turn these devilish machines against other Christians? If we want to convert the Turks to Christianity, let us first convert ourselves. They will never believe our teachings if they see that nowhere else does the practice most abominated by Christ rage more fiercely than among those who call themselves Christians.

Homer, pagan though he was, marvelled that while men could easily become sated with the good things of life, such as sleep, food, drink,

8. The story about Augustus is dubious in the extreme. He didn't have any direct male heirs; he actively disliked Tiberius (his stepson and actual successor) and despised his daughter Julia. The sentiments are by no means characteristic. Erasmus doubtless had someone else in mind.

dance, and song, their appetite for the savagery of war was insatiable;[9] this is especially true of those who have every reason to detest the very name of war. Rome, once the great warrior-state of antiquity, knew periods when the doors of Janus's temple were shut tight.[1] How does it happen that with us death never takes a holiday? What sort of face can you put on to preach the peace of Christ when you are continually torn among yourselves by internal faction-fighting? Imagine if you will what courage your squabbles inspire in the Turks. Nothing is easier than to conquer a divided enemy. If you want to be formidable in their eyes, make peace with one another. Why begrudge yourselves both the pleasures of this life and the rewards of the next? Though the life of mortal man is exposed to many troubles, peace is a lenitive for the greater number of these griefs, because one man can either help or console another. A stroke of good fortune is rendered all the more pleasant by being shared with a friend who can congratulate you and join in your exultations. How trivial and ephemeral are the occasions of disagreement between you two! Death hangs like a dark cloud over us all, kings no less than commoners; what business has a tiny animalcule raising a fuss when shortly he will disappear like a puff of smoke? Eternity waits for us in the wings; what's the point of struggling over these shadowy earthly realities as if this life were to go on forever? What wretched men they must be who don't believe in the happy future life of the true Christian, and therefore don't hope for it! How impudent are those who think the road to that felicity leads through wars when in fact it's nothing but an ineffable communion of joyful souls who already relish a foretaste of that full delight which Christ begged of the holy father when he implored that the disciples be joined together as he was joined with the father. How can any of you be deserving of that communion unless in the here and now you have been meditating on it with your entire spirit? A rakehell bully isn't abruptly transformed into an angel, nor a blood-soaked warrior into a fit companion of martyrs and virgins.

Come now! We've had enough and too much of shedding Christian blood—too much of letting human blood of any sort; enough of massacres on both sides, enough battles fought as if by devils out of hell, enough performances to delight the eyes of the onlooking Turks. After all the barely endurable miseries of the past, isn't it time for us to get just a little smart? Whatever insanities we endured in the past, let us write them off as the work of fate; it's time for Christians to be satisfied, as the pagans were before them, with putting away the evils of the past. Now is the time to turn to joint consultations on the path to peace, time to bind up the beast of war, not with mere ropes of hemp, but with adamantine shackles, never to be broken. I call upon you, princes, who hold power over most human affairs, and who bear the likeness on earth of Christ the King, to hear the voice of your own ruler calling for peace.

9. *Iliad* 13.615 ff.
1. When the empire was at peace, the doors of the

temple of Janus were shut tight, as several times during the reign of Augustus.

Remember that the whole world is weary of war's endless miseries, and demands peace of you. Even if some private individual holds out against this, it's only right that the public weal prevail. The task is too important to be held up over trifles.

I call on you priests, sanctified to God, to work zealously for what you know is closest to God's heart. Get rid of what you know he hates worst of all. I call on you theologians to preach the gospel of peace, and ring it in the ears of the people. I call upon you, bishops and other men of eminent dignity in the church, use your authority to establish peace in the church by unalterable edicts. I call on you dignitaries and magistrates, lend the strength of your authority to the wisdom of monarchs and the piety of popes. I call upon everyone who considers himself a Christian, everyone of every rank and condition, to join wholeheartedly in a conspiracy for peace. Through this common endeavor you can demonstrate the power of a united popular movement against the power of tyranny. In this endeavor all men's energies can be yoked together on a equal footing. Let a permanent peace unite all those whom, first nature, and then Christ have linked by so many common concerns; let all people act together since all have an equal stake in the successful outcome. All things press us in this direction, not only our natural instincts but what I may call our sense of humanity. So too does our supreme leader, the author of all our hopes for happiness, Christ himself; so too do the many obvious benefits of peace, so does the certain catastrophe of war. As if by God's special help, the minds of our present leaders are already well disposed to peace. Pope Leo, most benign and uncontentious of men, has given the signal to his flock, inviting them to be reconciled, and himself acting like a true vicar of Christ. "If you are really my sheep (he as much as said), follow your shepherd; if you are sons of the church, listen to your father." Francis, who is, and not just in name only, the most Christian king of France, invites you to join in the effort. He is not reluctant to pay the price for peace, and never places his own dignity ahead of the general welfare; his example teaches that the truly splendid and royal thing is to deserve as well as possible of the human race. Prince Charles, of noble birth and incorruptible temper, invites you to join in. The emperor Maximilian is not averse, neither is King Henry, lofty ruler of England.[2] Given the example of such eminent princes, it's only right for the others to come along.

Most people detest war and pray for peace. Perhaps a few mischief-makers, whose prosperity depends on the public misery, will still hanker after war. But you will judge for yourselves if it's right that their vicious propensities should outweigh the aspirations of all men of good will. Nothing has been accomplished so far by treaties, alliances, force, or

---

2. François I had been on the throne of France for only two years when Erasmus wrote; Charles, who was still under a regency, would not become king of Spain till a year later. It was easy and natural for Erasmus to express hopeful enthusiasm for these unproven monarchs. For the Emperor Maximilian and Henry VIII, his expressions of approval are considerably more tempered. They had not been very good friends of peace.

acts of retribution; now let us make the great experiment, how much can be done by mutual kindness and good deeds. We know that one war begets another, one act of revenge a counter-act; it is time for one gracious gesture to be answered by another, one token of kindness to invoke the response of another, so that he who behaves most liberally and generously may seem the most splendid king of all. Nothing will succeed that depends exclusively on human intentions, but Christ himself will favor pious measures of which he was the original author and sponsor. He will be right at hand to inspire and favor those who serve the cause he holds most dear; he will ensure that concern for public good prevails over private greed.

Dedication to universal peace will not prevent each individual from pursuing his own ends; the reign of princes will be more magnificent if the citizens over whom they rule are both virtuous and contented, governed by laws rather than soldiers. The respect rendered to noblemen will be more authentic and more profound; the priests will live more quiet lives; the people will be richer in their tranquility and more tranquil in possession of their riches; the Christian name will be more respected by enemies of the Cross. Finally, each individual citizen will be more agreeable and affectionate to his fellow-citizen, and more acceptable to Christ, whose good pleasure it is the highest of human delights to have deserved.

Two Forewords to the Latin Translation of the New Testament

Erasmus's 1516 edition of a Greek New Testament with a new Latin translation on facing pages was not an enduring work of scholarship. He did not have enough old Greek manuscripts to work with; he did not have adequate training in philology and palaeography; he had little background in the complex mixture of Hebraic and Hellenic cultures that everywhere underlies the teachings of the evangelists. There is nothing surprising about his deficiencies; he was a pioneer, and scholarship, which is largely a collective enterprise, quickly built beyond his first tentative structures, rendering them obsolete.

But the Paraclesis, or exhortation, in which Erasmus defended the basic principle of making the scriptures accessible to unlearned readers, resounded across Europe like a trumpet-call. There were three major parts to Erasmus's argument. He asserted first, and most resonantly, that the scriptures should become part of the daily life of plain folk—that meant translating them, not just into more accurate Latin, as he had done, but into the vernacular tongues, languages that peasants, women, and children could understand. With almost equal force he declared that the scriptures provided a clear and sufficient rule by which even princes, bishops, and theological doctors (the former monopolists of spiritual power) could and should be judged. And finally, by strong implication, he cast grave doubts on the adequacy of the old Latin version known as the Vulgate, which had passed without criticism for almost a thousand years. All these proposals, vehemently asserted in the Paraclesis, coincided with long-standing demands for church reform, not only by the humanists, but by groups like the Wycliffites in England, the Hussites in Bohemia, and the profuse variety of millenarian sects scattered across Europe—Waldenses, Picards, Joachimites, and (very close to Erasmus personally) the Brethren of the Common Life. To their scattered and often suppressed voices would soon be added the thunder-tones of Martin Luther. Calls of this general tendency for spiritual freedom and open access to religious truth provide the primary thrust of Erasmus's declamatory exhortation.

Famous as it became, the Paraclesis bears many marks of hasty and even careless composition. In the course of only a few pages, it repeats itself several times; it makes a couple of allusions that cannot be traced; and in the vehemence of its enthusiasm it overlooks a major set of problems to which Erasmus in later and more careful editions of his book addressed himself. He did not withdraw his idea of making scripture accessible to the unlearned;

but he devoted much more time and thought to the various preparations, precautions, and self-purifications that must be undertaken before an untrained mind plunges into the Word of God. For nothing is easier and more tempting, in interpreting a complex text that can be read on several different levels (as history, as parables, as allegory, as divine revelation, literally and figuratively) than to make it endorse one's own private interests or prepossessions. Being able to shelter one's personal concerns under the infallible cloak of holy writ is a terrible temptation for headstrong men. Nobody could appreciate that better than Erasmus, who opened the gates of biblical interpretation just a bit, and saw the irresistible floodwaters of the Protestant reformation come pouring through them.

For time moved very fast in the second and third decades of the sixteenth century. Erasmus, seeking to reform the old Vulgate, produced his new Greek-Latin text in 1516; by 1522 Luther had already published his German translation of the New Testament, Jacques LeFèvre produced a French version in 1524, Tyndale his English version in 1525, and in 1526 a Swedish version was begun. These were all ingredients of a word-war that immediately—and against the wishes of almost all the parties to it—turned violent on a scale never conceived before. It is hard to name an exact point in time when the wars of religion began, but the German peasant wars of 1524–25 and the ghastly sack of Rome in 1527 certainly marked major stages in the massive, continent-wide orgy of bloodshed and sectarian persecution that would not end till—well, in some parts of the world it has not ended yet. Erasmus did not foresee the full extent of that centuries-long holocaust; but he was given pause by the very threat of it. He did not retreat from his stance of 1516, if anything he widened his attack; but he also added to his third edition of the New Testament (1522) words of caution and self-restraint that render his final position characteristically balanced. The Paraclesis did not disappear altogether, but it was no longer called such; key phrases and concepts are retained in the new Introduction, but they become part of something larger, more careful, and, it may be thought, more wise. Both versions are given here; they will reward close comparison.

Paraclesis: or, An Exhortation (1516)

Erasmus of Rotterdam to the Pious Reader

The famous Lactantius Firmianus, oh best of readers, whose eloquence Jerome particularly admires,[1] when he undertook to defend the Christian religion against the pagans, begged for a gift of eloquence second only to that of Cicero—thinking, I suppose, that it would be impious to ask for equal gifts. For my own part, if prayer counts for anything in these matters, now that I am calling men—indeed, challenging them as with a trumpet's blast—to undertake the most sacred and salutary study

1. Lactantius, a native of North Africa, wrote the seven books of his *Divine Institutes* at the beginning of the fourth century; the passage in question is at the start of the third book. Saint Jerome expressed his admiration for Lactantius (popularly dubbed "The Christian Cicero") in a letter to Paulinus, no. 58, par. 10.

of the Christian religion, what I want most is an eloquence very different from Cicero's, less ornate than his, perhaps, but more effective. Indeed, if this is possible, I would like powers such as the ancient poets properly attribute to Mercury, who with magic wand and holy lyre sends sleep and dispels it as he chooses, leading souls down to hell and bringing them out again; or such powers as they ascribe to Amphion and Orpheus, one of whom moved heavy stones and the other oaks and ash-trees by the power of their song. Or else I'd like the power that the Gauls attributed to their Ogmius,[2] who is said to have led all mortals around by little chains reaching from his tongue to their ears—or perhaps the powers that ancient fabulators attributed to Marsyas—or else (not to linger too long among the fables) such a power as Alcibiades attributed to Socrates and the Old Comedy to Pericles[3]—a power which not only tickled the ears with momentary pleasure, but which fixed a stinging dart deep in the mind of the hearer, pulling him out of himself, transforming him utterly, and sending him away a very different person than he came. The great musician Timotheus, by playing Dorian melodies on the lyre, is said to have been able to rouse Alexander to martial fury.[4] Antiquity knew others who considered the incantations they called *epodes* just as efficacious. If there were any such magic formula, any power of harmony that could produce true *enthusiasm*, if Pytho has any power to stir the soul,[5] such power I would implore to persuade all men of the most wholesome truth there is. Although it would be even better if Christ himself, whose case is being pleaded, would so temper the chords of my lyre that this song might affect the minds and stir the souls of all—to effect which there really is no need of rhetorical argumentation and verbal agglomerations. For what I seek to declare is nothing but the truth itself, the simplest expression of which is always the most forceful.

And in the first place, it's not pleasant to raise the complaint, not altogether new but all too just and never more timely than in these days when men are applying themselves singlemindedly each to his own studies, that the philosophy of Christ is singled out for derision even by some Christians—is ignored by most and cultivated (coldly at that—I won't say insincerely) by only a few. In all other disciplines where human energy is invested, there's nothing so obscure and elusive that lawless curiosity has not explored it. Yet how does it happen that even those of us who lay claim to the Christian name fail to embrace this philosophy in full sincerity, as we should? Platonists, Pythagoreans, Academics, Stoics, Cynics, Peripatetics, and Epicureans[6] all know the doctrines of their

---

2. It is not known where Erasmus found the story of Ogmius.
3. Plato, *Symposium*; Aristophanes, *Acharnians* 530 ff.
4. The legend about Timotheus and Alexander is an old and probably inaccurate one; Dryden used it as the basis for his ode "Alexander's Feast."
5. *Enthusiasm* is given in the Greek; Pytho (from whom we get the name of the serpent genus *python*)

was a giant snake associated with worship of Apollo, also a secret genius or demon who entered men's minds and influenced their acts.
6. These are all names of ancient philosophical schools; Erasmus might have cited more modern instances, and doubtless wanted his readers to think of them, but he did not want to be responsible for naming them. This is sometimes called "Aesopian" language.

particular sects, they learn them by heart, and fight fiercely for them, ready to die rather than abandon the cause of their particular patron. Why then don't we stand up even more spiritedly on behalf of our maker and our leader, Christ? Wouldn't anyone consider it shameful for a professed Aristotelian not to know the opinion of the master on the causes of lightning, the essence of matter, or infinity? These are matters that neither render us happy when we know them nor make us wretched when we don't. Yet we, brought to Christ through so many initiations, confirmed by so many sacraments, think it no shame or disgrace to be ignorant of his teachings which promise supreme happiness to all. But what is the point of drawing out this argument, since it's a kind of impious madness in the first place even to think of comparing Christ with Zeno or Aristotle, or to pose his teachings against the trivial precepts of mannikins—not to put the matter more strongly—like that? Let the philosophical partisans cling to the leaders of their sects as hard as they can, as much as they want. Beyond doubt, only Christ was a teacher descended from heaven, only he (who was eternal wisdom itself) could teach positive certainties, only he (the unique author of human salvation) could teach us saving doctrine, only he could exemplify what he taught and grant us whatever he promised. Something which is presented to us as coming from the Chaldeans or Egyptians we examine with eager curiosity as the product of a remote part of the world, and that very strangeness becomes part of its value. Then frequently we are carried away by the speculations of a petty pedant, not to say an impostor, who wastes our time to no good purpose—there is worse I could say, but this is bad enough. Yet how does it happen that the same sort of curiosity does not intrigue Christian minds, who are firmly persuaded—as in fact is true—that their doctrine derives not from Egypt or Syria, but from heaven itself? Why don't we all reflect: this must be a new and marvelous philosophy since, in order to reveal it to mortals, he who was god became man, he who was immortal became mortal, he who was in the Father's bosom descended to earth? It must be a mighty doctrine, and by no means trite whatever else it may be, which that marvelous author came to teach after so many schools of excellent philosophers, so many famous prophets. Why don't we explore its details with pious curiosity, particular concern, avid interest? Especially since this special mode of wisdom, so extraordinary that it renders foolish all the wisdom of the world,[7] can be drawn from these few books as from the purest fountains, with far less labor than the doctrine of Aristotle can be extracted from his many thorny volumes and their immense body of commentaries by quarrelsome interpreters—and, I may say, with far more profit. For here there's no need to fortify yourself with all those laborious disciplines. The path is direct and ready for anyone to take. Only bring a pious, alert mind and above all one imbued with a pure and simple faith. Simply make yourself teachable, and you have made long strides in this philosophy. It

7. 1 Corinthians 1.18 ff.

supplies, of its own, the teaching spirit which nowhere finds shelter more gladly than in simple souls. Other philosophies, apart from the fact that they promise a false felicity, discourage the minds of many students simply by the difficulty of their teachings. This one adjusts itself to the capacities of everyone alike, lowering itself to the little ones and accommodating itself to their abilities; it nourishes them with milk,[8] carries them about, fosters and supports them, doing everything for them until they grow up in Christ. Yet it is not so fitted to the lowest that it does not present marvels to the very highest. In fact, the further you progress in this wisdom, the more you set it apart from, and above, the highest reach of any other. For the little ones it is a trifle, for grownups it is more than the greatest matter in life. It bypasses no age, no sex, no condition of fortune or rank of society. The sun itself is not so open and exposed to every gaze as is the teaching of Christ. It conceals itself from no one, unless some person, suspicious of himself, chooses to keep away.

I absolutely dissent from those people who don't want the holy scriptures to be read in translation by the unlearned—as if, forsooth, Christ taught such complex doctrine that hardly anyone outside a handful of theologians could understand it, or as if the chief strength of the Christian religion lay in people's ignorance of it. Perhaps the state secrets of kings have to be concealed, but Christ wanted his mysteries to be disseminated as widely as possible. I should prefer that all women, even of the lowest rank,[9] should read the evangelists and the epistles of Paul, and I wish these writings were translated into all the languages of the human race, so that they could be read and studied, not just by the Irish and the Scots, but by the Turks as well, and the Saracens. The first step is simply to understand. Many will ridicule, no doubt, but some will be intrigued. As a result, I would hope that the farmer might chant a holy text at his plow, the spinner sing it as she sits at her wheel, the traveler ease the tedium of his journey with tales from the scripture. Let all conversation between Christians draw from this source, for almost all of us are as our daily conversation forms us. Let each individual grasp what he can, and give expression to what he feels. Let the slowest not envy the quickest, and let the leader encourage the follower, not despair of him. Why should we restrict the allegiance of all to just a few? It makes no sense when baptism (in which we all first profess the Christian religion) along with the sacraments and the final reward of immortality are open equally to all, that doctrine should be confined to just a handful. I mean those to whom common opinion nowadays assigns the names of theologians and monks; not only are they a tiny minority of the Christian populace, but I could wish they were more like what their names signify. For among the theologians I fear too many can be found who betray the

---

8. 1 Corinthians 3.1–2.
9. Women in the sixteenth century got very little education, and if they were of the lower classes, none at all; to read one of the gospels, they would have to do so in a vernacular translation. If Erasmus did not translate into a contemporary vernacular, it was apparently because he did not know any one of them well enough to do it. His "native" tongue was Latin.

title they bear by dealing in earthly affairs, not divinity; and among the monks who profess the poverty of Christ and contempt for the world can be found something even worse than worldliness.

In my opinion he is truly a theologian who teaches, not by contorted syllogisms, but by his very demeanor and facial expression, by his eyes and the tenor of his whole life, that riches are to be despised, that the Christian should not rely on the protections of this world, but put his entire trust in heaven. He should not revenge injuries done him, should pray for those who wish him ill, should seek to do good to those who have done wrong, should choose as his special friends good men, wherever found, since they are all members of the same corporation, and should tolerate evildoers if he cannot correct them. He should believe that those who are stripped of their goods, spoiled of their belongings, and acquainted with grief are truly blessed, and not at all to be pitied; he should even think that death itself will be welcomed by the truly devout, since it is nothing but a passage to immortality. If anyone stirred by the spirit of Christ preaches doctrine of this sort and not only inculcates it but encourages, animates, and incites others to it, then indeed he is truly a theologian, whether he is a ditch-digger or a weaver. If anyone in his person and in his daily life exemplifies these doctrines, he is in truth a great doctor. Someone else, perhaps not even a Christian, may discourse more elegantly on the process by which the angels achieve understanding; but persuading us to live an angelic life, free from all stain, in the here and now—that in brief is the true task of a Christian theologian.

Someone may complain that these ideas are obvious and stupid; I can only answer that these obvious ideas are what Christ particularly taught, they are what the apostles repeat, these ideas (however stupid they may be) begot for us a multitude of true Christians and attracted a swarm of illustrious martyrs. This philosophy, unlearned as it appears to some, has brought under its sway the highest kings in the world, and nations and peoples without number—as neither mere force nor philosophical erudition could do. Certainly I don't object to that abstract philosophy being discussed by the learned, if they think it worth doing. But just as surely common Christian folk can content themselves with that general name, since the apostles and the church fathers, whether they understood these subtleties or not, certainly did not teach them. If princes put into daily practice these principles which I've described as plebeian, if preachers in their sermons set them forth, if schoolmasters would convey them to their pupils instead of that pompous erudition they derive from Averroes[1] and Aristotle—then Christendom might not be convulsed by these all-but-endless wars, people might not be racked by such an insane

---

1. Averroes was the twelfth-century Arabic (i.e., Moslem) philosopher through whose commentaries the works of Aristotle reached the west. Till the fall of Constantinople in 1453, Averroes was practically the only conduit of Aristotle's thought; he therefore had great, though often unavowed, influence on the scholastic philosophers.

fury to pile up riches any which way, sacred and profane business alike would not be torn up by such furious litigation, and finally we should not quarrel so much over mere manners and ceremonies with those who do not profess the philosophy of Christ.

The business of founding or advancing the Christian religion has been assigned to three classes of men in particular; to the princes and the magistrates who act in their behalf, to the bishops and their delegate priests, and to those teachers who inspire the young to seek knowledge. If these men, setting aside their own personal interests, were to work together heartily in behalf of Christ, we should no doubt see emerging everywhere not too many years hence an authentic and (as Paul says) a *genuine*[2] variety of Christians, people who would restore the philosophy of Christ not just in ceremonies and logical propositions but in the human heart and in the total life of the individual. By these weapons the enemies of the Christian name will be attracted to the faith of Christ far more quickly than by threats or weapons. To join all our energies together no force is more powerful than the truth itself. He is no Platonist who does not read the books of Plato—how can he be a theologian, let alone a Christian, who has not read the book of Christ? "Who loves me," he said, "keeps my word";[3] it is the very mark that he himself designated. Well, then, if we are really Christians in our hearts, if we actually believe he was sent from heaven to teach us what the philosophers could not, if we really expect from him rewards such as no prince however opulent could ever give us, why is anything more precious to us than this text? How can anything carry weight which is not in harmony with these teachings? Why, in dealing with these sacred texts, do we allow ourselves liberties such as, or even greater than, those assumed by profane interpreters in their discussions of secular laws or medical textbooks? Like performers on a public stage, we twist the text around, saying about it whatever comes to mind, distorting it and obscuring its sense. We drag down the teachings of heaven and force them like a Lydian rule[4] to fit our own life-patterns, and while we make great shows of erudition by gathering together scraps of pagan literature, we—I won't say we corrupt the main point of Christian religion, but—we restrict to a very few men matters that Christ wanted to be diffused as widely as possible; and that nobody can deny. The Christian philosophy is seated more deeply in the emotions than in learned syllogisms; for it, life is more than logic, inspiration is more than erudition, transfiguration more than argumentation. Very few can be learned, but no man is denied permission to be a Christian, no man is forbidden to be pious, and, I will add boldly, nothing prevents any man from being a theologian.

Our philosophy sinks easily into the human mind because it is so largely in accord with human nature. What else is this philosophy of Christ, which he himself calls being born again,[5] but renewal of a human

---

2. *Genuine* is given in the Greek.
3. John 14.15 and 23.
4. The Lydian rule was made of lead, therefore

flexible; it was used to model curves and irregular surfaces.
5. John 3.3.

nature originally well formed? By the same token, though nobody taught this philosophy more authoritatively and effectively than Christ himself, many things can be found in the books of the pagans that agree with his teachings. No philosophical school ever existed so crass as to teach that money makes a man happy. None was ever so impudent as to place the final good of life in the vulgar honors and pleasures. The Stoics recognized that no man was wise unless he was also good; they knew that nothing was truly good or honest except real virtue, nothing evil or shameful except dishonor alone. In Plato's dialogues Socrates repeatedly teaches that an injury should not be repaid with an injury; he also teaches that since the soul is immortal, those men are not to be bewailed who depart this life for a better one with a clear consciousness of having behaved virtuously.[6] He taught besides that the soul should be freed in every possible way from the claims of the body, and led toward those things which truly exist though they are not seen. Aristotle in his *Politics* wrote that nothing can be pleasant to us which is not in one degree or another degrading, with the solitary exception of virtue.[7] Even Epicurus concedes that nothing in man's life can be pleasurable unless he possesses a mind conscious of no wrong in itself—from which alone, as from a fountain, true delight gushes forth.[8] What shall we say of this, that a great part of Christ's doctrine is to be found in some of the philosophers, notably Socrates, Diogenes, and Epictetus? But since Christ taught his doctrine much more fully, and exemplified it even better, is it not monstrous that his teachings are ignored, neglected, or even mocked by Christians? Whatever in these writers of antiquity coincides closely with Christianity, let us follow by all means. But if there are certain things which alone can make a proper Christian, why do we look on them as almost more archaic and obsolete than the books of Moses?[9] The first step is to know what he taught, the second to put it in practice. I don't think anyone should consider himself a Christian simply because he can carry on a dispute about instances, relations, quiddities, and formalities, involving the question in a thicket of thorny abstractions—but only if he holds to the lessons that Christ taught and exemplified, holds to them, and exemplifies them himself. Not that I want to condemn the industry of those who exercise their mental powers in perfectly praiseworthy arguments of an abstract nature; it's no part of my intent to offend anyone. But it's my opinion—and a proper one, unless I'm badly mistaken—that the pure and genuine philosophy of Christ is drawn from no other source than the evangelical books and the letters of the apostles. Any man who piously reflects on these writings, praying rather than disputing, and seeking to be transformed within rather than armed for battle,[1] will cer-

6. Plato, *Gorgias*, and repeatedly in the *Phaedo*.
7. This sentiment has not been traced in Aristotle.
8. Cicero, *De finibus* 1.16.
9. The Old Law, as prescribed in Leviticus and Deuteronomy (traditionally written by Moses), was presumed to have been abrogated by the New Law of Christ.
1. This is the one brief passage in which the Paraclesis fleetingly considers the perils of putting an infallible book in the hands of passionate, willful, and self-centered men.

tainly find that there is nothing pertaining to the felicity of man, nothing relating to our conduct in this world, nothing about the great problems of life, that is not treated here, explained and resolved. If we want to learn something, why should any author be more agreeable than Christ himself? If we want a pattern for living, what model is more suitable than Christ the archetype? If we crave some medication against the foul lusts of the mind, why do we suppose a better remedy can be found somewhere else? If we want reading to stir up a soul grown torpid and weary, where, I ask you, will you find sparks so lively and vital? If you want to raise your mind above the vexations of this life, why should you suppose other delights will prove more alluring? Why have we regularly preferred to learn the lessons of Christ from the writings of men other than Christ himself? And because he promised to be with us even to the end of time,[2] he is present most especially in these writings in which even now he lives, breathes, and speaks to us, more forcefully (I might almost say) than when he lived among men. The Jews saw less and heard less than you see and hear in these evangelical writings, if you will only bring to them eyes to see and ears to hear him.

What sort of business is this, anyhow? We keep letters written by a friend, we kiss them, we carry them about with us, we read them over and over; and yet there are thousands of Christians who, though otherwise learned enough, have never read through the evangelists and the apostolic books even once in their lifetime. The Mohammedans hold to their tenets, the Jews even today study the books of Moses from their very cradles. Why don't we in the same way devote ourselves to the study of Christ? Those who follow the discipline of Benedict accept a rule written by a mere man, and what is more an uneducated man writing for men even less educated than himself;[3] yet they study it closely and incorporate it in their lives. The Augustinian monks learn all about their founder. The Franciscans adore the little traditions of their Saint Francis; they embrace the rule passionately, surround themselves with it, and carry it with them wherever in the world they go, not thinking themselves safe unless they have the little booklet on their person. Why do they honor more a rule devised by a mere man than the entire Christian church honors its rule which Christ granted to everyone, to which all of us alike have pledged ourselves in baptism? Finally, even if you should cite an infinitude of other rules, can any of them be more holy than this? Paul once said that by contrast with the glories of the evangelists the laws of Moses seemed less than splendid;[4] in the same way I wish that the gospels and the apostolic letters should be so highly prized that by contrast with them all the pagan writings would appear commonplace. Whatever tribute anyone wants to pay to Albertus Magnus, Thomas Aquinas, Aegidius Colonna, Richard of Saint Victor, or William of

2. Matthew 28.20.
3. Saint Benedict of the sixth century successfully avoided the Roman schools as hotbeds of sin.
4. Hebrews 3.3; the epistle "To the Hebrews" was still in Erasmus's time thought to be the work of Saint Paul.

Occam[5] is perfectly all right with me; I don't want to denigrate anyone or attack established courses of study. But let human teachings be as learned, as subtle, even (if you prefer) as seraphic as may be,[6] it must be confessed that these scriptural teachings are the most certain. Paul asks that the spirits inspiring prophets be judged whether they be of God.[7] Augustine, who read every book of every author with reserved discretion, asks nothing more than a similar reading for his own books.[8] In these sacred writings alone, what I cannot understand, I adore. It is no school of theologians that commends these writings to us, but the heavenly Father himself, speaking in his own divine voice, and on two separate occasions. One was by the river Jordan at the baptism of Christ, the other on mount Tabor at the transfiguration. "This," he said, "is my beloved son, in whom I am well pleased: hear him."[9] O solid authority, and truly, as the theologians say, irrefragable! What about this phrase, Hear him? Surely it means he is the one teacher, we should be disciples of him alone. Let every individual devote himself as much as he will to studying his own personal authorities, this injunction has been made without exception for Christ alone. On him alone the dove first descended to confirm the testimony of the Father.[1] Peter next assumes this spirit, to whom the supreme pastor, not only once but again and a third time, entrusted the feeding of his flock—and what were they to be fed but the sound staple of Christian doctrine? The same spirit was, as it were, reborn in Paul, whom Christ himself called a chosen vessel and illustrious beacon of his name.[2] What John drew from the holy wellspring of Christ's bosom he expressed in his letters. Let me ask what there is of a similar nature in Scotus (not that I would seem to be speaking invidiously), or what is there in Thomas? I may admire the ingenuity of the one and revere the sanctity of the other. But why should we do all our thinking only in the bounds laid down by these great men? Why must we carry them around with us, have them always to hand, why must we constantly hunt through them, scrutinizing their writings and looking into their implications? Why should a greater part of our life be given over to Averroes than to the evangelists? Why spend almost our entire life on the assertions of mere men and contradictory interpretations of them? Perhaps these interpretations are the work of sublime theologians, if that's what you want to call them; but it is from the teachings of Christ that the great theologian of the future will learn the first principles of his art.

May all of us who in baptism pledged ourselves in the very words of Christ, if we did so sincerely, imbibe the teachings of Christ even amid the embraces of our parents and the caresses of our nurses. For whatever

---

5. These are all medieval philosophical systems, highly esteemed in Erasmus's day.
6. Erasmus glances at adulatory titles for scholastic philosophers; Scotus was the "subtle doctor," Bonaventura the "seraphic doctor," etc.
7. The actual passage Erasmus has in mind is 1 John 4.1.

8. Augustine against Faustus the Manichaean, 11.5.
9. Matthew 3.17 andd 17.5.
1. The dove descending symbolizes the settling of the holy spirit on Christ.
2. Acts 9.15.

the new-formed soul first receives sinks deeply and clings tenaciously. May the first babblings of children be of Christ, may the first stages of infancy be modeled on the example of one whom I should like babes to know from their infancy and toddlers to love even as little children. For just as the strictness of some teachers causes students to hate good letters even before they know them, so there are some preachers who make the philosophy of Christ seem grim and sour, though really there is nothing more delightful. Let young people be trained in these studies, then, until by the silent passage of time they have matured into vigorous adults in Christ. Other men's writings are such that the effort devoted to them has often seemed vain in the end, and it happens that after devoting their entire lives to supporting some last-ditch cause, men change their minds and at the final moment defect. But happy the man whom death overtakes in the act of meditating this philosophy of Christ. Let us all, then, immerse ourselves in it, embrace it, practice it night and day, kiss it greedily, and die in it after we have been transformed into it, thus confirming the saying that "studies culminate in manners."[3] Anyone who cannot follow this path (but whoever really wants to can do it) may worship these writings as a treasure bequeathed by that divine bosom. If someone should show us the footprints of Christ, how eagerly would we Christians bow down in worship before them! Why then don't we venerate his living and breathing image in these writings? Should anyone produce a tunic worn by Christ, we would hurry to the ends of the earth to kiss it. But you might assemble his entire wardrobe, and it would contain nothing that Christ did not express more explicitly and truly in the evangelic books. To show our love of Christ we lavish gold and precious stones on a statue of stone or wood. But why wouldn't it be better to use these gems and golden ornaments—or anything else, more precious still, if it can be imagined—to adorn these writings which bring Christ before us more effectively by far than any graven image? An image, if it represents anything at all, represents only the form of the body, but these writings set before you the living picture of his sacred mind, Christ as he actually spoke, healed, died, and rose from the grave, rendering him so completely present that you would see less of him if you had him directly in front of your eyes.

Foreword to the Third Edition (1522)

Desiderius Erasmus of Rotterdam to the Pious Reader, Greetings

As I recall, most excellent reader, I've declared on a number of occasions that I disagree completely with those who say that laymen and the unlearned should be altogether excluded from reading the holy scriptures—that nobody should be admitted within those sacred precincts

---

3. The saying *Abeunt studia in mores* comes from Ovid's *Heroides*, "Sappho. to Phaon."

except the few who have devoted many years to the study of Aristotle's philosophy and scholastic theology. For the moment I won't argue the point whether academic minds are not best suited for reading and expounding volumes of arcane lore, to which they can certainly bring brains sharpened by training in the human disciplines. Let it be so, provided only that they attain this wisdom soberly and moderately, provided they don't harden into rigid opinions, provided they don't overvalue their own learning, provided they avoid arrogance and blind complacency, provided their vision remains clear and uncontaminated (such vision as that with which God himself scans the deep mysteries of scripture), provided their minds are not corrupted by worldly concerns, such as the Holy Spirit is quick to reject. Quite otherwise did the scribes and pharisees possess the sacred books, who, when asked about the coming of Christ, answered in the words of the prophets;[1] and who, when they were questioned about the special point of the law [condemning Christ] could reply very much to the point—for Caiaphas even uttered a prophecy of his own, that Christ would redeem the world.[2] But, "having eyes, they saw not," because their eyes were darkened with envy and hatred; "having ears, they heard not," because their hearing was deafened by the noise of evil desires; "having minds, they did not understand," because their spirits were dulled by the drugs of ambition and avarice.[3] And in fact no men resisted Christ more obstinately than these very men charged with guarding the books in which his coming is foretold and represented.

But exact knowledge of the holy books is not to be condemned simply because someone, through his individual fault, turns them to evil ends. Of its own nature, scripture is good and healthful. Even, then, if we concede the learned first place in teaching, I don't see why the unlearned should be kept from knowledge of the evangelists in particular, as the profane are barred from sacred places. For the evangelists wrote for the unlearned as well as the learned, for Scythians as well as Greeks, for slaves just as much as for free men, for women in addition to men, for humble artisans as well as kings. What they teach applies to everyone alike, their promises are extended to everyone in equal measure. And they are so written that they are more readily understood by a pious and modest man without learning than by an arrogant philosopher. It was natural for the Jews to wrap in mystery those doctrines of theirs which were delivered as from a dark cloud. But the light of the evangelists cannot be suppressed. In former days only the priest was allowed to approach the holy of holies. But when at the death of our Lord the veil of the Temple was rent,[4] all men were given access to Christ himself, who is the true holy of holies and the sanctifier of all persons; having himself risen from the earth, he draws everything to himself, because he yearns for all to find salvation. Some people cry out, as at a criminal

1. Matthew 2.4–6.   3. Mark 8.18.
2. John 11.49–50.   4. Matthew 27.51.

act, if a woman or a leather-worker expresses an opinion on the holy scriptures. There are plenty of girls whom I would rather hear speaking of Christ than various of these so-called supreme rabbis. Why should we be more exclusive than the Jews? They allowed the infant Jesus among their doctors to question them and to teach them, even though there was as yet no reason to suspect his divine nature. When his disciples tried to keep children from him, he rebuked them: "For of such," he said, "is the kingdom of heaven."[5] Neither should we hinder little children from reading the evangelists. Perhaps Jesus will raise them in his arms, touch them with his sacred hands, and bestow on them his blessing. Though the Pharisees begrudge them, children of tender years often sing a most welcome hosanna to the Lord. From people of this sort the evangelic spirit selected his disciples—not just fishermen and illiterates, but even the naturally retarded, as is frequently made apparent in the gospel stories. For these little children he thanks the Father: "I thank thee, God of heaven and earth, that thou hast hidden these things from the wise and prudent, and hast revealed them unto babes"—[6] that is, to those who in the judgment of the world are fools. Often indeed those who are most contemned by the world are most highly prized by Christ, and those whom the world considers most wise are idiots in Christ. Paul, writing to the Romans, describes them this way: "they became vain in their imaginations, and their foolish heart was darkened."[7] Professing themselves to be wise, they became fools. Nor do I say these things to take away authority from good doctors, or add to the arrogance of the unlearned who, because they think they grasp the mystic sense of Scripture, rely on their own ready wit and scorn the doctors of theology. Human wisdom has its own sort of arrogance, but so does human ignorance, and it is no less conceited than the other.

Paul will not allow a woman to speak in a church assembly, not even to teach; and he complains of women with a full catalogue of sins to discuss, who are always babbling and never arriving at knowledge of the truth.[8] On the other hand, Saint Jerome encourages virgins, widows, and wives to read the holy scriptures—yet he too would try to keep the unqualified from professing this sort of knowledge. In this matter, he says, the talky old woman, the maundering old man, and the prating sophist all presume to an opinion; they butcher the subject, because each wants to teach before he has learned anything. So far am I from thinking it proper for any layman, however worthy, to claim understanding of all scriptural problems, that such a claim doesn't seem to me tolerable even in men of learning. What is more arrogant than for a man to set himself up as a doctor in divine matters? But if there's no way for even learned men to assert with sufficient modesty their competence in these matters, I also think no man should be denied the right of pious

---

5. Matthew 19.14.
6. Matthew 11.25.

7. Romans 1.21–22.
8. 1 Corinthians 14.24–36; 1 Timothy 2.11–12.

and sober investigation, especially of those matters which might render his life better.

Wherever in gardens different varieties of delightful plants grow, each man is free to pluck whatever kind suits him. Only consider what sort of hearers Christ attracted—was it not an indiscriminate multitude, including the blind and the halt, beggars, publicans, centurions, artisans, women, and boys? Shall we prevent those people from reading—the very ones by whom he wanted to be heard? As for what I write, let the farmer read it, the workman, the stone-mason, the prostitute and her pimp, and, for all I care, the Turks themselves. If Christ did not bar them from hearing his voice, I'm not going to bar them from reading his books. How do you know that the same thing may not happen to them, as a result of these books, as befell the eunuch?[9] Among the books of the Old Testament there are quite a few from which the layman should be shielded. Such are the book of Ezekiel, the Song of Solomon, and some other books of the Old Testament—either because the stories related in them seem absurd on the face of things, or because the allegories are too obscure. Indeed, I wouldn't forbid the reading of them by any who are eager to learn more of Christian philosophy. They will acquire from this material some preliminary ideas and concepts useful in church assemblies; they will hear more gladly and recognize more readily matters with which they have some previous acquaintance, and for which they have already acquired a taste. But in the evangelical books the divine wisdom adapted itself so wonderfully to the capacity of the very meanest understanding that not even the simplest person is unfit for gospel philosophy. Let the mind only be brought to bear; however rude it may be, if only it be simple, pure, and free of those concerns and lusts which render even the most learned of men unfit for Christ. Before an unlearned man takes the scriptures in hand, he should offer a little prayer to season his reading: let him pray that the good Jesus, who died for even the humblest of men, will deign to impart that Holy Spirit of his which descends only on the humble and meek, such as tremble at his very words. And so, strengthened by the advice of James that "if any of you lack wisdom, let him ask of God that giveth to all men liberally and upbraideth not";[1] let him say with the psalmist, "Open thou mine eyes that I may behold wondrous things out of thy law,"[2] and elsewhere, "I am thy servant, give me understanding, Lord."[3] You see the petitioner seeks nothing else in this wilderness than escape from himself. He suffers from ignorance and implores that light may be forthcoming from any source. Perhaps he is tormented by hatred or envy, perhaps in the grip of lust, avarice, ambition or some other disease of the mind; he seeks the remedy here, and here he finds it. If someone is suffering from grief, let him seek to assuage it here, and he will be relieved. If he is

9. An accidental encounter with the apostle Philip brought spiritual light into the life of an Ethiopian eunuch in the service of Queen Candace. Acts 8.

1. James 1.5.
2. Psalms 119.18.
3. Psalms 119.125.

caught in some logical dilemma, there's no better place to look for help. Anyone who is tempted and about to give way can seek help from the evangelist. Anyone who is thirsting after justice will find here the purest of wellsprings, which, when he drinks of it, will be for him as a fountain raising him to eternal life. No longer will he thirst after the waters of this world, drawn from cisterns muddied by the hoofs of all the beasts on earth. If anyone hungers for the food of life, here is bread descended from heaven; he who eats of it will turn with all his strength and all his energy to Christ, until he reaches in the fullness of his manhood the utmost measure of Christ's plenitude. This is that fountain of paradise from which four streams depart to water the entire face of the earth. This is the bread of heavenly discourse with which Jesus even today feeds the motley crowd that flocks around him and even in desert places clings to him.

I know there are many pastors who take the bread broken by Christ and distribute it among the people. But what if there should be no more pastors? What if they turned into wolves? It is the duty of our shepherds to dig wells and draw from them the fresh water of heavenly doctrine to be shared among the flock, lest they perish of thirst in the desert. But what if the shepherds be turned Philistine,[4] and muddy the stream of living water by throwing dirt in it? What are the people to do? No doubt, implore the aid of the prince of shepherds, Jesus. He still lives, nor has he abandoned the care of his flock. Summoned by the public prayers of his followers, he will do as he promised in the words of Ezekiel: "As a shepherd seeketh out his flock in the day that he is among his sheep that are scattered; so will I seek out my sheep and will deliver them,"[5] and the other things that follow in this passage of the same prophet. Sheep stand for unlearned but rational men; out of these very sheep are created shepherds, and it sometimes befalls that a sheep is wiser than his own shepherd. And so, as it is not fitting for a layman to rebel seditiously against his priest (lest that order be confounded which Paul wishes to exist in the body of Christ),[6] so it is not fitting for priests to exercise tyranny over their flock, otherwise the sedition will be their fault. Therefore such priests as fulfill their duties properly are to be heard with reverence, as messengers of God through whom Christ himself speaks to us. If they teach corrupt doctrine, they should still be heard, but with discrimination, for whatever good may be mixed with the corruption. But if they depart altogether from the way, or preach doctrine in open conflict with the evangelist, then—just as when, on occasion, no doctor at all is to be had—let each man minister to his own needs by a private reading of scripture. Every person should draw from the wellspring of the Savior whatever he can make use of. From the sacred bread let each person eat what satisfies his hunger. The spirit of Jesus will not fail even a solitary person who in this frame of mind meditates religious matters.

4. I.e., unbelievers.   6. 1 Corinthians 14.40.
5. Ezekiel 34.12.

His promise was to be present wherever two persons were gathered in his name.[7] Six thousand souls might be gathered together, but in vain if they did not assemble in the name of Jesus. Everyone is enrolled in his name who seeks nothing but the glory of his rule on earth and eternal salvation hereafter.

Someone may say: Distinguishing spirits is a difficult matter, and the agent of Satan may sometimes transform his shape into that of an angel of light.[8] It is true; and for that reason I should avoid hasty judgment. Nonetheless the most certain witness for every man is the testimony of his own conscience, and the next surest is the consensus of the scripture and the life of Christ. Some things are too perspicuous to occasion doubt or require an interpreter. Naturally such teachings are offensive to those who have completely devoted themselves to this world—for no other reason than that such home truths interfere with their habits and desires. Why else was Christ so disliked by the scribes and pharisees—Christ, than whose doctrine nothing was more just, than whose life nothing was more innocent, than whose power nothing was more beneficent? But they already possessed their kingdom—of a sort. They were honored as learned men, revered as holy men, rich as they could desire, and they wanted that condition of theirs to last forever, though it was thoroughly immoral. And so they could not endure the light of evangelical truth, which they saw would expose the charade of their authority. How concerned we should be if this sort of authority were disgraced, Christ himself has told us: "Let them alone: they be blind leaders of the blind."[9] Certainly Christ never shut away from any pious person the nourishment of his gospel, not even from a swineherd. Rather, it was to humble shepherds that Christ imparted a share of his prophetic spirit. Therefore let everyone who seeks a Christian philosophy be practiced in these books. If he succeeds in his particular quest, let him give thanks to God. If still dissatisfied, he should not despair; let him seek, implore, knock. One who seeks is often rewarded by finding; to him who asks, it is sometimes given; for him who knocks, the door will be opened by one who holds the key—and what it opens can never again be shut, what it shuts can never again be opened. If you do not find the answer you seek, consult your neighbor; perhaps through him a secret spirit will speak to you, such as finds its way into the minds of men through more than one passage. Consult your pious curiosity, and your curious piety, but avoid presumption, avoid rash and stubborn assurance. To what you read and understand give your entire faith; but reject frivolous quibbles and impious curiosities should these by any chance obtrude on your mind. Say to yourself: "Things above our reach concern us not at all."[1] How the body of Christ rose out of a closed tomb is no question for you; enough that it happened. How the eucharist contains the body of Christ though before

7. Matthew 18.20.
8. As Lucifer is the name of both Satan and the morning star.

9. Matthew 15.14.
1. *Quae supra nos, nihil ad nos;* the origins of this saying are lost in the mists of antiquity.

it was only a wafer you need not ask; it's enough for you to believe that
this is the body of the Savior. How the Son can be distinct from the
Father though of one nature with him is not for you to know; for you,
it's enough to believe in the Father, Son, and Holy Ghost, three persons
but one God. But above all you must be careful not to twist the scripture
to satisfy your desires or your prejudices; rather, you should adjust your
personal wishes and pattern of life to its rules. Otherwise, this sacred
fount will prove the source of quarrels, contentions, conflicts, hatreds,
and even heresies, the bane alike of the faith and of Christian concord.
Yet this is no reason to conceal the sacred books from laymen, just
because some individual through reading them falls into error. The fault
there is not in the reading but in the man. Nobody in antiquity proposed
to forbid the reading of the gospels in churches just because the early
heretics drew from that source the seeds of their errors. Bees are not kept
from visiting flowers just because an occasional spider sucks poison from
them. Let everyone read, therefore, but let anyone who wants to profit
from his reading read soberly and alertly—not as if he were reading some
story of human history with no bearing on his life—but avidly, earnestly,
attentively. The truly pious disciple of Jesus will follow in all his footsteps; will observe what he said, what he did; will explore, analyze, examine
every detail; and he will find in that simple, unpolished scripture the
ineffable knowledge of divine wisdom. He will find in that foolishness
of God (if it's permitted to speak so), which at first glance seemed lowly
and despicable, what far surpasses all human prudence, however lofty
and admirable. Nothing is told there that does not have a bearing on
every one of us; nothing happens there that does not happen daily in our
own lives, more secretly perhaps, but just as truly. Christ is born within
us, and there is no shortage of Herods who try to destroy the weak,
unweaned baby. He grows up and passes the stages of maturation. He
cures illnesses of all sorts if only we devoutly implore his help. He does
not reject lepers or demoniacs or those suffering from an issue of blood;
he rejects neither the blind nor the halt. There is no affliction of the
mind so desperate or deep-seated that he will not relieve us if we say to
him from the heart: "Jesus, son of David, have mercy on us";[2] and
"Lord, if thou wilt thou canst make me clean."[3] He can raise the dead;
he teaches, he terrifies, he comforts, he consoles. He is opposed by Jews,
who do not want his light to cast their Moses in the shade. He has scribes
and pharisees who betray him—would that he had no more than two,
Annas and Caiaphas. He has his Iscariots who for money sell his guilt-
less blood. There is no lack of Pilates and their lackeys to flagellate him,
spit on him, and crucify him. He has those who say: "Lord, to whom
shall we go? Thou hast the words of eternal life."[4] In philosophy of this
sort it befits all men to be versed, whether laymen or illiterates. Nor will
there be lacking comfort for those who earnestly study it, such words of

2. Mark 10.47.   4. John 6.68.
3. Matthew 8.2.

comfort as will teach them everything they need for eternal salvation according to the prophecy of Joel: "I will pour out my spirit upon all flesh, and all shall be *theodidaktoi*, that is, learned in the spirit."[5] Paul does not wish to prohibit the spirit, but prefers that everyone prophesy.[6] And Moses, when asked to prohibit Heldad and Medad from prophesying, answered: "Would God that all the Lord's people were prophets, and that the Lord would put his spirit upon them."[7]

Some think it a fault, though venial, if the holy books are translated into French or English. But the evangelists had no hesitation about writing in Greek what Christ spoke in Syriac. Nor did the Latin fathers fear to turn the speeches of the apostles into Latin, thereby spreading the Word across the world in the form of the Vulgate. No law prevented Jerome from translating the Holy Writ into his native Yugoslav. I myself would like to see it turned into all the languages there are. Christ wants his gospel to be spread as widely as possible. He died for all; he wants to be known by all. It would serve that end if his books were turned into all the languages of all the nations; or else if, by decree of the princes, those three languages to which the divine philosophy has been entrusted were taught to all the peoples.[8] If the power of the Roman emperors could bring about within a few years that Frenchmen, Germans, Spaniards, Africans, Egyptians, Asians, Cilicians, and Palestinians all spoke Latin and Greek, even on everyday occasions—and for no better reason than to facilitate the commerce of an empire not destined to survive long in any case—how much more should we be concerned that the rule of Christ, which is to last forever, should be spread through all the regions of the earth? At present, Christianity is narrowly contracted, for what reasons I cannot guess, unless, as I suspect, there are men who would rather maintain their secular power under the pretext of Christianity in their own little corner of the world than see Christ himself ruling over the entire globe. But on this topic there will be more to say on another occasion, when it can be said more forcefully. Now let me hasten on with my task, and ask why it should seem improper that anyone should recite the Gospel in that language to which he was born, and which he understands—a Frenchman in French, a Briton in English, a German in German, an Indian in Indian? To me it seems much more improper, not to say ridiculous, that a layman or a woman should mumble their psalms or recite their prayers like trained parrots in a language where they don't understand what they are saying. I agree with Saint Jerome that the glory of the Cross would be more advanced and its triumphs made more splendid if it were celebrated by all the races of mankind, each one speaking its own language—if the farmer driving his plough could chant a passage in his native tongue from the mystic psalms, if

5. Joel 2.28.
6. 1 Corinthians 14.26.
7. Numbers 11.26–27.
8. The trilingual college, offering instruction in

Greek, Latin, and Hebrew, was a favorite project of the early humanists; foundations were actually established at Cologne, Louvain, and Alcala.

the weaver sitting before his loom could lighten his labor with a chapter from the gospel, if the sailor standing by his tiller could chant some favorite selection, if the matron sitting at her spinning-wheel could hear some scriptural story recited by her maid or niece. What is more remote from the mysteries of the prophets than the story of that eunuch in the train of Queen Candace who had been raised in a court, trained to womanly tasks, and furthermore was an Ethiopian, most effeminate of races: yet, while being drawn lazily along in his carriage, he read the prophecies of Isaiah about Christ. He was a profane man and unlearned; but since he read in a spirit of pious attention, an interpreter was promptly sent to him, Philip; the eunuch was turned to a man, washed in baptismal waters, and the black Ethiopian put on the snowy fleece of an immaculate lamb; and shortly thereafter, through her slave's influence, the queen herself became a servant of Christ.[9]

Now the fact that we have today many Christians so ignorant that they possess less knowledge of the faith than even its worst enemies, I attribute mostly to the priests. And I think I see a way in which we can render somewhat fewer of our people completely unfit for reading the scriptures. That would be if every year the substance of our Christian faith and doctrine could be proposed, briefly, clearly, and with learned simplicity, to the entire population. And lest the substance be adulterated by crafty preachers, it would be well to have a booklet composed by learned and judicious men, which could be recited by the assembled priests unanimously. I should like preaching to be done, not from the defective inventions of human minds, but from the evangelical sources, from the apostolic letters, from the creed, which—though I don't know whether it was produced by the apostles—certainly carries on it the marks of apostolic majesty and purity. The substance of our faith might, I think, be discussed not inappropriately at Eastertime; and I think this would be a great improvement over raising guffaws from the people with jokes that are always stupid and frequently obscene. Which demon out of hell introduced this custom into the church I don't know; for though the people must be given a bit of amusement to hold their attention, and even stirred up now and then, still this way of exciting laughter is the proper work of buffoons, not theologians. In addition, I think it would help in no small degree toward the end we desire if children who have been baptized, when they reach the age of puberty, should be ordered to attend sessions in which it would be made clear to them what was actually involved in the baptismal ceremony. Then let them be carefully examined in private by men of authority, to make sure they know and recall what the priest has taught them. If they have that material in hand, let them be asked further to give an account of what their sponsors promised in their name at their baptism. If they can give a good account of that, then let them renew their promises in public assemblies to the accompaniment of many solemn ceremonies—seemly, serious, chaste,

9. Acts 8.27 ff. See above, p. 130, n. 9.

and splendid—such as may befit that declaration of principles than which nothing can be more holy. What, after all, are human promises, but imitations, as it were, of this most sacred promise, recalls, so to speak, of Christianity's first fall into the world?

Monks know how to make a favorable presentation of their vows before the public by ceremonies of this sort; they perform the drama so vividly that often they wring tears from the onlookers. All the more it behooves us to do the same thing in enacting this promise, by far the most religious of all, in which we give bonds, not to men, but to God. What is more, we don't subscribe to the code of Francis or Benedict, but to that of the gospels. In this way it might actually come about that young people would understand what duties they owe their Prince and what exertions may raise them to true piety. When they are older it will help them realize in how many ways they have wandered from their first profession. What is performed in some of our churches now [by way of baptism] is a kind of comedy, not I suppose altogether wicked, about Christ's resurrection, his ascent to heaven, and the despatch of the Holy Spirit. How truly magnificent would be this spectacle if one could hear the voices of many young people dedicating themselves to Jesus Christ, many new recruits pledging loyalty to his cause, and renouncing this world which is fashioned only for evil—abjuring and rejecting Satan with all his pomps, pleasures, and worldly works! We should see many new Christs, bearing on their brows the insignia of their Prince; we should see the flock of candidates advancing from the holy fount, and hear the voices of a united society acclaiming Christ's recruits and wishing them well. These ceremonies I should wish to be publicly performed, so that the young may not simply receive the faith passively and in their cradles, but receive it publicly, before everyone, so far as that's possible. The ceremony will have more authority if it is performed by the bishops themselves rather than by parish priests or their curates; and if it is carried out as it should be, we'll have many more genuine Christians than we do now, or I'm much mistaken.

But here two scruples arise: first because the ceremony of baptism seems to be repeated, which is not right; and then there's danger that some young people, having heard what the promises are, may not approve of what was done for them by their sponsors. The first scruple is easily disposed of if things are so managed as to make clear that the second ceremony does nothing but ratify the first, just as when, in everyday life, we bless ourselves with holy water. The second problem is harder to solve, but every effort must be made to keep anyone from receding from his former faith. If his consent cannot be obtained, he must not be compelled, but left to his own conscience until he becomes wiser; nor, in the meanwhile, should he be subject to any penalty, apart from being barred from the eucharist and the other sacraments. But he should not be excluded from the church or church services, and I would want books of Christian philosophy to be put in his hands, where the pure image of Christ himself is presented, unclouded by Jewish ceremonies, uncom-

plicated by commentaries or human explanations. Neither should Christ
be represented as savage and fierce, but rather as he is, gentle and lova-
ble. Young people trained through observances of this sort will not come
altogether unprepared to the reading of the sacred scriptures. Nowadays
there are many fifty-year-olds who have no idea what vows they undertook in the baptism ceremony, who never even dreamed of what the
articles of faith demand of them, what Sunday prayers mean, or what
the sacraments of the church imply. We know this is often the case from
familiar conversations as well as from the secret confessional. But, what
is even more to be deplored, many of us who are priests are also of this
sort; we have never seriously considered what it is to be truly a Christian.
In name, in customs, in ceremonies we are Christian, rather than in
our minds. Either for lack of knowledge we don't have anything to teach
the people, or else, being corrupted with worldly lusts, we consult our
own advantage rather than that of Jesus Christ. What wonder, then, if
the people are sunk in darkness, when those who should be the light of
the world are also hidden in gloom? when those who should be the salt
of the earth know nothing worthy of Christ? when those who should be
a shining light for the entire house are themselves blind? when those
who should be as a strong city atop a lofty mountain, showing others the
way, are themselves bogged down in the filth of greed and lust? And
would there were not so many to whom that saying of Isaiah could be
applied: "his watchmen are blind; they are all ignorant, they are all dumb
dogs, they cannot bark, sleeping, lying down, loving to slumber. Yea,
they are greedy dogs which can never have enough, and they are shepherds that cannot understand; they all look to their own way, every one
for his gain, from his quarter."[1] And also from Jeremiah: "My people
hath been lost sheep: their shepherds have caused them to go astray."[2]
Again, Ezekiel declaims with great boldness against shepherds turned to
wolves, who feed themselves but let their flock scatter and be slaughtered.[3] In passage after passage the prophets recur to this charge, saying
that from the shepherds arise the calamities that befall the sheep. So says
Zechariah the prophet: "They were troubled because there was no shepherd."[4]

   Sometimes these afflictions fall deservedly on the flock, as when the
Lord allows the hypocrite and the figurehead to rule in place of the
proper shepherd; then, "having itching ears," as Paul says, "they will
turn away from the truth,"[5] and seek out doctors who will feed them on
fables. Then we have a lid worthy of the pot; and as the prophet Hosea
says, "then shall be like people like priest."[6] For the flock of the people
has mixed in with it wolves, foxes, leopards, and other wild beasts. For
the most part, to be sure, the common folk consist of sheep. Rough they
are, simple and unlearned, but of value to the Lord if ruled by the care

1. Isaiah 56.10.   4. Zechariah 10.2.
2. Jeremiah 50.6.   5. 2 Timothy 4.3.
3. Ezekiel 22.25–28.   6. Hosea 4.9.

of a faithful shepherd. The best of shepherds has taken care for their condition; he wants none of his flock to be lost, and when one sheep strayed into the mountains, Christ sought it out with great pains and brought it back on his shoulders.[7] But if now one should consider the great number of men, and at the same time reflect how little is done for them by the shepherds (who used to be priests, scribes, and pharisees), he must be moved to pity by the great number of dispersed and destitute sheep who have been altogether abandoned by their pastors. Happy that people whom Jesus has favored with his regard. His notice is not burdensome; he does not glare as with the evil eye, rather his glance is imbued with divine virtue. He looked on Peter who had denied him, and restored his wisdom.[8] And he understood one who, after changing his name, gave solid evidence of his faith.[9] On the mountain he looked into the hearts of his disciples and infused into them his celestial doctrine. What then, brothers? Let us labor to be like his sheep, putting aside all malice, pride, and wrath (none of them qualities befitting sheep), and with our prayers implore the most gentle Jesus that he will deign to turn his eyes even on us. He is the good shepherd, he will have mercy on us: either he will send us workmen fit to bring in his harvest if only we pray for them, as we read in Matthew;[1] or he will teach us himself, as Mark writes, "And he began to teach them many things."[2] Not only did he teach them but he supplied bread in the desert for that entire multitude whom the tyrannical pharisees would have allowed to perish of hunger. Today Jesus has not ceased to teach us, nor to feed us who, having left the cities, have followed him into the desert. He still pours forth his spirit on his disciples. The Lord's bounty is not yet grown scant, nor does the force of his spirit fail among pious souls. That we may deserve to receive it, let us do as the disciples did. Let us assemble for a meal, having beforehand purified our minds from all the dirty cares of the busy world. Let us all be of one mind, joining unanimously together in prayer, if we wish our vows to be heard. Let us speak with one voice, being of one mind, and seeking always the same thing. Let us petition in the name of Jesus, and the heavenly father will hear us.

Nowadays, what quarrels and endless contentions continually distress the Christian community! The secular rulers are all engaged in bloody wars; even bishops of the church are engulfed in waves of violence. The common people are caught up in vicious mutual hatreds. While the purity of Christian faith is corrupted in various ways, the peace of Christianity is being shattered. I don't want to pronounce here for one side or the other; wherever there is strife, there the devil is found. Who ever saw conflicts more atrocious and unrelenting among the pagans than those which for years now have raged between Christians? Without going into the causes, when was the ship of the church ever thus tossed about

---

7. Luke 15.4–5.
8. Luke 22.61.
9. This is clearly Saul/Paul.

1. Matthew 9.36–38.
2. Mark 6.34.

on the waves? Why don't we look into the causes of these events? When
we have found their source, we may be able to find a remedy for them.
In the gospels themselves I read that the apostolic ship was twice in
danger, always at night when Jesus was not available to help, as we read
in Matthew 14: "But the ship was now in the midst of the sea, tossed
with waves."[3] What wonder if tumults will arise in the church if Jesus
is not present? Whenever the spirit of Christ is absent, then the waves
and winds of this world toss about the ship and vex it sorely. What
wonder if now we have no saving counsel when the shadows lie so deep
that we would not even recognize Jesus if he approached, and would be
terrified at the coming of our own Savior as if he were a malignant ghost?
Indeed, if Jesus had not spoken to them in the voice they knew, bidding
them be of good cheer, they would all have died of fright. On that
occasion Peter judged that he would be safer in the waves with Jesus
than in the laboring ship. Let us imitate the faith of Peter; and then
Jesus, returned to the vessel, will promptly still the storms. Again the
ship was in danger in the eighth chapter of the same evangelist, this time
when Jesus was present but sound asleep. Mark adds to the story, saying
that he had placed his head on a pillow and indicating, not insignifi-
cantly, that this took place in the stern of the ship. Will you hear of the
perils that arose while Jesus slept? "There arose," he says, "a great storm
of wind and the waves beat into the ship so that it was now full;"[4] or, as
Matthew adds, "it was covered with the waves." A horrible wind is ambition, a pestilent wind is avarice, a pernicious wind is addiction to pleasure and the other earthly appetites. These are the winds that raise the
storm so that the waves of war and conflict flood the church. The result
is not only that the ship is endangered in which the apostles were
embarked, but so is all the rest of the enterprise that accompanies the
vessel of Jesus. For Mark adds that there were also with him other little
vessels.[5] What then means the sleep of Jesus? Would that he were not
so often asleep in the minds of the pastors who stand at the helm of the
ship, the post of highest honor, where a man must be a skilled skipper
to handle the tiller. What means the pillow on which he laid his head?
Was not this he who said, "the son of man hath not where to lay his
head?"[6] Surely Jesus had a place to rest, and it's only logical that he
didn't lack for a bed to sleep on. But someone who cares nothing for this
world, whose mind is wholly abstracted from it and totally devoted to
the study of heavenly matters, he really has nowhere to lay his head.
Oh, what a soft pillow is prepared for the ambitious man, the highest
reward spread before him, to be obtained by hook or by crook! What a
dainty bolster awaits the lover of riches when he has safely accumulated
his loot and piled it up in his house! But those who exercise public office
not for their own profit but for the benefit of others, who think an epis-
copal charge is a duty not a royal throne—for such there is no pillow

3. Verse 24.   5. Mark 4.36.
4. Mark 4.37.   6. Matthew 8.20.

inviting them to sleep, but rather a noisy bell that rings constantly in the ear, calling them to toil. But now we see some men so meltingly adapted to the pursuit of worldly affairs—one might almost say so intoxicated with the world—that they seem to sleep, not just on pillows, but the sleep of the drugged. Hence no doubt our present storm of misfortunes, since Christ is asleep in all of us.

But with things in such total turmoil, with everyone's safety at stake, what shall we think, my brothers? In great tempests, sailors are accustomed to take advice from anyone at all. Where can we find better counsel than in the scriptures? Discarding all other helps, let us call on Jesus, let us assail his ears, even pluck at them, till he is alerted to our needs. He can be roused in this way; it is what he wishes. Let us cry to him in woeful tones; "Master, carest thou not that we perish?"[7] Let us repeat with utter confidence, "Lord, save us for we perish."[8] And he who is ever kindly will hear us, and with his spirit will quickly settle the tempest excited by the gusts of the world. To the winds he will say "Quiet," and to the seas, "Be still, not a whisper." And what followed then? "The wind ceased and there was a great calm."[9] So long as the ship of the church is tossed about at the mercy of the winds, it remains in great peril. Even if a moment of tranquility interrupts the storm, another gust of wind from another direction will renew it. Though the south wind of avarice relents for a while, up springs the north wind of pride; if the west wind of pleasure dies down, along comes the cold east wind of rage. I have confronted now this wind and now that, and fought with each; but another quickly arises, with whom I undertake a new and more savage struggle, for there is no end of earthly lusts. The winds cannot be tamed unless Jesus rebukes them. Let us all take common counsel together, then, in the tranquility of the Christian name. Let each of us dismiss his personal desires. With minds in total agreement let us consider those matters which are worthy of the thoughts and aspirations of Christians. Let the populace devote itself to the study of true piety, and with ardent, unanimous prayers implore of Jesus Christ that he will turn the souls of our princes to the study of peace. Let the princes and above all the ecclesiastical authorities so arrange their thoughts and counsels that with sincere minds they may strive for just one thing: that through faith, charity, piety, concord, contempt of earthly values and love of heavenly things, Christ may reign, flourish, and rule as widely as possible. Then at last princes will be truly great if their authority serves the glory of the Eternal Prince and the salvation of the Christian flock. Then the people will be happy if ruled by such princes, as the princes themselves will be ruled by Christ. But if, on the contrary, we allow our strength to be sapped by civil strife, there is danger that God, offended by our misdeeds, may send upon us a Nebuchadnezzar,[1] who will use harsher

7. Mark 4.38.
8. Matthew 18.25.
9. Mark 4.39.

1. The cruel king of Babylon, who destroyed the temple and carried off the Jews into captivity.

measures to make us think more correctly. If we agree together, God will protect us with his concord; if we divide ourselves by our contentions, our enemies will despise us. Never, however, will we obtain concord if each man tries to hold stubbornly to his own opinion; nor will there ever be a firm, long-lasting peace if it is not sealed with true and solid reasoning. Nothing will last which is patched up with terror and threats, nor can anything endure which is woven of human tricks and devious counsels. If Christ be not summoned to our gatherings, if only to consider our troubles, the result can only be to bring even worse calamities on the world. Farewell, reader. I added these thoughts because the printer called for additional matter to fill up some empty pages; I didn't want them devoted to nothing but idle jokes.

Basel, 14 January 1522

Julius Excluded from Heaven

After a reign of ten hyperactive years, Pope Julius II died on February 21, 1513; he was seventy years old, and Leo X, a humanist and a peace-loving Medici succeeded him. Less than a year later the anonymous satire *Julius Excluded from Heaven* was published. There is no conclusive evidence that Erasmus wrote it, and he several times implied that he didn't—though without saying so explicitly. There were of course very good reasons for not avowing the publication, not least the possibility of retribution from ex-friends or -allies of Julius. The pamphlet was enormously popular and many times reprinted; but Erasmus had little to gain and much to lose from claiming it. Though he never actually did so, modern scholarship, basing itself on internal evidence, some cautious phrases in the later correspondence, and the lack of a credible alternative author, has had little hesitation in assigning the piece to Erasmus.

Actually, the relation of the satire to Julius II is more problematic than its relation to Erasmus. That Julius was one of the most secular-minded of many secular-minded Renaissance popes is not open to question; and Erasmus, who found that a fault, might have aggravated it, had he chosen, by emphasizing the pope's huge building programs in Rome, his patronage of Michelangelo, Bramante, and Raphael, his lavish purchases of antique sculptures and manuscripts for the Vatican collections. But these charges would not have blackened the dead pope's reputation as much as other abusive accusations that the satirist could pick up from the gutter or invent out of whole cloth. Pederasty, simony [the selling of church offices for money], nepotism, and subornation to murder are only a few of these invented charges; in addition, Erasmus unfailingly interprets all of Julius's behavior in the worst possible light. To comment in detail on all the misrepresentations and distortions of the satire would bury the dialogue under a dead weight of commentary. Suffice it to say that there is a wholly different side to the picture of Julius given by Erasmus, according to which he was a deft diplomat, a financier of genius, and one of the ablest administrators ever to occupy the chair of Peter. These aren't necessarily the qualities of the highest Christian visionary, but every so often they may be of great value to the church; and that value Erasmus was utterly unwilling to recognize.

Julius Exclusus, then, is not a portrait of a real pope but an extravagant caricature rising out of a theme dear to Erasmus's heart, a contrast between the spiritual and the worldly life. It is also a comic masterpiece, with roots in the Roman comedy of Plautus and the same sort of grotesque vitality that animates characters like Baron Munchausen and King Ubu. One should read it, with minimal care for its accuracy, as an exercise in malicious, playful fantasy, a *jeu d'esprit*.

Julius Excluded from Heaven: A Dialogue

Speakers: Julius, his Genius,[1] Peter

JULIUS: What the devil is this? The doors don't open? Somebody must have changed the lock or broken it.

GENIUS: It seems more likely that you didn't bring the proper key; for this door doesn't open to the same key as a secret money-chest. Why didn't you bring both the keys you have? This is the key of power, not of wisdom.

JULIUS: I didn't have any other key but this; I don't see why we need a different one when we've got this.

GENIUS: I don't either; but the fact is, we're still on the outside.

JULIUS: Now I'm really getting mad; I'll knock the doors down. Ho! Ho! Somebody come and open this door right away! What's the hang-up? nobody home? What's the matter with the doorman? He's asleep, I guess, or else drunk.

GENIUS: This fellow judges everyone else by himself.

PETER: A good thing our gates are of adamant, otherwise this one, whoever he is, would have kicked them in. He must be a giant of some sort, a general of the armies, a stormer of cities. But oh my God, what a sewer-stench is this! I certainly won't open the gates right away, but take a seat up here by a grated window where I can look out and keep an eye on the scene. Who are you and what do you want?

JULIUS: Open the door, will you? at least, if you can. And if you were really doing your job, it should have been open long ago, and decorated with all the heraldry of heaven.

PETER: Pretty lordly. But first tell me who you are.

JULIUS: As if you couldn't see for yourself.

PETER: See? What I see is new to me, like nothing I ever saw before, and I might say monstrous.

JULIUS: But if you're not stone-blind, you're bound to recognize this key, even if you aren't familiar with the golden oak tree.[2] You can certainly see my triple crown, as well as my cloak all gleaming with gold and gems.

PETER: That silver key of yours I do recognize, though there's only one of them, and it's very different from those that were given to me long ago by the one true shepherd of the church, that is, Christ.[3] But that glorious crown of yours, how could I possibly recognize it? No tyrant ruling over barbarian peoples ever ventured to wear one like it, much

---

1. Writers of antiquity sometimes liked to suppose that each man was born with a couple of tutelary spirits—daemons or genii—who controlled his instinctive sympathies throughout life, one for the better, the other for the worse. Erasmus doesn't assign the genius of Julius much of a part in the dialogue, but evidently found him an amusing and useful prop.
2. The Rovere family, from which Julius sprang, had, as its name implies, an oak tree for a crest.
3. Matthew 16.19.

less anyone who came here asking for admission. Your cloak doesn't impress me either; for I always used to consider gold and jewels as trash to be despised. But what does this amount to really? In all this stuff—the key, the crown, the cloak—I recognize marks of that rascally cheat and impostor who shared a name with me but not a faith, that scoundrel Simon whom I once flung down with the aid of Christ.[4]

JULIUS: Enough of these jokes, and watch yourself; for I, if you don't know, am Julius of Liguria,[5] and I don't doubt you recognize these two letters P.M., unless you've forgotten how to read.

PETER: I expect they stand for "Pestiferous Maximus."

GENIUS: Ha ha ha! This porter is as good as a wizard; he's got the needle's touch.

JULIUS: What it means is "Pontifex Maximus."

PETER: If you were triply great, greater even than Hermes Trismegistus,[6] you still wouldn't get in here unless you were supremely good, that is, holy.

JULIUS: Well, if it comes down to comparative holiness, you've got some nerve to keep me waiting outside here when for all these centuries you've only been called "holy," whereas nobody ever called me anything but "most holy." I have six thousand bulls to prove it—

GENIUS: That's what he said, bulls!

JULIUS: —in which I am not only named "Lord most holy," but addressed as "your holiness," so that whatever I chose to do—

GENIUS: —Even when he was drunk.

JULIUS: —people used to say that the holiness of the most holy lord Julius had done it.

PETER: Then you'd better ask those flatterers of yours to let you into heaven, because they're the ones who made you so holy. They provided the holiness, now let them provide the bliss. By the way, though I know you don't think it matters, do you actually imagine you were a holy man?

JULIUS: You really vex me. If I were only allowed to go on living, I wouldn't envy you your holiness or your bliss, either one.

PETER: The proper expression of a pious mind! But apart from that, when I look you over from head to foot, I see many a sign of impiety and none of holiness. What's the meaning of these many comrades of yours? They're certainly not a papal retinue. You have almost twenty thousand men at your back, and in this entire crowd I can't find one single individual who has so much as the face of a Christian. I see a horrifying mob of ruffians, reeking of nothing but brothels, booze shops, and gunpowder. They look to me like plain highway robbers

4. Peter, known as Simon Peter, shared a name with Simon Magus, a pseudo-Christ who appears briefly in Acts 8, but in later writers grew into a large and menacing magician. "Simony," or the buying of spiritual offices for money, gets its name from him.

5. Liguria, in northwest Italy, lies between the Piedmont to the north and Tuscany to the south.
6. "Thrice-great Hermes" is a title of the Egyptian god Thoth; he has various occult functions but is used here simply as the owner of a high-sounding name.

or spooks stolen out of hell and now intent on stirring up wars in heaven. As for yourself, the more I look at you, the fewer traces do I see of any apostolic character. What sort of unnatural arrangement is it, that while you wear the robes of a priest of God, under them you are dressed in the bloody armor of a warrior? Besides that, what a savage pair of eyes, what baleful features, what a menacing brow, what a disdainful and arrogant expression! I'm ashamed to say, and even to see, that there's no part of your body not marked with traces of outrageous and abominable lust; in addition, you belch and stink like a man just come from a drunken debauch and fresh from a fit of vomiting. Judging from the appearance of your whole body, you seem to me, not worn out by age or disease, but broken down and shrivelled up by drunken excesses.

GENIUS: How vividly he portrays the man in his own colors!

PETER: I see you threatening me with your lofty expression; but my feelings won't be suppressed. I suspect you may be that most pestilent pagan of all, Julius the Roman, returned from hell to make mock of our system. Certainly everything about you agrees well with him.

JULIUS: Ma di si![7]

PETER: What did he say?

GENIUS: He's angry. At that expression, every one of the cardinals used to take flight, otherwise they'd feel the stick of his holiness on their backs, especially if he hadn't had his supper.

PETER: You seem to me to have some understanding of the man; tell me, who are you?

GENIUS: I am the particular Genius of Julius.

PETER: His bad Genius, no doubt.

GENIUS: Whatever I may be, I'm Julius's man.

JULIUS: Why don't you stop all this nonsense and open the doors? Perhaps you'd rather I broke them down. Why do we need all this palaver? You see the sort of troops I have at my command.

PETER: I do indeed see some highly practiced thieves. But you must be aware that these doors can only be opened in other ways.

JULIUS: Enough words, I say. If you don't hurry up and open the gates, I'll unleash my thunderbolt of excommunication with which I used to terrify great kings on earth and their kingdoms too. You see, I've already got a bull[8] prepared for the occasion.

PETER: Just tell me, please, what you mean by all this bombast about bulls, bolts of thunder, and maledictions. I never heard from Christ a single one of these words.

JULIUS: You'll feel their full force, if you don't watch out.

PETER: Perhaps you used to terrify people with that bluster, but it counts for nothing here. Here we deal only in the truth. This is a fortress to be captured with good deeds, not ugly words. But let me ask you,

---

7. Perhaps short for *maledictus sis!* i.e., "Damn you!"

8. Papal bulls get their name from the leaden seal (*bulla*) authenticating them.

since you threaten men with the thunder of excommunication; what's your legal authority for that?

JULIUS: Very well: I take it you are now out of office and have no more standing than any other unbeneficed priest; indeed, you're not even a complete priest, since you lack the power to consecrate.

PETER: Doubtless because I happen to be dead.

JULIUS: Obviously.

PETER: But for the same reason, you have no more standing with me than any other dead man.

JULIUS: But as long as the cardinals are arguing over the election of a new pope, it counts as my administration.

GENIUS: He's still dreaming dreams about being alive!

JULIUS: But now, open the door, I tell you.

PETER: And I won't do a thing, I tell you, unless you give me a full account of your merits.

JULIUS: What merits?

PETER: Let me explain the idea. Did you distinguish yourself in theology?

JULIUS: Not at all. I had no time for it, being continually engaged in warfare. Besides, there are plenty of priests to do that sort of work.

PETER: Then by the holiness of your life you gained many souls for Christ?

GENIUS: Many more for hell, I'd say.

PETER: You performed miracles?

JULIUS: You're talking old-fashioned nonsense.

PETER: You prayed earnestly and constantly?

JULIUS: This is pure foolishness.

PETER: You subdued the lusts of the flesh with fasts and long vigils?

GENIUS: Enough of this, please; with this line of questioning, you're just wasting your time.

PETER: I never heard of any other gifts that an outstanding pope was supposed to possess. If he has some more apostolic talents, let him tell me about them himself.

JULIUS: Though it's a disgraceful thing for Julius who never lowered his crest before anyone else to yield to Peter—who was, to say nothing worse, a lowly fisherman and almost a beggar—still, just to let you know what sort of prince you're slighting in this way, now hear this. In the first place, I am from Liguria,[9] not a Jew like you; but I'm afraid that like you I was once a boatman.

GENIUS: It's nothing to be ashamed of, for there's still this difference, that Peter fished for a living, while Julius plied the oar on a barge for minimum wages.

JULIUS: Then, as it happened that I was the nephew of Pope Sixtus the great—

9. Liguria, as Julius uses the word, sounds like an empire at least; actually, it is a couple of thousand square miles around Genoa.

GENIUS: Great in vices, he means.

JULIUS: —on his sister's side, his special favor combined with my industry first gave me access to ecclesiastical office; and so I gradually rose to the dignity of a cardinal's cap. Having undergone many reverses of fortune, and been tossed to and fro by various accidents—having suffered, among other diseases, from epilepsy and the pox they call French[1]—I found myself quite overwhelmed; I was exiled, rejected, despised, despaired of, and almost given over as lost. Yet I never doubted that some day I would attain the papacy. That showed real strength of character, compared with you, who were terrified at the question of a serving girl, and gave up your faith on the spot.[2] She weakened your courage, but I got new courage from a woman, a soothsayer and prophetess of sorts, who when she saw me overwhelmed with misfortunes secretly whispered in my ear, "Bear up, Julius! Don't be ashamed of anything you have to do or put up with—some day you will attain the triple crown. You will be king of kings and ruler of all rulers." And in fact neither her prophecy nor my own instincts deceived me. Beyond all expectations I achieved my goal, partly with the help of the French who sheltered me in my hour of need, partly by the marvelous power of money in large quantities, which I increased by taking usurious rates of interest. And finally my own ready wit helped me—

PETER: What's this ready wit you're talking about?

JULIUS: —to coin money from the bare promise of ecclesiastical offices, making skillful use of brokers in the process, since the sums I demanded couldn't have been paid in cash by a man as rich as Crassus.[3] But it's useless to describe the schemes to you, since not even all my bankers understood them. Anyhow, that's how I made my way. Now as for how I bore myself in the pontificate, I'll venture to say that none of the early popes (who seem to me to have been popes in name only), nor even of the later ones, deserve so well of the church and of Christ himself as I do.

GENIUS: Only listen to the bragging of the beast!

PETER: I'm waiting to hear how you got away with it all.

JULIUS: I discovered a great many new offices (that's what they're called) which in themselves brought goodly sums into the papal treasury. Then I found a brand-new way by which bishoprics could be bought without any taint of simony. For my predecessors had made a law that any man appointed bishop should lay down his previous office. I interpreted it this way; "You are ordered to lay down your previous office; but if you don't have one you can't lay it down, therefore you must buy it." By this means each individual bishopric brought in its six or seven thousand ducats over and above those that are tradition-

---

1. I.e., syphilis.
2. When Christ was seized by the soldiers, several female onlookers accused Peter of being of his party; but he shamefully denied it. Matthew 26.69–75.

3. Crassus (the name means "fat") was a contemporary of Caesar's, famous almost exclusively for his legendary wealth.

ally extorted for bulls. Also the new money that I spread all over Italy brought in a very healthy sum.[4] And I never let up on accumulating money, understanding as I did that without it nothing is managed properly, whether sacred or profane. Now, to come to my major achievements, I conquered Bologna, which had long been ruled by the Bentivogli,[5] and restored it to the control of Rome. The previously undefeated Venetians I crushed with my army. For a long time I harrassed the duke of Ferrara, and nearly caught him in a trap.[6] I cleverly escaped from a schismatic council set up against me by convoking a fraudulent counter-council, and so, as they say, drove out one nail with another. Finally, I expelled from Italy the French, who at that time were the terrors of the whole world, and I would have driven out the Spanish too (for I had that project under way), if the fates had not suddenly removed me from the earth. And I ask you to admire my undaunted spirit throughout these trials. When the French looked like winners, I was already looking around for a good hiding place; when my position seemed almost desperate, I grew a long white beard as a disguise. But then the golden messenger of victory alighted unexpectedly on me at Ravenna,[7] where a good many thousand Frenchmen were killed; and that was the resurrection of Julius. In fact, for three days I was believed to be at death's door; I thought so myself; and yet here again, against everyone's hopes and even my own expectations, I lived anew. In fact my power and my political shrewdness are so great to this day that there's none of the Christian kings whom I haven't brought to blows, breaking up the treaties by which they had painfully made peace with one another, ripping them to pieces, and trampling them underfoot. Indeed, I was so successful in abolishing the treaty of Cambrai, made between me, the king of France, the emperor Maximilian, and several other rulers, that nobody ever mentions it any more. Over and above all this, I raised several different armies, celebrated many grandiose triumphs, put on splendid shows, built numerous impressive structures, and then at my death left at least five million ducats, which I would have increased even further if that Jewish physician who saved my life on one occasion had been able to stretch it out a little longer.[8] And I really wish now that some magician could be found to restore my earthly existence, so that I could put the finishing touches on the really marvelous projects that

4. During the years 1507 and 1508, Julius circulated throughout Italy a new and improved coinage. Like most people who do such things, he was accused of making millions out of the mint.
5. Giovanni Bentivoglio made himself de facto master of Bologna in 1462 and ruled the city with his two sons for almost half a century—although nominally it remained, as it had been before, a fief of the church. Giovanni did enrich and beautify the city, but Erasmus later in the dialogue greatly exaggerates his popularity with the Bolognesi.
6. This was Alfonso d'Este; Julius had him

imprisoned at Rome (the "trap"), but when the pope died, Alfonso escaped.
7. The terrible battle at Ravenna (11 April 1512) was technically a victory for the French, but their losses were so heavy that when twenty thousand Swiss descended on them from the Alps, they had no choice but to retreat. Julius was deathly ill over that summer.
8. When told of the Jewish physician who cured Julius in 1512, Erasmus complained that he could cure the fever in his body but not the madness in his mind.

I had under way. Still, on my deathbed I tried to ensure that none of the wars I had stirred up throughout the world should be settled; I ordered that moneys set aside for those wars should not be diverted elsewhere; and that was my last wish as I breathed out my dying breath. Now do you hesitate to open the gates for a pontiff who has deserved so well of Christ and the church? And I expect you to be all the more impressed because all this was achieved by my individual constancy of mind alone. I had none of those helpers and favoring circumstances that others have enjoyed; I had no ancestors, for I didn't even know my own father (which indeed I say proudly); I had no personal attractions, since most people shuddered at my face as at an ogre; I had no education, since with me it never took; I had no physical strength, for reasons mentioned above; I was not possessed of youthful energy, for I did all these things as an old man; popularity played no part, for there was nobody who didn't hate me; and I got no credit for clemency because I punished savagely those whom other rulers commonly let off scot-free.

PETER: What's this all about?

GENIUS: He talks very tough, but there's something soft in it.[9]

JULIUS: Thus, with everything against me—fortune, age, strength—briefly, without help from gods or men, by the unaided power of my spirit and my money, I accomplished in a few years so much, that my successors will be busy for at least a decade deciding what to do next. I've said all this about myself with the utmost truth and also, for that matter, with the utmost honesty. If one of those preachers who orate before me in Rome had been here to cover my account with his decorations, you'd have thought a god was being described, not a man.

PETER: Unconquerable warrior, since all these things you talk about are new to me and unheard-of, I beg your pardon for my amazement or inexperience; I hope it won't be too tiresome for you to answer a few clumsy questions about the details. Who, for example, are these little curly-headed striplings?

JULIUS: I brought them up for my diversion.

PETER: Who are these smoke-blackened and mutilated fellows?

JULIUS: They are soldiers and warriors who in behalf of me and the church bravely encountered death in battle. Some died in the siege of Bologna, many in the war against the Venetians, others still at Ravenna. They are all to be admitted to heaven by the terms of our contract, in which I promised, by promulgating some mighty bulls, to send anyone straight to heaven who died fighting for Julius, whatever his previous life had been like.

PETER: As far as I can see, these people must have been the very lot who before your coming were most hateful to me because they were

---

9. The implication may be that Julius's severity toward A sometimes concealed undue fondness for B, or perhaps A's wife. Erasmus's insinuation is too devious to be clear.

always trying to break in by force, using leaden bulls to force their way.

JULIUS: Then, as I understand it, you didn't let any of them in?

PETER: I! Not a single one of that crowd did I admit. That's what Christ told me; he didn't say to admit those who came here lugging heavy leaden bulls, but only those who had clothed the naked, fed the hungry, given drink to the thirsty, visited the prisoners, aided the pilgrims. If he wanted me to keep out those who prophesied in his name, cast our devils, and did wonderful works,[1] do you suppose he would want people let in who just walk up with a bull in the name of Julius?

JULIUS: If I had only known!

PETER: I understand; if some demon out of hell had told you about it, you would have declared war on me.

JULIUS: I would have excommunicated you first.

PETER: But go on, why do you go about wearing armor?

JULIUS: As if you didn't know the holy pope wields two swords; you wouldn't want me to go into battle unarmed, would you?

PETER: When I held your position, I followed that rule in the word of God which says to use no sword save that of the spirit.[2]

JULIUS: That would surprise Malchus, whose ear you cut off[3]—without a sword, no doubt.

PETER: I recall the event, and it's true; but at that time I was fighting for my master, Christ, not for myself; for the life of the Lord, not for loot or worldly booty; and I fought, not as pope, but as one to whom the keys had only been promised, not delivered, nor had I yet received the holy spirit. All the same, I was ordered to put up my sword as a clear warning that warfare of that sort was unbecoming to priests and even to Christians in general.[4] But more of this elsewhere. Why are you so careful about calling yourself a Ligurian as if it mattered what part of the earth the vicar of Christ came from?

JULIUS: But I consider it an act of the highest piety to shed renown on my people; that's why I have this title inscribed on all my coins, statues, structures, and arches.

PETER: So a man can recognize his fatherland who doesn't know his father? At first I thought you had in mind that heavenly Jerusalem, the home of all true believers and of its unique prince in whose name those believers are eager to be sanctified and exalted. But why do you describe yourself as "nephew to Sixtus on his sister's side"?[5] I'm surprised that this man Sixtus never showed up here, though he was pope and related to such a leader as yourself. Do tell me, if you will, what kind of man he was: was he a priest?

---

1. Matthew 7.21–23.
2. Ephesians 6.17.
3. At the taking of Christ, Peter cut off the ear of Malchus, the high priest's servant. John 18.10.
4. Matthew 26.52.

5. Julius was in fact nephew to Pope Sixtus IV (who built the Sistine chapel); Sixtus, a confirmed nepotist, did all he could to forward his nephew's career.

JULIUS: A might soldier he was, and a man of exemplary religion too; he was a Franciscan.

PETER: Indeed, I once knew a man named Francis,[6] a layman distinguished among his fellows for virtue as well as his scorn for wealth, pleasure, and ambition. Does that poor man now have command of military commanders like this?

JULIUS: As far as I can see, you don't want anyone to better himself; even Benedict was a poor man once, but now his followers are so rich that even I am envious of them.

PETER: Fine! but let's go back a ways: you are the nephew of Sixtus.

JULIUS: Glad to confirm it; I'd like to stop the mouths of those who say I'm his son. That's slanderous.

PETER: Slanderous indeed—unless perhaps it's true.

JULIUS: It's an insult to papal dignity, which must always be protected.

PETER: But I think popes should protect their own dignity by not doing anything offensive to the moral law. Speaking of papal dignity, let me ask you, is that the common and accepted way of achieving the papacy that you were describing just now?

JULIUS: For some centuries now, that's been the way of it, unless my successor is created by some other procedure.[7] For as soon as I achieved the papacy myself, I issued a formidable bull that no one else should seek the office by the means I had used; and I renewed that bull shortly before my death. How it will be observed is up to other people.

PETER: I don't see how anyone could describe a bad state of affairs any better. But this puzzles me, how anybody can be found to undertake the job, since so much hard work attaches to the office and so many difficulties must be overcome to acquire it. When I was pope, hardly anyone could be persuaded to accept the office of a presbyter or a deacon.

JULIUS: No wonder; for in those days the reward of bishops was nothing but hard work, sleepless nights, constant study, and very often death: now, it's a kingdom, with the privileges of a tyrant. And who, if he has a chance of a kingdom, won't grab at it?

PETER: Well, tell me now about Bologna. Had it departed from the faith that it had to be brought back to Rome?

JULIUS: Absurd! that wasn't the question at all.

PETER: Perhaps the Bentivogli were poor administrators and destroying the prosperity of the city.

JULIUS: Not a bit of it; the town was flourishing as never before, they had enlarged it and adorned it with many new buildings. That only made me more eager for it.

PETER: I understand; they had taken possession of it illegally.

JULIUS: No, again, the city was theirs by treaty.

---

6. Saint Francis of Assisi lived during the early thirteenth century.
7. Erasmus makes an exception for Julius's successor, Leo X, whom he admired, or at least did not want to offend.

PETER: Perhaps the citizens hated their ruler?

JULIUS: On the contrary; they clung to him tooth and nail, whereas they almost all loathed me.

PETER: What was the reason for it then?

JULIUS: Because, as the ruler arranged things, out of the immense sums that he collected from the citizens, only a few paltry thousands ever reached my treasury. Besides, its capture helped on some other plans that I had in mind. And so, with the French doing the work (mostly out of fear of my thunderbolt), I drove out the Bentivogli and put bishops and cardinals in charge of the town, so that all the money collected there, down to the last penny, came into the hands of the church of Rome. Besides, in the old days, all the titles and dignities of imperial rule seemed to belong to him. Now you see everywhere statues of me; my titles are inscribed everywhere, my trophies are admired; nothing to be seen but stone and bronze images of Julius.[8] Finally, if you had seen the royal procession in which I entered Bologna, you would surely despise all the triumphs celebrated by the Octavii and Scipios; you would understand that there were good reasons why I fought so hard for Bologna; and you would see that at the same time the church was fighting and triumphing alongside me.

PETER: So when you were the monarch, as I understand it, that condition had come about for which Christ ordered us to pray: "Thy kingdom come." Now tell me what the Venetians did wrong.

JULIUS: First of all, they ran after Greek fashions,[9] and they treated me almost as a joke, putting all sorts of obstacles in my way.

PETER: Were they right or wrong?

JULIUS: What does that matter? It's sacrilege even to mumble about the pope of Rome, except in the way of praise. Then they bestowed their priesthoods as they saw fit; they wouldn't allow lawsuits to be transferred to Rome; and they wouldn't allow the selling of dispensations. Do I have to go on? They inflicted unbearable damage on the authority of Rome, and took command of a significant part of your patrimony.

PETER: *My* patrimony? What patrimony are you talking about to me, who left all my possessions behind to follow, unclad, a barefoot Christ?

JULIUS: I say that various cities are the property of the Roman church, and it has pleased the most holy fathers to call by that name these their own special possessions.

PETER: Thus you use my shame to cover your own greed. And so this is what you call unbearable damage?

JULIUS: Why not?

PETER: Were their manners corrupted? Was piety growing cold?

8. Michelangelo adorned Bologna with a bronze statue of Julius, though bronze was not his usual medium. When the pope was driven out (1511), the statue was destroyed by an exultant mob.
9. Though Venetian ties with Byzantium had been close and long-standing, it's not clear what Julius refers to here; among Italian city-states, Venice was unusually independent in its relations with the papacy.

JULIUS: Forget it! you're talking about trifles. We were being deprived of thousands upon thousands of ducats, enough to furnish out a legion of soldiers.

PETER: A terrible loss for a usurer, I'm sure. And now about the duke of Ferrara, what was the matter with him?

JULIUS: What did he do, that most ungrateful of men? Alexander the vicar of Christ did this miserable rogue the honor of bestowing on him, as a wife, his second daughter, and with her he gave an enormous dowry, more than a man so base of birth could have expected.[1] Yet, indifferent to such humane treatment, he made nothing but trouble for me, accusing me of simony, pederasty, and mental instability. And besides, he held back some taxes, not the major ones, I concede, but still important enough not to be overlooked by a diligent shepherd.

GENIUS: Or a skinflint.

JULIUS: Besides, which is more to the point, Ferrara helped along the main project I had in mind to join this territory to my own because of its strategic location. At first I wanted to bestow the city on my kinsman, a man of energy who would have ventured anything in behalf of the dignity of the church. In fact, he recently killed the cardinal of Pavia with his own hands, in my behalf. As for my daughter's husband, he isn't the political sort.[2]

PETER: What's this I hear? Do popes have wives and children nowadays?

JULIUS: Proper wives they don't have; but what's so strange about their having children, since they're men and not eunuchs?

PETER: But what sort of events led to the calling of that schismatic council?

JULIUS: It's a long story, but I'll cut it short. For a long time some people have been discontented with the Roman church. They complained of the shameful money-grubbing, of monstrous and abominable lusts, of poisonings, sacrilege, murders, public sales of simoniacal positions, pollution of every description. They called me a simonist, a drunkard, a low villain swollen with earthly lusts, and on every count the man least worthy of occupying the position that in fact I occupied; they called me the greatest of all perils to the Christian community. And in this troubled state of affairs they thought help was to be sought from a general council of the church. They added that I had sworn when I was created pope to call a general council within two years, asserting that I was created pope only on that condition.

PETER: Were they right about that?

JULIUS: Absolutely. But when it suited my convenience to do so, I

---

1. The daughter of Pope Alexander VI was Lucrezia Borgia.
2. Julius's nephew Francesco Maria della Rovere did indeed stab Alidosi, cardinal of Pavia (24 May 1511), but on his own initiative, and to Julius's intense dismay. Julius's daughter Donna Felice was married to a Roman of the noble Orsini family, but neither of them took any part in the pope's wars.

absolved myself of my own oath. When a king wants to break his solemn oath, who has any doubt that he can do it? Keep your piety for another occasion, as the first Julius, my other self, used to say.[3] But only note the audacity of these men, the schemes they devised. Nine cardinals made a separation, notified me of a council to be called, and invited me to attend, even to preside. When I declined, they announced the council to the whole world in the name of the emperor Maximilian (under the pretext that years ago councils used to be called by Roman emperors) and likewise Louis of France, the twelfth of that name. What they proposed—I shudder to say it—was to rip up the seamless garment of Christ, which even those who crucified the Savior left untorn.

PETER: But were you the sort of man they said?

JULIUS: What has that got to do with it? I was pope. Suppose I was a worse rascal than the Cercopes, stupider than a wooden statue or the log from which it was made, more foul than the swamp of Lerna;[4] whoever holds this key of power must be revered as the vicar of Christ and reverenced as the holiest of men.

PETER: Even if he's openly evil?

JULIUS: As open as you like. It's just unthinkable that God's vicar on earth, who represents God himself before men, should be rebuked by any puny mortal or disturbed by any sort of popular outcry.

PETER: But common sense is outraged if we must feel warmly toward one whom we see to be evil, or speak well of one about whom we think ill.

JULIUS: Let every man think as he will, as long as he speaks well or at least holds his tongue. The pope of Rome cannot be censured by anyone, not by a general council.

PETER: This one thing I know, that Christ's vicar on earth should be as much like him as possible, and lead his life in such a way that nobody can blame any part of it, or justifiably speak evil of him. Things go badly with popes when, instead of earning men's commendations by good deeds, they extort praises with threats. Such popes cannot be praised without lying; indeed, they can't expect anything more than the sullen silence of those who hate them. Tell me now truly, is there no way at all to correct a criminal, infectious pope?

JULIUS: Absurd. Who is going to remove the highest authority of all?

PETER: That's exactly why he should be removed, because he's the highest figure; for the higher he is, the more pernicious his influence may be. If secular laws allow for a king who rules his land badly to be not only deposed but executed, why should the church be so helpless that it must put up with a pope who ruins everything, instead of expelling him as a public nuisance?[5]

---

3. Suetonius, *Life of Julius Caesar* 30.
4. The Cercopes (mentioned by Ovid, *Metamorphoses* 14) were a monkey-people famous for their malicious cunning; the wooden statue is specified in the text as Morychus, a much-ridiculed statue of Bacchus; Lerna was a foul swamp inhabited by the hydra who provided Hercules with one of his labors.
5. Because of its first clause, this entire sentence was dropped from an edition of the *Julius* printed at Oxford in 1669.

JULIUS: If the pope is to be corrected, it ought to be by a council; but against the will of the pope a council can't be called; otherwise it would be a mere convention, not a proper council. Even if it were called, it couldn't issue any decrees if the pope objected. And finally, my last defense is absolute power, of which the pope possesses more, all by himself, than an entire council. In short, the pope can't be removed from office for any crime whatever.

PETER: Not for homicide?

JULIUS: Not for parricide.

PETER: Not for fornication?

JULIUS: Ridiculous! not even for incest.

PETER: Not for the sin of simony?

JULIUS: Not for six hundred such sins.

PETER: Not for poisoning someone?

JULIUS: Not even for sacrilege.

PETER: Not for blasphemy?

JULIUS: No, I say.

PETER: Not for all these crimes poured together in a single sewer of a man?

JULIUS: Add if you like the names of six hundred other vices, each one worse than any of these, and still the pope cannot be removed from his throne for any such reasons.

PETER: This is a new doctrine about the dignity of the pope that I've picked up here; he alone, it seems, is entitled to be the worst of men. I've also learned about a new misery for the church, that she alone is unable to rid herself of such a monster, but is forced to adore a pope with a character that nobody would endure in a stable-boy.

JULIUS: Some say there is a single reason for which a pope can be removed.

PETER: What kind of good deed is that, please tell me—since he can't be removed for evil deeds, such as those I've mentioned.

JULIUS: For the crime of heresy; but only if he's been publicly convicted of it. In reality, this is just a flimsy thread of an exception, that doesn't limit papal authority by a single scintilla. The pope can always repeal the law, if it bothers him in the least. And then who would dare to accuse the pope himself, entrenched as he is behind so many lines of defense? Besides, if he were hard pressed by a council, it would be easy to save face with a recantation if a flat denial didn't dispose of the matter. Finally, there are a thousand different deceptions and evasions by which he could get away, unless he were a plain wooden stock instead of a man.

PETER: But tell me on your papal authority, who thought up such splendid laws as these?

JULIUS: Who else but the wellspring of all laws, the Roman pope? And by the same token, it's his privilege to abrogate the law, interpret it, expand it, or shrink it, just as suits his convenience.

PETER: A happy pope he must be if he can propound a law by which he can get around Christ and even a council. Though as a matter of fact, against a pope of the sort you've just described—an open criminal, a drunkard, a murderer, a simoniac, a poisoner, a perjurer, a skinflint, a man befouled in every part of his life with the most atrocious and disgusting lusts, and completely shameless about it all—I wouldn't propose a general council but a public uprising: the people should arm themselves with stones and expel such an infectious plague forever from their midst. —Tell me now, what reason you have as pope of Rome to avoid a general council?

JULIUS: You might as well ask monarchs why they hate senates and assemblies of the nobility. Because a gathering of so many excellent men casts a shadow over the royal dignity. Those who are learned gain assurance from their reading; those who answer only to a clear conscience speak their minds more freely than I like; those who have been granted dignities make use of their new authority. Among them some are always to be found who envy my glory, and approach every issue with an eye to diminishing the wealth and authority of the pope. In short, nobody sits in such assemblies who doesn't think himself entitled to put forth, under the authority of the council, something prejudicial to the pope—whom otherwise he wouldn't dare assail. Thus hardly any council concludes its work without the pope's suffering some diminution of his authority; he departs less supreme than he came. You yourself can provide an example of this, if you recall the incident; for although in those days only trifles were being discussed, not empires and kingdoms as now, nonetheless James ventured to add something to your decision. The case was that you had freed converted gentiles entirely from the Mosaic law, but James made an exception for fornication, idolatry, and crimes of blood, as if correcting your judgment.[6] Some people, if they were judging this matter today, would think the supreme authority of the church should be granted to James instead of Peter.

PETER: You think, then, that the only thing to be considered is the royal authority of the papacy rather than the welfare of the entire Christian community?

JULIUS: Every man must look to his own interests; I mind my own affairs.

PETER: But if Christ had felt this way, there would be no church for you to boast of ruling; and I still don't think it right that one who claims to be Christ's vicar on earth should follow a path different from Christ's. But tell me now, what tricks did you use to get rid of that schismatic council, as you call it?

JULIUS: I can tell you if you can follow the story. First of all I got to the emperor Maximilian (as they call him); he was the easiest to manipulate, and though he had solemnly proclaimed the council, by methods that I'd rather not describe, I got him to withdraw. Then I persuaded various cardinals in the same way that they ought to withdraw their support for the council as publicly as they had proclaimed it.

6. Acts 15.5–29.

PETER: Was that legal?

JULIUS: What isn't legal if the pope with his full authority approves it?

PETER: What! Then if he chooses to say so an oath is not an oath, since he can dissolve it whenever he wants, with regard to anyone?

JULIUS: Well, to speak frankly, this particular maneuver was a little shady, but I couldn't come up with a better one at the moment. Then when I saw that some people hostile to me were determined to have a council, and had drawn up the call so that, far from being excluded, I was humbly invited and asked to preside, see what a trick I made use of, taking a hint from my predecessors. I called a council of my own, declaring that the place and time set for the other were quite unsuitable. I called my council to meet on very short notice at Rome, where I knew nobody would come except a friend of Julius, or at least someone compliant to his wishes—it was a lesson I had taught many times over. And just to make things sure, I created a number of new cardinals with views favorable to my designs.

GENIUS: Criminal views, that is.

JULIUS: If I hadn't authorized the council, it would not have been one; yet it didn't really suit my purposes to assemble a great crowd of bishops and abbots, among whom there might conceivably be some honorable and pious men; so I decreed that in the name of economy, each district should send only one delegate, or at most two. Then when I still didn't feel quite safe enough, since there were so many districts that only a few from each would make a great number, when they were already on the way, I issued an order forbidding them to continue and putting off the council till a later date; for this I gave some trifling reason that lay to hand. Then, when I had excluded practically everybody, I called my council at Rome, anticipating the date I had set, and with nobody there except those I wanted. And even if a few were present who might disagree with me, I knew there was nobody who would dare to challenge Julius directly because I had the upper hand in both troops and weapons. And in this way I was able to bring enormous disrepute on that French council, sending out letters everywhere in which I talked about our sacrosanct council, but denounced theirs as a conventicle of Satan, a gathering of diabolic agents, a conspiracy of schismatics—and repeating these epithets over and over.

PETER: The cardinals and princes who instigated that council must have been very great rascals.

JULIUS: About their morals I never asked. The head of their group was cardinal d'Amboise of Rouen, who out of some quirk of conscience was always trying to reform the church; and so he did in a number of places. Death removed him from the arena, to my enormous gratification. His successor was cardinal Santa Croce, a Spaniard, a man of blameless life, but elderly, set in his ways, and a theologian; it's a breed of men particularly dangerous to the popes of Rome.

PETER: And did this theologian have no arguments to justify his behavior?

JULIUS: Plenty. He said the times had never been more disturbed, nor the church more afflicted with more intolerable diseases; and he called for a general council to heal them. He and his colleagues reminded me that when I was received into the papacy, I solemnly swore to call a council within two years; and the oath was so phrased that not even the college of cardinals could absolve me of it. Though I had often been reminded of it by my fellow cardinals, queried and prodded by princes, they said I would listen to anything rather than this, so that now it was apparent that during Julius's lifetime there would never be a council. They cited the examples of previous councils, and quoted various papal decrees, purporting to show that in refusing to call a council I was betraying the law itself; and with the connivance of the other princes, they declared it was the duty of the Roman emperor (who used to have sole responsibility in the matter) and the French king now to convoke a council.

PETER: No doubt they addressed you in vitriolic language?

JULIUS: No, the rascals were too smart for that; I'd have preferred some abuse. Painful though the matter was, they treated it with the utmost discretion and not only refrained from bad language but were careful to use all my titles of honor, begging and praying me by all things holy and good to behave as was worthy of me, and as I had promised, by calling a council and presiding over it, taking part with them in the work of curing the ailments of the church. I can't tell you how much hostility this gentle temper of theirs raised against me, especially since they grounded all their suggestions on holy scriptures—for apparently they had some men of learning in their camp. And meanwhile they fasted and prayed and maintained a marvelously frugal existence, to oppress me with the opinion of their holiness.

PETER: And you, on the other hand, on what grounds did you propose your council?

JULIUS: On the most magnificent grounds of all: I explained that it was my intention to reform first the head of the church, that is, myself; then all the princes of the Christian world; and finally the general population.

PETER: It sounds like a fine comedy; but what was the conclusion? I want to hear what those theologians in the assembly of Satan determined.

JULIUS: Horrible, abominable things; my mind shrinks from remembering them.

PETER: Good lord! Was it as bad as that?

JULIUS: Downright impiety, sacrilege, worse than heresy; if I hadn't opposed them tooth and nail, with every bit of my strength and craft, all the dignity of the Christian church would have gone to rack and ruin.

PETER: You make me even more eager to hear what it was.

JULIUS: Oh, I shudder to pronounce it. This is what the scoundrels were up to, that the church should be stripped of all her wealth and

all her splendor, returned to her primitive squalor and wretched frugality. That cardinals, who now outdo princes in the pomp of their
equipage, should be reduced to poverty; that bishops should live more
moderately, without retainers, and without so many horses in their
stables. They proposed that cardinals should not accumulate extra
positions, as for example bishops, abbots, and priests. Lest anybody
hold more than one bishopric, they proposed that those who by one
dodge or another, as they say, have accumulated livings by the hundred,
should be deprived of some of them, and forced to content themselves
with the income intended for a single frugal priest. They said that
nobody should be created pope or bishop or priest as a result of money
changing hands, or because of worldly favor or base flattery, but only
because of the purity of his life—which if he compromised, it would
be cause for removal. That a Roman pope convicted of flagrant crimes
might be deposed; that bishops guilty of whoredom and drunkenness
should be dismissed; that criminal priests should not only be deprived
but mutilated on some part of their body; along with many other notions
of the sort which it would weary me to recite but all tending to one
point, loading me down with religious duties and stripping me of my
wealth and power.

PETER: What was decreed in the other direction by the sacrosanct council
at Rome?

JULIUS: Now you seem to have forgotten what I told you, that I wanted
nothing out of my council except to drive out one nail with another.
After the first session had been devoted to a number of solemn ceremonies handed down from antiquity and generally acceptable, though
they had nothing to do with the matter to hand, two masses were said,
one to the holy cross and the other to the holy ghost, as if everything
was to be done in his name; and then there was a long oration full of
my praises. At the next session I turned the worst threats of my thunderbolt against those cardinals, declaring that whatever they had said
or would say in the future was worse than impiety, more vicious than
sacrilege, viler than heresy. In the third session I threatened France
with the same thunderbolt, transferring the trade fairs out of Lyons
and making an exception for certain parts of France, which I named,
in order to alienate the affections of the people from their king, and
stir up seditions among them.[7] And to give extra authority to all these
deeds, I issued a bull which I addressed to all the princes, especially
those who seemed inclined to favor me.

PETER: And that was all you accomplished?

JULIUS: I got what I wanted. I won out, at least if my decrees hold up.
In public ceremonies I deprived of their offices the three cardinals
who remained obstinate, conferring their posts on others in such a
way that they could not easily be restored. Their persons I consigned

---

7. By the pragmatic sanction of Bourges (1438), Charles VII regulated the legal and commercial status
of Italian merchants in France. That was what Julius altered.

to Satan, though if they'd fallen in my hands I'd have been glad to consign them to the flames.

PETER: But if what you say is right, the decrees of that schismatic assembly seem to me a good deal more holy than those of your sacrosanct council. I don't see that you produced anything but tyrannical threats, curses, and cruelty combined with cunning. If Satan inspired that other assembly, he seems closer to Christ than the spirit, for whom I don't even have a name, who presided over your council.

JULIUS: Watch your step now; for in all my bulls I cursed thoroughly anyone who in any way favored that assembly.

PETER: Wretch, in whom I seem to see old Julius born again! But what was the outcome of this business?

JULIUS: I left it in the state I described; how it will come out is up to the future.

PETER: So the schism survives?

JULIUS: It survives, and grows every day more dangerous.

PETER: And you as the vicar of Christ preferred a schism before a genuine council?

JULIUS: Three hundred schisms rather than find myself forced into submission and a reformation of my entire life.

PETER: So you're as guilty as that?

JULIUS: What's that to you?

PETER: I understand; you couldn't face the draining of that pestilential swamp. But which of the two groups do you think will win out?

JULIUS: As I said, it's in the hands of fortune, though we have more money. France is exhausted by her many long drawn-out wars; the English have mountains of gold still untouched. This I can confidently predict: if the French win (which God forbid), all the names will be turned around. My sacrosanct council will be an assembly of Satan; I will be, not a pope, but the idol of a pope; they will have acted on the impulse of the holy ghost, and everything we did will bear the mark of the devil. But I feel confident that the money I left behind will keep that from happening.

PETER: But what inspired this hatred of the French and their king, on whom your predecessors bestowed the title of the Most Christian King?[8] Especially since you admit you lived under their protection for a long time, and after they helped raise you to this more than imperial throne, you received from them Bologna and other cities—and since, finally, with their help you dominated the previously unbeaten Venetians? How did you wipe out the memory of such recent assistance, and break such firm bonds?

JULIUS: It would take a long story to explain the whole thing; but to put it briefly, the change wasn't an abrupt one; what I had been maturing

8. French kings since Louis XI (1472) have been known as "Most Christian Kings," often with about as much justice as English monarchs since Henry VIII (1521) have been known as "Defenders of the Faith."

in my mind for a long time I gradually began to put into effect. At first, things standing as they did, I had to dissimulate, then I came out openly. I never really liked the French, I tell you this from my heart, nor does any Italian actually like the barbarians—any more, for God's sake, than a wolf is fond of lambs. But I'm not just an Italian, I'm from Genoa;[9] I treated them like friends as long as I needed their help, in the way one always takes advantage of barbarians. In the process, I put up with a good deal, I concealed my feelings, I did plenty of pretending. I endured a lot; I achieved a lot. But then when things had reached the stage where I wanted them, I had only to act the role of the real Julius and drive that barbarian trash out of Italy.

PETER: What kind of animals are those you call barbarians?

JULIUS: They are men.

PETER: Men, then, but not Christians?

JULIUS: Yes, Christians too, but what does that matter?

PETER: Christians, then, but without laws or letters, leading a rude, uncultured life?

JULIUS: In some respects they're quite civilized; and besides, which is the thing we principally envy them, they are very rich.

PETER: Why then this name of barbarian? What's that you're grumbling?

GENIUS: Let me speak for him. The Italians when they were overwhelmed and completely submerged under a flood of really barbaric nations, as if from an overflowing sewer, picked up this mannerism from classical literature of calling everyone born outside Italy a barbarian; this epithet is more scornful, as they use it, than if they called someone a parricide or accused him of robbing a church.

PETER: So it seems. But since Christ died for all men, and showed no respect of persons; and since you claim to be Christ's vicar on earth; why don't you accept all men in the same spirit, seeing that Christ himself did not discriminate?

JULIUS: I would be delighted to accept everyone—Indians, Africans, Ethiopians, Greeks—as long as they can count money and pay taxes. But we were right to cut them all off, and especially the Greeks, because they are too stubborn in refusing to recognize the authority of the Roman pope.

PETER: So the court of Rome is to be, as it were, the treasure chest of the whole world?

JULIUS: Is it such a great matter if we collect all their carnal wealth, seeing we spread our spiritual gifts far and wide?

PETER: What spiritual gifts are you talking about? Up to now I've heard only about worldly things. No doubt you attract men to Christ by preaching his holy word?

---

9. Citizens of Genoa, a Ligurian city not far from the French border, presumably had particular reasons for disliking the French.

JULIUS: There are people who preach it, and I don't prevent them, as long as they don't in any way question my authority.

PETER: What then?

JULIUS: What then? Why are kings given whatever they demand except that individuals attribute to them whatever they have as if it were their gift even though in reality the monarchs have contributed nothing at all? In the same way, everything that's holy is imputed to us popes, even if we've done nothing but snore our life away. But we do more: we give extensive indulgences for very small sums of money; in more serious cases we provide dispensations for less than the maximum price; and wherever we go, we bless everyone, and for free.

PETER: I don't understand a word of this. But let's go back to our former subject: why does your most holy majesty hate the barbarians so much that you'll move heaven and earth to drive them out of Italy?

JULIUS: I'll tell you: there's a superstitious streak runs through the whole lot of these barbarians, especially the French; for I don't get along badly with the Spanish, whether you consider their language or their manners; though in fact I had to drive them out too in order to be free to act in my own independent way.

PETER: Apart from Christ, do they have any other gods?

JULIUS: No, the trouble is they worship Christ himself too precisely. You wouldn't believe how seriously these foolish people take certain obsolete, antiquated phrases.

PETER: Magic formulas?

JULIUS: You're joking. No, words like "simony," "blasphemy," "sodomy," "poisoning," "fortune-telling."

PETER: Fine words, indeed!

JULIUS: Just as you abominate them, so do they.

PETER: Never mind the names; the things themselves are found in your part of the world, aren't they? or are they perhaps common to all Christians?

JULIUS: I daresay the barbarians have vices of their own, but different from ours; they denounce ours and indulge their own, while we in turn flatter our own and despise theirs. We consider poverty a horrible crime to be avoided by any possible means; they seem to think it's barely Christian to enjoy your own money, even if it was innocently acquired. We hardly dare to speak of drunkenness (though in this particular I might not differ with them very sharply if on other matters we saw eye to eye); but the Germans consider it a minor and rather jolly error, not a crime. They hate usury; we consider money-lenders, of all men, most useful to the church of Christ. They view pederasty as such a disgraceful act that if someone even mentions it, you would think the atmosphere and the sun itself had been polluted; we look at it otherwise. Likewise with simony, a word long since completely antiquated and dropped from the common vocabulary; they still fear the very shadow of it and cling furiously to the outmoded laws made against it—not so with us. And there are many other matters of this sort in which we don't agree with the barbarians. Since we're so different in our manners of life, they have to be kept away from the mysteries of our business, which they will respect more if they don't understand them. For if once they knew all the inner workings of my court, they would spread the story abroad and noise about all the vices they would be quick to uncover. Already they write bitter and malignant letters to their people at home; they cry abroad that this is not the seat of Christ but the cesspool of Satan; they argue over me, asking whether, since I got the papacy as I did and live as I do, I should be considered a pope at all. In this way they threaten my reputation for holiness as well as my papal authority among the common folk, who formerly knew nothing about me, except that I was Christ's vicar and wielded power next to that of God himself. And from these events rise intolerable difficulties for the church of Christ: we sell fewer dispensations and get less for them; our revenues from bishoprics and priesthoods diminish; if we demand anything from the people, it's given only grudgingly; our revenues are off, our business ventures are losing money; people even care less and less about the terrible menace of my thunderbolt. If things once reach the point where they say I'm a scoundrel of a pope who does nothing and only pretends to wield a make-believe thunderbolt, then outright hunger will be staring me in the face. Now if they were at a safe distance (for barbarians aren't very smart), they would worship more zealously, and I could rule over them as I choose by written directives.

PETER: Things can't be going well with you if the apostolic authority depends only on their ignorance of your sly tricks and your way of life. In my day we wanted people to know all about us, whatever we did, even in our cells; we thought we would become many by becoming well known. But explain this to me, are the princes of the world so religious nowadays, and so respectful of priests, that at the beck of a single one—especially such a one as yourself—they will all at once plunge into war? For in my time we considered princes our most bitter enemies.

JULIUS: As far as the character of their life is concerned, they are not much like believing Christians. They openly despise us and consider us buffoons, except for a few of the weaker ones who may be a bit afraid of that terrible thunderbolt of excommunication—and even they are more upset by the publicity about it than by the thing itself. There are some princes who hope to share in our wealth or are afraid of it, and for those reasons they may defer to our authority; we've persuaded them, in addition, that some horrible misfortune awaits those who meddle in our priestly business. Almost all of them, having been thoroughly indoctrinated, feel respect for the rituals, especially as we observe them; for ceremonies are given to people as fairy stories are told to children. Meanwhile, the show goes on. Even if they are rascals, we bestow splendid titles on them, calling them "catholic," "your most serene highness," "most illustrious majesty," and "most worshipful monarch"; we also call them all our "beloved sons." Meanwhile in their letters they refer to us as "most holy father," and sometimes abase themselves so far as to kiss our feet; and when some really trivial question comes up, they go through the form of submitting to our authority, which gives them a great name for piety among the masses. We send them consecrated roses, crowns, swords; they in turn send us horses, soldiers, money, and sometimes boys; thus a pair of mules scratch each other, turn and turn about.

PETER: If that's the sort of men they are, I understand even less how you can incite such powerful kings to terrible wars and to the breaking of all their treaties.

JULIUS: If you can follow what I tell you, you'll pick up some better than apostolic wisdom.

PETER: I'll do the best I can.

JULIUS: The first thing I undertook to do was to acquaint myself with all the peoples and especially their princes—to know their minds, manners, emotions, their wealth and their ambitions, as well as who got along with whom, and who was at odds with whom. All this information was to be used for my own advantage. Then I found it easy to stir up the French against the Venetians because there was an ancient, ingrained hostility between the two parties. I knew the French were eager to expand their power, and the Venetians were occupying some of their towns, so I made the French cause my own. Then the Emperor, though otherwise no great friend of the French, saw he had no other hope of getting back from the Venetians what they held of his (and they held a number of fine cities); so he too made an alliance with the French for the time being. Then when I saw that the French were growing in power more than suited me (for the alliance had succeeded better than I wanted it to), I began to stir up the king of Spain against them. He was not all that strict about keeping his promises,[1] and he had a great interest in holding down the power of the French because he did not want to be barricaded out of his possessions at Naples. Then I pretended to take the Venetians back into favor, though I really didn't like or trust them, so that, playing on their grief over loss of the recent battle,[2] I could rouse them against the French. Next I took the Emperor, whom I'd recently joined with the French, and detached him from them. A major argument with him was money, which always works wonders with a man who needs it; I also sent letters and envoys to renew his ancient hatred of the French, which was always on the point of flaring up, even when he had no real chance to get at them.

     I knew the English at this time really hated the French, who were in close alliance with the Scots. They were a nation, as I well knew,

1. Toward the end of his long and eventful life, Ferdinand of Spain boasted that he had deceived Louis XII of France twelve times hand running.
2. The battle of Agnadello, 14 May 1509, was a catastrophe for Venice; in one day she lost possessions that she had been more than one hundred years accumulating. The "Emperor" in this gleeful story is the German Emperor, Maximilian.

of exceptional ferocity, eager for war and especially avid for loot—rather given to superstition as well, because far removed from Rome. Finally, they were enjoying at the moment a new liberty, resulting from the recent death of an old and very severe king.[3] Exuberant and almost riotous at their sudden release, they could easily be directed into any insane venture lying to hand—which was my dearest wish. My chances were improved by the temper of the new king, a young man little more than a boy, newly come to power, sharp, bold, and, like most young men, restless, even belligerent; he was naturally ambitious, and had been trained up to great deeds. From earliest youth he was said to have been planning an attack on the French; besides which, his marriage made him a kinsman of the king of Spain whom at that very moment I was inciting to war.

All these circumstances I turned to the advantage of the church, and by a great number of artfully composed letters managed to embroil all the princes in the most furious wars conceivable. I did my best not to leave anyone out, trying to involve the king of Hungary, the king of Portugal, and the duke of Burgundy, who is the equal of many monarchs. But since they had no particular interest in the war, I couldn't get them in. I knew that in any case, with those I already had involved, there would be no peace for anyone else. The combatants, though they really fought for their own interests, accepted distinguished awards and titles from me, as if the more death and destruction they visited on Christian folk, the more they might seem to be defending devotedly the church of God.

And so that you may appreciate the full extent of my luck or skill, I will tell you that though the king of Spain was warring at the time on the Turks,[4] and had enjoyed hitherto enormous success and taken lots of loot, I got him to abandon that enterprise and turn all his forces against the French. The Emperor too was bound to France by many treaties and even more by the enormous assistance he had received from them in regaining his possessions and cities in Italy. And he had major problems in Italy, because Padua had deserted to Venice—as well as in Burgundy, where the Gelderlanders had proved dangerous enemies of his grandson, then duke of Burgundy,[5] in a war he himself had provoked. And yet I arranged that he should neglect his own affairs in order to do my business.

Then, there is no people among whom papal authority counts for less than the English (that will be clear to anyone who looks over the life of Thomas archbishop of Canterbury[6] and the ancient constitu-

3. Henry VII; his son, the young king, is obviously Henry VIII.

4. In fact Ferdinand had been proceeding against Moorish pirates on the coast of North Africa—Mohammedans, indeed, but not "Turks." Erasmus uses the term loosely.

5. This was the future Holy Roman Emperor, Charles V. Gelderland, a small district of northern Holland, was a former duchy of the empire with inconveniently long-lived sentiments of independence.

6. Thomas à Beckett, archbishop of Canterbury, was murdered in 1170 for opposing the wishes of Henry II. After 350 years this event was still good evidence of the English character.

tions of the kingdom); yet that nation, though otherwise most impatient of impositions, almost allowed itself to be skinned alive by me. It's practically a miracle the way I got the priests, who used to skim off for themselves whatever they could, to bring in taxes to the king, without ever thinking of the precedent they were setting for future royal exactions—though indeed the king himself never noticed the example he was setting for action against his own and his successors' interests whenever the pope in Rome might become impatient with England.[7] In fact, the young king went at the matter with more energy than I wanted or advised, even though I thought he was erring in the right direction. But it would be a long story to explain in detail how artfully I stirred up these various princes to make war on their fellow Christians, when no previous pope had ever even been able to rouse them against the Turks.

PETER: But it may be that the flames of war that you fanned will spread out of control across the entire world.

JULIUS: Let them spread, as long as the Roman church retains its dignities and prerogatives. Actually, I've tried to let the whole weight of the war fall on the barbarians rather than the Italians; let them fight it out as long as they want, we'll stand by, and perhaps applaud their idiocy.

PETER: And is this the proper attitude of a pastor, a most holy father, a vicar of Christ?

JULIUS: Why did they stir up the schism?

PETER: But some evils must simply be endured if the remedy is worse. Besides, if you had permitted a council, there would have been no occasion for a schism.

JULIUS: Don't be silly! I'd sooner have six hundred wars than one council. What if they had removed me from the papacy as a simoniac and a buyer of the papal office, not a true pope at all? What if they learned the whole truth about my life, and made it public information?

PETER: Even if you were a true pope, you would have done better to resign the office than to protect your dignity by spreading such evils across the face of the Christian world. It's even worse when the office has been bestowed on an unworthy person, or not even bestowed but bought and snatched away by force. And it occurs to me that God in his wisdom may have created you as a plague for the French in retribution for their having raised you up to be a plague for the church.

JULIUS: By my triple crown, and by my heroic triumphs, I swear if you stir my anger, you, even you, will feel the wrath of Julius.

PETER: Oh, madman! So far I have heard nothing but the words of a warlord, not a churchman but a worldling, not a mere worldling but

7. Julius seems to be referring to the tax known as "Peter's pence." Henry VIII was a man of strong enthusiasms, and (before the troubles over his divorce) almost too loyal a son of the church. Thomas More tried unsuccessfully to tone down passages in Henry's defense of the church against Luther that undermined the position of the monarchy.

a pagan, and a scoundrel lower than any pagan! You boast of having dissolved treaties, stirred up wars, and encouraged the slaughter of men. That is the power of Satan, not a pope. Anyone who becomes the vicar of Christ should try to follow as closely as possible the example provided by Christ. In him the ultimate power coincided with ultimate goodness; his wisdom was supreme, but of the utmost simplicity. In you I see an image of power joined with the ultimate in malice and the ultimate in stupidity. If the devil, that prince of darkness, wanted to send to earth a vicar of hell, whom would he choose but someone like you? In what way did you ever act like an apostolic person?

JULIUS: What could be more apostolic than strengthening the church of Christ?

PETER: But if the church is the flock of Christian believers held together by the spirit of Christ, then you seem to me to have subverted the church by inciting the entire world to bloody wars, while you yourself remained wicked, noisome, and unpunished.

JULIUS: I think the church consists of the holy buildings, the priests, and especially the court at Rome, myself most of all, who am the head of the church.

PETER: But Christ made us servants and himself the head, unless you think a second head is needed. But in what way has the church been strengthened?

JULIUS: Now you're getting to the core of the matter, so I'll tell you. That hungry, impoverished church of yours is now adorned with a thousand impressive ornaments.

PETER: Such as? An earnest faith?

JULIUS: More of your jokes.

PETER: Holy doctrine?

JULIUS: Don't play dumb.

PETER: Contempt for the things of this world?

JULIUS: Let me tell you: real ornaments are what I mean. Those things you've mentioned are just words.

PETER: What do you mean then?

JULIUS: Regal palaces, spirited horses and fine mules, crowds of servants, well-trained troops, asiduous retainers—

GENIUS: —high-class whores and oily pimps—

JULIUS: —plenty of gold, purple, and so much money in taxes that there's not a king in the world who wouldn't appear base and poor if his wealth and state were compared with those of the Roman pontiff. Nobody is so ambitious that he wouldn't confess himself outdone, nobody so extravagant that he wouldn't condemn his own frugality, nobody so wealthy, not even a usurer, that he wouldn't envy my riches. These are what I call ornaments; I've protected what I inherited and added to them.

PETER: But tell me who first of all befouled and burdened with these ornaments of yours the church that Christ wanted to be supremely pure and unencumbered?

JULIUS: What does that matter? The main thing is that I've got them, I
    possess them, I enjoy them. Some people do say that a certain Con-
    stantine transferred all the riches of his empire to pope Sylvester—
    armor, horses, chariots, helmets, belts, cloaks, guardsmen, swords,
    gold crowns (of the very finest gold), armies, machines of war, cities,
    entire kingdoms.[8]

PETER: Are there any proper records of this magnificent donation?

JULIUS: None, except one codicil mixed in with some old decrees.

PETER: Maybe it's a fable.

JULIUS: I've often suspected as much. What sane man, after all, would
    bestow such a magnificent gift even on his own father? But still, it's a
    very pleasant thing to believe, and when anyone has tried to question
    it, I've been able to silence him completely with a timely threat or
    two.

PETER: And still I hear nothing from you but worldly concerns.

JULIUS: Evidently you are dreaming on about the old church in which
    you, with a couple of hungry bishops, acted out the role of a meager
    pope afflicted with poverty, labor, danger, and a thousand other trou-
    bles. The new age has changed all that for the better. Nowadays the
    high pontiff of Rome is another creature altogether; you were a pope
    in name only. What if you could now see all the holy churches dec-
    orated with the wealth of kingdoms, the thousands of priests every-
    where, many of them with splendid incomes, all the bishops equal in
    wealth and military power to so many kings, all the splendid episcopal
    palaces? If we were at Rome now, you couldn't fail to admire all the
    cardinals in their purple robes, attended by legions of servants, fol-
    lowed by riders on imperial horses and mules glittering with linen
    caparisons studded with gold and gems, shod with gold and silver
    shoes, like so many blazing suns. Then you might see the pope him-
    self born aloft on the shoulders of his guards, seated on his golden
    throne, and blessing as he passes all the adoring faithful. If you then
    heard the crash of the cannon, the applause of the people and their
    acclamations, if you could see the splendor of the massed torches,
    and the highest princes barely allowed to kiss the holy feet, if you saw
    the supreme pontiff of Rome placing a golden crown on the head of
    the Roman emperor who is king of all kings (that is, if written words
    carry any weight, though in reality he carries nothing but the shadow
    of a great name)—well, I say, if you heard and saw all this, what
    would you think?

PETER: That I had seen the worst tyranny in the world, the enemy of
    Christ, and the church's bane.

JULIUS: You would think very differently if you had seen just one of my
    triumphs, either the one that I celebrated at Bologna, or that which I
    held at Rome after subduing the Venetians, or that in which, fleeing

---

8. Lorenzo Valla proved in 1440 that the *Donation of Constantine* was a forgery; but his book was not
published till 1517, and the demonstration was not accepted as authoritative till many years later.

from Bologna, I returned to Rome; or the latest one, celebrating the defeat of the French, after almost all hope was gone, at Ravenna.[9] If you could see the long lines of steeds and stallions, the files of armed soldiers, the gaudy uniforms of the commanders, the choirs of specially chosen boys, the gleaming insignia, the wagon-loads of booty, the splendor of the bishops, the magnificence of the cardinals, the trophies, the piles of prize-money, the cheers of the people and the soldiers echoing up to the heavens, if you could hear the roars and thunders of applause, the blast of horns, the thunder of trumpets, the roar of cannon, and then if you could see me carried aloft like a very god, scattering coins among the people, the center and creator of all this splendor, then you would say the Scipios, Aemilii, and Augusti were shoddy, parsimonious fellows compared to me.[1]

PETER: Oh, enough of your triumphs, you braggart soldier! You surpass in hatefulness even those pagans—you who, while claiming to be the most holy father in Christ, have caused thousands of Christian soldiers to be killed for your own personal advantage, who have created only new legions of the dead, and who never by words or deeds brought one single soul to Christ! By the bowels of the Father! Oh you worthy vicar of that Christ who sacrificed himself for the good of all mankind! You, to preserve your own accursed skin, have driven to their deaths entire populations!

JULIUS: That's what you say because you are envious of my glory, when you see how puny your career as a bishop was, when compared with mine.

PETER: Have you the audacity, you scoundrel, to compare your glory with mine—though in fact my glory is the glory of Christ, not my own? First, if you concede that Christ was the best and true prince of the church, then it was he who gave me the keys of the kingdom, he told me to care for his flock, he approved of my faith by granting me his authority.[2] What made you pope was money in the first place, then flattery, and finally fraud—if in fact you should bear the title of pope at all. I gained thousands of souls for Christ; you drew just as many to death and hell. I first taught pagan Rome the lesson of Christ; you made yourself master of a kind of pseudo-Christian paganism. I with the mere shadow of my body healed the sick, exorcised the diabolically afflicted, recalled the dead to life, and wherever I went left my blessing on everything. What does that have in common with your triumphs? By a single word I could give over to Satan anyone I chose; and what I could do Saphira and her husband found out.[3] Yet what power I had I exercised for the good of all; you were not only

---

9. See above, p. 148, n. 7.

1. The two Scipios who conquered in Africa enjoyed tremendous triumphs in Rome; Plutarch describes in his life of Aemilius Paulus an immense triumph after the general's return from the east; while Octavius (Augustus) celebrated no fewer than five different triumphs.

2. Matthew 16.19; John 21.17; Matthew 16.16–17.

3. For withholding moneys promised to the church, Saphira and her husband, Ananias, were struck dead; Acts 5.1–10.

useless to everyone, but you used what power you had (and where didn't you have it?) to harm people throughout the world.

JULIUS: I'm surprised that when you list your achievements you don't include poverty, wakeful nights, heavy labor, criminal courts, prisons, chains, abuse, stripes, and last of all the cross.

PETER: You're right, and I'm glad you reminded me; for I've more reason to be proud of those sufferings than of miracles. It was in the name of these things that Christ told us to rejoice and be exceeding glad;[4] in the name of these he called us blessed. So Paul, my former fellow-apostle, when he prides himself on his achievements, has nothing to say of cities captured by armed force, or legions cut to pieces with cold steel, princes incited to war, or celebrations worthy of an autocrat; nothing but shipwrecks, chains, lashings, dangers, acts of betrayal.[5] There is the really apostolic triumph, that is the glory of the Christian leader. Let him boast of those whom he saved from sin, not of how many thousands of ducats he piled up. Then when we celebrate our perpetual triumph with Christ, even evildoers will join in our praise; but nobody will fail to curse you, except perhaps someone just like you or your flatterer.

JULIUS: What you say is unheard-of; I never heard the like.

PETER: I believe it; for when did you ever take time to read the gospels or to study the epistles of Paul and myself—busy as you were with so many delegations, treaties, schemes, expeditions, and celebrations? Even the other arts call for a spirit empty of sordid concerns; but the discipline of Christ requires a heart completely purged of any sort of earthly interest. For a teacher like the one we revere does not come down from heaven to give men any sort of facile or vulgar philosophy. Being a Christian is no lazy or comfortable profession. All the pleasures must be avoided like poison, riches trodden underfoot like dirt, and life itself treated as valueless; this is the profession of a Christian man. This sort of life, because it seems unbearable to those who do not act in the spirit of Christ, is easily reduced to a few idle words and empty ceremonies; and thus to a fraudulent head of Christ men add a fraudulent body.

JULIUS: What's left of me that's any good at all if you take away my money, strip me of my power, deprive me of my usury, forbid my pleasures, and even destroy my life?

PETER: You might as well say Christ was wretched when he, who had been at the peak of all things, was made a mockery before men. In poverty and painful labor, in fasts and deprivation he passed his entire life, and then died the most shameful of deaths.

JULIUS: He may find people to praise his example, but not to follow it, not in these days anyway.

PETER: But to praise him is really to imitate him.[6] Though Christ doesn't deprive his followers of all good things, in place of false goods he

---

4. Matthew 5.11–12; Matthew 5.3–11.
5. 2 Corinthians 11.23 ff.

6. Erasmus may have had in mind here the famous book of Thomas à Kempis. *The Imitation of Christ.*

provides them with true and eternal goods. But he does not enrich anyone who has not first renounced and rejected all the good things of this world. As he himself was altogether heavenly, so he wanted his body, that is, the church, to be exactly like him, pure from the contagions of mundane life. Otherwise, how could anyone be united with him if he were still contaminated with the filth of earthly existence? But when the church has got rid of all the pleasures of this world, and, what is more, of all secret hankerings after them, then Christ will reveal his true riches, exchanging heavenly joys for earthly ones (too often plentifully mixed with bitter flavors) and in place of lost riches substituting riches of another, far better, sort.

JULIUS: What are those, may I ask?

PETER: You shouldn't think the gift of prophecy, the gift of wisdom, and the gift of miracles are like any form of vulgar riches; you shouldn't suppose Christ himself is some common commodity that you can possess entirely and in him possess everything; and you shouldn't think that we here live a meager life. The more anyone is afflicted in the world below, the more delight does he feel in Christ; the poorer he is in the world, the richer in Christ; the more lowly in the world, the more exalted and honorable in Christ; the less he lives in the world, the more he lives in Christ. As he wished his entire body to be of the utmost purity, so he placed special importance on his ministers, that is, the bishops; and among these, the loftier anyone's position, the more closely he should resemble Christ in being completely free of and unencumbered by any worldly considerations. Now here, on the other hand, I see one who wants to be thought close to, and almost on a par with, Christ, yet who is immersed in all the dirty business he can find, in accumulating money, displays of wealth, possessions of every sort, wars, treaties, and private vices I won't even try to describe. And though you are utterly alien to Christ, you abuse the titles of Christ to serve your own pride. Hiding behind him who despised the rule of the world, you act the tyrant; and though really the enemy of Christ, usurp for yourself the honor due to him. While blessing others, you are accursed yourself; you open to others the gates of heaven, yet cannot get yourself admitted; as you consecrate, you are execrated; you excommunicate when you yourself are out of all communion with the sacred. What after all is the difference between you and the leader of the Turks, except that you pretend to use the name of Christ? You have the same sort of mind, you lead the same sordid lives; you are a worse misfortune for the church even than he.

JULIUS: I wanted to see the church adorned with every sort of good thing. But they say Aristotle distinguished three sorts of good: goods of fortune, goods of the body, and goods of the mind. I didn't want to change his order, so I began with goods of fortune, and I might have worked up to goods of the mind if untimely death hadn't called me away.[7]

7. Aristotle, *Politics* 7.1.

PETER: Untimely you call it, and you seventy years old! In any case, how could you expect to mingle fire with water?

JULIUS: But if we have to do without earthly shows, the common people won't respect us at all; as it is, they hate us almost as much as they fear us. Then the whole Christian community will go to rack and ruin when it can't defend itself against its enemies.

PETER: But if ordinary Christians recognized in you the real gifts of Christ, that is, a holy life, a sacred teaching, ardent charity, prophetic wisdom, and genuine virtue, they would look up to you as one purified from the impulses of the world; and the Christian community would expand even further if its leaders won respect from the unbelievers for the purity of their life, their contempt for pleasure, wealth, conquest, and death. As things stand, Christianity has shrunk within narrow bounds indeed, and if you look closely, even within those bounds you will find many merely nominal Christians. Let me ask you, didn't you ever consider, when you became supreme pastor of the church, how this church was born, how it grew, what sort of men gave it strength? Was this accomplished by wars, by chests full of treasure, by cavalry raids? No: by patience under suffering, by the blood of martyrs and our own, by enduring prisons and whips. You say the church has grown when all its ministers are burdened with earthly goods; you say it's been adorned when it's weighed down with worldly possessions and pleasures; you say it's being defended when the entire world is ripped apart by ferocious wars for the private gain of the priests; you say it's in flourishing estate when it's drunk on the pleasures of this world; you call it quiet when, because nobody complains about your riches, you are free to cultivate your vices; and you grant glorious titles to princes who recognize you as their teacher in the art of perpetrating shameless robberies and atrocious murders under the name of "the defense of Christ."

JULIUS: Such things as this I never heard before.

PETER: What did your preachers tell you, then?

JULIUS: I never heard anything from them but fulsome praise. They exercised their fanciest rhetoric in thundering out my glories, they compared me to Jove wielding his thunderbolt, they practically deified me, they called me the savior of the world, and a great many other things of that sort.

PETER: I'm not surprised there was nobody to give you good advice, for you yourself were the salt that had lost its savor.[8] For that is the special function of the apostles and those that follow them, to teach others the lesson of Christ, and in the purest form possible.

JULIUS: You're not going to open the gates, then?

PETER: To anyone, rather than a contagious disease like you. As far as you're concerned, we're all excommunicated anyway. But would you

---

8. The metaphor is repeatedly used by the evangelists, e.g., Matthew 5.13.

care for a word of practical advice? You have here a gang of muscle-men; you have a pile of money; you're a good builder. Go make your-self a new private paradise; but make it good and strong to keep the demons of hell from dragging you out of it.

JULIUS: I'll act in accordance with my own dignity. I'll take a couple of months to build up my forces; then we'll besiege you here, and if you don't surrender, drive you out. For I don't doubt to receive shortly, from the wars I started, fresh recruits of sixty thousand souls or more.

PETER: Oh, you hateful disease! Oh, the poor church! But tell me, Genius—for I'd rather talk with you than with this hideous monster!

GENIUS: What's your problem?

PETER: Are all the other bishops on earth like this one?

GENIUS: A good number are of this general type; but this one is, as you might say, outstanding.

PETER: Are you the one who stirred him up to such atrocious crimes?

GENIUS: I did hardly anything; he was so eager in his vices that even with wings I could hardly have followed him.

PETER: Well, I'm not surprised that we get so few candidates for admission, when monsters like this are in charge of governing the church. But perhaps the common people may be curable—or so I conjecture from the fact that because of the mere empty title of pope, they gave honor to such a filthy piece of garbage as this.

GENIUS: You've hit the nail on the head. But my master is getting under way, and has been shaking his stick at me. So farewell!

From The Colloquies

The *Colloquies* of Erasmus began as a series of model conversations, actually titled *Formulae*, illustrating the various Latin phrases appropriate to a particular social situation. Very often an interlocutor in one of these conversations would say the same thing four or five times over in slightly different words, as a way of laying out the possibilities. They were written down, not for publication, but as part of Erasmus's work as a private tutor in Paris. But the dialogue form offered dramatic as well as didactic possibilities beyond mere practice in colloquial Latin; as the number of colloquies grew, and the author found himself more at home with the form, Erasmus introduced moral and social conflicts of increasing complexity, till his dialogues became little plays or semi-dramatic essays on topics that could be thoroughly serious.

The chronology of the *Colloquies* extends over the last half of Erasmus's life. The first of them were evidently written in the last years of the fifteenth century, though they did not make their way into print till 1518, and then without Erasmus's knowledge and rather to his annoyance. But the little book proved spectacularly popular, and by 1552 Erasmus had written enough extra colloquies to practically double its size. With successive editions he continued to add to it, till in the end it contained fifty or more separate pieces. From the first, there were sporadic complaints from literal-minded readers that immoral and heretical ideas were to be found in the *Colloquies*, and they became serious when in 1526 the faculty of the Sorbonne (the University of Paris) formally voted to condemn the book. (Still later, after Erasmus's death, the *Colloquies* went onto the Index of Prohibited Books (1559), along with everything else that Erasmus ever wrote, including his translations of sacred texts and commentaries on them.) None of this disapproval prevented the spontaneous republication and widespread popularity of the dialogues. They added scenes from common life and touches of humor to the sometimes dull business of learning the Latin tongue; in lay terms, their flirtation with immoral attitudes added a fillip of interest; and for readers with little previous experience of drama and almost none of prose fiction, they opened up exciting imaginative possibilities. For Erasmus, who was one of the first men to make the printing press his pulpit, they became a major part of his ministry. He used them to teach virtue, to mock ignorance, to ridicule superstition, and—like any good teacher—to tickle his readers' risibilities while stimulating their minds.

For the two strongly religious colloquies, a few preparatory words may not be amiss. "The Religious Feast" may appear to a modern reader excessively unctuous in its piety. The lunch is fine and the country house is curious, but the conversation is not something most of us could sit through in patience. Erasmus, in portraying an ideal, overemphasized it. He wanted very much to show that ordinary men in discussing scriptural interpretation would not

be either silly or wicked. If his characters come off a bit bloodless, it's an
artistic flaw, no doubt, but a consequence of that program impressed on him
early by the Brethren of the Common Life for bringing Christian values into
intimate association with unprivileged laymen living and working in the
everyday world.

The dialogue entitled "An Inquisition into Faith," though it carefully
avoids the terms "Protestant" and "Catholic," is clearly about the differences
between those two communions. As Erasmus wrote, they were just on the
point of entering into a long, bloody, persecutory war that would spread
continent-wide and last for more than a century. Erasmus posits two intelligent, sincere spokesmen for the opposed groups and concentrates on showing how few of their differences concern matters defined by the Apostles'
Creed—that is, the fundamentals of Christianity. As always, his basic idea
is that reasonable men, talking directly to each other in good faith and without exaggerated invective, will find they're in pretty good agreement. That
the dialogue ends with the participants sitting down to a friendly lunch is no
accident; both classical and biblical sources suggested a sociable meal as an
emblem of relaxed friendship and easy, affable concord.

The Alchemy Scam

Speakers: Philecous, Lalus

PHILECOUS: What's the big deal with Lalus? I see him giggling to himself, breaking up completely every so often, then blessing himself with
the sign of the cross. I'll try to find out what tickles him. Greetings,
friend Lalus, you seem to be in a good mood.

LALUS: I'll be even happier if I can share the joke with you.

PHIL.:   Let me in on it, then.

LAL.   You know Balbinus?

PHIL.   An oldish fellow, quite respectable, and rather learned, is it?

LAL.:   The man himself; but nobody's wise twenty-four hours a day or
under all circumstances. For all his talents, and they're not to be
sneezed at, the man has this one weakness that he's cracked on the
art they call alchemy.

PHIL.:   That's not a crack, it's an epidemic disease you're talking about.

LAL.:   Whatever its title, Balbinus, though he's often been cheated by
men of this sort, really got taken to the cleaners this last time.

PHIL.:   How did it happen?

LAL.:   A certain priest came up to him, spoke to him politely, and raised
the subject in this way. "Most learned Balbinus, I don't doubt you're
surprised that a perfect stranger addresses you in public. I know you
have no time for any but the most sacred studies." Balbinus nodded;
he's extremely chary of words, and doesn't waste them.

PHIL.:   The mark of a cautious man.

LAL.:   But the other was no dummy either, and he went on: "But you'll overlook this impropriety when you know the motive that led me to it." "Tell me," says Balbinus, "but keep it short." "I'll put it to you," says the other, "as briefly as possible. You know well, most learned of men, what different fates we mortals undergo. Now I don't know whether to count myself lucky or unlucky. From one point of view I'm fortune's favorite, but from the other I couldn't be worse off." When Balbinus told him to get on with it, "I'll make it perfectly clear, most learned Balbinus," says he, "in just an instant. It's much easier for me to explain to a man who already understands this sort of business from the ground up."

PHIL.:   Sounds to me like a slick talker, not an alchemist.

LAL.:   We'll get to the alchemist bit soon enough. "Ever since I was a boy," he says, "I've been privileged to study the supreme art of all philosophy, the crown of all wisdom, the craft of alchemy." At the word "alchemy" Balbinus started involuntarily—just a twitch—then sighed and told him to hurry on with the rest. So the fellow went on. "But oh wretched me," says he, "that I happened on the wrong path." When Balbinus asked what was the wrong path, "You know very well, Excellency (for what can escape a man of your universal learning?), that there are two paths to success in this art, one called *longification*, the other *shortability*. And it was my bad luck to fall on the procedure of longification." When Balbinus asked what was the difference between the two procedures, the fellow said, "It's sheer presumption for me to talk about these matters before one who knows all about them; that's why I've approached you as a suppliant, to beg that you will take pity on me and condescend to explain to me the wonderful way of shortability. You are so skilled in the art, it will be no trouble for you to explain it to me. Don't deny this gift of God to your brother, who's perishing of grief; the Lord will reward you with gifts of infinite riches." Since there was no stopping his importunities, Balbinus had to confess that he didn't know the first thing about longification and shortability. When he asked the fellow to explain what the words meant, he said: "I know I've no right to speak in the presence of a master; still, since you ask, I'll explain. Those who have spent their entire lives on this work have been able to change the properties of matter in two ways. One is quicker but has an element of risk; the other takes longer but is more certain. Up to now, unhappily, I've been working on this second track, which is abhorrent to me, and I couldn't find anyone who would show me the other, after which my soul thirsts. Finally God inspired me to approach you, a man renowned for piety as well as learning. Given your erudition, granting my request will be easy; and your goodness will surely take pity on a brother whose whole destiny lies in your hands."

In a word, with palaver of this sort the rascal dissipated the last suspicion of fraud and made out that he knew all about the certain way. By now, Balbinus was itching with impatience. Finally, unable to restrain himself, he said: "Forget about that *shortability* business; I don't believe in it, and I doubt if I ever heard about it before. Tell me the truth now, do you understand *longification* thoroughly?" "Pshaw!" says the other; "I know every last detail of the process; I just can't stand the length of it." Balbinus asked how much time it took. "Too much," says the other; "almost an entire year. But it's really the surest method." "Don't worry," says Balbinus, "even if it takes as much as two years— as long as you're sure of your craft."

So in short they agreed the next day the project would get under way in Balbinus's house, on the understanding that the alchemist would do the work and Balbinus would put up the money. The profits would be shared equally, though the impostor in his modesty insisted that Balbinus must first get back all the sums he had advanced. Then they swore each other to secrecy as if they were to be members of a secret society. And now the coin is paid out with which the artist is to buy flasks, retorts, charcoal, and all the necessary apparatus. And our alchemist promptly spends it all—and very enjoyably—on whores, dice, and drink.

PHIL.:   That's one way of changing the properties of things, isn't it?

LAL.:   Balbinus was impatient that the work get under way at once; but the fellow said, "Don't you agree that a job well begun is half done? The great thing is to prepare the materials carefully." Finally he began to erect the furnace. Here again there was need for new gold—gold to attract more gold, so to speak. Without bait you don't catch fish, and alchemists can't make gold unless they have some to start with. Meanwhile Balbinus was all wound up in his calculations; assuming that for one ounce he would get fifteen, he was trying to figure his profit if he started with two thousand—for that was what he had decided to invest. When the alchemist had gone through his original stake, and for a month or two had pretended to be at work with bellows and charcoal, Balbinus finally asked him how it was going. First he was silent, then after being pressured he finally said, "Well, it's like all big projects, which are hard to get moving." The trouble was a mistake in buying the charcoal; it was made from oak wood, whereas pine or chestnut was called for. There went another hundred ducats, and they skipped cheerily away over the dice table.

New money, new charcoal; they went at the work harder than ever, just as in war, when troops have taken a beating they come charging back. When the furnace had operated for several more months, the golden harvest was still in the future, and not a grain of gold showed in the alembics (for the alchemist had made off with that too), another cause of their trouble was found. The glass vessels, it seems, hadn't been tempered properly. You can't make a statue of Mercury out of just any old wood; so, you can't make gold in vessels of common glass. Just because a lot of money had been spent already was a reason why they had to keep going.

PHIL.:   It's the gambler's argument. Just as if it weren't better to cut your losses than to lose everything.

LAL.:   Of course. The alchemist swore he'd never seen the like of it, but now the error had been detected, the rest would go smoothly, and the present little loss would be made up many times over. All the glass vessels were replaced, and the furnace heated up again. The alchemist now warned that the entire project would go better if some gold pieces were offered to the Virgin Mary, who, as you know, has a special cult at Paralia. After all, the art itself is sacred, and a project can hardly hope for much success without the good will of Heaven. This idea delighted Balbinus, an extremely pious man who never let a day pass without attending divine service. The alchemist undertook to deliver the holy offering—and so he did, to the nearest village, where he spent it all in the local brothel. When he came back, he announced that his best hopes had been realized, the business had come off perfectly, and the Virgin would certainly give her blessing to their endeavors.

When they had been sweating it out for several more months without a grain of gold appearing, and Balbinus showed some impatience, the alchemist declared that such a thing had never happened before in his entire professional life, and he couldn't imagine what was the cause of it. They pondered the matter deeply, and finally Balbinus was inspired to ask if the other had ever missed attending divine service, or failed to say his rosary prayers, as people call them: without these ceremonies, nothing whatever could be expected. Then the impostor cried aloud, "You've put your finger on the spot! I did forget to attend mass once or twice, and the other day after a late dinner I forgot to pay my respects to the Virgin." "Well," said Balbinus, "no wonder, then, if our project didn't succeed." The artist undertook to hear twelve holy services for the two he had missed, and for the single forgotten greeting to the Virgin, to give her ten.

Next time the prodigal alchemist ran out of money and couldn't think of an excuse to get more, he tried this trick. One evening he returned home, apparently half dead, and called in a perishing voice, "I'm a dead man, Balbinus, it's all up with me." Balbinus, stunned, asked what was the cause of such a catastrophe. "Somehow the police have got wind of what we're doing, and I expect they'll be at the door any minute, to drag me off to prison." At these words Balbinus turned deathly pale for you know in these parts it's a hanging offense to practice alchemy without a royal licence. But the other man went on: "It's not death I fear!" he cried. "Would that were all! No, I fear something worse." Asked what that could be, he said, "They'll bury me away in some dungeon, and there for the rest of my life I'll be forced to slave for my tyrants. Is there any form death could take that wouldn't be better than such an existence?"

They sat down to talk the situation out; it was a regular legal consultation. Balbinus, since he was a lawyer by trade, went over all the legal loopholes for getting out of trouble. "Can't you deny the fact?" says he. "No way," says the other, "their agents have all the evidence they need, and precedents we can't possibly escape." The law was so clear and so positive they had no hope of evading it. After they had gone over all the alternatives, and no way out appeared, the alchemist, who really needed some money in a hurry, finally said, "This is slow going, Balbinus, and all talk; we need a quick fix. I think I can hear the officers approaching right now, and they've got no good news for me." Then, when nothing occurred to Balbinus, the alchemist said, "Well, I see no way out and no way to save things; it comes down to facing death like a man. Unless perhaps this last idea may appeal to you. It's our only hope, and more useful than honest; I wouldn't consider it except under conditions of absolute necessity.

"You know," says he, "what sort of men these are likely to be—greedy for money, and easy enough to silence with a bribe. It's painful to give such scoundrels money that they'll only squander on dissipations; still, under the circumstances, I see no better alternative." Balbinus sees it the same way, and hands over thirty gold coins, the price of silence.

PHIL.: Wonderful munificence on the part of Balbinus, I'd say.

LAL.: No, in any honest business you'd sooner pull teeth from his mouth than money from his purse. Well, that's how the alchemist took care of himself. The only danger he ever ran was of not having money for his whore.

PHIL.: I'm surprised that Balbinus was so soft-headed in a matter involving so much money.

LAL.: This is the only subject on which he's soft-headed; everywhere else, he's rock-hard. —So new money is found for a rebuilt furnace, and special prayers are said to the Virgin Mary, to win her favor for the enterprise. A whole year has now gone by, while first one difficulty and then another held up the project and swelled the expense account. And now a new trouble comes up, and a ridiculous one.

PHIL.: What's that?

LAL.: The alchemist had begun a secret affair with the wife of a man at court; her husband got suspicious, and alerted some lookouts. One day he learned that the priest was visiting his wife's bedroom; he came home unannounced and began hammering at the bedroom door.

PHIL.: What was he going to do to the fellow?

LAL.: Do? Nothing very agreeable, I suppose. Either kill him or castrate him. There was the husband beating on the door and demanding that his wife open it, or he'd break it down; a tremendous uproar. How was the interloper going to get out of there? He looked around and found only one exit. Using his cloak as a rope, he climbed out that one narrow window, and lowered himself—at great risk, and with a couple of bad scrapes—down to the street, and so got away. Such stories spread quickly, as you know, and before long this one reached Balbinus, as the alchemist knew it would.

PHIL.: So there he was trapped for fair.

LAL.: No, he got out of this jam as easily as he got out of the bedroom.

You'll see what a tricky fellow he was. Balbinus didn't say anything directly, but the scowl on his face made it evident that he'd heard the general rumor. The fellow knew that in most respects Balbinus was a pious man; I might even call him superstitious. And people of that sort find it easy to condone major offenses when the perpetrator seems penitent. So one day the alchemist went out of his way to complain about the ill success of the operation; it wasn't going as well as he expected and wanted, and he couldn't imagine the reason why. That stirred up Balbinus, who otherwise might have remained silent; he wasn't, after all, a difficult man to provoke. "The trouble isn't hard to find," he said; "sin is the great obstacle to this enterprise, which should be directed by pure hands on a path of perfect purity." At these words, the con-artist fell to his knees, beat his breast, and cried in a woeful voice broken by sobs, "Balbinus, you've spoken the absolute truth; but it isn't your sins that cause the trouble, it's mine. I'm not ashamed to confess my shameful conduct before you, as I would before the holiest priest of God. I've been overcome by the weakness of the flesh, Satan drew me into his snare, and oh, to my misery, I abandoned my priestly vows to become an adulterer. But our offering to the Virgin Mary wasn't altogether in vain; I'd have perished for sure in this escapade, if she hadn't helped me. For when the husband was hammering at the door, I saw the window was too narrow for me to get out; in such desperate straits, I thought of the Virgin, I fell on my knees, I implored her that if our gift had been welcome, she would help me now. Immediately I returned to the window (for there was no time to waste), and found it had become wide enough for me to get out."

PHIL.:   And Balbinus believed that story?

LAL.:   Did he believe it! He forgave the man on the spot, and advised him earnestly not to show himself ungrateful to the blessed Virgin. Once again money was poured out for a donative, with many promises in return that from now on the business would be carried forward with pure hands.

PHIL.:   How did it all come out?

LAL.:   It's a long story, but I'll cut it short. When the fellow had toyed with Balbinus this way for a long time, and squeezed out of him a very healthy sum of money, another man learned of it who had known the rascal since he was a boy. It wasn't hard for him to guess that he was playing the same game with Balbinus that he had always been playing. So one day he paid a secret call and showed the master just what sort of artist he had in the house, warning him to kick the fellow out before he took off on his own with the contents of Balbinus's strong-box.

PHIL.:   What came of it then? No doubt Balbinus had him thrown in prison.

LAL.:   In prison? No, he gave him still more money to go on his travels, after swearing him by all the saints to keep quiet about what had happened. And I think he did wisely to handle it this way, instead of making himself the universal subject of tavern- and market-gossip. Besides, he ran the risk of having his goods confiscated. The impostor ran no risks at all. He knew about as much of the art as any donkey you'd pass in the street, and the law against swindling is not strict. Even if he was convicted of fraud, he could plead benefit of clergy, and escape the gallows; and nobody wanted to be at the expense of maintaining him in a jail cell.

PHIL.:   I'd feel sorry for Balbinus, if he hadn't enjoyed the process of his own deception.

LAL.:   Now I've got to be about my business. I have a lot of other stories for you, like this one, but some even sillier.

PHIL.:   When we have some time to kill, I'll be glad to hear them, and even add a couple of my own.

The Religious Feast

Speakers: Eusebius, Timothy, Theophilus, Chrysoglottus, Uranius, Sophronius, Eulalius, Nephelius, Theodidact

EUSEBIUS: Spring is here, the country grows green again; I'm surprised that anyone stays of his own accord in the smoky cities.

TIMOTHY: Not everyone is enchanted by blossoming flowers and greening fields, bubbling brooks and purling streams; or, if they are, there's something else that they like better. One pleasure counteracts another, as one nail drives another one out.

EUS.:   No doubt you're thinking of usurers, or of greedy merchants, who are just as bad.

TIM.:   Of those people indeed, my friend, but not just them; there are countless others, including even priests and monks, who for the sake of gain prefer to live in cities, and the more crowded the better. They follow the doctrines, not of Plato or Pythagoras, but of a certain blind beggar, who enjoyed being jostled by crowds because, he said, where there's lots of chaps, there's lots of chips.

EUS.:   Enough of your blind man and his chips; we're philosophers here.

TIM.:   Even Socrates, a philosopher himself, preferred the town to the country, because he was mostly interested in learning, and the cities contained a great deal from which he could learn.[1] No doubt in the fields there are trees and gardens, fountains and brooks which gratify the eyes, but they have nothing to say and so teach no lessons.

EUS.:   What Socrates says may be partly right if you go wandering alone in the woods. But I don't feel that even then nature is utterly mute; rather she speaks everywhere, and communicates a great deal to the contemplative man if she finds him attentive and patient. What else does this lovely face of burgeoning spring declare except that the Cre-

---

1. Plato, *Phaedrus* 2.

ator's wisdom is equal to his goodness? How many wonderful things did your Socrates teach to Phaedrus in their rural resting place, and learn from him also in return![2]

TIM.:   If people of that sort were always to hand, nothing could be more pleasant than a rural existence.

EUS.:   How would you like to try it? I have a little country house just outside town, not very grand but neat enough; would you like to join me there tomorrow for lunch?

TIM.   There's quite a few of us;[3] we may strip your larder clean.

EUS.:   It will be a very modest meal, prepared (as Horace says) from materials grown, not bought; the wine is of our own vintage and the trees practically drop melons, figs, pears, apples, and nuts into your lap, as if you were in the Fortunate Isles described by Lucian.[4] We might even get a chicken out of the poultry-yard.

TIM.:   There's no declining an invitation like that.

EUS.:   Let each one of you bring along his shadow, if he likes.[5] Since there are four of you, we'll be equal in number to the muses.

TIM.:   So be it.

EUS.:   One thing let me warn you of; everyone should bring his own condiments, since I'll furnish only the food.

TIM.:   What sort of condiments do you mean? Pepper or sugar?

EUS.:   No, something more basic and more agreeable.

TIM.   What's that?

EUS.:   A good appetite. A light meal today will provide it, tomorrow's walk will sharpen it, and you'll have a little stroll around my place too. When can I expect you?

TIM.:   We'll come about ten, before the sun gets too hot.

EUS.:   I'll have everything ready.

BOY: Master, the guests are at the gate.

EUS.:   You're right on time, and doubly welcome for coming promptly,

---

2. The *Phaedrus* dialogue is stage-set by the banks of the Ilissus, outside Athens.

3. Who is "us" in this colloquy? The four main guests of Eusebius are neither clerics nor in commerce; Timothy is said to be old, Uranius young; all or at least most are understood to be married. They bring with them four associates, referred to as "umbrae" [shadows] and sharing the same intellectual interests, but not otherwise defined. Everyone shares humanist assumptions, but it's not clear how anyone makes a living, or what relation prevails between the "umbra" and his originating "corpus"—so to speak. Doubtless Erasmus meant to leave the exact character of the group undefined—perhaps to imply that any group of thoughtful men could politely and profitably discuss scriptural questions.

4. Horace, *Epodes* 2.48; Lucian, "The True History." Note however that the rural idyll of epode 2 is revealed in the last lines to have been spoken by a gross usurer, and Lucian's "True History" is pat-

ently a joyful pack of lies.

5. "Umbra" [shadow] is an accepted Latin word for an uninvited guest who accompanies an invited one. But these "umbrae" are half-invited; they also have names made from adjectives, not nouns. They divide as follows:

Timothy has as *umbra* Sophronius or "sensible"

Theophilus has as *umbra* Eulalius the "fine speaker"

Chrysoglottus has as *umbra* the silent Theodidactus, "taught by God"

Uranius (also very silent) has as *umbra* Nephelius or "cloudy"

Eulalius is a very talky fellow; he reminds one of certain bright graduate students who have thought up flashy answers that they then attach to convenient problems. But otherwise the names of the participants don't suggest more than hazily their characters in the conversation. The muses are nine in number, and there will be one host plus eight guests.

along with your shadows, whom I'm delighted to see. I'm specially glad you come on your hour; people who arrive fashionably late are a host's abomination.

TIM.:   We came a bit early so as to have time to walk around and look at this palace of yours, which we hear is filled with wonderful things, every inch of it reflecting the owner's good taste.

EUS.:   You'll see a palace worthy of a king like myself. For me, though it's more like a little nest, it's more precious than any palace could be. And if a man reigns who lives exactly according to his heart's desire, then I'm a monarch here. But the first thing to do, I think, while the queen of the kitchen is putting together a salad and while the sun is still not too hot, is to look at the gardens.

TIM.:   There's another besides this one? For this one is so ingratiating that it seems to greet everyone and make him instantly welcome.

EUS.:   Here, then, let everyone pick a few flowers and leaves, of whatever sort he likes best, and bring them in to perfume the house. Take what you want, and don't be shy, for whatever grows here is practically public property. The door of this courtyard is never locked, except at night.

TIM.:   Here's Peter, guarding the gate.

EUS.:   I prefer him as a guardian, rather than the various Mercuries, Centaurs, and such strange creatures that other people have painted by their doorways.[6]

TIM.:   This is more suitable for a Christian.

EUS.:   He's not a silent guardian, either; he addresses the person who enters in three languages.

TIM.:   What is he saying?

EUS.:   Try reading it for yourself.

TIM.:   It's a bit too far away for me to make it out.

EUS.:   Here's a little spy-glass that will make you sharper-sighted than Lynceus.

TIM.   I see the Latin: "If thou wilt enter into life, keep the commandments."[7]

EUS.:   I can see the Greek all right, but it's Greek to me; let me give this little glass to Theophilus, who's at home in the language.

THEOPHILUS: "Repent ye therefore and be converted."[8]

CHRYSOGLOTTUS: I'll attempt the Hebrew: "The just man shall live by his faith."[9]

EUS.:   Doesn't he seem to you a very civil guardian who at the same time warns us against vices and invites us to the exercise of piety? Then he makes clear that our future life depends, not on the works of Mosaic law, but on faith in the gospels; and finally he emphasizes that the path to eternal life lies through faith alone.

6. Herms, or archaic figures of Hermes, otherwise known as Mercury, often stood by Athenian door-ways.

7. Matthew 19.17.
8. Acts 3.19.
9. Habbakuk 2.4.

TIM.: Now look through here; the path to the right leads us to a wonderful little chapel. On the altar Jesus Christ gazes toward heaven,
from which the Father and the Holy Spirit look down. With his right
hand he points upward, with his left he seems to invite forward the
passerby.

EUS.: He too is not silent. You see the Latin, which says, "I am the
way, the truth, and the life"; then in Greek, "I am the Alpha and the
Omega"; and in Hebrew, "Come ye children, harken unto me; I will
teach you the fear of the Lord."[1]

TIM.: Our Lord Jesus has certainly greeted us with glad tidings.

EUS.: But lest we seem uncivil to him, perhaps we should return his
greeting, and pray that, though we can do little or nothing ourselves,
he may out of his inestimable loving kindness preserve us from wandering off the path of salvation. May he lead us, when we have rejected
the Jewish formulas and deceits of this world, through the truth of the
gospels to eternal life; that is, may he lead us through himself to himself.

TIM.: It's only right, and the beauty of the place itself invites us to pray.

EUS.: The elegance of this garden has drawn many visitors, and they
have made it a custom that nobody passes Jesus without words of
greeting. I've placed him here, instead of that filthy Priapus,[2] to act
as guardian, not only of my garden, but of everything I possess, and
in fact of my soul as well as my body. Nearby as you see is a little
fountain bubbling over with pure water; it represents after a fashion
the unique heavenly fountain which with its pure stream refreshes all
those who are heavy laden, and for which the soul pants when worn
out by the cares of this world. Just so, according to the psalmist, does
the hart thirst after tasting the flesh of serpents.[3] Anyone who wishes
is welcome to drink of it; some people sprinkle themselves with it, and
some drink it, not from thirst, but for religion's sake.

I see that you don't want to be torn away from this spot, but time is
getting on and there's another garden to be seen; it's more cultivated
than this one, and occupies a big square area inside the walls of my
kingdom. What's to be seen inside the house you'll inspect after lunch
when the heat of the sun will force us to stay indoors for several hours,
like snails.

TIM.: Oh, wonderful! I think these must be the gardens of Epicurus
that I see.[4]

EUS.: This whole area could be called a pleasure-garden, but for honest
pleasures only, such as feasting the eyes, refreshing the nostrils, and
relaxing the mind. Nothing grows here but fragrant herbs, and not

---

1. John 14.6; Revelation 1.8; Psalms 34.11.
2. Priapus protected Greek and Roman gardens
with his enormous wooden phallus.
3. Psalms 41.2. The "flesh of serpents" phrase
appeared in early versions of the Bible, including
the Vulgate; modern editors have dropped it

entirely.
4. Epicurus, the Greek philosopher of the third
century B.C., lived and taught in a special garden
where (in line with his philosophy) he pursued an
austere and balanced pleasure.

the common varieties, but the rarest kinds only. Every variety has its own bed.

TIM.: I notice that your herbs also have something to say for themselves.

EUS.: You're right; other men may have more luxurious homes, I have a talkative one, lest I should ever feel lonely; when you've seen the whole place, you'll agree even more emphatically. As the herbs are divided into companies, so each company has its own banner with its own device. For example, this marjoram is saying, "Out of here, swine; my odor is not for you." In fact, though its fragrance is of the sweetest, hogs actively dislike it. In the same way, the other herbs have their own messages indicating something relative to the special quality of the herb.

TIM. So far I haven't seen anything more attractive than this little fountain, which seems to smile on all the herbs, and promises to keep them cool despite the summer heat. But now this little channel which spreads out the water so elegantly before our eyes, dividing the garden into equal sections, so that all the herbs can be reflected as in a mirror—is it of marble, may I ask?

EUS.: You flatter me; where would I get marble here? It's imitation marble, made of common cement, and painted white.

TIM.: Where does your little rivulet finally wind up?

EUS.: A clear case of human ingratitude. After it has refreshed our eyes here, it flows into the kitchen, after which it serves to carry refuse into the sewer.

TIM.: A perfect case of ingratitude, I agree.

EUS.: Or rather it would be, if in this trifle as well the benevolence of the deity weren't made manifest. For we are ungrateful in the same way when we take the fountain of holy scripture—a much more delightful stream than this, given us to refresh and purify our souls—only to befoul it with our vices and sordid lusts. Though we abuse in that way the inestimable gift of God, we don't really abuse this water when we use it in the various ways intended by him who provides unfailingly for human needs.

TIM.: You're exactly right. But, tell me, why are even the little fences dividing up your garden painted green?

EUS.: I don't want anything here that isn't green. Some people might prefer a spot of red by way of contrast with the green, but I like it this way. Every man to his own taste, even in the matter of gardens.

TIM.: The garden is beautiful in itself, but its beauty is almost overshadowed by the three pergolas.

EUS.: I often bring my book out here or stroll up and down, alone or with a friend; occasionally I have an open-air meal here.

TIM.: The line of columns supporting the roof, which shine with such a marvelous array of colors—surely they're marble, aren't they?

EUS.: The same sort of marble as the water channel.

TIM.: A beautiful delusion; I'd have sworn they were real marble.

EUS.: Let it be a lesson, not to judge by appearances, or swear rashly
to an impression. In this house we don't use money to achieve what
we can do with art.

(They turn to the frescoes on the walls.)

TIM.: You weren't satisfied with the elegant gardens outside, but you
had to have others, painted on the walls?

EUS.: A single garden couldn't possibly contain every variety of plant.
Besides, we get a double pleasure from seeing a painted flower in
competition with a real one; in one we admire the artifice of nature,
in the other the painter's skill, and in both the goodness of God, who
dispenses all these things for our use, and in all things is equally loving and generous. Finally, the real garden isn't always green and blossoming; this garden flourishes even in midwinter.

TIM.: But it isn't alive.

EUS.: But on the other hand, it needs no cultivation.

TIM.: It pleases only the eye.

EUS.: True; but it does so continually.

TIM.: Even a picture gets old.

EUS.: It does; but it's longer-lived than we are, and age adds to it a
beauty that it takes away from us.

TIM.: I wish I could contradict you there.

EUS.: In this gallery, which faces west, I pass the early morning hours;
in that which faces east I sometimes take the sun; and in the other,
which faces south but is also open to the north, I take refuge from
summer's heat. Let's walk over there, if you will, to see it from close
range. See, even the ground, the very paving stones, are colored and
sprinkled with painted flowers. This thicket that you see painted along
one wall provides a varied spectacle for me. First are the trees, of as
many different species as there are individuals, each one depicted with
the greatest accuracy as it occurs in the wild. Again, every bird that
you see is of a different species. I've tried especially to have here the
rarer ones and those that are somehow distinctive—there would be no
point, surely, in painting geese, hens, and ducks. Below are the various species of quadrupeds and of the birds that live on the forest floor.

TIM.: A wonderful menagerie and all lively; there's nothing that isn't
doing or saying something. What does that owl say, for example, who's
lurking under the branches and hardly visible there?

EUS.: Being an Attic owl, it speaks Greek, and says, "Use your wits; I
don't fly for just anyone."[5] In other words, he wants us to act with
good sense, since rash and thoughtless behavior often turns out badly.
Over here an eagle is devouring a rabbit while a beetle protests in
vain. Next to the beetle, a wren, bitter enemy of the eagle.

TIM.: What has the swallow got in her mouth?

---

5. Owls serve no less frequently as emblems of solemn obtuseness than as indicators of intelligence. The
explanation of Eusebius is very much called for.

EUS.:   Swallow-wort; it restores sight to her chicks, who are born blind. Don't you recognize the shape of the leaf?

TIM.:   Is this some odd sort of lizard?

EUS.:   Not a lizard at all, but a chameleon.

TIM.:   So this is the celebrated chameleon! I thought it was a beast even bigger than a lion, at least by a couple of syllables.

EUS.:   This fellow is always open-mouthed, always hungry. Nearby is a wild fig tree; in its presence he is always fierce, though peaceful otherwise. But he is poisonous; don't despise this wide-mouthed little creature.

TIM.:   But he doesn't change color.

EUS.:   True, because he doesn't change place; if he were to move, you'd see a different color.

TIM.:   What's the bagpipe player doing here?

EUS.:   Don't you see next to him a dancing camel?

TIM.:   It's a new kind of raree-show, a waltzing camel and a monkey musician.[6]

EUS.:   But you'd better save the close examination of all these details for another occasion, perhaps the full three-day tour. Let it suffice now to have given them a glance. In this next area are depicted, as accurately as possible, all the most remarkable medicinal herbs; though many of them are poisonous, you'll be surprised to know you can not only inspect them but touch them.

TIM.:   Here's a scorpion, a rare beast in these regions, though common in Italy. But I'm afraid the painter hasn't got the right color.

EUS.:   How so?

TIM.:   Because they are much blacker in Italy; this one is too pale.

EUS.:   You don't recognize the leaf on which he is resting?

TIM.:   Not really.

EUS.:   No wonder, for it doesn't grow in our local gardens. It is an aconite, and so poisonous that the scorpion touching it is stunned, grows pale, and prepares to give up the ghost. But when stricken by one poison, he seeks his remedy in another. You see right next to him several varieties of hellbore. If the scorpion could get himself off the aconite leaf and onto the white hellbore, he would get his original strength back, contact with a different poison serving to dissolve his paralysis.

TIM.:   Then it's all up with this scorpion, for he'll never get off his present leaf. I see that even the scorpions are eloquent here.

EUS.:   Yes, and in Greek too.

TIM.:   What is he saying?

EUS.:   "God will find out the guilty." In among the herbs and grasses you will uncover all sorts of serpents. Here is your basilisk with fiery eyes which themselves convey the most venomous poisons.

---

6. The waltzing camel is for Erasmus a frequent example of clumsiness on public display; but what he is doing in an otherwise serious natural history picture is not clear.

TIM.: He too has something to say.

EUS.: "Let them hate me as long as they fear me."

TIM.: A kingly sentiment indeed.[7]

EUS.: Kingly it isn't—the sentiment of a tyrant, rather. Here's a lizard at war with a viper. Here's a dipsas curled around the shell of an ostrich egg. Here you see a community of ants, whom we are advised to imitate, not only by the wise Hebrew, but by Horace.[8] Here you see the ants of India who dig up gold and hide it away.

TIM.: Good Lord, who could ever feel bored in this world of shifting scenes?

EUS.: Another time, as I said, you may look it over as much as you like. Now take a general view of the third wall. It shows lakes, rivers, and arms of the sea, containing the most noted kinds of fish. Here is the Nile, in which you see the dolphin, who is a friend to man; he is at war with the crocodile, who is man's worst enemy. Along the shores and on the banks you see the various amphibia, such as crabs, seals, and a beaver. Here's an octopus, predacious himself, but now captured by a giant shellfish.

TIM.: What's his motto? "The biter bit." The painter has made the water wonderfully clear.

EUS.: He had to, or we'd need different eyes. Next is a man-o'-war sailing cheerily across the surface of the water like a light skiff. You see a squid lying on the sand and blending with it perfectly; here you may safely touch him with your hand. But we must hurry on; these things please the eye but don't fill the stomach. We'll hurry over the rest.

TIM.: There's even more?

EUS.: You'll see now what we get to by going out the back door. Here is a fair-sized garden divided equally in two, one part for vegetables, where my wife and maidservant are in charge, the other medicinal herbs, particularly the rare ones. To the left is an open lawn, nothing but green grass surrounded by a hedge of thorns; there I sometimes stroll alone or chat with visitors. To the right is the orchard, in which, when you have time, you can inspect a great variety of exotic trees which I'm trying gradually to get used to our climate.

TIM.: I declare, you outdo Alcinous himself![9]

EUS.: Down by the wall, attached to the upper gallery which you'll see after lunch, is the aviary; many different bird-shapes to be seen, various bird-calls to be heard. Their tempers are very different too. Some recognize bonds of kinship and mutual affection; others are at open war. But they're all so tame and gentle that when I dine here with a window open, they fly in to sit on the table and take food from my hand. When I cross the arched bridge over there in conversation with

---

7. *Basileus* is the Greek word for "king"; *basilisk* means "little king."
8. Proverbs 6.6: the Horace reference is to *Satires* 1.1, 32–35. Dipsas was a deadly (but fortunately

mythical) reptile.
9. Alcinous, king of the Phaeacians in Homer's *Odyssey*; his gardens are elaborately described in books 6 and 7.

a friend, they fly up to listen, perching sometimes on my arms or shoulders. They're completely fearless, because they know nobody will harm them. At the end of the orchard is the kingdom of the bees, which furnishes a very pleasant spectacle; but for the moment I don't want you to see anything more, so that you can come back later as if to a new spectacle entirely. After lunch I'll show you the rest.

BOY: Your wife and maid complain that lunch is waiting.

EUS.: Tell them not to worry, we'll be right along. But let's wash up first, my friends, so that we may approach the table with clean hands and hearts. For if even the pagans held mealtimes in reverence, all the more so should we Christians, whom it should remind of that last supper which our Lord Jesus shared with his disciples. And for this reason washing hands is a custom by which we indicate that if our minds retain any shame or hatred, we should get rid of it before sitting down to our food. In fact, I'm convinced that food does us more good if it is eaten with a purified and tranquil mind.

TIM.: So say we all of us.

EUS.: Since Christ himself set the example of blessing the meal (for so I believe because in the gospels we often read that before breaking bread he blessed the food or gave thanks to the Father) and also of giving thanks afterward, if you agree, I'll repeat a short prayer that Saint Chrysostom praised very highly in one of his homilies and even undertook to explicate.[1]

TIM.: We beg you to do so.

EUS.: "Blessed God who hast nourished me from my youth, who supply food for all living creatures: fill our hearts with joy and gladness that, having abundance ourselves, we may abound in every good work through Christ Jesus Our Lord, to whom, with the holy spirit, be glory, honor, and dominion, world without end."

TIM.: Amen.

EUS.: Now take your seats one and all, and let everyone sit beside his own shadow. Your white hairs, Timothy, entitle you to a seat at the head of the table.

TIM.: In two words you have expressed the sum of my merits. Seniority is all I've got.

EUS.: God is the only judge of other merits; we can only go by what we see. Sophronius, you sit by your proper body.[2] You, Theophilus and Eulalius, sit along the right side of the table. Chrysoglottus and Theodidactus on the left side, Uranius and Nephelius the other two places; I'll take this corner.

TIM.: That we won't allow; as host, you should be at the top of the board.

EUS.: This whole house is mine and at the same time yours; but if I'm allowed to rule in my own kingdom, I think the host is entitled to

1. Chrysostom ("golden-mouth") of the fourth century A.D. was a famous and eloquent father of the church.

2. I.e., he is the shadow of Timothy.

whatever place he wants, Now may Christ who enlivens all men's hearts, and without whom there is no true delight, be pleased to attend our feast, and by his presence lighten our spirits.

TIM.: I hope he will be so pleased. But where will he sit now that we have taken all the places?

EUS.: I hope he will mingle with all our food and drink, so that everything tastes of him, but most of all I hope he will enter into our minds. To make ourselves worthy and better suited to receive so great a guest, I would like, with your permission, to have read a short scriptural passage, but in such a way that you can still partake of the eggs and lettuce, if you want.

TIM.: We'll eat with pleasure, but listen with even more pleasure.

EUS.: This custom seems to me commendable on many scores, because in this way we avoid asinine chatter and accumulate ideas for intelligent conversation. I have no patience with those people who don't enjoy a party unless it's full of dirty stories and loud bawdy songs. True gaiety rises from a clear, untroubled conscience; and really agreeable conversations are those which it's a pleasure to have heard or participated in, and which remain fragrant in the memory—not those that leave one feeling ashamed and secretly embarrassed.

TIM.: I hope we all take these words to heart, as their truth deserves.

EUS.: The passage I have chosen is not only clearly and certainly valuable, it is also quite cheerful when you've savored it for a while.

TIM.: Nothing is more proper than for us to get used to the very best thoughts.

EUS.: Speak out, then, loud and clear, my boy.

BOY: "The king's heart is in the hand of the Lord, as the rivers of water; he turneth it whithersoever he will. Every way of a man is right in his own eyes; but the Lord pondereth the hearts. To do justice and judgment is more acceptable to the Lord than sacrifice."[3]

EUS.: That's plenty; for it's better to learn a few things with enthusiasm than a great many things reluctantly.

TIM.: Better indeed, and not just of this book. Pliny wrote that Cicero's *Offices* should never be out of one's hands,[4] and I agree it should be carefully studied, especially by those going in for public service. And this little book of Proverbs is another that I've always thought we should never be without.

EUS.: Since I knew our meal would be bland as well as light, I provided this seasoning for it.

TIM.: There's nothing here that isn't of the best; yet if we had nothing but beets without pepper, wine, or vinegar, such a reading would give everything a savor.

EUS.: Still, I'd be better pleased if I understood more fully what I just heard. I wish we had here a good theologian who not only understood

3. Proverbs 21.1–3.
4. Pliny the elder, of the first century A.D., is best known for his *Natural History*; his remark about Cicero occurs in the preface to that book.

the text but could appreciate it. I don't know if it's proper for untrained laymen like us to discuss these matters.

TIM.: I think it would be perfectly all right for common sailors to discuss them, as long as they refrained from rash conclusions. Perhaps even Christ, who promised to be present whenever two men gathered in his name, will lend us his help, since there are so many of us.

EUS.: Then suppose we divide the three verses among the nine of us.

THE GUESTS: Agreed; only let the host lead off.

EUS.: I won't decline the post, though I'm afraid the intellectual fare I provide won't come up to the cooking. But I don't want to be a troublesome host, so here goes. Setting aside many conjectures that have been made about the passage, this seems to be its central moral sense: that other mortals may be influenced by warnings, suasion, laws, and threats; but if you oppose the king's will—since he fears nobody—you will only inflame it the more. And so whenever rulers start fighting over some matter, they should be left to themselves, not because what they want is necessarily the best, but because God sometimes makes use of their folly or malice to punish the wicked among their subjects. Thus he forbade resistance to Nebuchadnezzar, because he had determined to punish his people through the engine of that tyrant.[5] And perhaps this is what he meant in the thirty-fourth chapter of Job: "who maketh the tyrant reign for the sins of the people."[6] And the words of David are perhaps pertinent as well, when he deplores his sin in psalm fifty-one: "against thee only have I sinned and done this evil in thy sight."[7] It's not that kings don't sin against their people and do them great harm, but that no man is authorized to condemn them—though of course no man, however powerful, can escape the judgment of God.

TIM.: It's a good interpretation. But what is meant by "the rivers of water"?

EUS.: I have an analogy handy to explain it. The mind of a king, once aroused, is a violent and unrestrained force; it can't be directed here or there, but is born on by its own impetus, as if lashed by a divine frenzy. In the same way the sea spreads over the land, changing direction all the time till it has flooded fields, buildings, and obstacles of every kind; sometimes it even pushes underground. Men try vainly to stop its flow or push it in another direction. Great rivers behave the same way as we learn from the story of Achelous.[8] But you suffer less damage if you go with the flow than if you stand up to it directly.

TIM.: There's no remedy, then, for the fury of rulers?

EUS.: Perhaps the best would be, not to let the lion into the city. Next best would be to use the authority of the senate, the magistrates, and

---

5. Jeremiah 27.
6. Job 34.30. The moral emphasis in, for example, the Authorized Version, is quite different from that given here by Eusebius.
7. Psalms 51.4.

8. Achelous was a violent Greek river, which not even Hercules could easily control. The river in flood is used as a metaphor by Machiavelli, *The Prince* 25.

the people to limit his power and keep it from breaking out into a tyranny. But best of all is to train his mind in sacred teachings while he's still a boy and not yet fully aware that he's a ruler. Prayers and admonitions may also be useful, but only if they are gentle and polite. And the last resource is to implore God that he will direct the king toward conduct worthy of a Christian prince.

TIM.:   What did you mean by saying we were all "untrained laymen"? If I were a bachelor in theology I wouldn't be ashamed of such an interpretation.

EUS.:   Whether it's absolutely right I don't know; for me it's enough that the conclusion is neither impious nor heretical. But I've carried out your orders, and now, following the rule for parties, it's my turn to sit back and listen.

TIM.:   I think, if you'll make allowance for my white hairs, the passage lends itself to a deeper meaning.

EUS.:   I believe it does; I'm waiting to hear it.

TIM.:   The king may be understood as perfected man, who, having subdued all his carnal affections, answers only to the impulse of the holy spirit. Such a man is hardly to be compelled into conformity with human laws, he must be left to his master by whose spirit he is led. Neither is he to be judged by those standards which are necessary to attract the weak and silly to piety. Whatever he does that seems out of the way, we must say with Paul in Romans fourteen, "God hath received him; by his own master he stands or falls." And again, "He that is spiritual judges all things, but he himself is judged of no man."[9] Nobody prescribes laws to such a man except the Lord, who prescribed limits to the sea and the land; in his hand he holds the heart of the king, and directs it whither he chooses. What need is there to make laws for one who of his own free will does more than human laws can demand? What folly would it be to chain up in human regulations a man who can be seen by certain indications to be led by the inspiration of the holy spirit?

EUS.:   It's not just white hairs that make you venerable, Timothy, but the distinction of your mind. I only wish that among Christians, who all ought to be kings after this style, there were more worthy of the honor.

But now we've had enough of the eggs and salad; let's have the plates removed and others brought.

TIM.:   I'm well satisfied with this overture,[1] even if there's nothing else in the way of pageant or triumph to follow.

EUS.:   Yes, but since, with God's help as I believe, we have interpreted the first sentence correctly, I'd like your shadow to explain for us the next one, which seems to me a little more obscure.

SOPHRONIUS: If you'll favor me with your good will, I'll try my best to

---

9. Romans 14.3–4; 1 Corinthians 2.15.

1. The word "overture" tries to capture a pun on the Latin word for eggs, ova.

tell you how I see it. For it's quite a trick for a shadow to cast light into a dark place.

EUS.: So be it, in the name of the whole group; light from such shadows as these is doubtless best suited to our eyes.

SOPH.: This verse seems to teach the same doctrine as Paul; there are different styles of living that lead to piety. Some in the priesthood, others as bachelors, some in marriage, some in solitude, others in the buzz of business, men differ in their habits of body and mind. Again, one man eats absolutely anything, another discriminates between this food and that. One person distinguishes lucky from unlucky days, to his friend they are all the same. In such matters Paul wants everyone to follow his own feelings without interference from anyone else. Nor should anyone pass judgment on this sort of basis, but leave judgment to God, by whom our hearts are weighed. For it often happens that one who eats is more acceptable to God than one who abstains, and he who disregards a holy day pleases God better than one who pretends to observe it. This man's marriage may be preferable in the eyes of God to that man's celibacy. As a shadow, I have said my piece.

EUS.: I'd be glad to talk some more with shadows like this one. You've gone right to the heart of the matter, not with a probe, as they say, but with your tongue.—But look, here comes a fellow who has lived the celibate life, not a saintly type at all, far less one of those who castrated themselves for love of God. He was castrated, to be sure, but much against his will, to make better eating for us, and so he will, while this frame of things endures. He's a capon out of our own coop. I like boiled dishes. The sauce isn't bad; the greens in it are our best. Let every man help himself. I won't mislead you; after this comes the roast, then the dessert, and then the end of our discussion.

TIM.: But meanwhile we've excluded your wife from the feast.

EUS.: When you come with your wives, mine will be here too. But what part could she take here except that of a mute? She will be more at ease chatting with her women, and we will be more free to philosophize. Otherwise, the accident might befall us that happened to Socrates. When he was entertaining some fellow philosophers—who, as you know, would rather chatter on like this than eat—and when the discussion had run on for a while, Xanthippe in a rage turned over the entire table.[2]

TIM.: I doubt if we'd have anything of the sort to fear from your wife; she's a most mild-mannered woman.

EUS.: With me at least that's how she is. I wouldn't exchange her for any other if I could; and in this respect I consider myself particularly lucky. For I never liked the opinion of those who say the lucky man is the one who never marries. I much prefer what the wise Hebrew says, "He that hath a good wife has had good luck."[3]

2. The story of Xanthippe, Socrates' wife, is told by Plutarch, "On the Control of Anger."
3. Proverbs 18.22. Less cautiously, the Authorized Version renders the passage, "whoso findeth a wife findeth a good thing."

TIM.:   It's often our own fault if we have bad wives; either we pick that sort or we spoil them by not advising and guiding them as we should.

EUS.:   True enough; but meanwhile I'm anticipating an account of our third sentence, with which I suspect our theomantic Theophilus is thinking of obliging me.

THEOPH.:   You're quite mistaken; my mind was on my vittles. Still, I'll speak, since there's no penalty for being mistaken.

EUS.:   All the better if you're not letter-perfect; it will give us a chance to explore the topic together.

THEOPH.:   The idea seems to me the same as that which the Lord revealed in the sixth chapter of the prophet Hosea: "I desired mercy and not sacrifice, and the knowledge of God more than burnt offerings."[4] It is a doctrine vividly and forcefully interpreted by our Lord Jesus Christ in the ninth chapter of Matthew. The occasion was a dinner at the house of Levi the publican, to which the host had invited many publicans and sinners. Then the Pharisees, who gloried in their strict observance of the law—though in fact they neglected those very precepts on which the entire law depended, and the teaching of the prophets, as well—tried to turn the disciples against Jesus by asking them why their lord would sit at table with sinners. For they said all Jews who wanted to be considered holy stayed away from such people, and if they had to associate with them washed themselves all over as soon as they got home. When the untrained disciples had no answer to this challenge, the Lord answered for them and himself: "They that be whole need not a physician, but they that are sick. But go ye and learn what that meaneth: I will have mercy and not sacrifice: for I am not come to call the righteous, but sinners to repentance."[5]

EUS.:   You explain the passage admirably by relating it to parallel passages: it's an excellent method of interpreting scripture. But I'd like you to explain what is meant by "sacrifice" and what by "mercy." For how does it agree that God should here reject sacrifices when on so many other occasions he commanded that they be made to him?

THEOPH.:   The reasons for the Lord's rejection of sacrifice are explained in his own words in the first chapter of Isaiah. There are certain prescripts in the Jewish law that are presumptions, not proof, of holiness; such things are holy days, sabbaths, dietary laws, and sacrifices. Some of these things are to be observed always because their virtue lies, not in the fact that they have been commanded, but in the observance itself. God rejects the Jews, not because they observe the letter of the law, but because, swollen with pride over keeping to the letter, they neglect those larger commandments that he particularly imposes on us. They were so bloated with avarice, pride, greed, hate, envy, and other vices that they thought God himself should be grateful to them because they went to temple on holy days, offered burnt sacrifices, observed the dietary laws, and sometimes fasted. They grasped the

<hr>

4. Hosea 6.6.   5. Matthew 9.12–13. See also Matthew 12.7.

shadow and neglected the real thing. When he says "I will have mercy
and not sacrifice," I think this is an idiom of the Hebrew tongue for
"I want mercy rather than sacrifice." And this is what Solomon means
when he says, "To do justice and judgment is more acceptable to the
Lord than sacrifice."[6] For scripture uses the words "pity" and "charity" for acts that involve relieving the neighbor; the word for "charity"
derives from the word for "alms."[7] "Sacrifice" I believe is used for an
act that pertains to corporal ceremonies and has some affinity with
Judaism—for example, a special diet, a particular dress, fasting, ritual
prayers, and abstention from work on holy days. Though not completely unsuitable under certain circumstances, these observances
become hateful to God if someone relies on them to the neglect of
charity, as when the necessities of the neighbor cry out for relief. No
doubt shunning the company of the evil gives the appearance of sanctity, but this is no longer true when charity to the neighbor persuades
us otherwise. It is our duty to rest on holy days, but to let a fellow
creature perish out of respect for the day would be wicked. To keep
the sabbath day is in my opinion an act of sacrifice, but to be reconciled with one's neighbor is a work of mercy. Though it can well refer
to rulers, who do often oppress the weak, in my opinion it also agrees
not too badly with the passage in Hosea about preferring "the knowledge of God to burnt offerings." One does not observe the law if one
does not observe it according to the will of God. The Jews would
rescue an ass if it fell into a ditch on holy day; yet they abused Christ
who healed men on the sabbath.[8] This was a ridiculous judgment, far
removed from the knowledge of God; they did not realize the law was
instituted for man's sake, not *vice versa*. But you may think I'm talking
out of line here if it weren't that I'm speaking under your orders.

EUS.:   You're so far from being "out of line" that I would think the Lord
Jesus was speaking through your mouth.—But while we're generously
feeding our minds, let's not neglect their partners.

THEOPH.:   What are they?

EUS.:   Our bodies; they're partners of our minds, aren't they? I prefer
that term to calling them "instruments" or "houses" or "tombs" of our
minds.

TIM.:   This is real refreshment when the whole man is nourished at
once.

EUS.:   I see you're slow to help yourselves, so with your approval I'll
have the roast served round, lest instead of a tasty meal I give you a
tedious one. Here comes the main course of our meal; it's a small but
tasty leg of lamb, a capon, and four partridges. Those I got at the
market, but everything else comes from the estate.

TIM.:   What I see is an Epicurean, or even a Sybaritic meal.

---

6. Proverbs 21.3.   word *elemnon*, pitiful.
7. Charity, *eleemosyna*, derives from the Greek   8. Matthew 12.11–12.

EUS.: Barely a Carmelite one, I'd say.[9] But such as it is, take it for the best. Warm hearts and modest fare.

TIM.: Your house isn't silent, either; not only the walls talk, but the cup here has something to say.

EUS.: What has it said to you?

TIM.: "Nobody is harmed except by himself."

EUS.: The cup is preaching in behalf of the wine. Ignorant men, after drinking themselves into a hangover and a headache, blame the wine, when really it's their own fault.

SOPH.: Mine speaks Greek: "In wine there's truth."

EUS.: It's a warning to priests and royal servants to beware of wine because it brings up onto the tip of your tongue secrets that were hidden in your heart.

SOPH.: Among the old Egyptians, priests were forbidden to drink wine, even though men in those days didn't trust them with secrets.

EUS.: Nowadays everyone can drink wine; whether that's such a good idea, I don't know. Eulalius, what's that little book you're taking out of your sack? It looks very elegant, with all the gold embossing on its covers.

EULAL.: But the inside is even more precious, for these are the epistles of Paul, which I always carry with me, for my special delight. I bring it out now because your discussion reminded me of a passage that bothered me the other day, and that I still haven't got clear in my mind. It's in the first epistle to the Corinthians, chapter six: "All things are lawful unto me, but all things are not expedient: all things are lawful for me, but I will not be brought under the power of any." First, if we take the word of the Stoics, nothing is expedient that is not honest:[1] how then does Paul distinguish the permissible from the expedient? Certainly it is not permissible to run after whores or get drunk; in what sense then are "all things permitted"? But if Paul is talking about a particular class of things, all of which are permitted to him, I can't understand from the tenor of this passage what that class might be. From what follows in the text it's possible to conjecture that he's talking about choice of foods, for some people are said to have abstained from food offered to idols, and others from the foods forbidden by Mosaic law. Chapter eight deals with food offered to idols and so does chapter ten, where (as if explaining this passage) he says, "All things are lawful for me, but all are not expedient; all things are lawful for me, but all things edify not. Let no man seek his own, but every man another's welfare. Whatsoever is sold in the shambles, that eat."[2] What Paul adds here seems to agree with what he said above, "Meats

9. The ancient inhabitants of Sybaris were famous for gluttony; the Carmelite order of monks, dating historically from the twelfth century, for the strictness of their ascetic observance.

1. Not only dogmatic Stoics but moralists touched with stoicism, like Cicero (*De Officiis*), taught that

only honest behavior was truly expedient; see above, *Praise of Folly*, p. 12, n. 5.

2. Eulalius centers his discourse on 1 Corinthians 6; except where indicated otherwise, all the citations in his speech are from that chapter. This quotation is from 1 Corinthians 10.23–25.

for the belly and the belly for meats: but God shall destroy both it and them." And that throughout he had an eye to the Jewish dietary laws is made clear by the ending of chapter ten where he says, "Give offense to none, neither to the Jews nor to the Gentiles nor to the church of God. Even as I please all men in all things, not seeking mine own profit, but the profit of many that they may be saved." Here, when he says "Gentiles" he seems to allude to food offered to idols; "Jews" alludes to the dietary laws; and "the church of God" refers to those of both groups who are weak in the faith. It was permissible, then, to eat any sort of food whatsoever, on the score that to the pure all things are pure. But this may not be expedient. That all things were permitted was a matter of gospel liberty, but charity always keeps an eye out for what concerns the salvation of the neighbor, and so often abstains even when something is permitted, preferring the salvation of the neighbor to full exercise of one's liberty.

But here I'm troubled by a double scruple. First, because in the discourse nothing either precedes or follows that relates coherently to this interpretation. For he denounces the Corinthians as treacherous, given to whoring, adultery, and even incest, and for suing one another before infidel judges. How does this agree with "All things are lawful unto me but all things are not expedient"? And in what follows, he returns to matters of sexual morality which he had discussed before, dropping altogether the matter of lawsuits. "The body," he says, "is not for fornication but for the Lord, and the Lord for the body."

But I can partly overcome this scruple because of the way that carlier in a list of vices he mentioned idolatry: "Be not deceived: neither fornicators, nor idolaters, nor adulterers. . . ." Thus the eating of food offered to idols verged on idolatry; and soon thereafter follows "Meats for the belly and the belly for meats"—signifying that for the needs of the body and for the time being only one may eat anything except what jeopardizes the salvation of a neighbor; but flagrant immorality is always and everywhere to be condemned. Eating is a physical necessity which will be taken away with the resurrection of the flesh; but lust is a sin of ingrained evil.

The other scruple I cannot resolve is how the phrase "But I will not be brought under the power of any" agrees with this last passage. What he actually says is that he has all things in his power yet will not be brought under the power of any. But if one who abstains lest he give offense is in the power of another, that's just what he says of himself in chapter nine. "For though I be free from all men, yet have I made myself servant unto all, that I might gain the more."[3] Saint Ambrose, who was apparently troubled by this very scruple, thinks this is the real sense of the apostle, that he is here preparing the way for his assertion later in chapter nine that he has the power of doing what

---

3. 1 Corinthians 9.19. The citation of Ambrose is to the bishop of Milan (died 397) who wrote a commentary specifically on 1 Corinthians.

others, either apostles or pseudo-apostles, were doing—that is, receiving food from those to whom he preached the gospel. But though this was legal, he accommodated himself to the Corinthians whom he was denouncing for so many and such spectacular vices. In fact, whoever accepts a gift from another comes under the influence of the giver and loses a little of his own moral authority. He is less free to criticize, and the giver is less likely to accept moral rebuke from someone who is in his debt. On this occasion, then, Paul abstained from certain permissible liberties to preserve his apostolic liberty; he didn't want to lie open to reproof himself when he was about to protest as freely and vigorously as possible against the vices of the Corinthians.

I rather like this idea of Saint Ambrose's. But if one prefers to apply the passage to the question of diet, I think Paul's phrase "but I will not be brought under the power of any" applies there too. Take it this way: though I may sometimes abstain from food used in sacrifice or forbidden by Mosaic law, in order to promote my neighbor's salvation and the spread of the gospel, nevertheless my mind is free in the knowledge that to satisfy the needs of my body I may eat any food I want. It was the false apostles who tried to argue that certain foods were impure in themselves, and to be avoided, not only on particular occasions, but always and everywhere, as natural evils—in the same way that we are to refrain from homicide and adultery. Those who believed this were really "under the power of another," and deprived of their evangelical liberty.

Only Theophylact,[4] if my memory serves, reads this passage differently from everyone else. He would have it say, "We may legitimately eat of all foods, but only in moderation; for out of luxury rises licentiousness." This sense, though far from immoral, doesn't represent, in my view, what the passage is really saying.—Now I have showed you the scruples that bothered me; it will be a work of charity on your part to extricate me from them.

Eus.: Indeed, you answer to your name very well. Anyone who can raise such questions doesn't need another person to answer them. You've proposed your doubts so fully that I've quite given up doubting. Yet it's true that Paul in this epistle where he undertakes to handle many topics at once frequently slips from one theme to another, and then picks up again where he left off.

Chrys.: If I weren't afraid my palaver would interfere with your meal, and if I thought it proper to contaminate these sacred themes by mixing in something from the profane authors, I would introduce a passage I was reading this morning and that, far from puzzling me, filled me with delight.

Eus.: You shouldn't call anything profane that is decent and contributes to good morals. No doubt sacred writ commands our highest

---

4. Theophylact (died about 1100) was a Byzantine deacon who also wrote a commentary on 1 Corinthians. Eulalius's phrase "if my memory serves" is a patent bit of scholarly one-upmanship.

respect; but I often encounter ancient speeches in the pagan writings even of the poets, so chastely, nobly, and reverently expressed that I have to think some sacred being was hovering over the hand of the writer. Perhaps the spirit of Christ is more widely diffused than we like to think, and there are more saints at their synod in heaven than we have in our catalogues down here. Let me open my heart among friends; I can't read Cicero's books on *Old Age,* on the *Duties of Man,* or the *Tusculan Disputations* without sometimes kissing the book and blessing that noble heart, inspired as it was by a breath from on high. On the other hand, when I read some of these recent books on politics, economics, or ethics—good God, how flat they seem by comparison! The authors don't appear to have an ounce of feeling for what they're saying. I'd rather see the collected works of Scotus[5] go down the drain, along with all his fellows, than the books of a single Cicero or Plutarch. I don't condemn the new books entirely, but when I rise from the old one I feel myself a better man, while from the new ones I rise feeling more coldly inclined toward virtue and somehow more quarrelsome.—So don't hesitate to present your passage, whatever it is.

CHRYS.:   Many of the philosophical books written by Marcus Tullius [Cicero] seem to me to have something of the divine about them, but the one he wrote as an old man on old age I consider his "swan song," as the Greek saying has it. I was rereading it today, and memorized the following words, which particularly attracted my attention: "What if some God granted me the power to put off my years and become a boy again, as I was in my cradle? I would certainly refuse, and decline to go back to the starting line after already finishing the race. For in this life what gratification is to be found, or rather what anguish is not? Even if neither of the above, the most that can be hoped for is either satiety or grief. I don't want to rail against life as so many men, and learned men at that, have done. I am not sorry to have lived, since I've lived in such a way that I can't feel I was born in vain. So I can depart from this life as from an inn, not from my home. Nature provided us with a temporary lodging, not a place of permanent habitation. Oh, the glorious day when I depart for that company of spirits and leave behind this rabble of people and cesspool of appetites."[6] Those are the words of Cato. What more holy sentiments could be expressed by a Christian man? I wish all the conversations between monks, or of monks with nuns, were on the same plane as this speech of an old pagan to a group of pagan youths.

EUS.:   Someone will complain that the speech was composed by Cicero.

CHRYS.:   To me it doesn't matter whether the praise goes to Cato who felt these things and spoke them or to Cicero whose mind grasped the glorious reflections and whose pen clothed them in appropriate elo-

---

5. Duns Scotus, used here to symbolize the scho-   6. Cicero, *De senectute* 23.7.
lastic philosophers generally.

quence. Personally, I think that Cato, even if he did not speak these exact words, commonly said similar things in conversation. For Cicero was not such an impudent forger that he would concoct a Cato utterly different from the one who existed. He would not have neglected in his dialogue the element of decorum, most important in that sort of writing, especially when the memory of Cato was still vivid in the minds of his readers.

THEOPH.:   What you say is very likely; but I'll tell you what came into my mind as you were reciting. I've often wondered at the fact that—though all men want a long life and fear death—you'll hardly ever find an old man, or even one of advancing years, who if asked if he'd want to live life over again, with all its good and bad events, wouldn't answer like Cato, No, never. He'd be especially reluctant if he recalled all the things good and bad that befell him. For often the memory even of happy events is mingled with so much grief and shame that the mind shrinks from the thought of them just as much as from miserable events. I think the poets show this to us when they write that souls lose their desire for the bodies they left behind only after they have drunk long draughts of oblivion from the river Lethe.[7]

URANIUS.:   This is remarkable indeed, and I've often noted examples of it myself. But what struck me was the phrase "I am not sorry to have lived." Now how many Christians live so temperate a life that they could take over this expression of the old man's for their own? Most men think their life has not been vain if they've built up a pile of money to be left to their heirs. But Cato thought his life worthwhile because he had served the republic as a capable, responsible citizen and an incorruptible magistrate, leaving to posterity a name renowned for unflinching integrity. What speech could be more noble than his, "I depart as from an inn, not from my home"? After staying at an inn for a while, one gladly departs at a hint from the host; no man likes to be ejected from his own home. Yet men are often forced to move by sagging walls, a sudden fire, or some other mishap—or else just by the slow decay of a structure that warns the owner to move on.

NEPHELIUS.:   Just as eloquent is the speech of Socrates reported by Plato, to the effect that "the human soul is placed in this present body as in a garrison which it shouldn't abandon without orders from the commander, and in which it shouldn't linger any longer than its commander desires."[8] The thought is more forceful in Plato because instead of a "house" he specifies a "garrison." We simply occupy a house, but in a garrison we have a job to do, assigned by our commander; and this accords with the holy scriptures, which sometimes speak of life as a kind of warfare and often as a struggle.

URAN.:   Cato's phrases also agree very well with the language of Paul, who in second Corinthians chapter five speaks of the celestial mansions that we anticipate after this life as a home or dwelling; but the

---

7. The river of forgetfulness in Hades.   8. Plato, *Phaedo* 62.

body we inhabit in this world he calls a transient shelter: "For we that are in this tabernacle do groan, being burdened."[9]

NEPH.: In the same vein is that passage of Peter: "I think it meet, as long as I am in this tabernacle, to stir you up by putting you in remembrance; knowing that shortly I must put off this tabernacle."[1] What else does Christ tell us again and again but that we should live and watch as if we were to die tomorrow, but devote ourselves to good deeds as if we were to live forever? When we hear that "Oh, glorious day" don't we seem to hear Paul himself saying "I desire to depart and be with Christ"?[2]

CHRYS.: How happy are those who look forward to death in such a spirit! But in Cato's speech, splendid thought it is, someone might complain of an excessive assurance, amounting almost to arrogance, such as ought to be far from the mind of a Christian man. I don't believe I've ever read anything in the pagan authors that better accords with a truly Christian spirit than what Socrates said to Crito after drinking the hemlock. "Whether God will approve of my works," he said, "I cannot tell; certainly I have tried my best to please him, and I am in good hope that he will approve of my efforts."[3] Diffident as he was about his own achievements, yet he hoped by virtue of his strong desire to obey the will of God, that the Lord in his goodness would look kindly on him because he had tried to live well.

NEPH.: A really marvelous state of mind in one who never knew Christ or the sacred scriptures. When I read the lives of men like that, I can hardly keep from crying out, "Pray for us, Saint Socrates!"[4]

CHRYS.: I often find myself hoping just as confidently that the souls of Virgil and Horace are sanctified.

NEPH.: At the same time, I have seen all too many Christians meet their end in a spirit of chilly resignation. Some put their trust, where it shouldn't be placed, in things of this world; others, aware of their sins and haunted by scruples that ignorant counsellors place in their way, give up the ghost in absolute despair.

CHRYS.: No wonder if they die thus when all their life they never got beyond thinking about ceremonies.

NEPH.: What do you mean by "ceremonies"?

CHRYS.: I'll tell you, but first let me emphasize one point as strongly as possible. I don't condemn, rather I vigorously approve of, the sacraments and rites of the church. What I do condemn are certain superstitious or deceitful—or, to put it as gently as possible, certain simple or ignorant—men, who teach the people to put their trust in observances and to neglect those things that might make them real Christians.

---

9. 2 Corinthians 5.1–4.
1. 2 Peter 1.13–14.
2. Philippians 1.23.
3. *Phaedo* 69.
4. The phrase, which became famous, is often attributed to Erasmus in his own person; note that it is spoken by the "cloudy" Nephelius. Rather more surprising is Chrysoglottus's suggestion that Horace, the outspoken Epicurean, be sanctified.

NEPH.:   I still don't get your point.

CHRYS.:   Let me help you. If you look at the general run of Christian people, isn't it true that from beginning to end their life is tied up in ceremonies? In baptism, how scrupulously do they reproduce all the primitive rites of the church! The infant appears outside the church door, is subjected to exorcism, and hears the catechism recited; vows are repeated, Satan is abjured with all his pomps and pleasures; the baby is oiled, sealed with the sign of the cross, salted, and immersed; the godparents are charged with bringing up the child, and then, after paying a sum of money, exempted from the charge. So now at last the child is called a Christian—and so, in a manner of speaking, he is. In time he is anointed again, taught to say confession, makes his first communion, learns how to observe the holy days, to behave himself at church services, to fast every so often, and not to eat meat on Fridays. And if he does all these things he is considered an absolute Christian. He takes a wife, and there's another ceremony; or he takes orders, is once more anointed and consecrated, his garments are changed and prayers are repeated. And all these things as they are done I approve of; but that they are done from habit, not conviction, that I don't approve of. And that Christianity consists of nothing else, that I vehemently deny. The fact is that most men, while putting their trust in these ceremonies, struggle furiously to get rich, abandoning themselves completely to lust, wrath, envy, and ambition—until the moment when it's time for them to die. And here again some ceremonies are ready for them. They get confessed over and over, there's some more holy oil, the eucharist is administered, the candles are lighted, the cross is produced along with some holy water, a papal brief is hustled up or purchased on the spot for the dying man; an elaborate funeral is ordered, the will is made or remade. Someone is handy to shout instructions in the ear of the dying man; sometimes he hastens the process if (as often happens) he's loud of mouth or overtaken in drink. All these ceremonies serve some purpose, especially those that are vouched for by ancient traditions of the church; but there are other, more inward helps to bring us with cheerful spirits and Christian confidence toward our end.

EUS.:   Your sermon was pious and truthful, but meanwhile nobody has touched the food. Don't stint yourselves. I warned you before, there wouldn't be anything after the second course, and that's a rustic one. No use looking for pheasants, grouse, or Greek delights.[5] All right my boy, you may remove these dishes and bring on others. You see my horn, not of plenty, but of paucity. All this is the produce of the gardens you saw; don't hesitate to help yourself if there's something you fancy.

TIM.:   There are so many different things, we're refreshed just by the sight of them.

---

5. No specific goodies are implied here; Greeks (especially Corinthians) were noted for high living.

EUS.:   But if you're tempted to smile at my frugality, just reflect that
this meal alone would have provided food for that godly monk Hilar-
ion and the hundred disciples of his communion. For Paul and Anthony
this would have been food for a whole month.[6]

TIM.:   I doubt if even Peter, prince of the apostles, would have scorned
it when he was living with Simon the tanner.

EUS.:   Neither would Paul when, being short of cash, he had to work
nights as a tentmaker.[7]

TIM.:   All this bounty we owe to the goodness of God. But I would
happily go hungry with Peter and Paul if for lack of physical food I
could compensate with spiritual sustenance.

EUS.:   Rather, let us learn from Paul how to master both prosperity and
penury. In time of dearth we give thanks to Jesus Christ who provides
us with an occasion to exercise frugality and patience. When there is
a glut, we thank the munificence of him who by his liberality invites
us to love him; and as we enjoy in moderation the good things that
his loving kindness has showered on us, let us remember the poor,
who by the will of God lack what we possess, so that the occasion may
invite us to mutual acts of charity. We can win God's mercy by giving
our excess to the poor who need it; they, refreshed by our generosity,
will thank God for our good will and commend us to him in their
prayers. And that reminds me. Here, boy, tell my wife to send what's
left of the roast to our neighbor Gudula. She lives nearby, and is a
good woman; at the moment she's pregnant, and also very poor, because
her husband, a drunken spendthrift, died lately, leaving nothing for
his widow but a flock of children.

TIM.:   Christ bade us give to everyone who asks; if I did that, within a
month, I'd be a beggar myself.

EUS.:   I suppose Christ was speaking of those who beg out of necessity.
Some people beg—or rather demand, and even extort—great sums of
money that they spend on luxurious feasts or (what's even worse) on
their own filthy lusts; now to refuse people like that is actually a form
of charity. Just so, it's robbery to bestow money on people who will
waste it when it could be better spent to relieve the urgent necessities
of our neighbors. Thus I don't think those people can be held blameless who build elaborately decorated churches and monasteries at
inordinate expense, while at the same time so many living temples of
Christ are perishing of hunger, shivering in rags, and agonizing over
lack of the basic necessities. When I was in England, I saw the tomb
of Saint Thomas studded with innumerable gems of incalculable price,
not to mention other incredible treasures.[8] I myself would rather see
that immense sum of money distributed to the poor, than in the hands

6. These virtuous reflections on the great ascetics
could make one feel guilty about eating a dry bis-
cuit.
7. The poverty of Peter and Paul is detailed in Acts
9 and 18.

8. The extravagance of St. Thomas à Beckett's tomb
at Canterbury (goal of Chaucer's pilgrims) was
proverbial. Erasmus dwelt on it at length in another
colloquy specially devoted to pilgrimages.

of functionaries who sooner or later will steal the whole thing anyway. The tomb itself I would rather see decorated with branches and flowers; and I think that would be much more agreeable to the sacred man who occupies it. When I was in Italy, not far from Pavia I saw a Carthusian monastery constructed of white marble within and without from top to bottom; and everything inside was marble too, altars, columns, tombs. What was the point of spending all that money so that a few lonely monks could sing there in their marble temple—which is more trouble to them than it is a pleasure, since it's constantly crowded with visitors, who come there just to see the marble church.[9]

I learned something else there that's even odder; the monastery has a legacy worth three thousand ducats a year, to be spent on the structure; and there are actually people who say it would be sinful to spend that money on good works against the will of the donor. So rather than not build at all, they demolish what already exists and then build it again. These are striking examples, but I thought it proper to mention them; similar instances can be found everywhere. This isn't charity, it's ostentation. Rich men nowadays crave to have their tombs inside the churches, where once there was not even room for saints. They arrange to have themselves sculpted or painted with their names spelled out and the amount of money they gave; and with this display they fill up the greater part of the church. Before long, they'll be asking that their corpses be buried at the altar itself. Someone will ask, Do you think their money should be rejected? By no means, if what they offer is worthy of God's church. But if I were a priest or a bishop, I'd tell those crass courtiers and moneylenders that if they really want God to forgive their sins, they should give their money secretly for the relief of the truly poor. They may suppose their money is thrown away when it's given quietly, in small amounts, to meet the needs of the desperate; no monument will survive for posterity to gape at. But I think no money is better placed than that for which Christ himself will be our most certain guarantor.

TIM.:   Then you don't think money well invested which is given to monasteries?

EUS.:   Even to them I would give something if I were rich, but I would give for their necessities, not their luxuries, and I would give most where I felt the zeal for true religion was most fervent.

TIM.:   Many think money is not well spent which is given to public beggars.

EUS.:   There again something should be given, but with discrimination. I think it's a good idea for individual cities to take care of their own needy, and not tolerate vagabonds who wander cross country as they please. Least of all should they support the able-bodied poor, who, as I see it, need a job more than a handout.[1]

---

9. The Certosa near Pavia is still visited by many tourists; because it was constantly being added to, it is an anthology of architectural styles.

1. The idea that jobs may be hard to come by does not cross the mind of the comfortable company. Thomas More (*Utopia* 1) knew better.

TIM.:   Then where should we give our money? How much money and up to what point?

EUS.:   I find it very hard to draw the line precisely. The ideal thing would be to give to everybody. Then, bearing in mind my limited resources, I give what I can under the circumstances, first of all to those whom I know to be poor and honest. And if I don't have the necessary myself, I encourage others to give.

TIM.:   Will you allow me to speak freely in this kingdom of yours?

EUS.:   More freely than if you were in your own house.

TIM.:   You don't approve of lavish spending on churches; but you could have built this house of yours for much less.

EUS.:   Well, I think its virtues are those of neatness, or, if you will, of elegance; it's well short of luxury, if I'm any judge. Some people who live on charity build more splendidly than this. And yet these gardens of mine, such as they are, pay taxes to support the needy, and every day I cut back on my expenses, denying something to myself and my family, to contribute to the public good.

TIM.:   ⟨ If everyone shared that point of view, a great many people would be better off who now suffer from undeserved indigence; and a great many potbellies would get a chance to slim down by studying sobriety and temperance.

EUS.:   It may turn out that way. But now would you like to top off this rather flat dessert with something sweet?

TIM.:   We've had sweets enough and to spare.

EUS.:   But what I produce you'll welcome, even if you're crop-full.

TIM.:   What is it?

EUS.:   A codex of the gospels, which since I consider it my most prized possession, I offer you as the high point of the feast. Read the passage, my boy, from the place where you stopped.

BOY: "No man can serve two masters: for either he will hate the one and love the other; or else he will hold to the one and despise the other. Ye cannot serve God and Mammon.

"Therefore I say unto you, Take no thought for your soul,[2] what ye shall eat or what ye shall drink; nor yet for your body, what ye shall put on. Is not the soul more than meat, and the body than raiment?"[3]

EUS.:   Put back the book. In this passage Jesus Christ seems to me to be saying the same thing twice. In the first place he says "will hate" and then "will despise"; and then, having said "love," he repeats the idea in "hold to." The persons change, the ideas remain the same.

TIM.:   I'm not sure I follow you.

EUS.:   Let's put it in mathematical terms, if those will be clearer. In the first part put A for "the one" and B for "the other"; in the second part, reverse the order, and put B for "the one" and A for "the other." Now either he will hate A and love B or hold to B and despise A. Isn't it clear that A is twice rejected and B twice approved?

---

2. The Vulgate gives *animae*, i.e., "soul," in this passage; but the Authorized Version, agreeing with or maybe following the interpretation below, translates "life."

3. Matthew 6.24–25.

TIM.:   Perfectly clear.

EUS.:   But the conjunction "or," especially when twice repeated, implies contrary or at least different views. Otherwise we could offer absurd alternatives, couldn't we?—like "Either Peter beats me and I give up" or "I give up and Peter beats me."

TIM.:   A neat argument, so help me!

EUS.:   It will seem neat to me too, after you've showed me the solution.

THEOPH.:   My mind seems to be in a trance, or perhaps in labor; with a little encouragement I'll deliver, and you can be either the interpreters of my dream or the midwives of my brainchild.

EUS.:   It's supposed to be unlucky to describe your dreams at a feast, and it's hardly proper to give birth in the midst of so many men; but go on, deliver your dream or your brainchild, just as you choose: we'll be happy to have it.

THEOPH.:   In this passage as I read it, the distinction is between actions and not persons. I understand the expression "the one . . . and the other" to refer not to A and B. Rather, either expression refers to both persons, so that whichever one you choose is opposed to the other. As you might say, "either you exclude A and admit B" or else "admit A and exclude B." You see here that though the persons remain, the action is altered. And this is said of A in such a way that it makes no difference if you say the same thing of B, as in this formula: exclude A and admit B or else exclude B and admit A.

EUS.:   You've laid out the matter with perfect clarity; no geometrician could have done better with a diagram.

SOPH.:   I'm more troubled by the second sentence where he tells us to take no thought for the morrow, since Paul himself worked with his hands to earn his daily bread, and severely rebukes idle folk who prefer to live off others. He warns them sharply to get busy, saying manual labor is good for them and in addition enables them to help the really needy. Don't you think the labor is virtuous by which a working man supports his beloved wife and dear children?

TIM.:   Your question, in my opinion, can be answered in several ways. First, as relates to biblical times, the apostles when they travelled far and wide to preach the gospel had to be spared the time and trouble of earning a living; they had no time to ply a trade, especially when they had no other skill than fishing. Things are different now; we have plenty of time but we'd rather loaf.

Another solution is this: Christ didn't mean to discourage industry but overwork. He knew it's a common failing of men to concentrate on making a living, to the point that they let everything else slide and devote themselves only to this activity, like addicts. The Lord makes this point with special force when he says, "No man can serve two masters"—where "serve" implies wholehearted devotion. Therefore he wants the first, though not the only, consideration to be propagation of the gospel. For he says, "Seek ye first the kingdom of God, and all these things shall be added unto you."[4] He doesn't say "seek

4. Matthew 6.33; Luke 12.31.

ye only" but "seek ye first." As for the "morrow," I think this is an hyperbolic expression, meaning the distant future, because people who are concerned with this world generally concentrate on the future and try to make ready for it.

EUS.:   We accept your interpretation; but what does he mean by saying, "Take no thought for your soul, what ye shall eat."[5] It is true that the body requires clothing, but the soul doesn't eat food.

TIM.:   When he says "soul" here, I think he means "life."[6] Without food life is endangered, but it's not so with clothing, which we wear more out of modesty than necessity. Even if you're uncomfortable going naked, you don't die right away; but going without food is death for sure.

EUS.:   I'm not quite clear about the connection between this sentence and the next: "Is not the soul more than meat, and the body than raiment?" For if soul is so precious, we should be all the more careful to preserve it.

TIM.:   This argument doesn't lessen our anxiety, but increases it.

EUS.:   But that can't have been Christ's intent; we must be reading it wrong. Rather, by his argument he intensifies our faith in the Father. If the Father in his bounty freely gave what is more precious, surely he will add to it what is less so. He who gave the soul itself will not deny it nourishment; he who gave the body will somehow provide it with clothing. If we trust in his goodness, there is no reason why we should torment ourselves over trifles. What remains, then, except that— making use of this world, yet as if we were not using it—we direct all our affections and powers of devotion toward heavenly things, reject Mammon along with Satan and all his tricks, to serve the one God with all our heart and energy, since he will never forsake his children.—But meanwhile nobody has touched the dessert. Surely we are allowed to eat freely of these fruits which have been produced on the estate without any labor at all.

TIM.:   Our bodies are quite replete.

EUS.:   I hope your minds are too.

TIM.:   Even more so.

EUS.:   Then take away the dishes, my boy, and bring on the ewer. Let us wash our hands, my friends, so that if any fault has been committed during this meal, we can be cleansed of it before giving thanks to God. If you like, I'll finish the prayer from Chrysostom that I began before.

TIM.:   Please do.

EUS.:   "Glory to you, O Lord; glory to you, most holy; glory to you, our king. Now you have given us food, fill us also with joy and delight in the holy spirit, that we may be found acceptable in your sight, and that we be not shamed when you reward each according to his works."

BOY: Amen.

TIM.:   A thoroughly pious and elegant prayer.

---

5. Matthew 6.25,31.   6. See above, p. 205, n. 2.

EUS.:   It is one that Chrysostom himself thought deserving of an analysis.

TIM.:   Where is that to be found?

EUS.:   In his fifty-sixth homily, on Matthew.

TIM.:   I shan't fail to read it over this very day. But one thing I'd like to learn here, why do we pray three times for the glory of Christ, and under the three titles of "lord," "most holy," and "king"?

EUS.:   Because all glory is due to him, and the triple title is especially proper. By his sacrosanct blood he redeemed us from the tyranny of the devil, and claimed us as his own; thus we call him "lord." Then, not content with freely forgiving our sins, he bestowed justification on us through his holy spirit, that we might ourselves aspire to holiness; thus we call him "most holy" who sanctifies all mankind. Finally, because we expect from him the reward of a celestial kingdom where he will sit at the right hand of God the Father, we invoke him as our "king." And all this happiness we owe to his grace freely granted to us, so that now instead of the tyrant Satan we have as our master Jesus Christ; for the filth and squalor of sin we have innocence and holiness; and for hell we have the joys of celestial life.

TIM.:   Pious thoughts indeed.

EUS.:   Since this is the first time I've entertained you at a meal, I won't send you away without presents, such as my circumstances allow. Here, boy, bring out the favors. Whether you want to draw lots for them or just choose each his own doesn't matter; they're all of about the same value, that is, none at all. Neither are they like the gifts of Heliogabalus, who gave one man a hundred horses and the next man a hundred flies.[7] There are four booklets, two watches, a lamp, and a little case with reed pens. I think these will suit you better than a perfume-ball, a box of tooth-powder, or a looking-glass, if I know your characters.

TIM.:   They are all so fine that it would be hard for us to choose; we'd rather you distribute them as you see fit. That way, whatever each person gets will be specially welcome to him.

EUS.:   This little pamphlet in vellum contains the proverbs of Solomon; it teaches wisdom and is illuminated in gold because gold symbolizes wisdom. This I give to our white-haired friend so that, as the gospel says, wisdom may be added to the wise, and he shall abound in it.

TIM.:   I'll try not to depend on it completely.

EUS.:   Sophronius deserves the watch, which comes from outer Dalmatia (if you'll forgive my boasting in this way about my own present).[8] I know how he husbands his time, and hates to let a bit of that precious commodity slip away without serving some good purpose.

SOPH.:   Not really. You're prodding a naturally lazy man to be more diligent.

---

7. The story about Heliogabalus, one of the more degenerate Roman emperors, is told by his biographer Aelius Lampridius.

8. In modern terms, western Dalmatia would be like Czechoslovakia, apparently even in Erasmus's time the home of clever artisans.

EUS.:   This little vellum book contains the second chapter of Matthew;
it should have been given a jewelled binding, except that no cover or
container is more precious to it than the human heart. This then is
for you, deep-minded Theophilus, so you may be even more what
your name describes.[9]

THEOPH.:   I will try to give evidence that your gift has not been mis-
placed.

EUS.:   Here, Eulalius, are the epistles of Paul, which you like to carry
around with you; Paul is always on your tongue, and he wouldn't be
there so much if he weren't already in your heart. Now he will be
even more accessible to your hands and eyes.

EUL.:   This is not just a gift you give, but good advice, the most precious present of all.

EUS.:   The lamp is for Chrysoglottus, a tireless reader, and, as Cicero
says, "a mighty devourer of books."

CHRYS.:   I'm twice grateful: first, for the gift which is exquisite, and then
for the wakeup warnings it will convey to a sleepyhead reader.

EUS.:   The pen-case goes to Theodidactus, a most polished author; the
pens will be happy to serve the glory of our lord Jesus Christ under
the guidance of such a skilful writer.

THEODIDACT.:   I wish you could supply the inspiration as well as the
instruments.

EUS.:   This little book contains some of Plutarch's moral essays, selected
and transcribed by someone thoroughly skilled in Greek literature. It's
full of pious reflections, indeed it's almost miraculous that so many
Christian sentiments could be found in the breast of a pagan. This
will be for young Uranius, who's a lover of things Greek. There remains
just a watch, for Nephilus, who's a careful manager of his time.

NEPH.:   We thank you, not just for your keepsakes but even more for
your compliments. For you haven't bestowed gifts so much as eulogies.

EUS.:   And on my part I am grateful to you, on two scores: first, for
accepting so graciously my simple way of life; and then for refreshing
my mind with your conversation, which was no less learned than
devout. In what frame of mind you depart, I won't venture to guess;
but for my part, you leave me a better and a wiser man. I know you
have no taste for flute-players or clowns, much less dice. So if you
like we can pass another hour or so looking at the wonders of my
kingdom.

TIM.:   We were just about to suggest it.

EUS.:   No need to prompt someone who's already given his word. This
inner courtyard I suppose you've already looked over. It has a triple
exposure, and wherever you turn your eyes, you see the agreeable
greenery of gardens. The glass windows can be closed if you want to
keep out the weather on raw or windy days; and there are heavy shut-

9. Theophilus in Greek means "lover of God."

ters outside, as well as thinner ones inside, to keep out the sun if the
weather is hot. When I have a meal here, I seem to be eating in the
middle of a garden, not a house. The walls themselves are tinted
green and flecked with flowers; and there are some pictures of decent
quality. Here Christ sits at his last supper with the disciples. This is
Herod celebrating his birthday with the fatal feast. Here you see the
rich man of the gospel enjoying a splendid feast though soon to descend
to hell, while Lazarus is driven from the gates, though soon to be
received in Abraham's bosom.[1]

TIM.:   The story of this picture I don't recognize.

EUS.:   Cleopatra is competing in extravagance with Anthony; she has
already swallowed one pearl with her wine, and is reaching for another.
Here the Lapiths are rioting at the marriage feast, and here Alexander
has stabbed his friend Clitus with a spear. All the scenes warn us to
eat moderately, while avoiding drunkenness and sensuality.[2] Now we're
approaching the library; it's not enormous, but the books are choice.

TIM.:   The room seems infused with sanctity, everything glitters so.

EUS.:   Here you see the greater part of my wealth. At the dinner table
you saw only glass and pewter vessels; in the whole house there's only
one piece of plate, a gilt cup that I cherish in fond memory of the
man who gave it to me. This hanging globe puts the entire world
before your eyes. On the wall here, some particular regions are depicted
on a larger scale. On the other walls are portraits of famous authors—
of course depicting all of them would be an endless job. Christ occupies first place, seated on the mountain and stretching forth his hand.
Over his head looms the Father, saying "Hear ye him." Hovering on
outstretched wings, the holy spirit surrounds him with a nimbus of
brilliant light.

TIM.:   It is a work, so help me God, worthy of Apelles himself.[3]

EUS.:   Next to the library is a room for study, not very big, but neat.
Take away this shield and you have a fireplace, in case the weather is
chilly. In the summer it looks just like a solid wall.

TIM.:   It's a real jewel of a place; it also smells delightful.

EUS.:   I make a special point of keeping the house neat and fragrant.
Neither job is particularly expensive. The library has its own balcony,
looking down on the garden and leading to a chapel.

TIM.:   A place fit for a deity.

EUS.:   Now we come to the three galleries above the ones you saw next
to the kitchen garden. In these upper galleries you can look out, but
through windows that can be locked, especially where they don't open
on an inner courtyard; that makes the house more secure. Here on

1. The fatal feast of Herod is that at which the fate
of John the Baptist was sealed (Matthew 14); the
contrasting destinies of the rich man and the beggar Lazarus are described in Luke 16.
2. The Lapiths, invited to a marriage feast, got
into a brawl with some Centaurs who tried to carry
off the bride; as a social occasion, it was not suc-

cessful. Alexander, when drunk, killed his best
friend. The exclusive authority of moral values in
discussing works of art is very apparent here; it was
a frequent Renaissance aberration.
3. Nobody in the modern world ever laid eyes on
a painting by Apelles; his name is a byword, nonetheless.

the left, where there is more light and the wall is less interrupted by windows, is the whole life of Jesus as narrated by the four evangelists down to the sending forth of the holy spirit and the first preaching of the apostles, as described in the Acts.[4] Place names are added here and there, so the spectator can tell by what lake or atop what mountain the action is taking place. There are also subtitles indicating briefly the meaning of the scene; for example, the words spoken by Jesus, "I will: be thou clean."[5] On the opposite wall are types and prophecies from the Old Testament, especially the Prophets and the Psalms, which are little less than the life of Christ and the Apostles told in a different way. Here I often stroll, recalling the story and marvelling to myself at the wonderful wisdom of God in restoring through his Son the fallen human race. Sometimes I am joined by my wife or by some friend who takes pleasure in sacred subjects.

TIM.:   In this house who could possibly be bored?

EUS.:   Nobody who has learned to live with himself. Along the top of the wall are added, as if to form a frieze, the busts of the popes, with their mottos.[6] On the other side, busts of the Caesars, to help one remember history. In another corner of the gallery is a bedroom with balcony where one can take a nap or from which one can look out over the orchard and the aviary. Out there in the farthest corner of the field you can see a little garden house where we sometimes lunch during the summer season, and where anyone in the household who has contracted a contagious disease can be quarantined and cared for.

TIM.:   Some people say it's no use trying to avoid those diseases.

EUS.:   Why then do they step aside from a ditch or keep away from poison? Do they fear contagion less because they can't see it? Neither can you see the poison of the basilisk which he darts from his eyes. When the situation absolutely required it, I wouldn't hesitate to put my life in danger. But to take unnecessary risks with your existence is temerity; and deliberately to put others in risk of their lives is cruelty.

There are a great many other things for you to look at, and they are amusing enough; I'll ask my wife to show them to you. Stay here for the full three-day visit if you can, and make yourselves right at home. Please your eyes, feed your minds. But I have some business that calls me away. I have to take horse to some villages nearby.

TIM.:   Is it a matter of money?

EUS.:   Pooh! I wouldn't leave friends like you for a mere matter of money.

TIM.:   Hunting, then?

EUS.:   Yes, that it is; but not the hunt for boars or stags.

TIM.:   What then?

EUS.:   I'll tell you. I have a friend in one of the villages, who has taken to his bed, seriously ill. The doctor fears for his body, and I for his

---

4. I.e., as far as the events described in Acts 2.
5. These are the words with which Christ healed the leper; the story is told by three of the four evangelists.

6. The Latin text speaks of the titles of the popes, but popes don't properly have individual titles; informally and unofficially, they do have mottos.

soul. I don't feel he's properly prepared to die in a manner worthy of a Christian, so I'm going to visit him with words of good counsel. Whether he dies or recovers, they will be good for him. In another village a quarrel has broken out between two men—not bad fellows at heart, but both stubborn. If the quarrel is exasperated, others will join in, and I'm afraid it will turn into a gang fight. I'll try my best to reconcile them, for I've been friends with both for a long time. This is the quarry I'm hunting. If my enterprises succeed as I'd like, we'll celebrate a triumph here when I get back.

TIM.:   Success to your chase! We'll pray that Christ, no less than Diana the goddess of the hunt, will favor you.

EUS.:   I'd rather succeed in these projects than come into two thousand ducats.

TIM.:   Will you be back soon?

EUS.:   Not till I've tried every angle; so I can't set an exact time. Meanwhile, enjoy yourselves with my belongings as if they were your own, and farewell.

TIM.:   May the lord Jesus prosper your going forth and your coming back!

An Inquisition into Faith

Speakers: Aulus, Barbatius

AULUS: As the schoolchildren warble in the morning, "Give you good day"; only I hardly know whether it's right to express such a wish to you.

BARBATIUS: Frankly, I'd prefer one who'd make me well to one who just wished it. But why such misgivings, Aulus?

AUL.:   Why? Because, if you must know, you give off a whiff of sulphur, one of Jove's thunderbolts.

BAR.:   There are all sorts of Jovelets and anti-Joves[1] hurling natural thunderbolts, very different in their origin from the heavenly powers. But I suppose you're alluding to the anathema.

AUL.:   That's right.

BAR.:   I've heard some horrid rumblings, but nothing has hit me yet.

AUL.:   How so?

BAR.:   My digestion is none the worse, and I sleep as soundly as ever.

AUL.:   The danger may be even greater just because you're unaware of it. In fact those natural thunderbolts, as you call them, are dangerous when they light on mountains and ships at sea.

---

1. In the original, Veioves; Veiovis was an Etruscan addition to the eclectic Roman pantheon, an ill-defined god of the underworld never fully domesticated in the system, and so treated as here with a certain contempt.

BAR.: They strike, but don't do much damage. You can get lightning off a glass rod and thunder out of a brass pot.

AUL.: Even that scares people.

BAR.: Only boys. God alone wields the thunderbolt that wounds the soul.

AUL.: What if God is present in his vicar?

BAR.: If only he were!

AUL.: A lot of people are surprised that you haven't already been burnt blacker than a piece of coal.

BAR.: Suppose I were. As a sinner, my salvation should be hoped for even more fervently, if the doctrine of the evangelist holds true.[2]

AUL.: You could hope, of course, but you couldn't be sure.

BAR.: Why so?

AUL.: Because you must take warning from the thunder, and repent of your errors.

BAR.: If God deals that way with us, we're all doomed.

AUL.: Explain that.

BAR.: Because when we were God's enemies, worshippers of idols, and enlisted in the army of Satan, that is, outcasts on every possible score, then more than ever he communicated with us through his Son, and by his presence restored us to life even when we were as if dead.

AUL.: There you're quite right.

BAR.: It would be just as bad if a doctor abandoned his patients whenever the disease was at its height, and attended them only when it suited his convenience.

AUL.: But I'm afraid you'll bestow your disease on me sooner than I will be able to cure it; it often happens that one who visits a sick man has to be a wrestler as much as a healer.[3]

BAR.: So it may be in diseases of the body; but for those of the soul there is an antidote against every form of contagion.

AUL.: What is that?

BAR.: A fixed determination never to be swayed from one's positive opinions. And why then should one fear an arena where the matter is to be disputed only with words?

AUL.: There's something in what you say, provided we have some hope of improvement.

BAR.: The proverb says, "While there's life, there's hope"; and in Paul you will find that "Charity knows not despair because it hopes for everything."[4]

AUL.: That's not a bad reflection, and with this idea in mind I'd like to chat with you for a while; if you agree, I'll act as your physician.

BAR.: All right.

AUL.: Inquisitive people don't have a good reputation; but in medicine, it's the doctor's business to do some probing.

2. The sort of gospel passage that Barbatius has in mind is evidently like that at the end of Luke 7.
3. A wrestler either to hold the delirious patient in his bed, or against the disease transmitted to the doctor.
4. Approximately, from 1 Corinthians 13.

BAR.:   Inquire away, from heaven to earth, if you want.

AUL.:   I'll try; and for your part, do you answer truthfully from the heart.

BAR.:   I will; only let me know what you'll be looking into.

AUL.:   The Apostle's Creed.[5]

BAR.:   I accept the challenge, and you can consider me an enemy of Christ if I disappoint you in any particular.

AUL.:   Do you believe in Almighty God, who created heaven and earth?

BAR.:   And whatever is contained in heaven and earth, including the angelic minds.

AUL.:   When you say "God," what do you mean?

BAR.:   I mean a mind existing in eternity, having neither beginning nor end, than which nothing can be greater, wiser, or better.

AUL.:   Most reverently expressed.

BAR.:   By his omnipotent will he created all things, both visible and invisible; by his miraculous wisdom he controls and governs the universe, by his goodness he nourishes and preserves all things, and freely restores the fallen race of mankind.

AUL.:   These indeed are the three principal attributes of God; but what fruit do you derive from the knowledge of them?

BAR.:   When I consider his omnipotence, I submit myself entirely to him, compared with whose majesty there is nothing of any value in human or angelic kind. Then I believe with the fullness of faith in everything that the scriptures tell us he made or did, and in everything he promised for the future, since he can do with a single nod of his head whatever he will, however impossible it may seem to men. Thus, placing no trust in my own strength, I rely entirely on him who can do all things. When I consider his wisdom, I lose all confidence in my own, but I believe everything has been done by him absolutely rightly and justly, even if to human minds it seems absurd or wrong. When I consider his goodness, I see there is nothing in me that I do not owe to his grace freely bestowed; and I think there is no crime so great that he will not forgive a penitent sinner; nor is there anything he will not grant to one who implores it with sincere faith.

AUL.:   Do you think it enough that you believe all these things?

BAR.:   By no means. With sincere devotion I place all my faith and hope in him alone, detesting Satan and all forms of idolatry, as well as all magical arts. God alone I adore, placing none before him or on an equal footing with him; not an angel, not parents, not children, not a wife, not a prince; not riches, honors, or pleasures; prepared to

---

5. The official text of the Apostle's Creed runs:

I believe in God the Father, the Almighty, creator of heaven and earth.

And in Jesus Christ, his only son, our Lord, who was conceived by the Holy Ghost, born of the Virgin Mary, suffered under Pontius Pilate, crucified, dead and buried, descended to hell, the third day rose again from the dead, ascended into heaven, seated at the right hand of God the Father Almighty, whence he will come, to judge the living and the dead.

I believe in the Holy Ghost, a holy catholic Christian Church, communion of saints, forgiveness of sins, resurrection of the flesh, and an everlasting life. Amen.

lose my life in his cause should he so order, certain as I am that no man can perish who devotes himself entirely to God.

AUL.:   You seek nothing, then, fear nothing, and love nothing save God alone?

BAR.:   If I revere, love, or fear anything save him, I revere, love, and fear it for his sake, referring all to his glory, always giving thanks to him, whether good or evil befalls me, whether life or death be decreed for me.

AUL.:   Certainly your answers are admirable so far. What are your feelings about the second person?

BAR.:   Make your question.

AUL.:   Do you believe Jesus was both god and man?

BAR.:   Indeed I do.

AUL.:   How could it be that the same person could be both an immortal god and a mortal man?

BAR.:   He who can do whatever he will could easily do that. And because of his divine nature, which he shares with the father, whatever immensity, wisdom, and goodness I recognize in the father, I also attribute to the son. Whatever I owe to the father, I owe to the son as well, except that it was the father who chose to create everything through the son, and through him to bestow all upon us.

AUL.:   Why then do the scriptures more often call the son "Lord" than "God"?

BAR.:   Because "God" is the name of authority and sovereignty which belongs particularly to the father, who is the absolute beginning of all things and the source of his own deity. "Lord" is the word for a redeemer and liberator. Indeed, the father redeems, but through the son, and the son is god, but by derivation from the father. Only the father derives from nothing else, and among the divine persons takes first place.

AUL.:   Then you place your trust in Jesus as well?

BAR.:   Of course.

AUL.:   But the prophet denounces a curse on anyone who places his trust in man.[6]

BAR.:   But to this one man alone was given all power in heaven and on earth; so that at his name every knee should bow, of things in heaven, on earth, and in the nether regions. And I should not venture to fix, as they say, the anchor of my faith and hope in him, unless he were divine.

AUL.:   Why does the Creed call him the son?

BAR.:   Lest anyone should be deluded into thinking him a creature.

AUL.:   Why "only"?

BAR.:   To distinguish from adoptive sons the natural son, the honor of whose cognomen is imparted to us;[7] to keep us from expecting another son besides this one.

---

6. Jeremiah 17.5.   7. I.e., we are known as "Christians."

AUL.:   Why did god wish his son, who was also a god, to become a man?

BAR.:   That as a man he might reconcile other men to god.

AUL.:   Do you believe he was conceived without the agency of a man, by the work of the holy spirit, and born of the immaculate Virgin Mary, having received a mortal body from her substance?

BAR.:   I do indeed.

AUL.:   Why did he choose to be born after this fashion?

BAR.:   Because it was fitting for god to be born in this way; just so should he be born who was to purify the filth of our conception and birth. God wished to be born the son of man so that we, being reborn in him, might be recreated true sons of god.

AUL.:   Do you believe that he lived on earth and there performed those miracles and taught those doctrines set forth in the gospels?

BAR.:   With greater certainty than I believe you to be a man.

AUL.:   I'm not an inverted Apuleius, that you should suspect an ass to be lurking under my human form.[8] But do you believe this same Christ to be that Messiah whom the types and figures of the Old Testament describe, whom the oracles of the prophets foretold, whom the Jews were anticipating for so many centuries?

BAR.:   There's nothing of which I'm more convinced.

AUL.:   Do you believe that his doctrine and life suffice to produce perfect piety?

BAR.:   Absolutely.

AUL.:   Do you believe he was seized by the Jews, bound, beaten and abused, spat upon, derided, and flagellated under Pontius Pilate, and finally nailed to a cross, where he died?

BAR.:   Implicitly.

AUL.:   Do you believe he was exempt and free from all manner of sin?

BAR.:   Of course. A lamb without spot.

AUL.:   Do you believe he suffered all these evils of his own free will?

BAR.:   Not only so, but gladly, even eagerly; but through the will of the father.

AUL.:   Why should the father want his only son, utterly innocent and supremely dear to him, to undergo such atrocious tortures?

BAR.:   That through this victim he might reconcile us sinners to himself when we placed our faith and hope in his name.

AUL.:   Why did God allow the entire human race to fall? And if he allowed it, wasn't there some other way of redeeming us from ruin?

BAR.:   Faith rather than human reason convinced me that it could not possibly have been done differently or in a manner better suited to our salvation.

AUL.:   Why was he best pleased with this manner of death?

BAR.:   Because in the eyes of the world it was most shameful, crucifix-

---

8. In his merry yet reverent tale "The Golden Ass," Lucius Apuleius imagined that, without losing his human mind, he had been transformed into the outward shape of an ass.

ion being agonizing and slow; because it was fitting that he should die with outstretched limbs since he was to call all the nations to salvation through him, and invite men, who are, as it were, nailed to the cares of this world, to raise themselves heavenward. Besides, he wanted to allude to the brazen serpent that Moses fixed on a pole, the sight of which healed everyone who turned his eyes toward it of the serpent's bite.[9] Finally, he wanted to fulfil the faith of the prophet who wrote: "Tell it to the nations that the lord has reigned from a tree."[1]

AUL.:   Why did he choose to be buried so particularly with myrrh and ointments, enclosed in a tomb newly cut from solid rock, its entry sealed and protected by public guards?

BAR.:   To make perfectly clear that he was indeed dead.

AUL.:   Why didn't he return to life immediately?

BAR.:   For this reason, that if his death had been doubtful, his reincarnation would have been doubtful too. But he wanted it to be absolutely certain.

AUL.:   Do you believe his soul descended to hell?

BAR.:   This topic, Cyprian tells me, was not originally in the Roman Creed, nor is it in the Creed of the Eastern Churches, and Tertullian, one of our earliest writers, says nothing about it.[2] Nonetheless, I firmly believe it; first because it accords with the words of the prophet in the psalms, "thou wilt not leave my soul in hell," and again, "Lord, you have delivered my soul from the lowest hell."[3] Also because the apostle Peter in the first of his epistles (the authorship of which has never been questioned) says that Christ was "put to death in the flesh but quickened by the spirit" (Chap. 3)—"by which also he went and preached to the spirits in prison."[4] But, though I believe he descended to hell, I do not believe he went there to suffer any sort of punishment; he went to destroy for our benefit the rule of Satan.

AUL.:   So far I hear nothing in the least impious. But if he died to bring us out of the depths of sin and back to new life, why was he resurrected himself?

BAR.:   For three very good reasons.

AUL.:   Yes?

BAR.:   First, that he might convey to us a positive hope of resurrection. Then, that we might be sure he is immortal and will never die, since we have placed in him faith in our own salvation. Then that we, being dead to sin through our repentance, and being buried with him through baptism, might be recalled by his grace to a new life.

AUL.:   Do you believe the same body which died on the cross, which

9. Numbers 21.9.

1. Psalms 96.10. The words "from a tree" (*a ligno*) were long ago judged an apocryphal addition and removed from the text.

2. Cyprian of Carthage (martyred in 258) wrote an important early book on the unity of the Catholic church. Barbatius, in appealing to one of the ear-liest and most revered of the church fathers, is putting solid ground under his feet. Tertullian, also a Carthaginian, was the very earliest of the church fathers and after Augustine the greatest.

3. Psalms 16 and 86.

4. 1 Peter 3.

revived in the tomb, and which was seen as well as touched by the disciples, then ascended to heaven?

BAR.:   Absolutely.

AUL.:   Why did he choose to leave the earth?

BAR.:   So that we should all love him spiritually, and nobody on earth should lay any special claim to Christ, but all should raise their spirits equally to heaven, knowing that our head is there. For if men quarrel nowadays over the cut and color of their habits, if some go around showing off the blood or the foreskin of Jesus or the milk of the Virgin, what would be the consequences if Christ himself had remained on earth, wearing clothes, eating, and preaching? What squabbles would arise over the different elements of his bodily existence!

AUL.:   You believe then that he was raised to immortality and a seat by the right hand of God?

BAR.:   Of course—so that he might be master of all things and a sharer in his father's reign. That is what he promised to his disciples and actually showed to Stephen his martyr.[5]

AUL.:   Why did he show it in that way?

BAR.:   Lest we remain in fear and uncertainty; so we might know how mighty a patron and master we have in heaven.

AUL.:   Do you believe that he will return in his original body to judge the living and the dead?

BAR.:   I am just as sure as I am that those things came to pass which the prophets told of Christ; so certain I am that everything will come to pass that he taught us to expect. Before his first coming we were taught by the oracles of the prophets that he would appear in humble guise to teach and redeem us. In the second coming he will be seen sublime in the glory of the father; before his tribunal will be forced to plead all men of every nation, of every condition, king and commoner alike, Greeks and Scythians; and not just those who are living at the moment of his return, but everyone who died from the beginning of the world to that moment. They will all suddenly arise and each one, restored to his own body, will behold his judge. Also present will be the blessed angels as faithful attendants, and the punitory demons. Then from on high he will pronounce his unalterable sentence, by which the devil and those who have adhered to him will be consigned to eternal torment lest they do any further harm; the faithful he will receive into the communion of the celestial realm, where they will dwell safe from all harm. But the exact time of this great event he has preferred to keep hidden from us.

AUL.:   So far I've heard nothing out of line. Let's consider now the third person.

BAR.:   As you please.

AUL.:   Do you believe in the Holy Spirit?

BAR.:   I believe it is the true God, at one with the Father and the Son.

5. Acts 7.55, 56.

I believe this was the spirit that inspired the writers of the Old and New Testaments, and that without his help nobody achieves salvation.

AUL.:   Why is it called a spirit?

BAR.:   Because as our bodies live by the breath of our nostrils, so do our souls live by the silent breath of the spirit.

AUL.:   Is it not proper to call the Father himself a spirit?

BAR.:   Indeed it is.

AUL.:   Aren't the persons of the Trinity mixed together then?

BAR.:   Not at all. For the Father is referred to as a "spirit" because he is incorporeal; and that is common to all three persons because of their divine nature. But the third person is called a spirit because it bloweth where it listeth,[6] and transfuses itself invisibly into souls as mists rise from the ground or from rivers.

AUL.:   Why is the second person accorded the name of the "son"?

BAR.:   Because of the perfect likeness of his nature and will to his father's.

AUL.:   Is the son more similar to the father than is the Holy Spirit?

BAR.:   Not insofar as they share equally in the divine nature, except that the Holy Spirit's proceeding from the Son as well implies that the Son has a fuller affinity with the Father.

AUL.:   What then prevents the Holy Spirit from being called the Son?

BAR.:   Because with Saint Hilary,[7] I nowhere read that the spirit was begotten, nor do I read of God as a father in this context. What I do read is that it is a spirit and proceeds from the Father.

AUL.:   Why in the creed is the Father alone declared to be God?

BAR.:   Because, as I said, he is the absolute creator of all things that exist and the source of all deity.

AUL.:   Speak more clearly.

BAR.:   Because nothing can be named which does not trace its origin to the Father. So the very statement that the Son and the Holy Spirit are God must include the Father as well. Special authority inheres in the Father, therefore, by reason of his originating nature, because he alone derives his origin from nobody. In the creed, however, it can be understood thus, that the name of God is not confined to any one person, but has a general application, the three elements of the unity being distinguished as God, Son, and Holy Spirit, that is, three persons.

AUL.:   Do you believe in the holy church?

BAR.:   No.

AUL.:   What are you saying? You don't believe?

BAR.:   I believe in a holy church which is the body of Christ, that is, a universal assemblage of all those throughout the world who agree in the evangelic faith, who worship God the Father and only him, who place their entire assurance in his Son, and who act by the inspiration

---

6. John 3.8.

7. Saint Hilary, of the fourth century, wrote an important treatise on the Trinity.

of his Spirit. Whoever is guilty of a deadly sin is separated from this society.

AUL.:   Why do you shrink from saying, "I believe in the holy church"?

BAR.:   Because Saint Cyprian[8] taught me to believe in God alone, in whom we should place all our faith. The church as properly defined, though it consists of none but good men, yet it consists of men who from being good may turn bad, who can be deceived and fall into error.

AUL.:   What do you think of the communion of the saints?

BAR.:   This article is not specifically handled by Cyprian, though he does indicate by name in which churches it has more or less authority. He does tie it with other subjects, in this way: "in line with this doctrine are those of the holy church, the remission of sins, and the resurrection of this flesh." And to some readers this part seems no different than what was said above, but only to explain and emphasize what had previously been said of the holy church: that the church is no other than the belief in one God, one gospel, one faith, one hope, a joining in one spirit and the same sacraments: briefly, such a particular communion of all good and pious men as have existed from the beginning of the world to its end, like the unity of the different parts of a single body. In this way the flourishing state of some parts sustains the welfare of others, so long as the body's various parts are alive. But outside this society no individual acts, however good, can lead anyone to salvation unless he is reconciled to the whole congregation. And from this follows remission of sins, since out of the church there is no remission of sins, however much penitential torment a man may undergo, however many works of devotional charity he may perform. Not in the church of heretics, I say, but in the holy church, meaning thereby the church assembled in the spirit of Christ, remission of sin comes through baptism, and after baptism through penitence and the keys given to the church.

AUL.:   So far, these are the views of a wise man. Do you believe in the future resurrection of the flesh?

BAR.:   All my other beliefs would be vain if I didn't believe in this, the keystone of the entire arch.

AUL.:   What do you mean by "the flesh"?

BAR.:   The human body animated by a human soul.

AUL.:   Will each individual soul seek out the same body from which in death it departed?

BAR.:   The very same that it had before. And so in the creed of Cyprian, the words are explicit—resurrection of *this* flesh.

AUL.:   How can it be that a body completely changed from one shape into others can be restored to its original shape?

8. The ancient explanation of the creed, to which Erasmus refers as "Cyprian's," was actually by Rufinus Tyrannus or Aquiliensis (from the Tyrrhenian sea, or from Aquileia); Erasmus knew the correct authorship, but also knew that the book would be better recognized and more authoritative if assigned to Cyprian.

BAR.: He who can do what he will created it from nothing; will it be hard for him to return to its original shape anything that was once changed out of it? I don't much worry over the ways in which this will be done, knowing that he who promised it is so truthful he cannot possibly lie, and so powerful that by a simple nod of his head he can accomplish whatever he chooses.

AUL.: What need will we have for our bodies at that time?

BAR.: So that every man who in this life suffered for Christ may be altogether glorified with Christ.

AUL.: What does the creed mean by adding "and eternal life"?

BAR.: It protects us from thinking that we may be reborn as frogs are reborn in the springtime, only to die again. For in this world death has a double nature: there is death of the body, which comes to all, whether good or bad, and death of the soul, which is sin. After the resurrection, the faithful will enjoy eternal life both of the body and of the soul. Nor will the body be liable ever again to sickness, old age, hunger, thirst, pain, weariness, death, or any other disability; but, become all spirit, it will be moved at the impulse of the spirit. Nor indeed will the spirit suffer any grief or affliction, but will enjoy for eternity the highest of all goods, which is God. On the other hand, eternal death will swallow up the ungodly, both body and soul. Of if the sinner's body is preserved, it will be only for undying torment, and his soul will be harrowed without hope of pardon by continual pangs of anguish.

AUL.: You believe all this in your heart, and seriously?

BAR.: Yes, I tell you; no less assuredly than I believe I'm talking with you now.

AUL.: When I was in Rome itself, I did not find in everyone there such a sincere belief.

BAR.: Wherever you look, you will find many folk who are not fully persuaded of these matters.

AUL.: Since you agree with us in so many and such difficult points of faith, what prevents you from being altogether of our party?

BAR.: That's something I'd rather hear from you. For to myself I seem to be utterly orthodox, even if I can't claim that my life—however hard I try—altogether corresponds with my profession of faith.

AUL.: Well then, what's the reason for all those hostilities between you and the orthodox?

BAR.: Ask yourself. But come now, Doctor,[9] if you're not dissatisfied with these preliminaries, why don't you join me in a little lunch, after which you can explore some more particular points at your leisure? You may inspect both arms and check into my evacuations, liquid as well as solid. Then you can look me straight in the face, which is the best index to what's in my heart, and form your judgment from that.

---

9. The title is used ironically, referring back to Aulus's proposal, at the start of the colloquy, to "act as your physician."

AUL.:   But I'm not supposed to share a meal with you.

BAR.:   Doctors are not above this practice when they want to find out what's the matter with their patients.

AUL.:   But I'm afraid I may seem to be favoring heretics.

BAR.:   In fact, nothing is more holy than to favor heretics.

AUL.:   How so?

BAR.:   Didn't Saint Paul desire to be made anathema for the Jews, who were worse than heretics?[1] Doesn't anyone favor a sinner when he strives to make a bad man good or raise a live soul from one that is dead?

AUL.:   Absolutely.

BAR.:   Well, make the effort; there's nothing to be afraid of.

AUL.:   I never heard a sick man speak so much to the point. Come, let's go to lunch.

BAR.:   You'll get mainly health food, as is natural when you eat in an invalid's house. We'll be careful of our stomachs so that our minds will be better prepared for argumentation.

AUL.:   So be it. I hope the birds will be of good omen.[2]

BAR.:   I'm afraid the fishes will be of bad; perhaps you've forgotten, today is Friday.

AUL.:   That wasn't part of the deal.[3]

The Abbot and the Learned Lady

Speakers: Antronius, Magdalia[1]

ANTRONIUS: What sort of decorations are these?

MAGDALIA: You don't think them very elegant?

ANT.:   How elegant they are I don't know; certainly they're not very suitable for a girl or a married woman.

MAG.:   And why not?

ANT.:   You have books all over the place.

MAG.:   You're a man of good birth, an abbot, and a courtier; haven't you ever seen books in the houses of ladies?

ANT.:   Yes, but they were written in French; here I see Greek and Latin books.

MAG.:   I suppose one can learn wisdom only from books written in French?

---

1. Romans 9.3. In behalf of the Jews, Paul actually wants to take Christ's curse on himself.

2. The prospect of chicken for dinner, the hope that good fortune may attend this first small effort at reconciliation.

3. The discussion has been of the creed, i.e., *symbolum*; but a *symbola* is a contribution to a feast. The root of the word is Greek, *syn-ballein*, meaning to throw or put together, hence to compare, agree, strike a deal. There's a lot of rather esoteric punning going on here, which doesn't come through in English.

1. Via a proverbial Greek expression, "Antronius" could be understood to imply "an ass from a cave"; "Magdalia" may be intended to recall Mary Magdalen, who was one of the women closest to Christ in his last days. There is no particular reason for identifying her with the unnamed "fallen woman" of Luke 7.37.

ANT.:   That's the sort of book for ladies, to drive away boredom.

MAG.:   Only ladies are entitled to have some knowledge and live pleasantly?

ANT.:   Having knowledge and living pleasantly aren't the same thing at all. Women shouldn't have knowledge, but ladies are entitled to live pleasantly.

MAG.:   Isn't everyone supposed to live well?

ANT.:   I suppose so.

MAG.:   But who can live pleasantly who doesn't live well?

ANT.:   Rather, who *can* live pleasantly who lives well?

MAG.:   Then you approve of those who live badly but pleasantly?

ANT.:   I think those people live well who live pleasantly.

MAG.:   But this pleasure, where does it come from? from external things, or from the mind?

ANT.:   From external things.

MAG.:   Oh, what a subtle abbot, and what a dull philosopher! Tell me, what are the things by which you measure pleasure.

ANT.:   Sleep, good food, freedom to do as you please, money, honors.

MAG.:   But if to these things God added wisdom, would you live pleasantly?

ANT.:   What do you mean by wisdom?

MAG.:   Just this: that if man cannot be truly happy unless his mind is active and vigorous, then neither riches, honors, nor high descent render him any happier or better.

ANT.:   Then good-bye to that wisdom of yours.

MAG.:   What if I enjoy reading a good book more than you do hunting and drinking and shooting dice? You wouldn't think I was living pleasantly?

ANT.:   I couldn't endure such a life.

MAG.:   I'm not asking what you would prefer, but what ought to be the quality of a good life.

ANT.:   I'd be very unhappy to see my monks too much given to reading books.

MAG.:   As a matter of fact, my husband is very proud of my reading. But why wouldn't you want your monks to read books?

ANT.:   Because I know they would be less docile; they would answer me back by citing Decrees, Decretals, Peter and Paul.

MAG.:   Your orders, then, run contrary to Peter and Paul?[2]

ANT.:   I don't even know what they say, but I have no use for a monk who answers back; I wouldn't want any of my flock to know more than I do myself.

MAG.:   That wouldn't happen if you took some pains to know as much as possible.

2. Decrees are formal, authoritative church decisions; decretals are interpretations of church law which in codified form make up the body of canon law. Clerics familiar with these materials, and with the epistles of Peter and Paul, might be hard to boss around.

ANT.: There is no time.

MAG.: Why not?

ANT.: I don't have the leisure.

MAG.: No leisure to be wise?

ANT.: No.

MAG.: What's the problem?

ANT.: I have prayers to recite, an establishment to oversee, my hunting, my horses, my attendance at court.

MAG.: And so those things are more important than wisdom?

ANT.: That's the way custom decrees things.

MAG.: Now tell me this: if some Jupiter gave you the power to turn your monks and yourself into any animal you chose, would you turn them into pigs and yourself into a horse?

ANT.: No way.

MAG.: But if you did that, you could be sure none of them would know more than you.

ANT.: I don't care what sort of beasts my monks become, as long as I can be a man.

MAG.: Do you think anyone is a man who doesn't know, and doesn't want to know, anything?

ANT.: I know myself.

MAG.: And so do pigs know themselves.

ANT.: You seem to me some kind of female sophister, you twist things so.

MAG.: I'd rather not say what you seem to me. But why don't you like my library?

ANT.: Because the distaff and the knitting needle are the proper implements of a woman.

MAG.: Isn't it a wife's job to run the household and raise her children?

ANT.: Of course.

MAG.: And do you think that sort of work can be carried on without wisdom?

ANT.: I suppose not.

MAG.: But that wisdom I acquire from my books.

ANT.: I have in my abbey sixty-two monks, but you won't find a single book in my study.

MAG.: A happy outlook for those monks.

ANT.: I can put up with books, but not with your Latin ones.

MAG.: And why not those?

ANT.: Because that language is not fit for female ears.

MAG.: I'm waiting for a real reason.

ANT.: It's not compatible with woman's native modesty.

MAG.: So you think those French books stuffed with frivolous fables[3] are good for our modesty?

3. The French books at issue are probably "romans," i.e., tales of chivalry and romance, or even "fabliaux," spicy stories.

ANT.: There's something else.

MAG.: Tell it then, whatever it is, straight out.

ANT.: Women are safer from priests if they don't know any Latin.

MAG.: That's the least dangerous part of your projects. Whenever you're soliciting us that way, *you* don't know any Latin.

ANT.: Anyhow, that's the popular opinion, since it's very rare and unusual for a woman to know Latin nowadays.

MAG.: Why do you quote popular opinion at me, the very worst guide of all to good behavior? Why do you talk about popular customs, which authorize evil of every sort? We should accustom ourselves only to the highest standards; thus, what used to be unusual will become common, what used to be disagreeable will become pleasant, and what was once improper will become perfectly proper.

ANT.: I hear you talking.

MAG.: Don't you think it proper for a woman born in Germany to learn French?

ANT.: Very much so.

MAG.: Your reason?

ANT.: So she can converse with people who know French.

MAG.: And yet you think it improper for me to learn Latin so that every day I can converse with the many authors, the many preachers, the many scholars, the many philosophers, the many different supporters of my faith?

ANT.: Books absorb so much of the female intellect that they have very little left over.

MAG.: How much excess brain power you have I don't know; whatever little I have I would rather spend on good books than on prayers repeated mindlessly, on all-night feasts, on gulping down enormous flagons of liquor.

ANT.: Too much book-learning leads to insanity.

MAG.: Don't you consider all those drinking parties, with their clusters of parasites and buffoons, a form of insanity?

ANT.: They serve to pass the time.

MAG.: How does it happen, then, that such agreeable companions as mine lead to madness?

ANT.: They have that reputation.

MAG.: But the events themselves say otherwise. And how many more people do we know for whom excessive drink and immoderate eating, riotous nights and violent passions, lead to insanity?

ANT.: Personally, I wouldn't want a learned wife.

MAG.: But personally, I'm delighted to have a husband very different from you. Learning renders him dearer to me, and me dearer to him.

ANT.: To acquire learning requires enormous effort, and then comes death.

MAG.: Tell me, you splendid thinker, if you had to die tomorrow, would you rather die a stupid or a learned man?

ANT.: If I could do so without effort, I'd rather be wise.

MAG.: But nothing in this life comes without effort; and yet, whatever you possess, and however you acquired it, in the end it must be left behind here. Why should it distress us to invest a little labor in the most precious endeavor of all, the fruits of which will accompany us to the other life as well?

ANT.: I've often heard the common saying that a learned woman is twice a fool.

MAG.: It's a common saying indeed—always on the tongue of fools. A really wise woman doesn't think she knows anything, whereas one who knows nothing thinks she knows everything—and therefore really is twice a fool.

ANT.: I can't fully account for it, but just as a saddle doesn't fit on a cow, so letters don't suit a woman.

MAG.: But you can't deny a saddle would look better on a cow than a miter on an ass or a swine. What's your opinion of the virgin Mary?

ANT.: The highest.

MAG.: Wasn't she a reader of books?

ANT.: She was indeed, but not in these.

MAG.: In which books then?

ANT.: She read her book of hours.[4]

MAG.: According to which order?

ANT.: Saint Benedict's.

MAG.: So be it. What about Paula and Eustochius,[5] weren't they skilled in interpreting the sacred scriptures?

ANT.: Nowadays such accomplishments are very unusual.

MAG.: In the same way an abbot without learning used to be a very rare bird; nowadays nothing is more common. Once upon a time princes and emperors were as remarkable for their learning as for their prowess. Still, learning in women is not as unusual as you think; in Spain and Italy there are a number of women of the highest nobility who could compete in learning with any man. In England there are the daughters of the More family, in Germany the girls of Pirckheimer and the Blaurers.[6] So that unless you men look sharp, things may take such a turn that we will preside in the schools of theology, preach in the churches, and take over the wearing of your miters.

ANT.: God forbid.

MAG.: Not at all; it's entirely up to you. Because if you keep on as you've begun, you'll find the geese preach themselves rather than put up with you dumb pastors. You see how the world is turned upside down these days; either you must drop your mask entirely or be prepared to play your role to the full.

---

4. Books of hours were illuminated calendars to enable bored medieval ladies to keep track of the seasons. As reading matter for the Virgin, they are a comic anachronism as gross as the introduction into her life of Saint Benedict.

5. Saint Paula and her daughter Julia Eustochium were leading members of the cenacle of devout women who gathered around Saint Jerome, rather to the scandal of his censorious contemporaries.

6. Like More, Willibald Pirckheimer and the brothers Ambrosius and Thomas Blaurer were members of the humanist circle closely acquainted with Erasmus.

ANT.:   How did I get involved with this woman? If and when you come
to visit us, I myself will receive you more graciously.

MAG.:   How so?

ANT.:   We'll dance, we'll drink deep, we'll go hunting, we'll play and
laugh.

MAG.:   I've got enough to laugh at already.

Letters

Like Voltaire, with whom it's commonplace to compare him, Erasmus was a prodigious correspondent; and because, throughout much of his life, he was a famous man, his letters were preserved in unprecedented numbers. Not everyone who writes is capable of writing a good personal letter; to Erasmus the form came naturally, and he used its freedoms to fill his letters with jokes, gossip, news, arguments, complaints, exhortations, scholarship—all the things that filled his restless, active life from day to day. The classic Allen edition of the *Opus Epistolarum* took forty years to prepare and fills eleven volumes. From such a wealth of material, limitations of space allow us to choose only a couple of highlights. The letter to Dorp is essential to the understanding of *Folly*; the journey from Basle to Louvain gives a glimpse of the frightful difficulties of getting around Europe in the sixteenth century; the late letter to the bishop of Cracow, showing Erasmus still deeply involved in the world yet ironically distanced from it, suggests a final tempered perspective.

To Martin Dorp †

[A *Defense of* Folly]

Antwerp, end of May 1515

I haven't yet received your letter, but a friend here at Antwerp showed me a copy; how he got hold of it, I have no idea. You complain of the

† Martin Dorp was a young Dutch theologian at the University of Louvain; Erasmus had known him during his stay there (1502–4). Three years after the first publication of *The Praise of Folly* (Paris, 1511), Dorp wrote a letter mainly about it (September 1514); its contents are fairly represented in Erasmus's reply, and the full text may be consulted in P. S. Allen's edition of the *Opus Epistolarum* (2.10–16). In 1514 Dorp was thirty years old, Erasmus about forty-five. Because misgivings about *Folly* were far more widespread than the "two or three" theologians to whom Erasmus attributed them, his reply to Dorp provided a good opportunity for a general public defense; the letter as given here was many times appended to early editions of the *Folly*—often in conjunction with the very apologetic annotations of Gerard Lister.

Erasmus's attitude toward Dorp as a person is complex, not to say artful. He praises the young man's integrity, yet assumes throughout that he is acting as front for a cabal of unnamed, malicious others. He makes much of his intellectual attainments but is not gentle in intimating that without Greek he has no business discussing Erasmus's work on the New Testament—or, for that matter, theology in general. Elsewhere in the correspondence, Erasmus refers to Dorp as "stolid," but for publication the adjective was deleted. In any case, the present letter is very feline, compounded of purrs, compliments, and some pretty ferocious scratches. The ending mixes an act of real kindness with a fairly blunt put-down: Erasmus reminds Dorp that the young man's supporters and patrons thought themselves honored to be mentioned in the writings of the great Erasmus—he was, after all, a European figure writing to an obscure (and, on the evidence, not particularly brilliant) student of theology.

The controversy did not end with this letter; Dorp replied, and Erasmus wrote again (October 1515). Neither convinced the other (naturally), but, more surprisingly, they did not become enemies, and when Dorp died prematurely in 1525, Erasmus wrote an epitaph for him.

Folly, poorly printed as it was, you strongly approve of my work in restoring the text of Saint Jerome,[1] and you discourage my proposed edition of the New Testament. In what you say there's so little that's offensive to me, old friend, that henceforth you will be even dearer to me than you were—dear though you always were. For your advice is sincere, your warnings friendly, and your criticisms constructive. Christian charity has this quality, that however sharply a criticism is framed, its basic sweetness shines through. Every day I get letters from scholars who call me the pride of Germany, the sun and the moon of scholarship—grandiose titles that embarrass more than they embellish me. But among all these letters, not one, I swear, has ever given me as much pleasure as this critical letter from my friend Dorp. Paul was right when he said charity can do no wrong;[2] whether she praises or criticizes is all the same, the aim is always to be of help. And I really wish I had the leisure to answer your letter in a way that would give satisfaction to such a good friend. In whatever I do I truly want to have your good opinion because I value so highly the sharpness of your insight, the depth of your learning, and the strength of your judgment, that I'd rather earn the esteem of one Dorp than that of a thousand others. But up to this point I'm still recuperating from seasickness followed by a long horseback ride, not to mention the problem of getting all my luggage together; still, I thought it better to answer any way at all, rather than leave a friend in the frame of mind you expressed—whether the ideas were all your own or suggested to you by others who encouraged you to write that letter in order to insinuate their views behind the mask of your person.

First, then, to speak frankly, I'm almost sorry myself that I published the *Folly*. The book has gained me a certain amount of reputation, or, if you prefer, notoriety; but I don't care for fame when it's accompanied by envy. What, in the name of heaven, is fame (as the vulgar call it) but the emptiest of names left over from pagan times? A few such words linger on among us Christians; we tend to call the reputation we leave to posterity by the name of immortality, and put the label of "virtue" on any sort of interest in the arts. In whatever books I've published, I always aimed exclusively at the same single objective, to do some good by my efforts, or at least not to do any harm. We often see men, even men of ability, abusing their literary skills by subordinating them to their personal emotions, as when one man serenades his foolish mistress, another flatters his superiors, still another uses his pen to revenge some slight, and a fourth composes panegyrics on himself that go beyond any characters on the comic stage.[3] Whatever modest talents I have I've always tried to use for someone's benefit, or at least without doing anyone harm. Homer took out his rage against Thersites in some very ugly lines; Plato in his dialogues arraigned all sorts of individuals, and by name. Whom

---

1. Erasmus's corrected edition of the writings of Jerome was only the first of a series of editions that extended to include Cyprian, Hilarius, Irenaeus, Ambrose, Augustine, Chrysostom, Basil, and Origen. He had many helpers, but the task was a monumental one all the same.

2. 1 Corinthians 13.4–7.

3. Erasmus mentions a couple of specific characters from the comedies of Terence, whose names I have omitted.

did Aristotle spare when he didn't spare either Plato or Socrates?[4] Demosthenes had an opponent, Aeschynes, on whom he emptied the vials of his wrath; Cicero went after Piso, Vatinius, Sallust, and Anthony. Think of all the people whom Seneca ridiculed and attacked by name! Among more recent authors, Petrarch sharpened his pen against a certain doctor, Valla wrote against Poggio, and Politian against Scala.[5] Can you name me anyone at all so meek that he never wrote a bitter word against anyone? Saint Jerome himself, a man of utmost gravity and piety, couldn't keep himself from hot words against Vigilantius, bitter insults against Jovinius, and some sour expressions about Rufinius. It's traditional for learned men to commit their joys and sorrows to paper as the most faithful and intimate of companions, to whom they could entrust all the passions of their hearts. You can even find a few who wrote books of set purpose, to let off steam against their enemies and to pass on the reasons for their animus to posterity.

But in all the many books I've written, in which I've praised so many different men to the skies, have I ever blackened the reputation of a single one? Whom have I ever spattered with a spot of mud? What nation, what class, what individual have I ever attacked by name? Do you have any idea, my dear Dorp, how many times I've been provoked by all but intolerable insults to take my revenge? But I've always been able to cool my anger and to think more about how posterity would view me than about the punishment the malicious provokers deserved. If others knew the facts of the matter as I did, nobody would have considered me a spiteful man, but rather a candid, a modest, and a moderate one. On thinking it over, I always asked, What do other people care about my private feelings? Will people from another country or in another century pay the slightest attention to my grievances? Whatever I did wasn't done to gain their acclaim, but from my own sense of self-esteem. Besides, nobody is so hostile to me that I wouldn't prefer to have him as a friend if I could. Why should I cut him off and write something against an enemy that I might later regret having written against a friend? Why blacken a reputation that I could never restore to its pristine whiteness, even if the person should so deserve? I'd rather err on the side of charity to the undeserving than risk abusing an honest man. If you overpraise someone, it's put down to your good nature; but if you paint a rascal in his proper colors, however, much he deserves it, your criticism is attributed, not to his behavior, but to your ill nature. I'll say nothing of how huge conflicts often arise out of mutual insults and dangerous conflagrations from a simple exchange of epithets; but, as it's not Christian

4. Homer's Thersites can perfectly well be understood as a literary creation, not a character drawn from life. Aristotle, though he often differed from Plato, never satirized him. Erasmus's classical justifications (for satire that he says he didn't write) are perfunctory. Cicero (in the next sentence) was a lawyer, and as such attacked a lot of people, but Sallust wasn't one of them; that diatribe belongs to another author.

5. Early humanists were often vitriolic in controversy. Lorenzo Valla and Poggio Bracciolini, Poliziano and Bartolomeo Scala were famous antagonists. Petrarch wrote an "Invective against a Certain Physician," but not because he disliked any individual; he hated doctors in general.

conduct to repay one insult with another, so it's hardly dignified to pay off an injury by getting into a slanging match with your opponent, like a couple of fishwives.

By reasoning of this sort I long ago persuaded myself to keep my writings clean of personal invective and uncontaminated by insults. And this same principle is observed in the *Folly* as in my other works, though it follows a slightly different path. In the *Enchiridion* I laid out very simply the pattern of a Christian life; in my little book on *The Education of a Christian Prince*, I declared directly the things that a prince ought to be taught. In the *Panegyric of Philip*, under the guise of praise, I did the exact same thing that elsewhere I did openly and directly.[6] And now *Folly* says, though jokingly, precisely the same thing as the *Enchiridion*. I wanted to mock, not to attack; to benefit, not to wound; to comment on men's manners, not to denounce them. Plato, a serious philosopher indeed, approves of deep drinking at parties because he says that certain follies and flaws can be mentioned when one is high that in all solemnity can hardly be discussed. And Horace reminds us that a joking admonition, no less than a solemn one, can convey a serious point:

> Telling the truth in a joke—
> What's wrong about it?[7]

The wisest men of antiquity understood this very well, when they preferred to set forth their soundest precepts about human life in the form of ludicrous or childish stories because they knew that even a bitter dose of truth, if sugar-coated, goes down readily. In the same way, Lucretius tells us, doctors rub a bit of honey on the rim of a cup from which a patient is to drink a bitter dose.[8] For the same reason, princes are fond of bringing fools into their courts, under cover of whose special license certain minor failings may be discussed without offense to anyone, and so corrected. Perhaps it's not proper to introduce Christ into this list, but if divine doings hold any proportion with human ones, don't his parables have something in common with the fables of the ancients? The truths of the gospel enter the mind more easily and retain their savor longer when enclosed in these narratives than they would if presented as bald doctrine. It's a point that Saint Augustine illustrates at length in his work *On Christian Doctrine*.[9] I saw the people being corrupted by the most stupid opinions, and that in the most public occasions of life; their recovery was a matter for prayer rather than anticipation. And then I felt I had found a way to insinuate myself in these diseased minds, and minister to them under the guise of pleasure. I'd often seen before that this sort of jocose and cheerful medication yields good results with many patients.

---

6. The *Enchiridion*, or *Handbook of the Militant Christian*, had been published in 1503, *The Education of a Christian Prince* in 1515. Erasmus was touchy about his 1504 *Panegyric of Philip* (this was Philip I "The Handsome," son of the emperor Maximilian) because it had been seen as flattery— which it actually was, of the grossest sort. But here he says it was really teaching.

7. Horace, *Satires* 1.1.24–25.
8. Lucretius, *De rerum natura* 1.936 ff.
9. Augustine, *De doctrina christiana* 2.6.

Perhaps you will say that the mask I assumed was merrier than should have been adopted for the discussion of serious topics; and I'm disposed to agree with you. The charge of having gone clumsily to work I won't dispute; that of excessive satiric bitterness I certainly do. In fact, I could put up a defense for that too, if only on the basis of the many thoroughly serious authors who wrote before me, in the same vein, and whose names I cited in the little preface to the book itself. What else could I do? I was on my way back from Italy, and stayed for a few days with my friend More, where kidney trouble kept me briefly indoors. My books had not yet arrived, and even if I had had them, the pain of my disease wouldn't have allowed me to resume serious studies. Out of boredom I began to play with the notion of praising folly—not, certainly, with the idea of publication in mind, but merely as a distraction from the pain of my disease. I showed some parts of the first draft to a few friends, hoping to improve the joke by sharing it. They were delighted, and urged me to go on with it. So I went on, and put about a week more or less into the exercise—about all I thought such a trivial argument deserved. Then the same people who had asked me to write it took the manuscript to France, and there it was printed from a faulty and mutilated text. Its popularity is shown by the fact that within a few months seven editions appeared, and in several different cities—much to my amazement.

If you want to call all this clumsiness, my dear Dorp, you have here my open confession, or at least my plea of no contest. As a result of too much leisure and some importunate friends, I played the fool for the first time in my life. Well, who's wise all the time? You yourself admit that my other writings have received and deserved the highest praise of pious and learned men. Who are these strict censors, or rather these severe judges seated on their Areopagus,[1] who won't forgive a man for one single error? They must be fearfully morose of disposition if, because of a single silly little book, they deprive me on the spot of the credit won by years of long and serious labor. I could produce far more curious performances by other men, even mighty theologians, who dig up vexed long-deceased questions, ridiculous trifles over which they then do battle as if their very existence were at stake. What's more, they act out these ridiculous charades and comic carnivals without even putting on masks. I show a little more propriety when, to play the fool, I put on the mask of Folly herself; and, just as Socrates, when he wanted to sing the praises of love assumed a false person,[2] so I too act out my comedy from behind a mask.

You write that even people who dislike the argument agree in admiring the wit and learning of the book, but they are offended by the freedom of the biting satire. But these critics give me more credit than I deserve. I'm not in the least eager for such praise, coming as it does from people in whom I recognize neither wit nor learning nor eloquence.

1. A high and strict Athenian court which concerned itself particularly with morals and manners; cf. Milton's essay "Areopagitica."

2. In the *Phaedrus*, Socrates "veils his face" before speaking of love.

Believe me, my dear Dorp, if they were better endowed that way, they wouldn't be offended by jokes which aren't simply witty or learned, but convey a good moral point. By all the muses, I beg you to tell me what sort of eyes, ears, and palate do these people bring to their reading when they claim to be offended by the sharpness of my little book? What sharpness can there possibly be where not a single name appears except for my own? Why don't they recall what Jerome said repeatedly, where the discussion of vices is general, there can be no insult to any individual? If anyone is offended by that sort of talk, he has no quarrel with the speaker; let him accuse himself as his own betrayer, when he makes a personal application of what was spoken about everyone and no one. Of course anyone can claim an application to himself if he wants to. But don't you see that in the whole book I've been so careful about using individual names that I didn't even ridicule one nation more than another? When I accuse each nation of having its own special form of self-love, I give the Spanish credit for military prowess, the Italians literary taste and eloquence, the English good food and good looks, and similarly throughout, something for everyone, things that anyone will recognize for himself and hear with a smile. Again, when I review, according to the plan of my book, the various classes of men, and note the vices of each, let me ask you did I ever write anything vulgar or virulent? When did I open up a sewer of vices? We all know how many things could be said about bad popes, scandalous bishops and priests, corrupt princes— if, like Juvenal, I had not been ashamed to write down what many are not ashamed to act out. But I considered only absurd and ridiculous things, not disgraceful ones; and I touched on them in such a way as to make perfectly clear I was alluding indirectly to important matters about which it's important for people to know.

I realize you don't have time for dabbling in such trifles; still, when you have a moment, you might look a little more closely at those ridiculous jokes of Folly's; you'll find that they agree much better with the teachings of the evangelists and the apostles than do those splendid (as they consider them) disputations which are supposed to be worthy productions of our great theological masters. In your letter you yourself admit that most of the things I say are true. But you think it's not seemly

> To wound the tender ear with cutting truth. [3]

But if you think it's never right to speak out and declare the truth plainly except when it doesn't offend, why do physicians use bitter herbs as medications, among others of high repute *hiera picra*? If they do that in ministering to ills of the body, why shouldn't I do the same thing to cure diseases of the mind? "Preach the word," says Paul, "be instant in season, out of season; reprove, rebuke, and exhort." [4] The apostle wants vices to be attacked in every possible way; do you want to say now that this sore spot or that shouldn't be touched?—especially when it's done

---

3. Persius 1.107. *Hiera picra* is a fierce cathartic.   4. 2 Timothy 4.2.

so gently that no individual can possibly suppose he's been wounded unless he deliberately turns the point against himself. If there's one rule above all for correcting men's vices without wounding anyone, it's to avoid mentioning names; the second rule is to avoid discussing matters so offensive in themselves that simply raising the subject would offend respectable feelings. Thus in tragedies, for example, certain actions are too horrifying to be placed before the eyes of spectators, hence they are only described; similarly, certain details in the lives of men are too obscene to be described in detail, so they are avoided. A last rule is to put everything that's said in the mouth of a fictitious character given to jokes and frivolities, so that the comic quality of the speech effaces every chance for offense. Don't we often see how, even in the courts of the most severe tyrants, a timely and opportune joke breaks the tension? I ask you what prayers or serious speeches could have softened the anger of great king Pyrrhus as well as the rough joke of a soldier?[5] "If only we'd had another bottle," he said, "there's a lot worse things we could have said about you." The king laughed and forgot the insult. It was with good reason that the two supreme orators Cicero and Quintilian taught the art of raising a laugh. Wit and humor have such force that we enjoy good jokes even when they are directed against ourselves; examples can be found in the letters of Julius Caesar.[6]

If you grant that what I wrote is true, and that it was more pleasant than obscene, what better approach can you imagine for treating the common ailments of mankind? Pleasure is what catches readers in the first place, and holds them once caught. In other respects each man looks for some special value of his own, but pleasure attracts everyone alike, unless perhaps someone who is too stupid to respond to written material at all.

People who take offense when no name has been mentioned seem to me like those high-strung women who, if anything is said against women of loose manners, get all excited, as if every woman in the world was being disgraced; and then if anything is said in praise of a good woman, they are as complacent as if words spoken about one individual or another applied to the entire sex. Men should have better sense than this, especially men of learning, and theologians most of all. If I hear of someone being charged with a crime of which I am innocent, I'm not offended; in fact, I congratulate myself on being free of a crime to which others are subject. If some sore spot is touched on, and I see myself there as if in a mirror, that's all the more reason why I shouldn't be offended. If I have any sense, I'll conceal my feelings and try not to betray my fault to the public. If I'm a person of integrity, I'll take the warning to heart and make sure I'm not charged directly for a failing which here I was able to recognize without my name attached to it. Why don't we allow this little pamphlet the liberties that even marketplace audiences allow to popular comedies? How many shafts are launched there, in perfect freedom, against monarchs, priests, monks, wives, husbands, and—who isn't fair game? And yet, since nobody is attacked by name, the audience has its laugh, and the individual either frankly confesses his failings or prudently conceals his feelings. The gloomiest of tyrants put up with their jesters and fools, even when the jokes strike pretty close to home. The emperor Vespasian took no revenge on a joker who said he had a face like a man taking a dump.[7] And who, now, are these people with such delicate ears that they cannot bear to hear Folly herself sporting with the common life of mankind, yet never uttering a word of personal blame? The Old Comedy would never have been hissed off the stage if it had refrained from mentioning eminent men by name.

But you, my good Dorp, write almost as if you thought this one little book of Folly had made the entire order of theologians my enemies. "What need was there," you ask, "to wound the order of theologians so severely?" and you deplore all the troubles I've brought on myself. "Formerly," you say, "everyone read your books eagerly and was hoping to meet you face to face. Now Folly, like Davus, has made a mess of everything."[8] I know you don't write out of malice, and I won't play games with you either. Let me ask you, do you think the order of theologians has been insulted when something is said about foolish or bad theologians, men altogether unworthy of the title? If that's the way you think, then you must suppose the entire human race is insulted whenever someone talks about rascally men. What king was ever so brazen as to claim there were never any bad kings, unworthy of the honor? What bishop was ever so arrogant as to make the same claim about his own order? Is there any one order of theologians that in its entire body numbers not a single stupid, ignorant, or quarrelsome member, but shows us nothing but Saint Pauls, Saint Basils, and Saint Jeromes? Isn't it rather the case that the loftier a group's principles, the fewer members there will be who live up to those principles? You will find more good sailors than good princes, more good doctors than good bishops. It isn't a question of insulting the order, but rather of praising the chosen few who in an admirable order have comported themselves admirably. Tell me, if you will, why the theologians should be more offended—if any of them really are—than the kings, primates, judges, bishops, cardinals, and the popes themselves?—or, for that matter, the merchants, husbands, wives, lawyers, and poets?—for Folly takes as her province the entire human race. Of course anyone is free, if he's that silly, to take to himself personally what was said in general about bad men. Saint Jerome wrote to Julia Eustochium[9] on the subject of virginity, and in his diatribe described the manners of corrupt nuns so vividly that Apelles himself couldn't have depicted them more sharply. Was Julia offended?

7. Suetonius, *Life of Vespasian*.
8. The seventh satire of Horace's second book is about the Saturnalia, a Roman festival when slaves were momentarily free; Horace's slave Davus uses the occasion to tell the poet exactly what he thinks of him.

9. Julia Eustochium was one of Jerome's conclave of devout ladies; she took vows of virginity in 383 and later directed a convent at Bethlehem under the supervision of Jerome himself. Apelles was the legendary, almost mythical, Greek painter.

Did she bring charges against Jerome that he had dishonored the entire order of nuns? Not a bit of it. And why not? Because as a wise virgin, she didn't take to herself criticisms levelled at her bad sisters; rather, she welcomed them as warning the good sisters against evil ways and urging the evil sisters to improve. Jerome wrote to Nepotianus about the lives of the clergy and to Rusticus about the lives of the monks, describing the evil behavior of both groups and devastating them with bitter sarcasms. Neither of the men to whom he wrote took offense, because both understood the criticisms were not directed against them. Why didn't William Mountjoy, not the least eminent of the noble Englishmen at the royal court, get angry with Folly because she mocks courtiers?[1] Like the eminently sensible and magnanimous man he is, he realized that what was said about evil and foolish noblemen had no bearing on him. Think of all the jokes Folly cracked about wicked and worldly bishops. Why wasn't the archbishop of Canterbury upset? Because as a man of absolute virtue and broad intelligence, he knew none of the shafts were directed at him.

I won't even try to list here the names of princes, bishops, abbots, cardinals, and scholars of distinction not one of whom has given the slightest sign of being angry at *Folly*. And in fact I doubt if any clerics could be produced who are really bothered by the book, unless perhaps a few who either don't understand it or are so sullen by nature that they don't approve of anything. It's an admitted fact that among theologians there are some so deficient in wit and judgment that they're unfit for study of any sort, let alone theology. After they've memorized a few rules out of Alexander of Villedieu and jumbled together a few logical paradigms, they learn by rote some ten propositions of Aristotle, add to them the same number of questions from Scotus or Occam, and top off their education with a smattering from the *Catholicon*, the *Mammatrecton*, and some similar compendia which act as their horn of intellectual plenty.[2] And now, since nothing is more arrogant than ignorance, just see how high they raise their crests! These are the people who, because they don't understand Saint Jerome, scorn him as a mere grammarian. These are the ones who despise Greek, Hebrew, and even Latin literature, and who, though they are more stupid than swine and don't even have ordinary common sense, fancy themselves the defenders of the fortress of learning. They judge, they condemn, they pass sentence, they have no doubts or hesitations, and there's absolutely nothing they don't know. Yet this is the handful of rogues that often stirs up the greatest commotions, since there's nothing more impudent or persistent than ignorance. These fellows are engaged in a great conspiracy against humane letters because they want to cut a figure in the assembly of theologians, and

1. William Blount, Lord Mountjoy, was one of Erasmus's pupils; William Warham, archbishop of Canterbury, was one of his patrons.
2. Alexander of Villedieu (thirteenth century) wrote a versified Latin grammar; Duns Scotus and William of Occam were scholastic philosophers. The *Catholicon* and *Mammatrecton* were compendia of biblical information; Erasmus's point is that this is all pretty elementary stuff.

they are afraid that if polite learning flourishes and the world gets a little wiser, they will be recognized as ignoramuses, though before they wanted to appear before the world as know-it-alls. They are the ones who raise outcries, they thunder objections, they form conspiracies against the men trained in good literature. *Folly* displeases them because they don't understand her, whether it's Greek or Latin she speaks. They aren't theologians but theological play-actors; if something rather sharp is directed against creatures of this nature, what is that to the most respectable order of good theologians?

If they're really motivated by religious zeal, why have they concentrated their fire on *Folly?* How much did Poggio write that was impious, foul, or pestilent?[3] Yet he is everywhere considered a Christian author, and has been translated into many languages. Pontanus pursued the clergy with the most amazing insults and imprecations; yet he's read as a witty and amusing author. What a quantity of obscene matter is found in Juvenal, which doesn't prevent him from being cited frequently in the pulpit. How maliciously Tacitus wrote against the Christians, what an enemy of the faith was Suetonius, how scandalously Pliny and Lucian ridicule the immortality of the soul! Yet for the sake of learning everyone reads them, and rightly so. Only *Folly*, because she tosses a few barbs, not at good theologians worthy of the name, but at the silly little problems raised by the ignorant and at their ridiculous title of "Our Masters," only *Folly* is not to be endured.

The fact is that two or three rascals impersonating theologians are trying to stir up hostility against me as if I had wounded or insulted the whole order of theologians. Really, I have so much respect for theological learning that it's the only sort I allow to be learning at all. I admire and reverence this order so much, that it's the only one in which I aspire to be enrolled.[4] Only modesty prevents my laying claim to such a splendid title, conscious as I am of the special gifts for learning and strict living that the name of theologian requires. I'm not sure that the teaching of theology isn't beyond the capacity of man; surely, it's a profession for bishops only, not for men like me. I find it enough to have learned that saying of Socrates, that I know nothing at all, and to devote my energies to helping other people with their studies.

The fact is, I don't know where to locate those two or three godlike men lurking among the theologians who you say take a dim view of me. Since the *Folly* was published, I've visited a number of countries, stayed in several universities, frequented quite a few populous cities; and I never found a theologian who was angry with me, unless perhaps one or two of those who bear a standing grudge against humane letters, and not even these spoke to me face to face. What they said behind my back I

3. Poggio, mentioned above (p. 230, n. 5) as a controversialist, was a comic author as well; his *Facetiae* were as notable for their anticlericalism as for their indecency. Pontanus was a Neapolitan scholar and poet, famous if not notorious for the erotic

freedom of his verse and the satiric point of his dialogues.

4. In fact Erasmus had received in 1506 a doctorate of theology from the University of Turin.

don't know or care, because I have the judgment of so many good men to sustain me. If I weren't afraid of speaking more out of arrogance than truth, my dear Dorp, I could recite for you a long list of theologians famous for the holiness of their lives, distinguished by their preeminent authority—some of them even bishops—who have never been more friendly to me than since the publication of *Folly*, and whom that book pleases far more than it does me. I would give you their names and titles here and now if I weren't concerned that their liking for *Folly* would earn them the continuing hostility of those three malignant theologians. I suspect one of them is behind this present distress of yours; at least that's my best guess. If I were to set him forth in his true colors, nobody would be at all surprised that *Folly* displeased this sort of man; indeed, she wouldn't please me at all if she didn't displease men of his ilk. She doesn't in fact please me all that much, but she certainly displeases me the less for not pleasing men of his disposition.

I give more weight to the opinion of some judicious and learned theologians who are so far from complaining of bitterness in my book that they praise my candor and moderation in handling a theme rather provocative in itself without adding provocation, and playing with edged tools, yet not cutting anyone. But if I'm to answer just now only to the theologians, who are the only ones I've heard of being wounded, who can be ignorant of all the things that are commonly said about the manners of bad theologians? *Folly* doesn't so much as touch on that topic. Her jokes are all about the trivial, empty arguments in which they engage, and even of those she doesn't disapprove entirely; she attacks only those who put, as they say, the whole "stock in trade" of theology in these painful nothings, and get so embroiled in their own word-wars (it's Saint Paul's expression)[5] that they have no time to read the evangelists, the prophets, or the apostles.

And I only wish, friend Dorp, there were fewer men guilty of this fault. I could show you some eighty-year-olds who've spent so much of their life on claptrap of this sort that they've never glanced at the text of the gospels; they told me so themselves when I asked them. Even under the mask of Folly, I didn't venture to say what I have often heard many theologians deploring—but authentic theologians, serious and learned men, who have drawn their doctrine from the very wellsprings of Christianity. Whenever they are among people with whom they can speak their minds freely, they deplore this new-fangled theology that's been unleashed on the world, and yearn for the old sort. What could be more sacred and more sublime than the old beliefs; what could be so well suited to contain and reflect the divine teachings of Christ? But the present mode—not to mention the base barbarity of its crude and artificial dialect, its deliberate ignorance of all good literature, its indifference to languages—is so contaminated with the teachings of Aristotle, the inventions of petty human beings, and the laws of the pagans, that I can

5. 1 Timothy 6.4.

hardly taste in it a faint flavor of the pure undiluted Christ. For while the new theology has kept its eyes focused on human traditions, it has ignored its own original archetype. Thus it often happens that the more cautious theologians are forced to say in public something very different from what they feel in their hearts or say to their intimate friends. And often they don't have an answer to give those who consult them wanting to know why Christ teaches one thing and human traditions another. What, I ask you, does Christ have in common with Aristotle? How do these intricate sophistical questions relate to the mysteries of eternal wisdom? Where do we get by following out that labyrinth of problems, many of which are meaningless and most of the others positive nuisances because they beget only quarrels and contentions? Some deserve study, perhaps a solution: I don't deny it. But there are a great many others that are better ignored than explored (it's an important part of knowledge not to know certain things), and still others where we're better off withholding judgment than making a decision. Finally, if a question does have to be decided, I'd like to have the decision reached reverently, not peremptorily, and on the basis of holy scripture, not some petty rationalizations worked out by men. Now there's no end to all these niggling questions, and all they lead to is a proliferation of quarrels and factions with a never-ending stream of pronouncements. Briefly, things have come to the point where a decision in any matter depends not so much on the rule made by Christ as on the definitions of the schoolmen and the power of the bishops, whoever they happen to be. And this process has muddled everything till there's not the least hope of recalling the world to true Christianity.

All these matters and others of the sort are seen and deplored by many men of the utmost holiness and deepest wisdom; and they lay the principal cause of it all on this brash and irreverent breed of new theologians. Oh, friend Dorp, if you could only enter silently into my thoughts; you would understand only too well how many things I am leaving prudently unspoken in this place. And Folly herself either says nothing at all about these matters or touches them only lightly lest anyone should be offended. I preserved the same caution everywhere, not to write anything indecent, nothing libellous or seditious or that implied in any way any sort of insult to any class of people. If anything is said about worship of the saints, you will always find a clear and explicit statement nearby that what's being challenged is the superstition of those who worship the saints in the wrong way. Likewise, in what's said about princes, bishops, and monks, I always add a statement that the order itself is not being blamed, only its corrupt and unworthy members. I carefully avoided wounding the good in the course of pursuing the vices of the bad. And all this time I was careful to keep personal names out of it, lest I should sully the reputation even of a bad man. Finally, I filled the whole story with quips and jests, telling it through the mouth of an imaginary speaker, to make sure that even solemn and sour readers would take it in the right spirit.

But now you tell me that I'm condemned, not only as too sharp in my writings, but as impious in addition; for, you ask, how can pious ears endure to hear me calling the felicity of our future life a sort of madness? I beg of you, my dear Dorp, tell me who deceived your honorable nature into making this underhanded and libellous accusation? Or rather, as I prefer to think, what sly scoundrel abused your unsuspecting disposition into launching this calumny against me? This is the way of those pestilent detractors; they pluck a couple of words out of context, carefully changing them to leave out anything that might soften or explain them. Quintilian knew this trick, and taught it in his *Institutio*.[6] You lay out your own position at large, with supporting testimonies and anything else that will soften, explain, or render your position more acceptable; then you lay out the adversary's position perfunctorily, without any supports, and phrase it in the most odious language conceivable. My enemies have learned this trick, not from Quintilian, but from the resources of their own malice; and in this way things that would be perfectly agreeable if presented as I wrote them become odious in their representations. Reread the original passage, I beg of you, and take note of the several stages and gradual approaches by which I worked up to saying that ultimate felicity is a kind of madness; pay particular attention to the exact words in which I expressed the idea. You will find nothing there to offend pious ears, rather, a great deal to gratify them. The offense lies in the way you repeat the idea, not in my book.

When Folly in the course of her lecture showed that all human affairs fall under her sway, and taught that the sum of human happiness resided in foolishness, she surveyed the entire human race up to kings and popes; then she continued on to the apostles, and even Christ, whom we find the holy scriptures themselves describing as, in a way, foolish. But there's no danger anyone will suppose they were literal fools, only that because of the infirmities of human nature and in consequence of their human feelings, there was some element in them which, compared with the pure and perfect wisdom of eternity, might seem less than wise. But this very foolishness far surpasses human wisdom. In the same way the prophet Isaiah compares the justice of mortal men to filthy rags[7]—not because the justice of the righteous is a polluted thing, but because the purest of human things are to some extent impure if compared with the ineffable purity of God. Thus I described a wisdom that is folly, a sanity that is madness, a derangement that is eminently sane. In order to soften what was to follow about the ultimate happiness of the blessed, I prefaced an account of Plato's three madnesses, of which the happiest is the madness of lovers, which is nothing but a particular form of ecstasy. In its turn, the ecstasy of the pious is simply a kind of foretaste of future bliss, by which we are totally absorbed in God, to exist forever in him rather than in ourselves. And this is what Plato calls madness, when someone is rapt out of himself into the object of his love and enjoys it completely. Didn't

---

6. Quintilian's book on oratory 5.13.25–28.   7. Isaiah 64.4.

you notice how carefully, a little later on, I distinguished between the varieties of folly and madness, so that no simple-minded reader could possibly mistake my words?

Well, you say, it's not a matter of the substance, but the ears of the pious will be offended by the words themselves. But why aren't those same ears offended when they hear Paul talking of "the foolishness of God" and "the folly of the cross"? Why don't they object to Saint Thomas when they find him writing in this way about Peter's ecstasy: "in his pious folly he began a sermon on tabernacles"? He calls that sacred and pious rapture by the name of folly; and to this day his words are chanted as part of the sacred service.[8] Why, may I ask, didn't they complain about a prayer I wrote some years ago, in which I called Christ a mage and an enchanter? Saint Jerome calls Christ a Samaritan, though in literal fact he was Jewish. Paul says he was "made sin," which is a stronger expression than "a sinner," and says he was "accursed."[9] What impious blasphemy is this if anyone chooses to interpret it maliciously; what holy reverence if one reads it in the spirit that Paul wrote it! Along the same lines, if one called Christ a grave-robber, an adulterer, a drunkard, and a heretic, don't you suppose all pious folk would clap their hands over their ears? But if an interpreter softened and explained these expressions, carefully bringing the reader up to them as if leading him by the hand, he might show that Christ by the power of the cross redeemed his body from the grave and led it in triumph before the Father; that he took to himself the synagogue of Moses as David did the wife of Uriah, so that from here might be born a people of peace;[1] that he was drunk with the sweet wine of charity when he sacrificed himself for us; and that he introduced a new kind of doctrine far different from the teaching of his predecessors, whether wise or unwise. Now who, I ask you, could be offended with that, especially when we find that in holy scriptures all these expressions are frequently used with favorable connotations? I myself in my collection of Adages (for that suggests itself in this context), have called the apostles Sileni, and indeed referred to Christ himself as a sort of Silenus.[2] An evil-minded interpreter could in a short phrase twist these expressions into something intolerable; but let a candid and fair-minded reader consider what I have written, and he will see the allegory and approve of it.

I'm surprised your hypercritical friends haven't noticed how cautiously I express myself and how careful I am to soften my words with modifiers. For example, Folly says, "But now that I've 'got on my high

---

8. The words are from a hymn for the feast of the Transfiguration; the notion that Saint Thomas wrote them is peculiar to Erasmus. Erasmus's own prayer was written early in his career. The allusions to Paul are to first Corinthians 1.3.
9. 2 Corinthians 5.21 and Galatians 3.13.
1. The child of David and Bathsheba was Solomon, the peaceful prince; an allegory with the relations between Christian church and Jewish synagogue followed naturally.
2. Beginning with just a few, Erasmus expanded his collection of adages (proverbial sayings) to include thousands. Silenus was a drunken, obese companion of Bacchus, but in the form of little statuettes he often served to contain precious perfumes and ointments. This is the point of Erasmus's comparison.

horse,' I want to take the next step and argue that the happiness after which Christians strive so passionately is nothing but a certain kind of folly amounting to madness. Don't startle at the words but look at the realities." You hear what she says? First because she is Folly and discussing such an arcane topic, I temper her boldness with a proverb to indicate that she's already embarked on a lofty theme. And I don't call bliss simply folly or madness but a kind of folly amounting to madness, by way of helping you to distinguish this pious and joyful madness from other sorts, according to the formal distinction which follows close at hand. Not content with this, I add "a certain" kind, to make plain that the language is metaphorical, not literal. Furthermore, I apologize for any offense the sound of the words may give, and warn the reader to pay more attention to the substance of them than to the words themselves— all this in the course of my first laying out of the argument. And then in the further development of the idea, what one word is there that isn't set down with reverence and circumspection—more reverently, indeed, than is altogether appropriate to the character of Folly? But in this matter I preferred to violate somewhat the decorum of her character than to fall short of the dignity of the subject—dispensing with rules of rhetoric rather than those of piety. And then at the end of the whole discourse, lest anyone should be upset because I'd set Folly, a comic character, to talking about sacred topics, I had her beg pardon in these words: "But I've long since forgotten myself and 'overstepped my boundaries.' If you think I've been too cheeky or long-winded, remember you've been listening to Folly and a woman."

You see how careful I was not to give the slightest occasion for offense. But people trained to hear nothing but propositions, conclusions, and corollaries close their ears to nuances of this sort. Didn't they notice that in the preface to the book, I tried to forestall all spiteful complaints? I don't doubt that what's said there will satisfy any fair-minded reader; but what can I do with people who are determined ahead of time not to be satisfied, or who are so stupid they don't even know when they are satisfied? Just as Simonides said of the Thessalians that he couldn't deceive them because they were too dumb,[3] so you can find some men too dense even to know they've been pleased. Their natural companions are those who never lack an occasion for calumny because that's all they ever look for. Let anyone of that disposition read the writings of Saint Jerome; he will find a hundred passages on which to ply his censorious trade, and even in this most Christian doctor of all, there will be no lack of expressions over which spiteful souls can cry, "Heresy!" I'll say nothing of Cyprian, Lactantius, and other doctors of the church. Finally, who ever heard of a comic pamphlet being subjected to theological scrutiny? If this passes, why won't the same test be applied to the songs and farces of the poets? All sorts of obscenities are waiting to be discovered there, passages redolent, no doubt, of ancient paganism. But as these aren't

3. Plutarch, "How to Study Poetry."

considered serious works, no theologian has yet tried to take them in charge.

All the same, I don't want to conceal myself behind the shelter of works like these. Even as a joke I wouldn't want to have written anything that could offend a Christian conscience; only grant me a reader who understands what's in front of him, a fair-minded and unprejudiced reader who tries to understand what he reads, not to misrepresent it. But if one were to reckon up the number of readers who have neither wit nor judgment to understand; then add the number of those that know less than nothing of good literature because they've been infected rather than instructed by muddled and careless teaching; and finally tot up the lot of those who hate anyone who knows what they don't know, and who bring to their reading nothing but a fixed determination to blacken anything that by some chance they do understand; then indeed the only way to avoid calumny would be to write nothing at all. A good number of these accusers are attracted to their dirty work by the hope of glory, for there's no creature on earth more ambitious than an ignorant man who wants to give the impression he knows something. Such people suffer a violent thirst for fame but can't achieve it by their own talents, so they imitate the young man of Ephesus who, rather than live in obscurity, set fire to the most celebrated temple in the entire world.[4] So critics, unable to publish anything of their own that's fit to read, take out their jealous rage by ripping to pieces the works of celebrated authors.

I'm talking, of course, about other people, not myself, for I'm nobody, and don't care a straw about my little book of *Folly*; I wouldn't want anyone to think I'm upset over it. There's nothing surprising in the fact that people of the sort I've been describing pick occasional passages here and there out of a larger work, in order to show them as scandalous, irreverent, ill-sounding, impious, or smacking of heresy—not that they find such passages in the book, but they import them from their own stock. How much more sociable it would be, and suitable to the candor of Christians, if they would speak up to encourage the work of learned men, and if some error should escape them, either let it pass or interpret it for the best, rather than searching out points to quarrel over like an enemy, or acting like a paid informer more than a theologian. Surely we ought to be able to teach and learn from each other reciprocally, and (to use the words of Jerome) scrimmage together on the field of scriptural interpretation without inflicting deadly wounds. But my critics are amazingly unaware of moderation. Certain authors they read with such partisan approval that, no matter what manifest errors they fall into, they must be defended by one frivolous quibble or another; while other authors are considered so iniquitous that nothing they say, however cautiously it's phrased, can escape malicious misrepresentation under one pretext or another. How much better it would be if, instead of bickering back

---

4. The man who burned the temple of Diana at Ephesus to make a name for himself is known; but there's no reason to gratify his stupid vanity by recording his name here.

and forth to the great waste of everyone's time, they would set to work
learning Greek, Hebrew, or even something about Latin literature! These
tongues are so valuable for the study of holy scriptures that it seems to
me only a grossly impudent man could set up for a professor of theology
without knowing them.

And so, my dear Martin, having only your best interests at heart, I
want to beg of you, as I've often done before, to include at least the study
of Greek literature among your other studies. You have a mind of unusual
sharpness; your prose style, strong yet nervous, fluent yet sparkling,
bespeaks a mind not only vigorous but exuberant. At your time of life,
you're at the peak of your powers, and you've successfully completed the
standard curriculum. Believe me, if you added to these brilliant preliminaries the crowning glory of Greek letters, I would think, with everyone else, that a great future lay ahead of you, such as no other recent
theologian could anticipate. You may suppose that by comparison with
true devotion all merely human learning is despicable, that you can
attain your final end more directly by a certain transfiguration in Christ,
and that all other things worth knowing will take on a richer luster when
seen in the light of faith than when studied in the books of mere mortals.
And of course I readily subscribe to those sentiments. But if you imagine
that, as things now stand, you can gain real knowledge of the art of
theology without command of the languages, especially that in which
most of the holy scriptures are written, then you are badly mistaken.

I would really like to persuade you on this point, partly because of my
affection for you, partly because I'm concerned about your studies—
which means I'm really fond of you and deeply interested in your work.
Perhaps I cannot alter your judgment, but won't you, simply to gratify a
friend, try how the Greek works out? I will bet anything you like that
you will find your friend was true and his advice good. In the name of
our old friendship, our common country, my long devotion to scholarship (I won't call it erudition) and my advanced age (for by the calendar
I'm old enough to be your father), won't you grant me this favor—out
of friendship or respect for authority, if not as a result of persuasion?
You like to say I'm eloquent; I won't believe it unless I can wring this
concession from you. If I succeed, we will both be happy, I for having
given the advice, you for having profited by it; and though you are now
the dearest of friends, in the future you will be even dearer, because I
will have rendered you even dearer to yourself. If I fail, I'm afraid that
when you are older and more experienced in the world, you will see the
rightness of my opinion and the error of your own—recognizing your
mistake, as often happens, when it's too late to mend. I could name
many men who when they were old went back to study like schoolboys
because they had finally realized that, without knowledge of Greek,
scholarship is lame and blind.

But we've had more than enough of this. To return to your letter, you
think there's just one way for me to placate the angry theologians and
get back into favor with them, which would be to write a kind of 'retrac-

tion' in favor of wisdom, as a sort of counterweight to my praise of folly—and this you strongly advise me to do. For my part, friend Dorp, I have no worse enemy than myself, and if I could, I'd much prefer to be on good terms with everyone. Actually, I wouldn't mind undertaking this job, if I didn't foresee the consequences. Whatever envy has built up in that handful of insidious, ignorant men would be inflamed rather than diminished by such a project. I think it will be quite enough if we 'let sleeping dogs lie,' and 'don't go raking around in this cesspool.' If I'm not mistaken, the snake will die of natural causes before long.

Now I come to the second part of your letter. You greatly approve of my efforts to restore the text of Saint Jerome, and encourage me to undertake other work of this nature. As I'm already hard at it, I don't need encouragement as much as help; it's a tremendous, troublesome job. But you must never believe me again if I don't foretell accurately how this matter will turn out. The same people who took offense at *Folly* will be unhappy with the edition of Jerome too. In fact, they don't like Basil, Chrysostom, or Nazianzen[5] any better than they do me, except that they can get at me more easily—though sometimes, when specially irritated, they don't hesitate to vent their spleen on those lights of the church. They are afraid of good literature and terrified for their own dictatorship. And just so you won't think I'm saying this without good reason, let me tell you that when the project was first set on foot and word of it got out, I was visited by several solid (as they're considered) and substantial men, theologians (as they pronounce themselves) of great distinction, who begged me by all that's sacred not to let the printer admit into the edition any Greek or Hebrew. There was great danger in those languages, they declared, and nothing good would come of them; at most, a sampling might be given, just as a curiosity. Even before that, when I was in England, I happened to be seated at table with a certain Franciscan, a Scotist of the first water, who was popularly supposed to know a lot, and in his own opinion knew everything. When I spoke of the Jerome project, he was amazed that there was anything in the writings of the saint that wasn't already well known to theologians—a man so ignorant that I doubt if there are three lines in all the works of Jerome that he could interpret correctly. He was kind enough to tell me, this urbane fellow, that if I had any problems with Jerome's prefaces to his biblical commentaries, the commentator from Brittany had explained everything brilliantly.[6]

I ask you, my dear Dorp, what can be done with such theologians? What prayer can one even offer for them, unless for a good brain-surgeon? Yet this is the stuff of which many are made who shout loudest in the assembly of the theologians; these are the creatures who define Christianity for us. They shrink in horror, as if confronted by deadly poison, from the doctrines that Saint Jerome expounded and that Ori-

---

5. All three of these famous saints wrote in Greek.
6. William of Brittany was a thirteenth-century

commentator on Jerome's prefaces—not the last word in sixteenth-century scholarship.

gen, even as an old man, was still laboring over, in order to make himself a proper theologian. Saint Augustine in *his* last years, when he had long since been created a bishop, expressed grief in his *Confessions* that as a young man he had avoided works of literature which would have been of the greatest use to him in interpreting scripture. If there's danger in these studies, I'm not afraid to face perils that men of such distinction have sought out. And if linguistic study is just an idle curiosity, I have no desire to be more single-minded than Saint Jerome. When they dismiss as idle curiosity what he worked hard to acquire, let them decide for themselves what right they have to pass judgment on him.

An ancient papal decree is still in effect setting up public lectureships in the various languages; but nothing of the sort was ever decreed about teaching the tricks of the dialectic or Aristotelian philosophy—apart, of course, from various decretals calling into question whether it's proper to teach that material at all. In fact, many authoritative writers disapprove of it. Why do we neglect completely what the pope directly commands, and rush into what is questioned or even reproved? Actually, our theologians run into the same problems in reading Aristotle as in reading scripture. Everywhere their contempt for language brings down on them the same punishment; everywhere, and here particularly, they wander as in a cloud, dreaming dreams, groping through a mist, blundering into obstacles, and producing nothing but monsters. To these splendid theologians we owe the fact that very few of the notable authors described in Jerome's list of famous men[7] have come down to us; "our masters" couldn't understand what they wrote, and so got rid of them. Because of theologians like these we possess Saint Jerome himself in a text so depraved and mutilated that it's almost more work for others to restore it than it was for Jerome to write it in the first place.

Now for the third point. What you write about the New Testament really makes me wonder what's happened to you. You used to be pretty sharp-sighted; are you trying now not to see what's in front of you? You don't want me to change a single thing unless an idea is expressed more significantly in the Greek, and you deny that in the edition we know as the Vulgate there's any error at all. You think it would be sacrilege to alter in any way a text authenticated by agreement over so many centuries and endorsed by so many councils. But if what you say is true, let me ask you, most learned Dorp, why Jerome often cites scripture in a form that varies from ours, and Augustine in another form, and Ambrose in still another? Why does Jerome censure and correct many specific passages which still remain uncorrected in the Vulgate? What will you do when all the sources combine against you, that is, when the Greek manuscripts agree on a different reading, when Jerome cites them as conclusive evidence, when the oldest Latin versions confirm their reading, and when the passage in that form agrees better with its context?

7. Jerome wrote a book on famous men; that "theologians" were responsible for the loss of their writings is Erasmus's invidious addition.

Are you going to dismiss all these authorities to follow a manuscript that may be full of scribal errors? Nobody says that the scriptures contain lies, though you seem to assume this is my attitude; nor does the matter relate in any way to the various controversies between Jerome and Augustine.[8] But the situation cries aloud; it would be plain, as they say, to a blind man: often, because of the ignorance or carelessness of a translator, the Greek has been imperfectly rendered, and often the original true reading has been corrupted by an ignorant copyist. We see this happen every day; texts are changed by thoughtless or sleepy scribes. Who does more to promote a lie, the man who corrects and removes a mistake, or the man who, out of reluctance to make a change, lets it stand? Besides, it's the nature of corrupt texts that one error leads to another. For a fact, more of these changes that I've made relate to the emphasis than to the basic sense, though frequently the emphasis is itself part of the sense, and not infrequently the whole passage has been drawn out of shape. When such a thing happens, I ask you, where does Augustine turn, where do Ambrose, Hilary, and Jerome look, if not to the Greek originals? Though this is the process approved by ecclesiastical decrees, you still try to refute, or rather evade it, by verbal hair-splitting and equivocations.

For you write that, though in earlier ages Greek manuscripts were more correct than Latin, nowadays it isn't so, and we shouldn't put any trust in the books of those who have deserted the Roman church. I can hardly believe that you really mean that. What are you saying? that we shouldn't read the books of those who have deserted the Christian faith? Why then is so much authority granted to Aristotle, a pagan who never so much as heard of the Christian faith? The entire Jewish race departed from Christ, are we to pay no attention to the psalmists and prophets who wrote in their native language? Think over, if you will, all the points on which the Greek church differs from the orthodox Latins; you'll find nothing there that rises from the words of the New Testament or pertains to them. Something there is about the word "hypostasis,"[9] the procession of the Holy Spirit, the ceremony of consecration, the poverty of priests, and the power of the pope—that's where the controversy lies. But none of this has to do with any disputed texts. What do you say when you see interpretations based on Greek readings in Origen, Chrysostom, Basil, and Jerome? Was somebody falsifying Greek texts even in that early age? Who ever proved that a single passage in a single Greek manuscript had ever been falsified? Why would they conceivably do so, since they don't defend their beliefs on this basis? Even Cicero, though generally no friend to the Greeks, confesses that their manuscripts were generally more correct than ours. For the different shapes of letters, the use of accent marks, and the general difficulty of the writing are reasons why their texts were less subject to careless corruption, or if corrupted could more easily be restored.

---

8. Jerome and Augustine had some rather testy disagreements on scriptural questions.

9. The total personality of Christ as distinct from his two contrasted natures (human and divine).

When you say that the Vulgate shouldn't be changed because it was approved by so many church councils, you put yourself on a level with the vulgar ruck of theologians; whenever anything has established itself in common usage, they claim it has ecclesiastical authority. Can you name me a single council in which this edition was endorsed? How could anyone endorse it when nobody knows who wrote it? That Jerome wasn't its author his own prefaces make clear. But suppose some council did approve it; did they approve it so categorically as to preclude any future corrections from the Greek manuscripts? Did they approve all the mistakes which by one oversight or another might slip in? Did the decree of our council fathers take some such form as this: "We don't know who prepared this edition, but we approve of it anyway; we don't want it changed in the least, even to agree with the most correct Greek manuscripts. Even if Chrysostom, Basil, Athanasius, or Jerome should read a passage differently, even if it agrees better, as they read it, with the sense of the gospels, we don't want it changed; all the same, in every other matter, we hold those authors in the highest esteem. If hereafter, by whatever means, any ignorant, careless scribe—whether absent-minded, sleepy, or drunk—commits any sort of error, oversight, omission, or slip of the pen, we authenticate the same by our full authority; and once it has become part of the text, we forbid anyone to change it, ever." A ridiculous decree, you'll say. But this is how it must have been if the authority of a council is to deter me from the work in hand.

Finally, what's to be said when different copies of the Vulgate differ from one another? Did the council approve in advance this variety of readings, foreseeing somehow the changes that different copyists would make? I really wish, my dear Dorp, that the popes could find a little free time to establish some sensible rules in these matters. Provisions could then be made for correcting the texts of good authors, for preparing proper editions of them, and preserving them in libraries. But I would not want the members of such a commission to be those self-styled theologians who have nothing in mind but establishing their own teachings as absolute truth. For what have they actually taught that isn't at the same time clumsy and confused in the highest degree? Put them in charge, and the world would be forced to reject the best authors of antiquity and instead accept as words of oracular wisdom the insipid foolery of the moderns—foolery so devoid of proper learning that unless they pick up a bit of scholarship I would sooner be a common shoemaker than the best of them. These are the men who want nothing corrected, lest their own ignorance be made manifest. These people throw up imaginary obstacles like the supposed authority of councils, they exaggerate the terrible perils to Christian faith, they spread fantasies about the danger to the church, as if it rested only on their shoulders—shoulders which in fact would be better employed holding up a dung-cart. With smoke-screens and fulminations of this sort, they delude the ignorant and superstitious mob; and since those are the only people among whom they can pass for theologians, they are careful not to risk their reputations. At bottom, they're afraid that when they cite scripture, as they're fond of doing, someone who knows Greek or Hebrew will tell them what the passage really means, so that what they pronounced with oracular assurance will be shown up as mere bluff. Saint Augustine, a mighty man and a bishop besides, was not ashamed to be instructed by a tiny toddler.[1] These theologians would rather turn everything topsy turvy than admit there's some element of full and perfect learning with which they're unfamiliar. As a matter of fact, I don't think there's anything in this whole business that bears on the fullness of the Christian faith; though of course if it did, that would only be a greater reason for exploring the matter more thoroughly.

Neither is there the slightest reason to suppose that mankind will suddenly abandon their faith if word gets out that there is something in scripture that an ignorant or sleepy scribe wrote amiss, or that some unknown translator rendered ineptly. The church's real danger comes from another quarter, about which I will maintain, for the moment, a discreet silence.

How much more Christian it would be if we could forget all these squabbles, and just allow every man to contribute what he could to the common store, without ulterior motives. Let each man learn in modesty what he needs to know and teach without invidium what he knows already. If some are too illiterate to learn anything, or too arrogant to accept instruction, let them go their ways (there will only be a few of them), so that we can concentrate on the good, or at least promising, minds. I recently showed my notes, still very rough, and fresh, as they say, off the griddle, to some true scholars, first-rate theologians, and learned bishops; they agreed that even from these preliminary jottings they had received major assistance toward their understanding of the gospels.

What you say about Lorenzo Valla I knew long before I entered on this task, since I had a hand in editing his *Notes on the New Testament*; I was also acquainted with Jacques LeFèvre's *Commentaries on the Epistles of Paul*.[2] I only wish those men had completed the job so there wouldn't be any more for me to do. Indeed, I consider Valla worthy of the highest praise; though a rhetorician rather than a theologian, he was thorough enough in his study of scripture to have compared the Greek and Latin texts throughout—whereas there are plenty of theologians who haven't so much as read the New Testament all the way through. I do, however, disagree with some of his conclusions, especially in matters of theology. As for Jacques LeFèvre, he already had his commentaries under way when I was getting my project ready; but unluckily neither of us ventured, even in the course of our intimate conversations, to tell the

1. The story, if not true, is neat. Augustine, walking on the beach in profound meditation, saw a child carrying sea water in his cupped hands and pouring it into a hole in the sand. Asked what he was up to, the child replied with another question: Why are you trying to get the mystery of the trinity to fit within the human mind? A wise child indeed;

a very dubious story.
2. Almost fifty years after Valla's death (1457), Erasmus found the manuscript of his *Notes on the New Testament*, and had it published (Paris, 1505). In 1512 Jacques LeFèvre published an edition of Paul's epistles, in Latin, but making use of Greek materials for the annotations.

other what he was about. Though I had no advance notice of what he was up to, I warmly approved of his book when it appeared. Here too I differ on a number of points, though unwillingly, because I would like to be "of one mind" with such a friend on all matters. But truth comes before friendship, especially in discussion of religious matters.

Why you bring up these two men is not very clear to me. You're not trying to discourage me on the score that the job has already been done, are you? Even though two such able men preceded me, I have ample reason to assume the task. Or were you insinuating that not even their labors met with the approval of the theologians? Their hatred for Valla was of long standing; his book didn't increase it that I could see. I gather that LeFèvre's work met with general approval. In any case, don't you see that my undertaking is quite different from theirs? Valla annotated only a few passages, in passing, as it were, and lightly. LeFèvre's commentaries deal only with the Pauline epistles, which he translated in a version of his own and then annotated where there seemed to be problems. I have translated the entire New Testament afresh from the Greek originals with a Greek text across the page for easy comparison. My annotations are separate; they show, partly on the evidence and partly on the authority of the ancient theologians, that my emendations were not rashly undertaken, that they can be accepted with confidence, and that they cannot be lightly dismissed. I only hope I have succeeded in a venture which has cost me so much labor. As far as the book's acceptance by the church is concerned, I shouldn't hesitate to dedicate the product of my late-night studies to any bishop whatever, any cardinal, or even pope, so long as he's the sort of man we have now.[3] Finally, I don't doubt that you too will congratulate me on the book you now deplore, provided only that you acquire a little taste of that language without which you can't possibly form a reasonable judgment of the matter.

So you see, friend Dorp, for one letter you've earned double thanks; first from your theologian friends, for whom you've duly performed your ambassadorial services; and then from me, because the friendly manner of your comments made clear your personal affection for me. Will you on your side take my free and open explanation in good part? I think in prudence you should prefer my advice, which is given only with your interest in mind, over that of a party which wants to enlist your talents (capable of infinitely better things) for their particular faction. I'm not surprised; they would be greatly strengthened by the addition of such a gifted leader. Let them improve their position if they can; if not, continue to strive for the best on your own; and if you can't render them better—certainly you should try—at least make sure they don't render you worse. And this too I would ask, that as you presented their case faithfully to me, so you present mine to them just as faithfully. If they can be placated to any extent, you will do it; and you may persuade

3. I.e., like Leo X.

them that I follow my own course, not out of contempt for people without literary skills, but for the public good, the general interest. Literature is open to all who want to acquire it; it puts no pressure on anyone who prefers to do without it. And you will add that if anyone appears who can or will teach me better doctrine than I now maintain, I will be the first to renounce my own opinions and subscribe to his.

My best greetings to Jean Marais, who should be told about this fuss over the *Folly* because the commentaries on it were dedicated to him by my friend Lister.[4] Give my regards also to the learned Jean de Nève and the most congenial Nicholas of Burgundy, lord of Beveren and provost of Saint Peter's. You have high praise for abbot Menard, and given your strict integrity, I don't doubt he deserves it; for your sake I'm willing to rate him very high indeed, and won't fail to make honorable mention of him in my writing at the earliest opportunity. And to you, dear Dorp, as the best of friends, a fond farewell.

To Beatus Rhenanus

[The Hardships of Travel]

(ca. 15 October 1518)

Herewith, dear Beatus, the full tragicomedy of my journey.[1] I left Basle, as you know, in a languid and enervated state, not having fully recovered my health despite a long stay at home, because it had been occupied with constant work. The boat trip was not disagreeable except that around midday the heat of the sun became oppressive. We dined at Breisach, but after a fashion that couldn't have been more disagreeable. The stench of the place was atrocious and the swarms of flies even worse. For half an hour we sat around the table, waiting for the people to bring out their food; and when finally it arrived, it was absolutely inedible: a gray mush, lumps of greasy meat, pieces of fish reheated for the sixth time—enough to turn your stomach. I didn't get to see Gallinarius. The man who reported he was suffering from a slight fever also added a choice tidbit; it seems that Minorite friar with whom I had a quarrel over *haecitas*[2]

4. Gerard Lister had been a student of medicine at Basle, where he got to know Erasmus, who assisted him in compiling notes on the *Folly*. But the result was not (apparently) satisfactory, for Erasmus refused Lister permission to annotate any of his other writings. Among the compliments and salutations of the final paragraph Erasmus takes care to include dignitaries and authorities who will be both impressive and useful to Dorp.
1. As the crow flies, the distance from Basle in Switzerland to Louvain in Belgium is about 260 miles; when Erasmus undertook this journey in the fall of 1518, he elected to follow the great waterway of the Rhine to cover much of the distance. Then from Cologne to Louvain, a scant hundred miles or so, he could proceed by horse or light

carriage. How he made out, his letter describes. It was addressed to his good friend and associate Beatus Rhenanus (who acquired his last name because his father came from Rheinau and his first name from a cheery disposition). Rhenanus had worked alongside Erasmus in John Froben's Basle printing house.
The towns at which the traveling scholar stopped are indicated on an outline map (p. 252); among the people he encountered—many of them casual acquaintances of his or of Rhenanus—it has seemed desirable to annotate only the most prominent.
2. Literally, "thisness"; the scholastic word for the individuating essence that defines the special reality of an object. Erasmus objected to the word not only as barbarous Latin but as pretentiously obscure.

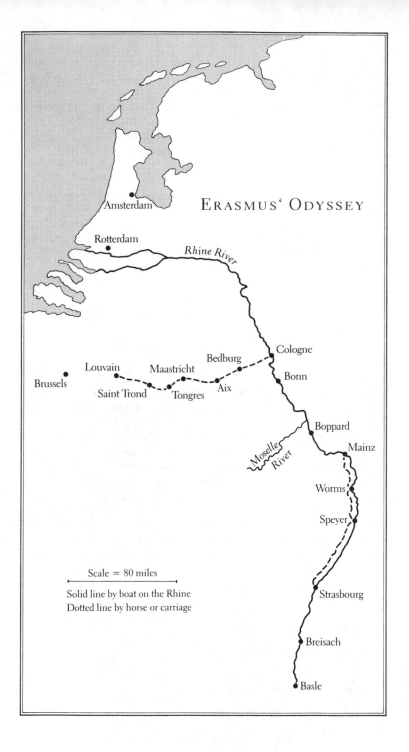

Erasmus' Odyssey

Amsterdam

Rotterdam

Rhine River

Cologne

Bedburg

Louvain   Maastricht

Brussels

Saint Trond   Tongres   Aix   Bonn

Boppard

Mainz

Moselle River

Worms

Speyer

Scale = 80 miles

Solid line by boat on the Rhine
Dotted line by horse or carriage

Strasbourg

Breisach

Basle

managed to steal and pawn a holy church chalice. Now there's Scotist subtlety for you! Just before dark we were pushed off the boat into some icy little village: I didn't want to know its name, or if I knew it then to remember it now: I nearly perished there. I think there were more than sixty of us in one small overheated room, a ragtag collection of men from ten o'clock on; oh what a stench and what an uproar, especially after they got liquored up. And of course they had no sense of time, so the racket went on all night.

In the morning while it was still dark, we were routed out of bed by the shouts of the boatmen. For my part, I'd had no sleep, and I got on the boat without any breakfast. We reached Strasbourg well before lunchtime, about the hour of nine; and there we were better received, especially with Schurer[3] supplying the wine. There were also some members of a literary society of which the other members soon arrived to greet me, but nobody more obligingly than Gerbel. Gebwiler and Rudolphingen stood treat for me, which for them is no new practice. From there we set off on horseback for Speyer; on the way we saw not the least sign of soldiers, though rumor had spread frightful stories about them. My English horse gave out when we had barely reached Speyer; may the rascally smith who shod him so badly have both his ears pierced with red-hot nails! At Speyer I slipped away from the inn and betook myself to my Maternum[4] nearby. There the dean, a man of learning and humanity, detained me with his polite hospitality for two days; and there by chance I encountered Herman Busch.

From Speyer I took a carriage to Worms and from there to Mainz. As it happened, one of the Emperor's secretaries was in the same coach, a man named Ulrich Farnbul, which is to say Feinhill. Throughout the whole journey he took incredible pains to look out for me, and when we couldn't get into Mainz,[5] he led me off "in the fullness of his knowledge" to the house of a certain canon; and then, on my departure, he took me down to the boat. Again the boatride was not disagreeable, since the weather was fine, though the sailors worked hard to make the trip longer than necessary. There was also a good deal of stink from the horses aboard. My kind companions on this first day were John Longicampianus, who used to teach at Louvain, and a certain lawyer friend of his. There was also a Westphalian, Doctor John, who was a canon of Saint Victor's outside Mainz—a most agreeable and jolly companion.

When we reached Boppard, where the boat had to pass a customs inspection, we passengers debarked and strolled along the bank when someone pointed me out to the customs agent: "there's the man." The agent was, if I'm not mistaken, a certain Christopher Cinicampius, in

---

3. Schurer, a printer at Strasbourg, had been an employer of Beatus Rhenanus. Note that Erasmus, leaving the house of Froben at Basle, could rely on a network of printers and publishers stretching across Europe, for the comforts (and sometimes the necessities) of existence.
4. Maternum: perhaps the cathedral church at

Speyer, perhaps an Augustinian monastery in the neighborhood; Erasmus still maintained contact with his old order.
5. Either because there was no room at the inn, or for fear of the plague, prevalent that fall in many cities of Germany.

the vulgar tongue Eschenfelder. You wouldn't believe how the man carried on in his ecstasies. He takes us to his house, where on a table among various business papers lie some volumes of Erasmus. He declares himself overjoyed, he calls in his wife and children and all his friends. When the sailors start calling for us to return, he sends them a couple of bottles of wine, when they call again he sends them more, he promises that when the boat returns he will pass them duty-free, in gratitude for having brought such a man to him. From here as far as the juncture of the Moselle we were accompanied by Doctor John Flamming, prefect of the nunnery, a man of angelic purity, sane and sober judgment, and uncommon learning. At the juncture, Doctor Matthias, chancellor to the archbishop, carried us off to his house; though he is a young man, his manners are polished, his Latin excellent, and he is an accomplished lawyer. We had a merry dinner at his house.

At Bonn, the canon left us, to avoid the city of Cologne;[6] I would rather have avoided it too, but my servant with the horses had preceded me there, and nobody in the boat was confident that I could send a messenger to recall him; I was particularly doubtful about employing any of the sailors. So the next day we reached Cologne before six o'clock of a Sunday morning under an already menacing sky. Having reached the inn, I ordered the servants of the host to hire a shay and prepare me a meal for ten o'clock. But the meal was put off so I could hear mass, and nothing happened about the shay. I tried to get hold of a new horse, for my own horses were useless. Nothing happened. Finally, I caught on; they were trying to keep me there. I promptly ordered my own horses saddled, loaded one of my saddlebags on them, and left the other for the host to forward by boat. Then, climbing on my limping nag, I set off toward the count of Neuenahr.[7] It was a five-hour journey before I found him at Bedburg.

At this man's house I remained very comfortably for five days, enjoying so much calm and leisure that I was able to carry out a good many revisions on my manuscript—for I had brought with me part of my New Testament edition. I only wish you were acquainted with this man, my dear Beatus! Young he is, but of a wisdom greater than years generally bring; a man of few words, but as Homer says of Menelaos, "clear and judicious," learned without ostentation and not just in one narrow subject, utterly frank, and a warm, genial friend. Now I felt vigorous, even a bit robust, and soon I looked forward to greeting, in the fullness of my health, the bishop of Liège, and to appearing in fine fettle among my friends in Brabant.[8] What merry dinners, what brave compliments, what rich conversations I promised myself! I even thought, if the autumn proved fine, of going to England and accepting there what the king has so often offered to me. But oh, the foolish hopes of mortal men! oh, the

6. Cologne was definitely hard hit by the plague.
7. Herman, count of Neuenahr (1492–1530).
8. Brabant is a district of southern Holland and northern Belgium where Erasmus had spent much of his youth. Through his various agents, Henry VIII held out many inducements for Erasmus to settle in England—so various and so vague that it's hard to know which ones he has in mind here.

sudden and unexpected twists of human affairs! From all these dreams of felicity I was tumbled abruptly into the pit of misfortune.

My shay was to be ready next morning. The count, unwilling to say his goodbyes the night before, promised to come and see me off in the morning before I left. That night a savage windstorm blew up, which had made itself felt even the day before. I rose nonetheless just after midnight, having certain things to communicate to the count. When seven o'clock came, and the count had not yet appeared, I sent a servant to wake him up. He came, and in his usual gentle way asked whether under such inclement conditions I was still determined to leave; he said he feared for my safety. At that point, my Beatus, some god, I know not which, or some evil demon, took away, not half my mind, as Hesiod says,[9] but the whole thing; for half my mind was already missing when I decided to go to Cologne. And I only wish that he had warned me, as his friend, more sharply, or that I had listened more submissively to his concerned, and perfectly accurate, warnings. But the power of fate was on me; what else is there to say? I got into the uncovered shay, the wind blowing

> as from the high peaks it descends
> To rend the trembling oaks.[1]

It was a south wind, laden with nothing but pure pestilence. I tried to huddle under my robes, but the wind in its violence drove right through them. Showers of rain swept down on me from the dark sky, more pestilent even than the wind. I reached Aix exhausted by the bumping of the shay, which rattled over the cobblestone roads so painfully that I would rather have been sitting on a horse, however lame he was. In Aix a certain canon, whom the count had recommended as my guardian, dragged me out of my inn to the house of the precentor. There, as usual, several canons were deep in drink. My appetite had been sharpened by a very light lunch; but they had nothing to eat except some carp, and it was cold. I ate it. The drinking went on till late at night. I excused myself on the ground that I'd had very little sleep the night before, and went to bed.

Next morning, I was taken to the house of the vice-provost, for it was his turn to entertain visitors. Here, since there was no manner of fresh fish except eel (doubtless the storm was to blame, since as a rule he is said to set a magnificent table), I had to make do with that dried fish which the Germans call, after the stick with which it is pulped, *stockfish*. Ordinarily, I find it palatable; but a good part of this was practically raw. After lunch, since the weather was still threatening, I went back to my inn, and ordered a fire to be lit in my room. The canon, who was a man of good heart, sat with me for about an hour and a half, making conversation. But all the while, my stomach was acting up; and when it continued in turmoil, I sent him away, went to the latrine, and emptied my

9. Hesiod, "The Shield of Hercules" 149.   1. Horace, *Epodes* 10.

bowels. That still brought no relief, so I stuck my finger down my throat again and again, until finally that raw fish came up, but nothing else. Lying down after my fit of vomiting, I didn't so much sleep as doze, but without pain either of head or body; then, having arranged with the driver to bring up my bag, I found myself invited to another nocturnal drinking-bout. I made excuses, but unsuccessfully. I knew that my stomach could endure nothing but warm broth. For the same thing happened one night at Basle, when, not realizing that my stomach would be terribly distressed by putting slimy food into it, I raised it to fury; a month passed after that before my stomach could accept regular food again. The meal was splendid that night, but it wasn't for me. When I had soothed my stomach with a bit of broth, I went home—for they had me sleeping in the precentor's house. As I left the party, my empty body shivered violently under the cold night sky. It was a long night.

Next morning I breakfasted on a bit of warm beer and a few crusts of bread, then mounted my lame and ailing horse; more ungainly riding you never saw. By now I was so distressed as to be more fit for a bed than a saddle. But there's no part of the world more wretched, uncouth, or disagreeable than this, such is the degradation of the people. My only thought was to get away. Fear of robbers, who flourish in these parts, was wholly dispelled by the pains of my illness.

Back in Basle, I used sometimes to scratch parts of my groin as a way of stimulating my bowels and once, scratching particularly hard, my nail made a little break in the skin inside my left leg. The same thing happened on my right thigh, but without causing any pain or infection. The sore on my left leg got a little irritated on my two-day ride from Strasbourg to Speyer, but I still felt it only when I sat on it heavily. My most recent horseback ride had inflamed this sore spot even further, since that was where I pressed hardest on the saddle; the whole area was tender. In addition, the sore on my right leg swelled up a little, like an abscess under the skin, but still without pain. On the top of my left leg a further hard swelling developed, but again without pain and without infection. When I rode a horse, these parts were not well protected from the wind.

After a trip of about sixteen miles, I reached Maastricht, where after sipping some more broth to keep my stomach warm, I took once more to horse, and reached Tongres; the distance was about twelve miles. This last stage was by far the most painful to me. The irregular gait of the horse caused me great pain about my kidneys, and I thought I might get along more comfortably on foot; but I feared to work up a sweat and there was danger lest night overtake us in the open country. And so, suffering from incredible pains throughout my body but especially in the kidneys and liver, I got to Tongres. At this point, what with hunger and weariness, every muscle in my body was unstrung; I couldn't either stand or walk steadily. But with my tongue—which was still operative—I covered up the extent of my debility, soothed my stomach with a bit of broth, and went to bed.

Next day I ordered a covered shay. My plan was to ride a horse where the road was paved with stones, until I got to a smoother dirt road. I saddled the bigger horse because he was more sure-footed on cobblestones. But hardly was I mounted in the chill morning air than my sight failed, everything went black. I called for a cloak, but promptly fainted away. They revived me by rubbing my arms and legs. With the help of several bystanders, my servant John held me on the horse and brought me to my senses. When I had recovered a little, I got into the shay. Somewhat later, I felt the need to move my bowels; I got out, did my business, and shortly felt some color return to my face and a certain liveliness to my limbs. By now we were near the town of Saint Trond. Once more I mounted the horse, lest, being carried in a shay, I might seem an invalid. As evening fell, I suffered once again from nausea, but there was no more fainting. I offered the driver of the shay a double fee to drive me next day as far as Tirlemont: it's a town about twenty-four miles from Tongres. He accepted the offer. Here a fellow traveler whom I knew told me how hurt the bishop of Liège had been at my leaving for Basle without paying him a courtesy call.[2] I took a little broth for my stomach, and went to bed. The night was extremely painful, especially because of the sore on my left leg; it was now infected and covered with a big scab. But here by good luck I was able to take a stage coach on its way to Louvain (about twenty miles away),[3] and I flung myself into it. The trip was horribly, almost unbearably, painful; but at last, about seven o'clock of that day, we reached Louvain.

I was in no mood to seek my own quarters because I suspected they were icy cold, and also because I didn't want to be responsible—if rumors of the plague got about—for disrupting the work of the college. So I turned aside to the house of Theodoric the printer.[4] He is such a good friend that, if I had my way, I could be happy with his acquaintance alone. That night, during my sleep, the biggest of my boils burst, and the pain diminished. Next day I went to the doctor, who applied poultices. Now a third sore broke out on my back; it had been made by a servant at Tongres when he was trying to relieve the pain of my kidneys, and in rubbing my back with oil of roses dug too deeply into my ribs with his horny finger. Afterwards this sore began to fester, another swelling appeared, moving around in the neighborhood of my right nipple; but it didn't come to a head, and after a while it slowly disappeared of its own accord. As the doctor departed, he secretly told Theodoric and his servant that I had the plague, that he would send over more poultices, but would not return himself to look after me. I sent a urine specimen to the doctors, they said it showed no evidence of sickness; I consult other doctors, they say the same thing. I call in a Jewish doctor, he says

<hr />

2. The complaint dates back four months, to May of 1518, when Erasmus left Louvain for Basle.
3. It's doubtful whether the last stage of Erasmus's trip took him from Tirlemont or from Saint Trond to Louvain. Dates and distances are not altogether

distinct in his account.
4. Theodoric Martinus, another in the network of Erasmus's printer-friends. To take in a man who might be suffering from the plague was a heroic act.

on the evidence of the specimen my body is just as healthy as his. When the original doctor did not return for a couple of days, I asked Theodoric what was the matter. He made some vague excuse, but I suspected the truth. "What!" I said, "does he think it's the plague?" "That's it," he told me; "he says confidently that there are three plague sores." I laughed heartily, and put all thoughts of the plague out of my mind.

After a couple of days the father of the original doctor shows up, looks me over, and reaches the same conclusion; he tells me to my face that I have the plague. I summon on the side another physician of great reputation. He looks me over, and as he's a blunt man, says, "I wouldn't hesitate to get in bed with you; and if you were a woman, we could have fun together." The Jew agrees with him. Finally, I went to the very best doctor in Louvain—for in fact good doctors are pretty scarce here. I asked if the urine specimen showed anything bad; he said no. I told him the story of my sores, showing in various ways that they couldn't be plague sores. They weren't new sores, they hadn't appeared of their own accord. At the beginning the sores moved about, the one on my left thigh always did so. I had no fever, no particular headache except from being constantly shaken about; I wasn't unusually sleepy, and my palate always felt clean. The vomiting wasn't spontaneous, I provoked it myself, and I threw up nothing but that fish. Once free of that, my stomach recovered; that I rejected food for a time is simply a special mannerism of mine. The urine showed no signs of the plague. Most of this discourse he listened to bravely enough; but whenever I mentioned my sores and boils, I felt the man getting uneasy. I gave him a gold crown, and he promised to return after lunch; but instead, having been terrified by my account, he sent his servant. I kicked him out, and, being thoroughly sick of doctors, commended myself to Christ as my physician.

Within three days my stomach was back to normal after I had drunk a bowl of chicken soup and a bottle of wine from Beaune. I promptly returned to my studies, working over some passages in my New Testament that needed filling out. After seventeen days my wounds gave off some black and putrid matter, as the doctors had predicted would happen. The swelling on my left thigh grew even larger, though without any pain, but it caused me some worry. Then a ridiculous suspicion entered my mind—I hope it's wrong—that this infection came from contact with my horse. For I often slapped barehanded at the flies that settled on him, and then proceeded to touch these parts of my body, either when urinating or when getting dressed. But my new physician calmly advises me to be secure of mind. Now the swelling is going down and getting softer, but it doesn't change its position. The sores are all out of danger, that lump on my right breast having vanished of its own accord.

After recuperating for almost four weeks at Theodoric's house, I returned to my own quarters. During that time I had been so weak that I went out only once to hear mass. If it was the plague, I overcame it by determination, by other distractions, and by strength of mind, for very often the worst part of a disease is the thought of it. From the day of my return I decreed that nobody should come near me unless summoned by name, since I didn't want anyone to be frightened or to have his kindness turned to his disadvantage. Nevertheless, Dorp came to see me first of all, and then Ath. Mark Laurin and Pascal Bersel, who stopped by every day, relieved me during much of my illness with their delightful conversation.

My dear Beatus, who would suppose this thin little body of mine, delicate to begin with and now worn out with age, after going through the pains of so many journeys and the drudgery of so much study, would be able to survive so much sickness? You know how hard I worked at Basle recently, and not just off and on. I had a premonition that this year would be fatal for me; and in fact one trouble succeeded another, each more serious than its predecessor. When the illness was at its height, I was not much disturbed, either by a yearning for life or by a fear of death. My entire trust was in Christ alone, of whom I asked only that he give me whatever fate he thought best. In my youth, as I recall, I used to shudder at the very name of death. At least I have profited from the passing years in fearing death less and in estimating human happiness less in terms of longevity. Already I have passed my fiftieth year; since so few out of so many reach that stage, it's only right for me to ask if I haven't already lived long enough. Besides, if this enters in, I've already prepared the monument by which posterity can know I existed. And perhaps, to quote the poets, when heard from the funeral pyre the voices of envy grow still while glory sounds more loudly.[5] Though, of course, it's no part of the Christian spirit to care for earthly glory; quite enough if I experience that supreme glory of rendering myself acceptable to Christ. Farewell, my dear Beatus. You will learn the sequel from my letter to Capito.[6]

From Louvain, 1518

To Peter Tomiczki, Bishop of Cracow †

[A Tempered Perspective]

Basle, 31 August 1535

Your letters are so full of learning and eloquence, most distinguished of prelates, that they quite shame me out of trying to reply to them. But

5. Ovid, Amores 1.15.39.
6. Wolfgang Capito (1478–1541); Allen reprints Erasmus's letter to him as his no. 877.
† Toward the end of his life, Erasmus had become a European figure, his correspondents no less impressive for their social eminence than for their wide geographic range. Partly this was the natural outcome of humanism, which united scholars continent-wide. But Erasmus corresponded, not just with other scholars, but with princes, prelates, and dignitaries; he discussed with them, not just points of scholarship, but the destiny of Europe. The bishop of Cracow and vice chancellor of Poland was both a friend and a patron; Erasmus entertains him with a smattering of gossip and flattery—and a tragic piece of news from far-distant England.

on the other hand, they bear such evident marks of humanity that I don't shrink from answering them quite off the cuff. This is almost always the case with me; and so by writing a great deal and hastily, I have got in the habit of writing badly.

That I respect and admire your excellence is no credit to me; I should be more monstrous than any Scythian [1] if I didn't love wholeheartedly a man endowed with so many virtues and such extraordinary gifts of fortune, combined with such singular modesty. It pleases you to call by the name of friendship your favor toward me and my reverence toward you— either playing down your own role or much exaggerating mine. It's quite enough dignity for me to be enrolled in the number of your clients. The same modesty appears in your comparing my accomplishments with yours. It's what the Greek proverb calls a matter of the ant and the camel. [2] Nor do you simply make the comparison, but in important respects you give the advantage to Erasmus. I only wish that out of all my writings some good might proceed, especially in the way of piety. About the extent of my fame I'm really not much concerned, though it's not the part of a good man to neglect his reputation. But the judgments of men are very different; and what, I ask you, could be more turbulent than this age of ours? In the same chorus, what discordant voices, what clashing opinions! so that anyone who in this age wants to set something before the public can hardly avoid exposing himself to the tongues of innumerable assassins. There's nothing to do then, but (in the words of Paul) to follow the right path through glory and shame, through good fame and bad. [3] If years ago I had known what it meant to have a celebrated name, I would have tried with all my might to keep the name of Erasmus from being known except to my servants; now, it's idle for me to wish for that "easy way of life" recommended by Epicurus. But since this is the prudence of Epimetheus, [4] to be wise after the event, my only concern now (and to it I am devoting my whole soul) is to leave this world with the good graces of Christ.

As for these labors of mine, in which you suppose I indulge myself joyously, my mind is wholly set on having done with them. But partly it is necessity that keeps me at them, and partly the pressure of importunate beseechers. It's a matter of necessity for me to correct some things of mine that were hastily written and thrown on the world without proper care. I have to rework these things since I can't prevent the printers from publishing all the foolishness I ever wrote, down to my schoolboy jokes. For the sake of a bit of money, they sometimes even put out under my name things written by other people. As for the importunate beseechers, they are of two sorts. Some of them are out for their own profit, like the printers who always want new books on which they can turn a penny. Then there are others who have a claim on me, and who beg of me

---

1. From a Greek vantage, Scythians were barbarians, and all barbarians could therefore be called Scythians.

2. Comparing an ant with a camel, the first thing to strike anyone would be the disparity in size.

3. 2 Corinthians 6.8.

4. The brother of Prometheus the far-sighted, Epimetheus was gifted only with hindsight, and so opened Pandora's box, containing all the evils of the world.

some discourse that they think will serve the public interest; or if I don't directly owe them, they speak with such authority that their request is equivalent to a command. Thus I must write a book *On the Mercy of God* for Christopher, bishop of Basle; a commentary on a couple of psalms for the bishop of Lincoln; another commentary for Turzo, bishop of Olmutz. Then there are two other books, one *On the Creed* for the earl of Wiltshire, and another on *Christian Dying*. Even more importunate are the people who remind me of past promises or actually have a letter that I wrote. Among others of this sort is the book on *Ecclesiastes* which I must now produce in good earnest, though it was promised only in jest—my fate being like that of many girls who accept for fun something of which they can be delivered only with grief and groans. What will be the fate of the book I don't know; certainly, my own spirit never undertook an argument more reluctantly. Still, I preferred to make this roll of the dice rather than be accused of welshing. But what are my petty troubles compared with your immense labors, since—by your sound doctrine, your wise counsel, your integrity, generosity, wisdom, and authority—you have earned the highest praise from the king, the kingdom, and the church of Poland? Though our years agree, there's a great difference between your flourishing old age adorned with dignities of every sort and my declining years, bent before all the threats that envy can muster, like a worn-out horse, not to say a mule.

If the return of spring restored your excellency to the vigor of youth, it's reason for us to thank God. But until the ides of May, the weather here handled me very roughly, so that unless I sought relief from those continually lowering skies (for in prolonged illnesses, that's the anchor on which doctors always hang their faith), I was threatened with certain death as the end of my troubles. Weak as a woman, I was brought on a stretcher to Basle, a city by no means paltry or unattractive, whose hospitality I had previously enjoyed for several years. Here, in expectation of my return, people had prepared a house for my use, such as they knew would suit me. In it, I could work on my *Ecclesiastes*, which in many places might have turned out incoherent, almost shapeless, if I had not been present. The city itself, which about seven years before I had left in a state of turbulence, I found to be perfectly tranquil and quite disposed to resume the quiet tenor of its ways. Now I am not avoided by men whose opinions differ from mine, and most minds seem less inclined to dark suspicions than to candor. In fact I think that— either because of my age, or my experience of the world, or perhaps because of the bit of learning I've picked up—it's now safe for me to live just about anywhere.

In fact, I wouldn't have left my nest [at Freiburg] in order to settle permanently in Basle, unless compelled to do so by the utmost necessity. My original intention was, if I could, to settle at Freiburg in the house I had bought and furnished for my purposes; it was quite splendid enough for me. But if the climate changed, I thought of leaving that home for Brabant or else Burgundy. In Brabant, apart from many other considerations, I would be welcome at the Emperor's court and given a pension on condition of living there. But in addition the Emperor Charles vigorously recommended me to the senate and the clergy of Besançon, if I should choose to settle there. The wines of Burgundy are important to my health. One could make light of it, but the stuff is very expensive to bring here, and the containers often arrive half-empty because of thieving carters—or else the wine has been much diluted with inferior vintages. Indeed, the university of Freiburg is reputed to be one of the best and most flourishing in almost every branch of learning. In addition, I lived quite splendidly in the favor of King Ferdinand, from whom I received many marks of his most distinguished consideration. But the climate of the town never seemed to agree very well with my poor constitution, and even my house, elegant though it was, did not escape suspicion. Here, I'm a little less badly off; I've given up hope of being really well, at least in this life. From boyhood I suffered from a delicate physique and a frail constitution (as the doctors put it), and was very sensitive to an inclement climate. But the vigor of maturity enabled me partly to ignore and partly to overcome those difficulties. Now, after a lifetime of study and (much more wearing) of constant controversy and cruel condemnations, I find my body wasted away to skin and bone. As it weakens, it naturally becomes more susceptible to changes in the atmosphere. The truth is, I'm getting so ethereal myself that the least puff of air changes my disposition, for better or worse. But troubles are more easily borne when one knows they can't last forever. I was much pleased with what you wrote, wittily and sensibly, about Roscius the comic actor, that with advancing years he changed his style of fluteplaying; I only wish I could come close to playing the same part in the church that Roscius did in the theater. In fact, necessity has forced me to imitate what reason taught him to do. As for us two, there is this big difference: you are called away from your scholarly pursuits by the need to bring as much prosperity as possible to the state—something that only you can do; whereas I am driven reluctantly onward to a continual succession of new labors. In any event, your advice, or rather consolation, has been most welcome, and will in future reconcile me better to the difficulties of my ill health, and, whatever happens, will enable me to bear it with a calmer mind.

Your letter contains good news about Jaroslav Laski; a rumor had reached us here that he had been executed with Gritti.[5] Many things are being written about the victories of the Emperor, and many other stories noised about; but I don't believe all these "windy rumors," if I may use the Homeric expression. The people of the imperial faction here lit a lot of bonfires as signs of public rejoicing, and the same thing happened at Rome. The Pope, however, refused to follow suit until the facts were

5. Jaroslav Laski was a freewheeling Polish diplomat in the troubled region of the eastern Balkans; he conspired with Gritti, the Venetian adviser of the grand vizier, and survived the failure of this conspiracy only to die in the next one.

confirmed by letters written directly to him by Charles in person. The rumor has held constant for some time that Guleta, built on the ruins of ancient Carthage,[6] has been captured, and I suppose it is true. Everything else is doubtful. From here I have no good news to send. The plague has spread through many cities of Germany. The city of Munster in Westphalia, which has been occupied by the double-dippers,[7] has been taken by storm, with punishments for everyone more than twelve years of age. For the moment, that rabble has been crushed but not exterminated. The Anabaptists are swarming out of Holland into those regions by troops, and they make no secret of their profession; they are tolerated and ignored, so long as they make no public disturbance. What will come of it all, God knows. The hearts of kings are in the hand of God, and I pray the projects of our Charles may, with Christ's favor, turn out well. But many people feel he would have done better to defend lower Germany from the pests assailing her than to be capturing Guleta. For the quarrels here don't consist any longer of "word wars,"—things have reached the stage of swordplay and bloodshed. The combatants capture cities by treachery or trickery or outright force; they win adherents to their sect by threatening death and violence, they create new kings and queens daily, pronouncing new laws according to their latest whim.

Last month I heard from the Reverend Doctor Joannes Faber, bishop of Vienna and counsellor to King Ferdinand, that a delegate had arrived from the Turk, and then a little later, a second messenger, a Bulgar from official;[8] nothing is certain yet, but it's thought their mission was peace, to which the prince is strongly inclined; and in the present state of German and Hungarian affairs, it makes sense. Our age has produced no person more holy and humane than this prince; I hope God will give him a fortune equal to his virtues, so that he may perform as much good in this world as he wants and is able to do. The landgrave of Hesse, who held the duke of Wurttemberg in his power, is said to have released him on most honorable terms. Around the ides of August, two sisters—Mary the former queen of Hungary, and the queen of France—held a conference at Cambrai; we'll see what comes out of this little conclave. I hope it will turn out better than that session in ancient Rome over which the mother of Heliogabalus presided.[9] Last winter there was a savage reaction in Paris against some men who raised a set of dangerous riots, perilous even to the monarchy itself; they had been undertaking to carry out the will of God (so they said) by putting up placards everywhere against the royal council. In Paris alone some twenty-four of those responsible were executed by various forms of torture, and a great many

---

6. Carthage/Guleta is now called Tunis.

7. Erasmus's word is *retincti*; though the Anabaptists denied the validity of infant baptism, they also denied that what they practiced was rebaptism. Latin is strained to the limit to express their position.

8. The long, tangled wars between the Sultan Suleiman and Charles, Holy Roman Emperor, were often interrupted by threats of truce.

9. Julia Soemias, mother of Heliogabalus, presided over the senate and signed some of her son's decrees. But the comparison is jocose.

others took flight, among them several noblemen. But shortly the king, turning more lenient, called them back, restored their privileges, and (so they say) granted them freedom to follow their own judgments in matters of dogma, provided only that they make no attempt against the kingdom. The authors of this moderate policy—so it's said—were the king of England and Paul the Third. You will learn from a fragment of a letter that I'm enclosing[1] what fate befell the bishop of Rochester and Thomas More, than whom England never bred a better or a more holy man. In More's death I seem to undergo my own; we two seemed to share, as Pythagoras thinks possible, a single soul between us. But such is the tumult of human affairs.

But now I am burdening you with too much gloomy news; here's something for you to laugh at. Paul the Third lately got the notion of creating some more cardinals in a future synod, especially learned ones— among whom even Erasmus was proposed, "a cabbage among the lilies."[2] But there were problems, among them a fortune too meager to support the dignity, in addition to his age and a state of health that could hardly support the weight of church business. And so now the project is being pursued with a great canvassing of votes, so that this burden can be put on me, though I don't want it, reject it with all my strength, and will always reject it. A frail ephemerid like me must take up the cudgels against competitors of unlimited leisure, wealth, and power—and all so that I may die rich! I send you the Pope's brief so that we may join in laughter over it. Believe me, they'll never be able to get a saddle on the cow.[3] The bishop of Rochester received his cardinal's hat in prison, when he was already condemned to death.

In behalf of your king, who in his wisdom is a most devoted partisan of peace, my prayers invoke all good things; he deserves better neighbors. For the blessings of your generosity—neither sought nor expected—I thank you with all my heart. So learned and so friendly a letter, even if it comes "without gifts," will always be most precious to me. Nor did I ever receive from you a letter that did not bring solace to my soul. The students of magic say this is a special quality of evil spirits to diffuse terror and despair, whereas good spirits spread joy and liveliness. No wonder then if your letters bring an aura of light that dispels gloom on the spot, coming as they do from a noble and truly Christian spirit. I would send you the volume on *Ecclesiastes* if I could find someone to carry it; but it will have to reach you through commercial channels. Since I couldn't compete with your letter in elegance of expression, I've tried to make up for it with loquacity. May the Lord preserve your Excellency in safety.

Basle, the day before the Calends of September 1535[4]

1. The letter was probably that from Conrad Goclenius, dated 10 August, which Allen reprints as his no. 3037. It reported that John Fisher, bishop of Rochester, and Thomas More, late lord chancellor of England—both long-time friends of Erasmus—had been executed by order of Henry VIII.

2. From Zenobius, a Greek sophist of the later Roman empire, who compiled a book of proverbial sayings.
3. The glancing allusion is to Horace, *Epistles* 1.14.43.
4. I.e., August thirty-first.

CRITICAL COMMENTARY

H. R. TREVOR-ROPER

Desiderius Erasmus †

Desiderius Erasmus was a scholar who, in the early days of printing, sought to give his contemporaries clear and accurate texts of certain neglected works. He re-translated the Bible, and edited the Christian Fathers. He also wrote, in his clear, elegant Latin, colloquies, satires and works of evangelical piety; and he carried on, mainly with scholars, a gigantic correspondence. Offered opportunities of practical responsibility, he consistently evaded them, and in the crisis of his time he appeared to many a timorous neuter. He was neither a courtier in the age of courts, nor a revolutionary in an age of revolution. Though a friend of kings, his ideal society was the republican city-state. In religion, Luther and Rome alike accused him of tepidity. He was not even an admirer of fashionable classical culture: ancient Rome displeased him both by its paganism and by its empire. His personal character was not heroic. He was a valetudinarian, comfort-loving, timid and querulous. He lived in his study and died in his bed.

And yet Erasmus is a giant figure in the history of ideas. He is the intellectual hero of the sixteenth century, and his failure was Europe's tragedy. For his failure seemed, at the time, immense and final: as immense as his previous success.

Consider his success. Born the illegimate son of an obscure priest, he rose, merely by his pen, to a position of undisputed supremacy in Europe. Cosmopolitan in an age of awakening nationalism, he was born in Holland, studied in Paris, found his intellectual home in Oxford, took his doctorate in Savoy, travelled to Germany and Italy, published his works impartially in Louvain, Paris, Venice and Basel, and had disciples throughout Europe. When he travelled, customs-officers treated him as a prince, princes as a friend. The royal bastard of Scotland was his pupil, the King of Poland his correspondent; the King of Portugal tried to lure him to Coimbra; the King of France wrote twice, and in his own hand, to tempt him to Paris. He was offered professorial chairs in Bavaria and Saxony, bishoprics in Spain and Sicily. The Emperor made him his Privy Councillor, the Pope offered him a cardinal's hat. His disciples formed a European *élite*: they included, he once proudly wrote, 'the Emperor, the Kings of England, France and Denmark, Prince Ferdinand of Germany, the Cardinal of England, the Archbishop of Canterbury, and more princes, more bishops, more learned and honourable men than I can name, not only in England, Flanders, France and Germany, but even in Poland and Hungary. . . .' Such was the fame of Erasmus in 1524, when it was almost at its peak.

Eleven years later, his failure seemed complete. The great crisis of the

† From *Men and Events: Historical Essays* (New York: Hippocrene Books, 1977) 35–60.

Reformation had split his followers, and Popes and Princes could not help him. To save his independence, Erasmus had declined their gifts, avoided their courts, and fled to die in a republican city in Switzerland. He died defeated, foreseeing the future. Soon his name and works would be condemned, his disciples persecuted, his patrons unavailing. 'If that is a crime', protested a Spanish thinker whom the Inquisition accused of having corresponded with Erasmus, 'it is a crime committed also by many great princes, many men of all conditions in all countries . . . among whom I see the Pope, our Lord the Emperor, and most Christian princes, as well spiritual as secular. . . .'[1] It was in vain. By mid-century Erasmus had become a heretic. In Catholic countries it was dangerous even to have known the last great thinker of united Catholic Europe.

How did this great tragedy come about? For it was a real tragedy, not only of one man but of a whole generation. The disciples of Erasmus, in the early sixteenth century, were the spiritual and intellectual *élite* of Europe. There is scarcely a great name in those years which is not among them. They were the saints, the humanists and the reformers who, by their universal diffusion, might have created a new Europe but were in fact swallowed up in the great and widening gulf which they had sought to bridge. To understand this tragedy of a generation it is not enough to study their leader only. We must consider the century which produced both him and them.

In the fourteenth century the decline of Medieval Europe began. The great age of medieval industry, medieval art, the medieval Church was then over. Particularly of the Church, whose vitality then began, as it seemed, a long, uninterrupted ebb. This spiritual ebb was accompanied by other developments. First, the wealth of the Church was increased. New religious orders were not founded, but the old became increasingly rich, and none more arrogant, more ostentatious of their wealth, than the former 'Mendicant' orders, the Franciscans and Dominicans. This increasing wealth of the Church led, as a natural consequence to greater aristocratic control. The system of 'commendation'—'the leprosy of the Church' as Montalembert called it—made the Church, in the fifteenth as in the eighteenth century, into 'a system of outdoor relief for the upper classes'. Hence those aristocratic teen-age bishops, those highly promoted papal bastards who so enliven the history of the pre-Reformation Church. Meanwhile, as spiritual life ebbed away from religion, new forms of piety were developed upon its arid crust. In the schools, Thomism triumphed: a mechanical dissection of dead doctrine; among the people 'works' replaced 'faith': mechanical devotions—pilgrimages, veneration of images and relics, ostentatious ceremonies, and finally, the sale of indulgences. Genuinely religious spirits turned away from this oppressive incrustation of religion to an inner mysticism. It was not for nothing that the fifteenth century was the great age of mysticism. Mysticism, as so often, was the refuge of the defeated.

1. Juan de Vergara, quoted in M. Bataillon, *Erasme et l'Espagne* (Paris 1937), p. 493.

But Christianity was not everywhere defeated. Sporadically, throughout Europe, the evangelical protest was raised. In England the Lollards appealed to—and translated—the Bible. In Medicean Florence, the new Platonists, Ficino and Pico della Mirandola, challenged the formalism of the schools and Savonarola, the puritan friar, preached his crusade against the mechanical 'works' of religion. In the other great centre of European wealth, the Netherlands, Gerard Groote founded the evangelical order of the Brethren of the Common Life, whose new primitive Christianity spread through the monasteries of Northern Europe and produced the greatest mystical work of the century, *The Imitation of Christ*. But all these remained local movements, doomed (it seemed) to local extinction. By the end of the fifteenth century the Lollards had been crushed in England, Savonarola had been burnt in Florence, and the Brethren of the Common Life remained rude and parochial in their Northern simplicity. None of these was able, by themselves, to mobilise the scattered forces which demanded the reform of the Church.

For all over Europe there were practical men eager to reform both the Church and society. Princes, noblemen, officials, clergy, lawyers, scholars only asked to be inspired and used. Already serious efforts had been made within the Church itself, but the machinery was clogged by its own vested interests, against which even a reforming Pope was to prove helpless: the prisoner of his own patronage and the powerful monastic orders around his throne. Other reformers obtained local successes by invoking the lay power: which, however, had dangerous appetites. So Cardinal Ximenes in Spain, thanks to royal support, was able to purge monasteries, to reduce papal patronage, to advance biblical study, and to found the new humanist university of Alcalá. But Ximenes was exceptionally fortunate: generally these early reformers were broken by the impossibility of their task or achieved success only among a few disciples. They remained a scattered minority of enlightened men in an apathetic or hostile world. Then Erasmus appeared and gave them not a constitutional programme but a message, not new machinery but a new spirit. He turned the disconnected reformers into an army which seemed—for a time—invincible.

How did he do it? One technical advantage which he possessed must not be overlooked. Erasmus had the good fortune to coincide with the spread throughout Europe of the printing-press, first used ten years before his birth. The great printers of his time were his natural allies. They were scholars and humanists, members of that educated urban patriciate from which the reformers naturally sprang. Thierry Martens of Louvain was a pupil of the Brethren of the Common Life; so was Josse Badius of Paris, who had also studied in Italy; and Aldus Manutius of Venice was a humanist and a Greek scholar. These men, his publishers and friends, lent their services to Erasmus and his contemporaries as they could not have done to his predecessors. The printing-press, coinciding as it did with a European Church, a European movement of reform, and an international language, gave to the educated classes a weapon of sudden, miraculous potency: a new way to learning, to the Scriptures, even to heresy, by-passing the control of the Church. The age of Erasmus was that golden age which lay between the European discovery of printing and the discovery of its antidote, the *Index Librorum Prohibitorum*. [2]

But of course this was not the only reason for Erasmus's success. Erasmus did not go to the printing-press: the printing-press came to him. He was the first modern best-seller, the first great writer whose works publishers competed to commission, to print and to distribute. They did so because he had discovered, as none other had done, a universal idiom. Behind his lucid, nimble, pungent style he had united the intellectual appeals of all the reformers: Lollard biblicism, Dutch piety, Italian scholarship and Florentine Platonism. Fusing all these, he had made them into one message. And finally, there was his irony, which carried that message everywhere. Like Pascal after him, he discovered that in moral questions it is not earnestness but irony that kills.

This great achievement, the uniting in one cosmopolitan message of the various local protests of the fifteenth century, occupied Erasmus for the first forty years of his life as a wandering scholar. The process began in his native Holland, where he studied under the Brethren of the Common Life at Deventer and there discovered the deep evangelical piety which marked him for life. In Holland also he made his first contact with the exact classical scholarship of Renaissance Italy, and particularly of Lorenzo Valla, the papal secretary who had exposed the false Decretals of the Church. As a scholar, Valla remained Erasmus's master all his life; it was by Valla's strict and disconcerting textual methods that Erasmus would afterwards delete, as spurious, the only reference to the Trinity in the New Testament. But Erasmus's most fruitful contact with Italy was not with the Italy of the philologists: it was with the Platonist Florence of Ficino, of Pico and of Savonarola; and he made that contact not in Italy, where it was already extinct, but in England. There, in Oxford, English scholars—Grocyn, Linacre, Colet—returning from Italy, had grafted Florentine Platonism on to the stump of Lollard Biblicism and produced a new movement, Platonist and Pauline, by which Erasmus, coming to England in 1499, was at once inspired. From that moment, Oxford became his spiritual home. He became a disciple of Colet, the fellow-pupil of Thomas More, and for the rest of their lives remained intimately attached to both of them. After that discovery, Erasmus's intellectual experience was complete. He visited Italy, only to be disappointed by the cold, proud cult of pagan antiquity which had now replaced the Florentine renaissance. He went to Cambridge, but, as his biographer observes, '*l'esprit de Cambridge n'est pas l'esprit d'Oxford*', [3] and he was disappointed there too. Thus, from four sources, from Wyclif and Gerard Groote, from Lorenzo Valla and Savonarola,

2. The *Index of Prohibited Books*, published in 1557 and repeatedly revised thereafter [Editor].
3. A. Renaudet, *Erasme et l'Italie* (Geneva 1954), p. 110 ["The spirit of Cambridge is not the spirit of Oxford"—Editor].

Erasmus drew together his philosophy of reform. Out of these separate elements he had created a single cosmopolitan force, a combination of Latin and Northern piety capable of inspiring the army of reformers throughout Europe and conquering, from its northern base, even orthodox France, even Jewish Spain, even pagan Rome.

And what was this philosophy? Erasmus himself called it *Philosophia Christi*, the philosophy of Christ. Rebelling against the dead intellectual apparatus of the Schoolmen and the mechanical devotions which monks and friars had multiplied among the ignorant people—the 'works' which seemed no longer to express or illustrate but to have replaced that 'faith' which St. Paul had preached—he urged men to turn to the Bible and, in particular, to the New Testament, and there to discover the primitive spirit of Christianity, as it had been before a jealous priesthood had desiccated it in formal dogma and overlaid it with 'judaic' observances. After all, thanks to the new art of printing, the Bible need not any longer be withheld from the Christian world; thanks to the new scholarship of Italy, the text could be cleaned of all excrescences and incrustations and presented widespread in its original form. The message of Christ, he wrote, was not either complex in itself or a mystery of state which princes, out of prudence, must conceal: it was simple, and it should be spread. 'I would have women read the Gospels and the Epistles of St. Paul; I would have the ploughman and the craftsman sing them at their work; I would have the traveller recite them to forget the weariness of his journey. Baptism and the sacraments belong to all Christians; why should knowledge of doctrine be reserved to a few men only, theologians and monks, who form but the smallest part of Christendom and often think only of their lands and goods? True theology is possessed by every man who is inspired and guided by the spirit of Christ, be he a digger or a weaver.' The theologian, said Erasmus, by his expert knowledge, has a duty to divulge the simplicity of the Scriptures; but it is the layman who, if he understands it, is the measure of Christianity.

This teaching was soon to become 'Protestant' teaching; but when Erasmus first advanced it 'Protestantism' had not yet been heard of. Luther had not yet spoken, nor the Church panicked. Therefore clergy and laity alike listened to it without alarm. It seemed a new and fruitful message, capable of renewing the Church from within. In all Erasmus's works this 'Philosophy of Christ' is expressed. It is in his *Adages*, in his *Paraphrases*, in his *Colloquies*, in his *Praise of Folly*, in the introductions and dedications of his great scholarly editions, in the vast correspondence by which he held together, throughout Europe, the ever-growing Erasmian *élite*. But most simply it appears in one of his earliest works, *Enchiridion Militis Christiani*, 'the Manual of a Christian Soldier'. When the *Enchiridion* was first published, in 1504, it attracted little notice, for Erasmus was not yet famous. But in 1508, with the publication in Venice of the great Aldine edition of his *Adages*, his fame was established, and in 1516, his wonderful year (for it saw the publication of his New Testament, his edition of St. Jerome and his *Institutio Principis Chris-*

tiani), it swept over Europe. In that year the *Enchiridion* was rediscovered and began its conquest of Germany. Two years later a new edition, prefaced by a new manifesto of the Philosophy of Christ, was printed at Basel. Translations soon appeared in German, Dutch and French. The great French reformers—Lefèvre d'Etaples and his friends—accepted Erasmus as their leader. And meanwhile (for in 1517 the Archduke Charles, ruler of the Netherlands, had gone with his Flemish court to be King of Spain) the works of Erasmus had crossed the Pyrenees. In 1522 began that extraordinary phenomenon, the Erasmian conquest of the Peninsula. 'It is astonishing,' wrote one of his disciples, 'this devotion to Erasmus among all classes of Spaniards, learned and ignorant, clergy and laity alike.' 'They say', another reported to him, 'that in reading your works they feel illuminated by the spirit of God. They say that you alone know how to publish the teaching of God for the peace and consolation of men's souls.' In 1524, the *Enchiridion* was translated into Spanish. The translator himself was astonished by his success. 'At the court of the Emperor,' he wrote, 'in the towns, in the churches, in the monasteries, even in the inns and on the roads, everyone now has the *Enchiridion* of Erasmus. Hitherto it was read only in Latin by a few scholars, who did not always understand it; now it is read in Spanish by men of all conditions, and those who had previously never heard of Erasmus now know him through this little book.' From Spain the *Enchiridion* soon conquered bilingual Portugal. In 1531 an Italian translation was published at Brescia. The rest of his works soon followed. The piety of the North had triumphed throughout Europe.[4]

Thus Erasmus conquered the *élite* everywhere. He conquered them because they were ready to be conquered. Particularly they were ready for him in Spain, where the reformation of Cardinal Ximenes had prepared the ground and the upper classes were deeply penetrated by a leaven of converted Jews. This connexion between Erasmianism and the Jews in Spain is interesting. The fact is indubitable; it is also somewhat paradoxical, for Erasmus himself was anti-semitic and hated Spain and Portugal, which he declined ever to visit, precisely because of their indelible Semitic tincture; 'Italy', he once wrote, 'contains many Jews, but Spain scarcely contains any Christians'; and he dismissed Portugal (whose 'Grocer-King' had been offended by Erasmus's strictures on the royal spice-monopoly) as 'that Jewish race'.[5] But in fact the paradox is explicable, and explicable partly by Erasmus's own confusion of terms. To him Judaism was a religious term: it meant Talmudic formalism,

4. The Erasmian conquest of Spain has been the subject of one of the greatest historical studies of Erasmus and his work, M. Marcel Bataillon's *Erasme et l'Espagne* (Paris 1937). For the cult of Erasmus in Portugal, see M. Bataillon's volume of essays, *Etudes sur le Portugal au temps de l'Humanisme* (Coimbra 1952). For his influence in France, see Margaret Mann, *Erasme et les Débuts de la Réforme Française* (Paris 1934); for

his influence in Italy, see A. Renaudet, *Erasme et l'Italie* (Geneva 1954).
5. The connexion between Erasmianism and the Peninsular Jews is amply documented by M. Bataillon. For Erasmus's antisemitism see the accumulation of references given by P. S. Allen, *Opus Epistolarum Des. Erasmi Roterodamensis* (1906–47), IV, 46.

pharisaical observances—in fact, precisely those 'mechanical devotions' which, in his eyes, had stifled, in official Christianity, the Philosophy of Christ. But the Spanish Jews of his time were of course converts to Christianity—the believing Jews had been expelled from the Peninsula before he had begun to publish; and being converts, newly arrived at Christianity, they had not acquired, and were not prepared to acquire, that heavy apparatus of dogma which the born Christian has more gradually learnt to wear. Ironically, it was the born Christians, the *cristianos viejos*, who, in Spain, represented the 'judaism' hated by Erasmus, and who, mobilised by the Orders and the Inquisition, ultimately destroyed Erasmianism in Spain: it was the 'new Christians', the *conversos*, who were the natural Erasmians. Thus the Spanish Jews, by that same emancipation from dogma which afterwards made them prominent among the Spanish mystics, provided Erasmus with some of his greatest disciples and helped to make Spain, for a time, the bulwark of Erasmianism in Europe.

Such then was the position in the early 1520's. At that time the ultimate triumph of Erasmianism in the Church must have seemed almost certain. For what power had the corrupt Court of Rome against so unanimous a Europe? And this Erasmian Europe was, moreover, politically mobilised under an Erasmian sovereign. Since 1516 Erasmus had been a privy councillor of his own native sovereign the Archduke Charles, ruler of the Netherlands, to whom he afterwards dedicated his *Education of a Christian Prince*. By 1520 the Archduke was not only King of Spain, the most powerful military monarchy of the day, but also, as Emperor in Germany, the greatest lay sovereign in Europe; and both Spain and Germany were now deeply penetrated by movements of reform. Further, the Emperor was surrounded and advised by what has been called an 'Erasmian general staff'. Mercurino Gattinara, his Piedmontese chancellor, was a devoted disciple of Erasmus. So also was Alonso de Valdés, his indispensable secretary. Finally, in 1521 the Pope himself was a Netherlander. He was the Emperor's old tutor, Adrian of Utrecht, a compatriot, almost a friend of Erasmus, and he had taken to Rome, just as the Emperor had taken to Spain, an entourage of Netherlanders, familiar with the Christian revival of the north. To complete his triumph, all that Erasmus required was a period of peace: for it is peace, not war, he always insisted, that forwards spiritual movements among men. Unfortunately, Europe did not obtain peace. Moreover, two other forces threatened from either side the victory which Erasmus sought: two rival fanaticisms to which his whole spirit was hateful: Luther and the Monks.

From first to last monks were the bane of Erasmus's life. Between them there was no peace. He hated and despised them as the irreconcilable enemies of learning and true piety, and they in turn pursued him with the vindictiveness of a depressed class whose very livelihood is threatened by reform. For if the spirit of monasticism was now dead—save among the Carthusians whom Erasmus himself, like More and

Colet, excepted from his condemnations[6]—its vested interests were still living, and these vested interests were threatened at their very base by Erasmus's Philosophy of Christ. Were there monks in the New Testament or in the primitive centuries of the Church? What did monks do, asked the Reformers, except perpetuate among the ignorant people those mechanical devotions, those 'works', those pilgrimages, those relics, those indulgences which the Philosophy of Christ had never admitted? In the last two centuries, all agreed, monks had contributed nothing to religion, nothing to society, nothing to learning. They had become a mere religious vested interest, a pressure-group which, by its wealth and its influence with the illiterate people, could intimidate even the sometimes liberal court of Rome. In the early sixteenth century all liberal men believed that monasticism must be abolished: it was a disease in the Church. In the same year in which that practical reformer, Thomas Cromwell, was legislating against it in England, a committee of cardinals, appointed by the Pope, and including Cardinal Pole and the future Pope Paul IV, advocated its gradual abolition throughout Christendom. The battle-cry against the monks had been uttered thirty years before, by Erasmus, in his *Enchiridion: Monachatus non est pietas*, Monkery is not piety. It was a phrase which the monks would remember and revenge.

The monks, of course, had their answer. The Philosophy of Christ, they could say, was all very well for educated men: for bishops and cathedral clergy, princes and officials, cultivated merchants, lawyers, scholars—that educated bourgeoisie in which Erasmus found his disciples. But what of the poor and unlearned who could not understand such an intellectual message? For them visual images, 'mechanical devotions', pilgrimages, relics, ceremonies, were the necessary evidence of the Church. The images which the Reformers attacked were the Bible of the illiterate. Erasmus might credit the ploughman and the craftsman with a capacity for apprehending the truth apart from such visual aids, but he was wrong: he romanticised the gross faculties of the fallen plebs. And as for the monks and friars, the religious tribunes of that plebs, the recruiting-sergeants of that Christian army, who purveyed to their crude senses this necessary trash and *bric-à-brac* of religion—was it not their living also? Pigs'-bones and indulgences, spiritual necessities to the ignorant people, were bread-and-butter to their tub-chaplains. . . . Unfortunately, this argument, though strong as a cement to rally the monks in defence of their interests, did not seem very cogent to the Princes of the church—at least as long a those Princes were not frightened. Unfrightened, the educated classes turned naturally to Erasmus: it was only if they were frightened and needed an army that they would turn to the recruiting-sergeants, and lower their intellectual standards in deference towards them. Fortunately for the monks, a benefactor arose who

6. Both More and Colet at one time contemplated becoming Carthusian monks, More at Sheen, Colet at Richmond. Erasmus's respect for the Carthusians is shown by his colloquy *Militis et Carthusi*- *ani*, as also by a letter of 1527, written to a monk, evidently a Carthusian, who was contemplating a return to the world (Allen, *Opus Epistolarum*, vol. VII, No. 1887).

did so frighten the upper classes in the Church and drove them into dependence on these hitherto despised allies. This benefactor was, appropriately enough, a renegade monk: Martin Luther.

When Luther made his frontal attack on the Roman Church, he incorporated in it, of course, many of the criticisms already made from within the Church by Erasmus. Consequently he naturally looked to Erasmus for support against Rome. But Erasmus, though a critic, was still a Churchman. He would support the Church of Rome, he replied, until he saw a better: and although he sympathised with Luther's criticism, he did not think that Luther offered a better alternative. Consequently the Roman Church also looked to Erasmus for support against Luther. From 1519 onwards both sides began to court Erasmus: each hoped that the greatest uncommitted spiritual writer in Europe would declare roundly against its adversary.

What was Erasmus to do? He could not support Luther, whose philosophy he rejected and who was seeking to disrupt the Church. On the other hand he could not denounce him completely, without repudiating his own criticism of the Church—in other words, without ceasing to be Erasmus. The more he was pressed, the more he refused to commit himself, or use his unique position to endorse the rage of either party. He urged the Elector of Saxony to protect Luther against the Catholic fanatics; he urged Luther to persevere 'against the tyranny of the See of Rome and its satellites, the mendicant monks'; on the other hand he disavowed the heretical views of Luther. But the proper answer to Luther, he insisted, was not condemnation, for 'the accusations of Luther against the tyranny, the rapacity, the corruption of the Court of Rome' were only too true—'would to God', he wrote to the Pope's chaplan, 'that they were not'. The true remedy for Lutheranism was not denunciation, it was 'to cut the roots from which the evil continually springs: of which one is the hatred of the Court of Rome, with its intolerable avarice and tyranny, and other certain human ordinances which weigh heavily upon Christian liberty'. These 'human ordinances' were, of course, monasticism and mechanical devotions.

To this philosophy of reform Erasmus remained constant. He sacrificed to it his comfort, his influence, his friends, his peace of mind. He has often been accused of timidity, but in fact his refusal to take sides is a sign rather of consistency: consistency to his ideal of a still united Church peacefully reformed from within. Pressed by Luther, he refused to support him or separate himself from Rome. Pressed by Rome, he refused to deny the truth or justice of Luther's criticism. 'All the Princes urge me to write against Luther,' he said; 'I will not, or if I do, I shall so write that the Pharisees will wish I had kept silent'; and rather than be converted into an inquisitor in the Netherlands, he fled to the free city of Basel to preserve his intellectual integrity. The monks were delighted. From now on Erasmus, though he had opposed Luther and been spurned by Luther, could be blackened as a Lutheran. The monasteries set to work: packs of monks dived into Erasmus's writings; and soon a series of clerical tally-hos denoted the flushing, in many a deep theological thicket, of suspected heresy. In reply to the Erasmian phrase 'Monkery is not piety', a monk of Cologne invented a rival battle-cry which was to become just as famous: '*Erasmus posuit ova, Lutherus eduxit pullos*. . . . . Erasmus laid the eggs, Luther hatched them. God grant that we may smash the eggs and stifle the chicks.'

But Erasmus's patrons were not yet prepared to abandon him to such enemies. In 1527 the Spanish monks prevailed on the Inquisitor-General to permit a general inquest on the works of Erasmus by an assembly of theologians in Valladolid. Erasmus was attacked for his doubting spirit, his inconvenient scholarship, his insinuating style. Had he not advocated toleration in religion, basing it on uncertainties which the monks in no way felt? Had he not maintained that questions of *hypostasis* and *homoousia* did not justify setting fire to the world?[7] But it was no good. The great of the world stood by Erasmus. The Inquisitor-General himself championed him. The Emperor wrote personally to promise his support. Even the Pope would not favour the monks. From the Conference of Valladolid Erasmus, thanks to his great patrons, emerged triumphant. Alas, it was his last triumph. In the very same year an event occurred which led to the loss of those patrons and precipitated the ultimate defeat of Erasmus, the ultimate victory of Luther and the monks.

For in 1527 the Spanish Erasmists appealed to the sword. Erasmus hated war. Only in peace, he thought, could the spirit reform the world. It was his great grievance against the kings who patronised him that they treated war so lightly, as a royal sport. Never did Erasmus's basic republicanism express itself more eloquently than when he attacked the whole tribe of kings for their crimes against peace, their cynical profusion in dissipating the prosperity built up by the ceaseless labour of 'that despised and humble crowd', the people. Rightly, he once declared, was the eagle chosen as the symbol of royalty, since it is 'neither beautiful, nor musical, nor fit for food, but carnivorous, greedy, hateful to all, a curse to all, able and eager to do more harm than all.' Even Popes, instead of controlling the warlike rage of kings, now joined and encouraged them in their crimes in order to establish their families in Italian duchies. Even theologians and clergy committed *la trahison des clercs*,[8] prostituting their learning in support of secular wars. Even the Erasmians, he was now to discover, were not exempt from this disastrous fever. In 1527 the government of Charles V, fired by Erasmian visions of reform, launched the invincible Spanish *tercios*[9] against the corrupt Court of Rome, and the Spanish Erasmists applauded both the war and the violent sack of Rome which it accidentally entailed. Meanwhile the Erasmian chancellor Gattinara applied to Erasmus to re-edit, as an imperial manifesto against the Papacy, Dante's *De Monarchia*. Once again Eras-

---

7. I.e., the nature of Christ's entire personality (as both God and man); and the question whether the Son is *like* the Father in every way or actually *identical* with him [Editor].

8. The treason of the clerks—a catch-phrase from the 1920s applied to sixteenth-century behavior [Editor].

9. Infantry regiments [Editor].

mus refused; he declined to be the agent of the Messianic Erasmianism of Spain.

He was wise in his refusal. The sack of Rome was, for him, a fatal turning-point. Shocked by his own action, the Emperor himself lost his nerve; he moved gradually over to the papal side. And the Pope, shocked by his own failure, decided—if only the Emperor would secure his family in the duchy of Florence—to become an imperialist. On these terms the bargain was sealed. The Medici returned to Florence, the Pope decided to live and die an imperialist, and the Emperor decided not, after all, to clean up the Papacy. Thus the Emperor abandoned the Erasmians, and soon afterwards they suffered still further blows. In 1530 Gattinara died, in 1532 Valdés. Five years after the sack of Rome the 'Erasmian general staff' was dissolved. Against Luther and the monks the Erasmians were left to rely on themselves. At once they began to feel the increasing pressure of persecution. Already his books had been censured in Paris, his French translator burnt at the stake. In Spain, too, some of his disciples were burnt and even the Inquisitor-General could not save them. From now on the pace quickened. Rome, said its nuncio with satisfaction, was only waiting for Erasmus to die in order then to declare him formally a heretic.

Erasmus died in 1536 in Basel, already by then a Protestant city. He died uncondemned—indeed it was in his last year that he was offered, by a new 'Erasmist' pope, the cardinal's hat: but this honour he refused, as he had always refused other than purely intellectual authority. Nevertheless, he died defeated and defeatist. His hope, which had once seemed so near to fulfilment, of seeing the Philosophy of Christ accepted throughout Europe, was broken. Already, on the first emergence of Luther, he had foreseen the future: the recrudescence of monkery, the defeat of the Philosophy of Christ, the victory, within the Roman Church, of the Council of Trent. 'A fine defender of evangelic liberty is Luther!' he had then written. 'By his fault the yoke which we bear shall become twice as heavy. Mere permissible opinions shall become articles of faith. It will become dangerous to teach the Gospel. . . . Luther behaves like a wild man; his adversaries goad him on. But if they prevail, we shall be left to write only the epitaph of Christ, dead without hope of resurrection.' Erasmus was a true prophet. After his death all this came about. Nevertheless, a whole generation passed before his ideals were formally defeated; and the fate of this generation is interesting, for it bears some resemblance to our own. It was the generation of the liberals who were obliged to choose between rival orthodoxies.

The period from about 1530, when Erasmus lost his protectors, until 1559, when his teaching was most emphatically condemned by Rome, was the generation of the Erasmian *epigoni*,[1] the men who had grown up under his influence and who were now feeling the ever-increasing

---

1. Descendants or followers, often degenerate ones.

pressure, on either side, of Lutheranism and the Monks. What were they to do in such a crisis? Liberal men, believers in the Philosophy of Christ, they wished to remain true to that ideal, but they could no longer hope to realise it within an undivided Church: they must make the difficult choice between opposing bigotries. Some, in hope, chose Catholicism: but it was a 'Protestant' Catholicism, the Catholicism of Erasmus himself and, after his death, of the 'reforming' cardinals, Contarini, Sadoleto, Morone, Pole. They believed in such 'Protestant' doctrines as Justification by Faith, the renovation of the soul by Grace, and in the cult of mental prayer. They looked back, through Erasmus, to Savonarola and *The Imitation of Christ*, and their favourite contemporary book was a little work which a Benedictine disciple of the Spanish Erasmian, Juan de Valdés, had composed in a monastery on Mount Etna, *The Benefit of Christ*.[2] Others, in despair, chose Protestantism, but it was a 'Catholic' Protestantism, the Protestantism of the German Melanchthon, the Swiss Bucer, the Spaniard Encinas, still hoping for reunion across the narrowing Erasmian bridge. But ultimately such attempts proved futile: the gulf widened, the bridge crumbled, and the Erasmians who sought to meet upon it had to scramble to opposite sides or perish in the intervening abyss. The middle position became impossible.

Thus, little by little, in the generation after Erasmus's death, the Erasmian *élite* was dissolved. Death, desertion or martyrdom carried away its members and they were not replaced. But before each desertion, or each martyrdom, what a crisis of conscience occurred! Wherever we look, it is the same: groups of friends broken up by the agony of divergent choice and retrospective recrimination. Of the liberal cardinals who in 1538 had proposed the abolition of monasticism, one—Caraffa—became a reactionary, persecuting Pope and threw another of them, Morone, into prison as a heretic; a third, Pole, died in disgrace, accused of heresy. The little book of devotion which they had read together, *The Benefit of Christ*, was so thoroughly dealt with by the Inquisition that 300 years afterwards no copy of it could be found.[3] It had become a Protestant work, like its precursors, *The Imitation of Christ* and the devotional writings of Savonarola.

Everywhere it was the same story. But perhaps the most famous of these Erasmian separations was that which divided not the living but the dead, the separation of Erasmus himself from his closest friend, Sir Thomas More. In all their lives, More and Erasmus had never diverged. Florentine Oxford had been the inspiration of both. Both had admired

2. For Juan de Valdés and his connexion with Erasmus see Bataillon, *Erasme et l'Espagne*, pp. 373–92. He was the twin brother of Alonso de Valdés, Charles V's Erasmian secretary, and founded an Erasmian circle in Naples.

3. Before its total condemnation in 1570, *The Benefit of Christ* was often reprinted and widely circulated in Italian, and translated into French, Spanish, Croat and perhaps other languages. After 1570 it was translated into English (from the French version) and reprinted three times before 1640. By Macaulay's time the original was thought to be 'as hopelessly lost as the second decade of Livy'; but by 1855 two copies had been discovered in Cambridge and Vienna, and the Cambridge text has been twice reprinted. See Churchill Babington, *The Benefit of Christ's Death* (Cambridge 1855) and G. Paladino, *Opuscoli e Lettere di Riformatori Italiani del Cinquecento* (Bari 1927).

Pico della Mirandola and translated Lucian (afterwards a suspect author). Both had rejected monasticism, but exempted the Carthusians from that rejection. They had influenced each other's work, shared each other's irony, believed alike in toleration and republican city-government. And yet these inseparable allies were separated after death by rigid divisions of belief which they had never admitted. In the foundering of the Erasmian 'Third Church', More was converted into a saint of post-Tridentine Rome; Erasmus was utterly disowned by the same Rome, discarded, and accepted, as a Protestant. Already in the Protestant England of Edward VI his *Paraphrases* were printed for use in churches; by 1559 all his books were on the Roman Index; thereafter, while the Inquisition was obliterating even his name from Catholic Europe, his works, which had once been universal, were printed only in Protestant cities. The imprints of Paris, Augsburg, Mainz, Alcalá, Seville, Zaragoza, Venice, Modena gradually disappear from their title-pages, to be replaced by Basel, Geneva, Amsterdam, Leyden, Hanover, Heidelberg, Leipzig, Oxford, Stockholm, Aberdeen.[4]

Thus by 1560 the division seemed complete. The Reformers were outside the Church; and within the Church the Counter-Reformation, as it was formulated by the last session of the Council of Trent, was a victory for the monks. Every specifically Erasmian position was emphatically rejected by Rome and declared a mark of Protestant heresy. Thereafter the remaining Erasmists in the Church, however distinguished, were summarily dealt with. Even an Archbishop of Toledo, Primate of all Spain, was persecuted by the Inquisition and thrown into prison to die because of his Erasmian views. To avoid such a fate, the European Erasmists went over to the Protestantism of which they were accused, the Spanish Erasmists took refuge in mysticism—only to find that mysticism was persecuted also as an 'Erasmian' deviation. And on the other side, all that Erasmus had attacked in the Roman Church was now strengthened, reasserted, multiplied. Instead of appeasing the Reformers, Rome had decided to defy them. New monastic orders, new relics, new images, new devotions—this was now the order of the day, and art was called in to advertise ever more ostentatiously this reinvigorated apparatus of belief.[5] Of the old concessions to reason nothing was left. Even the achievements of Erasmian biblical criticism were rejected, by both sides; the Book of Revelation crept back into the canon of the New Testament, the Epistle to the Hebrews was restored to St. Paul, the spurious *comma iohanneum* returned, for two centuries, into the New Testament.[6] Erasmianism, it seemed, was killed stone-dead.

4. This protestantisation of the works of Erasmus appears clearly in A. van der Haeghen, *Bibliotheca Erasmiana* (Ghent 1893).
5. The use of art as official propaganda in favour of challenged Roman doctrines and practices has been brilliantly illustrated by E. Mâle, *L'Art Religeux après le Concile de Trente* (Paris, 2nd edition, 1951).
6. In the first epistle of John, verses 7 and 8 of chapter 5 were long thought to refer to the Trinity; if authentic, the passage would be important, as giving apostolic authority for that doctrine. But, as Erasmus pointed out, and as all scholars now agree, the passage is a late interpolation *[Editor]*.

It would be easy to end here, as has often been done; but it would, I think, be unfair. Political programmes may be defeated entirely, but not ideas: at least, not great ideas. Political circumstances may alter around them, ideological frontiers may be formed against or across them, but such convulsions merely alter the terrain: they may divert or divide, but they do not permanently dam the stream. The idea of ideological blocs systematically opposed to one another in intellectual matters is a naïve idea such as can only occur to doctrinaires and bigots. The Age of the Reformation had of course its bigots: monks who, in sixteenth-century Spain, denounced Liberal Catholics as 'Lutheran' heretics, puritans who, in seventeenth-century England, denounced Liberal Protestants as 'popish' conspirators. But the historian of ideas is not interested in these stunted McCarthyites. The victims of persecution are always more interesting than their persecutors; and if we wish to discover the heirs of Erasmus, rather than to assume too easily that they were crushed by the Counter-Reformation, we should not accept as final and mutually exclusive the barren categories of 'Protestant' and 'Catholic' into which Christendom was officially and superficially divided. There was an Erasmianism after Erasmus, a secret stream which meandered to and fro across those loudly proclaimed but ill-guarded frontiers, creating oases of rational thought impartially on either side.

In Protestantism this stream is, of course, more easily identified, for the Protestant Churches openly adopted Erasmus and used his name. In some ways his direct heir was Calvin. Calvinism, at least in its early days, had a double appeal: it appealed to the laity in general, the simple gentry revolting against the privileges and usurpations of the priesthood, and it 'exercised its most profound attraction not on this or that economic class but on the intellectual *élite* of all classes'.[7] Now these were precisely the two social groups to whom Erasmus also had appealed. The ideal of Erasmus had been the ideal of lay piety, simple, sincere, animated by faith, nourished by prayer, free from the ostentatious trappings of priestly 'works'; and his scholarly rationalism had drawn to him too 'the intellectual *élit'* of all classes'. When Rome had yielded to the monks, the intellectual *élite* moved over to Protestantism: from Italy, Spain and Marian England there was an exodus of Erasmists to Geneva and Basel;[8] and Calvin, for those harder times, cast the ideas of Erasmus into his harder mould. It is easy, if we are blinded by the later, less intellectual

7. I take this phrase from a most interesting passage in J. H. Hexter's book, *More's Utopia, the Biography of an Idea* (Princeton 1952), p. 93. The intellectual ascendancy of Calvinism *in the early period* of the Counter-Reformation deserves further study. In my opinion a great deal of historical error has been caused by failure to distinguish the successive phases of religion, e.g. between the intellectual Calvinism of Calvin's own time (contrasting with the intellectual poverty of Rome), and the backward Calvinism of the early seventeenth century, which appealed to different classes and

contrasted with the intellectual revival of Rome. For the influence of Erasmus on Calvin see Margaret Mann, *Erasme et les Debuts de la Réforme Française* (Paris 1934), pp. 161 foll.
8. For the flight of the humanists to Switzerland in the 1550's see (for Spain) Bataillon, *Erasme et l'Espagne*, p. 749; (for Italy) Delio Cantimori, *Gli Eretici Italiani del Cinquecento* (Florence 1939), pp. 88–92, and A. Pascal, 'Da Lucca a Ginevra', a series of eight articles in *Rivista Storica Italiana* 1932–5; (for England) G. H. Garrett, *The Marian Exiles* (1938).

form of Calvinism, to overlook its earlier character; but if we look more closely, it is clear. Calvin was brought up under the influence of Erasmus and himself professed the 'Philosophy of Christ'; the inspiration of Erasmus is clear in his works; and it was in Basel, the capital of Erasmianism, that Calvin, in the last years of Erasmus's life, wrote and published his *Institutes*. Admittedly Calvinism had also many features which Erasmus would have condemned, and in theocratic Geneva was dogmatic and intolerant; but as practised under more tolerant lay rulers in England and the Netherlands, it could become, in many ways, the continuation of Erasmianism. Unfortunately, Calvinism, becoming intolerant, was unable to retain for long the intellectual Erasmian *élite*. Falling back therefore on its other basis, the poorer gentry, it degenerated into a religion of backwoods squires: the Huguenot *hobereaux* of Southern France, the Covenanting lairds of Scotland, the Orangist *petite noblesse*[9] of Gelderland. With this change, the spirit of Erasmus left Calvinism and sought, within Protestantism, another body.

It found it in the 'rational theology' of the seventeenth century, a theology which was 'unitarian' in origin and began with Erasmus. Erasmus, on purely scholarly grounds, had correctly rejected from his New Testament the Trinitarian interpolation in the Epistle of John. Under pressure from the orthodox, he had in the end wearily restored it, but he had made it clear—to the fury of the monks—that he only did so for the sake of peace. Erasmus was therefore regarded as a unitarian, the founder of a rationalist unitarian school. The other founders were the French and Italian rationalists, Castellio, Acontius and the two Sozzini who, fleeing from the Inquisition to the Erasmian city of Basel, there formulated their views and published the first systematic defence of toleration, *De Haereticis an sint Persequendi*.[1] Afterwards the younger Sozzini went on and preached these views, under the name of Socinianism, in the italianised kingdom of Poland. Thus fathered, Socinianism incorporated not only antitrinitarian conclusions but also Erasmian tolerance, Erasmian rationalism, and Erasmian respect for the Bible as the purest source of Christianity. In the late sixteenth century England and Poland were the two most tolerant countries in Europe, and it was no accident that they proved the most accommodating homes for the unorthodox spirit of Erasmus. But by the next century the Jesuit reconquest of Poland was complete; the Socinian university of Rakow, 'the Sarmatian Athens', was snuffed out, and the Erasmian professors fled to a new area of tolerance which had been reconquered from the Counter-Reformation: the United Provinces of Erasmus's own home, the Netherlands. There already Calvinism had begun to harden into a rigid, illiberal system. The fresh breath from Erasmian Poland suddenly regenerated

9. Lesser gentry; *hobereaux:* squires [*Editor*].
1. [Whether Heretics Should Be Persecuted—*Editor.*] The book is anonymous, but according to Cantimori (*op. cit.*, p. 160) Castellio and Fausto Sozzini were certainly the principal contributors to

it. Toleration was afterwards regarded, and attacked, as an exclusively 'Socinian' doctrine. See quotations given by H. J. McLachlan, *Socinianism in Seventeenth-Century England* (1951), p. 9, note.

it, creating in its midst the liberal, tolerant 'Arminianism' of Amsterdam;[2] and from Amsterdam the same refreshing air was carried back to
increasingly puritan England and there recreated the religious liberalism
which Erasmus himself had found there 130 years before.

What an extraordinary revenge it was! In 1500 Erasmus had helped
to create in Oxford that Florentine, Platonist piety which challenged the
rigid Catholicism of the Middle Ages. Now, in 1630, his spirit, having
fled first to Poland, then to Holland, had returned to Oxford to challenge the rigid Calvinism which had at one time seemed his more direct
inheritor. Throughout the 1630's 'Socinian' books poured into England
from Amsterdam. Their ideas penetrated both parties in the church alike,
showing themselves both in Independency to the Left and in Laudian-
ism to the right of strict Calvinism. It was in high-church Arminianism
that they first made themselves noticed. Lucius Cary, Viscount Falkland, and 'the incomparable John Hales of Eton' were each described as
'the first Socinian in England'; William Chillingworth and Jeremy Taylor were also, for their tolerance, called Socinians; and Archbishop Laud
himself, for all his illiberal politics, was regarded as too liberal towards
such ideas. The great patron of this 'Socinian' reception, Lord Falkland,
who built up a fine Socinian library and made his house at Great Tew
into the centre of such studies, was a particular admirer of Erasmus; and
it is from the famous *convivium theologicum* of Great Tew, the head-
quarters of the new Oxford Movement, and from the Cambridge Platonism of the next generation, that rationalist Christianity ultimately spread
over England.[3]

Meanwhile, what of the Catholic Church? Ostensibly, of course,
Erasmus had no place in it. His name and works were carefully blotted
out of its official records. But if Sir Thomas More could ultimately find
a place in Rome of the Counter-Reformation, could Erasmus really be
excluded? Silently, secretly, anonymously, he returned. He returned by
two roads: first with the Jesuits; afterwards, when they had degenerated
from his exact spirit, with the great mystical revival of seventeenth-century France.

For although the Counter-Reformation was, ostensibly at least, a victory for the monks, it was not *only* a victory for the monks. That indeed
would have been impossible. The Holy Office might condemn all Erasmian doctrines; it might repudiate the Erasmian cult of prayer, the Erasmian teaching of grace and faith; it might burn the books of Erasmus in
Rome; it might forbid the translation of the Bible in whole or in part; it
might reject rational criticism; and instead of all these it might offer
again, redoubled, the old apparatus of religion on whose dead weight

---

2. Arminius himself explicitly based his teaching
on that of Erasmus. See A. W. Harrison, *Armin-
iamism* (1937), p. 17. He was also regularly accused
of Socinianism (*ibid.*, 25, 37).
3. For this reception of Socinianism in England,
and its consequences, see H. J. McLachlan's

important work, *Socinianism in Seventeenth-Century England* (1951), and J. Tulloch, *Rational
Theology and Christian Philosophy in England in
the Seventeenth Century* (1872); and cf. C. J.
Stranks, *The Life and Writings of Jeremy Taylor*
(1952), pp. 23–4, 229.

Erasmus had poured his irony, the other reformers their scorn. But if it had done no more than this, how could Rome have reconquered, as it did, a third of the provinces lost to Reform? In fact the Counter-Reformation was more positive than this. It rejected Erasmus indeed, but in name only. It stole his spirit and used it not to purge away but to reanimate the lifeless cumber of monastic religion. The first to do this, the real architects of the Counter-Reformation, were the newest order, the Jesuits. It was they who showed that both the new learning and the new piety of Erasmus could be used to reinvigorate the old forms of religion. The *Philosophia Christi* of Erasmus could become the Spiritual Exercises of Loyola; his fluent Latinity could be continued in their polished schools; his Biblical criticism could become ultimately the astringent scholarship of the Bollandists. Thus refreshed, the spirit of Christianity could carry still that deposit of previous centuries whose dead weight Erasmus had sought to lessen: perhaps it could even be enriched by it.

The Jesuits, of course, had to walk warily, especially in Spain and at Rome where the power of the orders was greatest. They had to denounce one half of Erasmianism before they could safely appropriate and exploit the other. Thus Loyola himself had read Erasmus's *Enchiridion*, and he based his *Spiritual Exercises* fundamentally upon it; but he was careful to ensure that his pupils read it only in an expurgated and anonymous version, and he added to the *Spiritual Exercises* the rigorous and corrective *Rules for Thinking with the Church*.[4] And of course the Jesuits, like the Calvinists, rejected altogether the Erasmian belief in toleration. Even so they often found themselves in trouble on account of their 'Erasmian' innovations. They were distrusted by Pope Paul IV, whose total condemnation of Erasmus they deplored. Their 'Erasmian' cult of 'mental prayer' was attacked as heretical by Dominicans and Pope alike. They supported, against the Pope, Cardinal Morone, who was accused of heresy for disseminating the Erasmian book *The Benefit of Christ*; their support, against the Inquisition, of the Erasmian Archbishop Carranza nearly compromised their order and they had to wriggle out of their commitments; and they were constantly suspected of 'illuminism'—that heresy of direct contact with God, without the expensive and oppressive help of the Church, for which the Spanish Erasmists were persecuted by the Inquisition. Nevertheless, by opportune denials, tactical tergiversations and firm discipline over their indiscreet members, the Jesuits survived these difficulties: they made room for some at least of the ideas of Erasmus in the monk-ridden Church of Rome; and thereby, in half Europe, they saved it. It is not surprising that the writers of Counter-Reformation Europe in whom the spirit of Erasmus has been most

4. For the Erasmian inspiration of Loyola's *Spiritual Exercises* see Henri Brémond, *Histoire Littéraire du Sentiment Réligieux en France*, XI, 60; M. Bataillon, *Etudes sur le Portugal au Temps de l'Humanisme*, p. 255 and note. For Loyola's expurgation of the *Enchiridion* see François de Dainville, S.J., *La Naissance de l'Humanisme Moderne* (Paris 1940), p. 230.

observed were often the pupils, sometimes the admiring pupils, of the Jesuits.[5]

The intellectual supremacy of Jesuits in the Catholic Church, like that of the Calvinists among the Protestants, was brief. In the seventeenth century it soon declined into mere intellectual smartness. But just as the desiccated Calvinist orthodoxy of the seventeenth century was refreshed by the 'Socinian' spirit from Poland, so the courtly vapidity and moral 'laxism' of the seventeenth century Jesuits was challenged— at least in Northern Europe—by a new liberalism: the great mystical revival which triumphed in France. Once again, since it was a Catholic movement, the name of Erasmus was suppressed: Erasmus was still, in the eyes of orthodox French Catholics, 'malheureusement catholique, s'il est encore digne de ce nom,'[6] and only a bold writer, like Claude Joly, could openly name him as the source of his inspiration.[7] But the ideas of the new mysticism were his: they were, in the words of one of its historians, 'idées érasmiennes débaptisées';[8] and they came into France not from Italy, dominated by the now disreputable Jesuits, nor from Spain, reconquered by brute monkish reaction, but from the Catholic Rhineland and, above all, from the Catholic South of Erasmus's home, the Netherlands.[9] Just as the Protestant Netherlands received back the 'Socinian' spirit of Erasmus and therewith refreshed the wooden Calvinism of Holland and England, so the Catholic Netherlands, recreating the mystical spirit of Erasmus, discharged it upon France to refresh the wooden orthodoxy of the Sorbonne. The result was what the Abbé Brémond called 'the mystical invasion' of France: an invasion which, like the 'Socinian' invasion of England, flowed alike in all parties in the Church, bearing fruit in the 'dévots' and the Jansenists, in Bérulle and Pascal, in St. Francis of Sales and St. Vincent de Paul—the great figures who gave to Catholicism in seventeenth-century France a warmth, a richness and a humanity which it could claim nowhere else. At the beginning of the new century the fact could be admitted. In his 'Apology or Justification for Erasmus', a French Catholic, in 1713, paid a last open tribute to 'that great man' whose work, so long resisted, had at last been achieved. The age of rational, tolerant piety had begun.[1]

5. The differences between the Jesuits and the official Church—always on an 'Erasmian' issue— can be followed in L. Pastor, History of the Popes (English translation), vol. XIV, pp. 246–58, 278, 302, and in Bataillon, Erasme et l'Espagne, pp. 747, 757, 760, 795, 814–15. Melchor Cano, the Dominican high-priest of orthodoxy, denounced the whole Jesuit order as illuminists and Gnostics such as the Devil had constantly thrust into the Church. He urged their ruin, as did another Dominican, Fray Alonso de la Fuente de Llerena. See H. C. Lea, Chapters from the Religious History of Spain (Philadelphia 1890), p. 291, Fermin Caballero, Conquenses Illustres, II, Melchor Cano (Madrid 1871), pp. 347–67. For the Erasmianism of Cervantes, a pupil of the Jesuits, see Bataillon, op. cit., pp. 819 foll.

6. ["Unfortunately Catholic, if he is even worthy of the name"—Editor.] From André du Val, quoted by J. Dagens, Bérulle et les origines de la Restauration Catholique (Bruges 1952), p. 42.
7. Brémond, op. cit., IX, 328, note.
8. ["Defrocked Erasmian ideas"—Editor.] From Dagens, op. cit., pp. 78–9. For an instance of the widespread, if unavowed, influence of Erasmus on French devotional literature of the seventeenth century, see Brémond, op. cit., IX, 358–59.
9. See the statistics of Dom Huyben quoted in Dagens, op. cit., p. 105, note.
1. Marsollier, Apologie ou Justification d'Erasme, quoted in Dagens, op. cit., p. 79. This revival of Erasmus within the Catholic Church even penetrated—timidly and for a brief period—to Spain. See Jean Sarrailh, La Crise Religieuse en Espagne

That age now seems to be closing. Therefore it may be useful to consider Erasmus, who was, in a sense, both its prophet and its martyr. What does a humanist do when bigotries swell, black and red, on either side? There are some to-day who say that intellectuals should line up on either side as a species of army chaplains to encourage the troops. I well remember the spectacle, five years ago, in Berlin, when a so-called 'Congress for Cultural Freedom' mobilised the intellectuals of the West and invited them to howl in unison against the rival intellectuals similarly mobilised in an opposite 'Intellectual Congress' in Breslau. But I do not think that Erasmus, if he had yielded to political pressure and joined the Gadarene stampede of Lutherans or monks, would have had so lasting and beneficent an effect in the history of thought as he did by continuing to advocate peace for the diffusion of unarmed sense. Intellectuals may be citizens; they may even, as such, have to become soldiers; but it is not their business to be recruiting-sergeants. If their rational message is not heard in their time, let them still utter it rather than turn it into 'a battle-cry: it may still be heard tomorrow. For history, closely considered, suggests that opposite sides in an ideological struggle, for all their high-sounding abstract slogans, are not so opposite as they think that they are. The humanist message in fact can be understood by both. It may take a long time and a devious route; it may have to survive by stealth; but there is no proper alternative to it. Whether we think of secular or religious ideologies, the words of a sensible eighteenth-century Whig bishop remain true; 'the Church, like the Ark of Noah, is worth saving: not for the sake of the unclean beasts that almost filled it, and probably made most noise and clamour in it, but for the little corner of rationality that was as much distressed by the stink within as by the tempest without.' In the ideological struggles before the Age of Reason, that 'little corner of rationality' was occupied by Erasmus; and it is he, not Luther or Calvin, the Pope or the Jesuits, who still speaks to us with a human voice.

R. S. ALLEN

The Transalpine Renaissance †

Hitherto we have viewed the age mainly through the personality of individuals. It remains to consider some of the features of the Renaissance when it had spread across the Alps—to France, to Spain, to Switzerland, to Germany, to England—and some of the contrasts that it presents with

---

à la Fin du XVIIIᵉ Siècle (Oxford, Taylorian Lecture, 1951), L'Espagne Éclairée (Paris 1954), pp. 193, 637, 681. Even when Erasmus is not cited by name, the programme of religious reform described by M. Sarrailh, with its cult of 'interior religion', its biblicism, its lay piety, its opposition to 'pra-

tiques machinales, purement extérieures', is in fact the Philosophia Christi of Erasmus.
† From The Age of Erasmus (London: Clarendon Press, 1914, 1963) 252–75. Strictly bibliographical footnotes have been omitted.

the earlier movement in Italy. The story of the Italian Renaissance has often been told; and we need not go back upon it heie. On the side of the revival of learning it was without doubt the great age. The importance of its discoveries, the fervour of its enthusiasm have never been equalled. But though it remains pre-eminent, the period that followed it has an interest of its own which is hardly less keen and presents the real issues at stake in a clearer light. Awakened Italy felt itself the heiress of Rome, and thus patriotism coloured its enthusiasm for the past. To the rest of Western Europe this source of inspiration was not open. They were compelled to examine more closely the aims before them; and thus attained to a calmer and truer estimate of what they might hope to gain from the study of the classics. It was not the revival of lost glories, thoughts of a world held in the bonds of peace: in those dreams the Transalpines had only the part of the conquered. Rather the classics led them back to an age before Christianity; and pious souls though they were, the scholar's instinct told them that they would find there something to learn. Christianity had fixed men's eyes on the future, on their own salvation in the life to come; and had trained all knowledge, even Aristotle, to serve that end. In the great days of Greece and Rome the world was free from this absorbing preoccupation; and inquiring spirits were at liberty to find such truth as they could, not merely the truth that they wished or must.

Another point of difference between Italy and the Transalpines is in the resistance offered to the Renaissance in the two regions. The scholastic philosophy and theology was a creation of the North. The greatest of the Schoolmen found their birth or training in France or Germany, at the schools of Paris and Cologne; and with the names of Duns, Hales, Holcot, Occam, Burley and Bradwardine our own islands stand well to the fore. The situation is thus described by Aldus in a letter written to the young prince of Carpi in October 1499, to rejoice over some translations from the Greek just arrived from Linacre in England: 'Of old it was barbarous learning that came to us from Britain; it conquered Italy and still holds our castles. But now they send us learned eloquence; with British aid we shall chase away barbarity and come by our own again.' The teaching of the Schoolmen made its way into Italy, but had little vogue; and with the Church, through such popes as Nicholas V, on the side of the Renaissance, resistance almost disappeared. The humanists charging headlong dissipated their foes in a moment, but were soon carried beyond the field of battle, to fall into the hands of the forces of reaction. Across the Alps, on the other hand, the Church and the universities stood together and looked askance at the new movement, dreading what it might bring forth. In consequence the ground was only won by slow and painful efforts, but each advance, as it was made, was secured.

The position may be further illustrated by comparing the first productions of the press on either side of the Alps: in the early days, before the export trade had developed, and when books were produced mainly for the home market. The Germans who brought the art down into Italy,

Sweynheym and Pannartz at Rome, Wendelin and Jenson at Venice, printed scarcely anything that was not classical: Latin authors and Latin translations from the Greek. Up in the North the first printers of Germany, Fust and Schoeffer at Mainz, Mentelin at Strasburg, rarely overstepped the boundaries of the mediaeval world that was passing away or the modern that was taking its place.

The appearance of the *Epistolae Obscurorum Virorum* [1] in 1515 exposed the scholastic teachers and their allies in the Church to such widespread ridicule that it is not easy for us now to realize the position which those dignitaries still held when Erasmus was young. The stream of contempt poured upon them by the triumphant humanists obscures the merit of their system as a gigantic and complete engine of thought. Under its great masters, Albert the Great, Thomas Aquinas, Duns Scotus, scholasticism had been rounded into an instrument capable of comprehending all knowledge and of expressing every refinement of thought; and, as has been well said, the acute minds that created it, if only they had extended their inquiries into natural science, might easily have anticipated by centuries the discoveries of modern days. [2] In expressing their distinctions the Schoolmen had thrown to the winds the restraints of classical Latin and the care of elegance; and with many of them language had degenerated into jargon. But in their own eyes their position was unassailable. Their philosophy was founded on Aristotle; and while they were proud of their master, they were prouder still of the system they had created in his name: and thus they felt no impulse to look backwards to the past.

In the matter of language they had been led by a spirit of reaction. The literature of later classical times had sacrificed matter to form; and the schools had been dominated by teachers who trained boys to declaim in elegant periods on any subject whatever, regardless of its content; thus carrying to an extreme the precepts with which the great orators had enforced the importance of style. The Schoolmen swung the pendulum back, letting sound and froth go and thinking only of their subject-matter, despising the classics. In their turn they were confronted by the humanists, who reasserted the claims of form.

There was sense in the humanist contention. It is very easy to say the right thing in the wrong way; in other spheres than diplomacy the choice of language is important. Words have a history of their own, and often acquire associations independent of their meaning. Rhythm, too, and clearness need attention. An unbalanced sentence goes haltingly and jars; an ambiguous pronoun causes the reader to stumble. An ill-written book, an ill-worded speech fail of their effects; it is not merely by sympathy and character that men persuade. But of course the humanists pushed the matter too far. Pendulums do not reach the repose of the mean without many tos and fros. Elegance is good, but the art of rea-

---

1. *Letters of Obscure Men* [Editor].

2. Cf. F. G. Stokes, *Epistolae Obscurorum Virorum*, 1909, p. xvii.

soning is not to be neglected. Of the length to which they went Ascham's method of instruction in the *Scholemaster* (1570) is a good example. He wished his scholar to translate Cicero into English, and then from the English to translate back into the actual words of the Latin. The Ciceronians did not believe that the same thing could be well said in many ways; rather there was one way which transcended all others, and that Cicero had attained. Erasmus, however, was no Ciceronian; and one of the reasons why he won such a hold upon his own and subsequent generations was that, more than all his contemporaries, he succeeded in establishing a reasonable accord between the claims of form and matter in literature.

In their neglect of the classics the Schoolmen had a powerful ally. For obvious reasons the early and the mediaeval Church felt that much of classical literature was injurious to the minds of the young, and in consequence discouraged the use of it in schools. The classics were allowed to perish, and their place was taken by Christian poets such as Prudentius or Juvencus, by moralizations of Aesop, patchwork compositions known as 'centos' on Scriptural themes, and the like. The scholars, therefore, who went to Italy and came home to the North carrying the new enthusiasm, had strenuous opposition to encounter. The Schoolmen considered them impertinent, the Church counted them immoral. To us who know which way the conflict ended, the savage blows delivered by the humanists seem mere brutality; they lash their fallen foes with what appears inhuman ferocity. But the truth is that the struggle was not finished until well into the sixteenth century. Biel of Tubingen, 'the last of the Schoolmen', lived till 1495. Between 1501 and 1515 a single printer, Wolff of Basle, produced five massive volumes of the *Summae* of mediaeval Doctors. Through the greater part, therefore, of Erasmus' life the upholders of the old systems and ideals, firmly entrenched by virtue of possession, succeeded in maintaining their supremacy in the schools.

Between the two periods of the revival of learning, the Italian and the Transalpine, a marked line is drawn by the invention of printing, c. 1455: when the one movement had run half its course, the other scarcely begun. The achievements of the press in the diffusion of knowledge are often extolled; and some of the resulting good and evil is not hard to see. But the paramount service rendered to learning by the printer's art was that it made possible a standard of critical accuracy which was so much higher than what was known before as to be almost a new creation. When books were manuscripts, laboriously written out one at a time, there could be no security of identity between original and copy; and even when a number of copies were made from the same original, there was a practical certainty that there would be no absolute uniformity among them. Mistakes were bound to occur; not always at the same point, but here in one manuscript, there in another. Or again, when two unrelated copies of the same book were brought together, there was an antecedent probability that examination would reveal differences: so that in general it was impossible to feel that a fellow-scholar working on the same author was using the same text.

Even with writers of one's own day uniformity was hardly to be attained. Not uncommonly, as a mark of attention, an author revised manuscript copies of his works, which were to be presented to friends; and besides correcting the copyists' errors, might add or cut out or alter passages according to his later judgement. Subsequent copies would doubtless follow his revision, and then the process might be repeated; with the result that a reader could not tell to what stage in the evolution of a work the text before him might belong: whether it represented the earliest form of composition or the final form reached perhaps many years afterwards. To understand the conditions under which mediaeval scholars worked, it is of the utmost importance to realize this state of uncertainty and flux.

Not that in manuscript days there was indifference to accuracy. Serious scholars and copyists laid great stress upon it. With insistent fervour they implored one another to be careful, and to collate what had been copied. But there are limits to human powers. Collation is a dull business; and unless done with minute attention, cannot be expected to yield perfect correctness. When a man has copied a work of any length, it is hard for him to collate it with the original slowly. Physically, of course, he easily might; but the spirit is weak, and weary of the ground already traversed once, urges him to hurry forward, with the inevitable result.

With a manuscript, too, the possible reward might well seem scarcely worth the labour, for how could any permanence be ensured for critical work? A scholar might expend his efforts over a corrupt author, might compare his own manuscript with others far and near, and at length arrive at a text really more correct. And yet what hope had he that his labour was not lost? His manuscript would pass at his death into other hands and might easily be overlooked and even perish. Like a child's castle built upon the sand, his work would be overwhelmed by the rising tide of oblivion. Such conditions are disheartening.

Thus mediaeval standards of accuracy were of necessity low. In default of good instruments we content ourselves with those we have. To draw a line straight we use a ruler; but if one is not to be had, the edge of a book or a table may supply its place. In the last resort we draw roughly by hand, but with no illusions as to our success. So it was with the scholar of the Middle Ages. His instruments were imperfect; and he acquiesced in the best standards he could get: realizing no doubt their defects, but knowing no better way.

But with printing the position was at once changed. When the type had been set up, it was possible to strike off a thousand copies of a book, each of which was identical with all the rest. It became worth while to spend abundant pains over seeking a good text and correcting the proofs—though this latter point was not perceived at first—when there was the assured prospect of such uniformity to follow. One edition could be distinguished from another by the dates on title-page and colophon; and work once done was done for all time, if enough copies of a book were taken off. This necessarily produced a great change in methods of study. Instead of a single manuscript, in places perhaps hopelessly entangled, and always at the mercy of another manuscript of equal or greater authority that might appear from the blue with different readings, the scholar received a text which represented a recension of, it may be, several manuscripts, and whose roughnesses had been smoothed out by the care of editors more or less competent.

The precious volumes to which modern book-lovers reverently give the title of 'Editio princeps',[3] had almost as great honour in their own day, before the credit of priority and antiquity had come to them; for in them men saw the creation of a series of 'standard texts', norms to which, until they were superseded, all future work upon the same ground could be referred. As a result, too, of the improved correctness of the texts, instead of being satisfied with the general sense of an author, men were able to base edifices of precise argument upon the verbal meaning of passages, in some confidence that their structures would not be overset.

But the new invention was not universally acclaimed. Trithemius with his conservative mind quickly detected some weaknesses; and in 1492 he composed a treatise 'In praise of scribes', in vain attempt to arrest the flowing tide. 'Let no one say, "Why should I trouble to write books, when they are appearing continually in such numbers? for a moderate sum one can acquire a large library." What a difference between the results achieved! A manuscript written on parchment will last a thousand years: books printed on paper will scarcely live two hundred. Besides, there will always be something to copy: not everything can be printed. Even if it could, a true scribe ought not to give up. His pen can perpetuate good works which otherwise would soon perish. He must not be amazed by the present abundance that he sees, but should look forward to the needs of the future. Though we had thousands of volumes, we must not cease writing; for printed books are never so good. Indeed they usually pay little heed to ornament and orthography.' It is noticeable that only in this last point does Trithemius claim for manuscripts superior accuracy. In the matter of permanence we may wonder what he would have thought of modern paper.

The first advance, then, rendered possible by the invention of printing was to more uniform and better texts; the next step forward was no less important. To scholars content with the general sense of a work, a translation might be as acceptable as the original. Improved standards of accuracy led men to perceive that an author must be studied in his own tongue: in order that no shade of meaning might be lost. Here again the two periods are easily distinguished. Nicholas V set his scholars, Poggio and Valla, to translate the Greeks, Herodotus and Thucydides, Aristotle and Diodorus. The feature of the later epoch is the number of Greek

---

3. First edition [Editor].

editions which came out to supplant the versions in common use. The credit for this advance in critical scholarship must be given to Aldus for his Greek Aristotle, which appeared in 1495–9; and he subsequently led the way with numerous texts of the Greek classics. At the same time he proposed to apply the same principle to Biblical study. As early as 1499 Grocin in a letter alludes to Aldus' scheme of printing the whole Bible in the original 'three languages', Hebrew, Greek and Latin; and a specimen was actually put forth in 1501.

In this matter precedence might seem to lie with the Jewish printers, who produced the Psalms in Hebrew in 1477, and the Old Testament complete in 1488; but as the Jews never at any period ceased to read their Scriptures in Hebrew, there was no question of recovery of an original. Aldus did not live to carry his scheme out; and it was left to Ximenes and the band of scholars that he gathered at Alcala, to produce the first edition of the Bible complete in the original tongues, the Complutensian Polyglott, containing the Hebrew side by side with the Septuagint and the Vulgate, and for the Pentateuch a Syriac paraphrase. The New Testament in this great enterprise was finished in 1514, and the whole work was ready by 1517, shortly before Ximenes' death. But as publication was delayed till 1522, the actual priority rests with Erasmus, whose New Testament in Greek with a Latin translation by himself appeared, as we have seen, in 1516.

Thus by an accident Germany gained the credit of being the first to assert this new principle, the importance of studying texts in the original, in the field where resistance is most resolute and victory is hardly won. And now it was about to enter upon a still greater contest. Erasmus' New Testament encountered hostile criticism in many quarters; conservative theologians made common cause with the friars in condemning it. But at the very centre of the religion they professed, the book was blessed by the chief priests. The Pope accepted the dedication, and bishops wished they could read the Greek. Far otherwise was it with the impending struggle of the Reformation: there the cleavage of sides followed very different lines. Into that wide field we cannot now expatiate; but it is important to notice an element which the German Renaissance contributed to the Reformation, and which played a considerable part in both movements—the accentuation of German national feeling.

At the middle of the fifteenth century Italy enjoyed undisputed preeminence in the world of learning. The sudden splendour into which the Renaissance had blazed up on Italian soil drew men's eyes thither more than ever; and to its ancient universities students from the North swarmed like bees. To graduate in Italy, to hear its famous doctors, perhaps even to learn from one of the native Greeks brought over out of the East, became first the ambition, and then the indispensable requirement of every Northern scholar who could afford it; and few of Erasmus' friends and colleagues had not at some time or other made the pilgrimage to Italy. Consequence and success brought the usual Nemesis. The

Italian *hubris*[4] expressed itself in the familiar Greek distinction between
barbarian and home-born; and the many nations from beyond the Alps
found themselves united in a common bond which they were not eager
to share. We have seen the kind of gibe with which Agricola's eloquence
was greeted at Pavia. The more such insults are deserved, the more they
sting. We may be sure that in many cases they were not forgotten. Celtis
returning from Italy to Ingolstadt in 1492 delivered his soul in an inau-
gural oration: 'The ancient hatred between us can never be dissolved.
But for the Alps we should be eternally at war.' In other countries the
feeling, though less acute, was much the same. Thus in 1517 spoke
Stephen Poncher, bishop of Paris, after his first meeting with Erasmus:
'Italy has no one to compare with him in literary gifts. In our own day
Hermolaus and Politian have rescued Latin from barbarism; and their
services can never be forgotten. When I was there, too, I met a number
of men of rare ability and learning. But with all respect to the Italians, I
must say that Erasmus eclipses every one, Transalpine and Cisalpine
alike.'

Of the foreign 'nations' at the universities of Italy none was more
numerous than the German, a title which embraced many nationalities
of the North: not merely German-speaking races such as the Swiss and
Flemish and Dutch, but all who could by any stretch of imagination be
represented as descendants of the Goths; Swedes and Danes, Hungarians
and Bohemians, Lithuanians and Bulgars and Poles. That they went in
such numbers is not surprising. The prestige of Italian teaching was great
and well-established, whereas their own universities were few and scarcely
more than nascent; indeed, when the Council of Vienne had ordained
the teaching of Greek and other missionary languages in 1311, its
injunctions went to France and Italy and England and Spain: but Germany had no university to which a missive could be directed. From
Southern Germany, too, and Switzerland and Austria, the distance was
small, notwithstanding the obvious Alps and the difficulties of the passes.
Even Celtis, in spite of his denunciations, sent on his best pupils to Italy.
So there were many who brought home with them to the North recol-
lections of lofty condescension and of ill-disguised contempt for the for-
eigner: insults that they burned to repay.

Italy might vaunt the glories of ancient Rome; but Germany also had
deeds to be proud of. Rome might have founded the World-empire; but
Charlemagne had conquered the dominions of the Caesars and made
the Empire Germanic. Classic antiquity, too, could not be denied to
the land and people whom Tacitus had described; and Germans were
not slow to claim the virtues found among them by the Roman historian. Arminius became the national hero. German faith and honour,
German simplicity, German sincerity and candour—these are insisted
upon by the Transalpine humanists with a vehemence which suggests
that while priding themselves on the possession of such qualities, they

4. Arrogance [*Editor*].

marked the lack of them in others. We may recall Ascham's horror of the Englishman Italianated. Not that Germans could not make friends in Italy. Scheurl loved his time at Bologna, and was eager to fight for the Bentivogli against Julius II. Erasmus was made much of by the Aldine Academy at Venice; and ten years later Hutten was charmed with his reception there. But with many, conscious of their own defects[5] and of the reality of Italian superiority, the charge of barbarism must have rankled. To Luther in 1518 Italian is synonymous with supercilious.

The rising German feeling expresses itself on all sides in the letters of the humanists. A young Frieslander, studying at Oxford in 1499, writes to a fellow-countryman there: 'Your verses have shown me what I never could have believed, that German talents are no whit inferior to Italian.' Hutten in 1516 writes of Reuchlin and Erasmus as 'the two eyes of Germany, whom we must sedulously cherish; for it is through them that our nation is ceasing to be barbarous'. Beatus Rhenanus, in editing the poems of Janus Pannonius (died 1472), says in his preface, 1518: 'Janus and Erasmus, Germans though they are and moderns, give me as much satisfaction to read as do Politian and Hermolaus, or even Virgil and Cicero.' Erasmus in 1518 writes to thank a canon of Mainz who had entertained him at supper. After compliments on his host's charming manners, his erudition free from superciliousness—if he could have known Gibbon, he surely must have used those immortal words of praise, 'a modest and learned ignorance'—and his wit and elegance of speech, he goes on: 'One might have been listening to a Roman. Now let the Italians go and taunt Germans with barbarism, if they dare!' In 1519 a canon of Brixen in Tirol writes to Beatus: 'Would to God that Germany had more men like you, to make her famous, and stand up against those Italians, who give themselves such airs about their learning; though men of credit now think that the helm has been snatched from their hands by Erasmus.' This is how Zwingli writes in 1521 of an Italian who had attacked Luther and charged him with ignorance: 'But we must make allowances for Italian conceit. In their heads is always running the refrain, "Heaven and earth can show none like to us". They cannot bear to see Germany outstripping them in learning.' Rarely a different note is heard, evoked by rivalry perhaps or the desire to encourage. Locher from Freiburg could call Leipzig barbarous. Erasmus wrote to an Erfurt schoolmaster that he was glad to see Germany softening under the influence of good learning and putting off her wild woodland ways. But these are exceptions: towards insolence from the South an unbroken front was preserved.

In another direction the strong national feeling manifested itself; in the study of German antiquity and the composition of histories. Maximilian, dipping his hands in literature, stimulated the archaeological researches of Peutinger, patronized Trithemius and Pirckheimer, and

---

5. Thus a worthy abbot in the Inn valley, writing to Erasmus in 1523, manages to achieve a Latin letter, but apologizes for only being able to write in German characters.

even instituted a royal historian, Stabius. Celtis the versatile projected an elaborate *Germania illustrata* on the model of Flavio Biondo's work for Rome; and his description of Nuremberg was designed to be the first instalment. As he conceived it, the work was never carried out; but essays of varying importance on this theme were produced by Cochlaeus, Pirckheimer, Aventinus and Munster. The most ardent to extol Germany was Wimpfeling of Schlettstadt, a man of serious temperament, who was prone to rush into controversy in defence of the causes that he had at heart. His education had all been got in Germany, and he was proud of his country. His first effort to increase its praise was to instigate Trithemius to put together a 'Catalogue of the illustrious men who adorn Germany with their talents and writings'. The author's preface (8 Feb. 1491) reveals unmistakably the animosity towards Italy: 'Some people contemn our country as barren, and maintain that few men of genius have flourished in it; hoping by disparagement of others to swell their own praise. With all the resources of their eloquence they trick out the slender achievements of their own countrymen; but jealousy blinds them to the great virtues of the Germans, the mighty deeds and brilliant intellects, the loyalty, enthusiasm and devotion of this great nation. If they find in the classics any credit given to us for valour or learning, they quickly hide it up; and in order to trumpet their own excellences, they omit ours altogether. That is how Pliny's narrative of the German wars was lost, and how so many histories of our people have disappeared.'

The book was sent to Wimpfeling, who collected a few more names and added a preface of his own (17 Sept. 1492) in the same strain. 'People who think that Germany is still as barbarous as it was in the days of Caesar should read what Jerome has to say about it. The abundance of old books in existence shows that Germany had many learned men in the past; who have left carefully written manuscripts on oratory, poetry, natural philosophy, theology and all kinds of erudition. All down the Rhine you will find the walls and roofs of monasteries adorned with elegant epigrams which testify to German taste of old. To-day there are Germans who can translate the Greek classics into Latin; and if their style is not pure Ciceronian, let our detractors remember that styles change with the times. Mankind is always discontented, and prefers the old to the modern. I can quite understand that our German philosophers adapted their style to their audiences and their lofty subjects. So foreign critics had better let this provocative talk alone for ever.'

A few years later Wimpfeling edited a fourteenth-century treatise by Lupold of Bebenburg entitled 'The zeal and fervour of the ancient German princes towards the Christian religion and the servants of God'; the intention of which clearly fell in with his desire. In his preface, addressed to Dalberg, Agricola's patron, he tells a story which explains a peculiarity occasionally found in mediaeval manuscripts; of being written in sections by several different hands. Some years before, the Patriarch of Aquileia was passing through Spires. To divert the enforced leisure of a halt upon a journey, he prowled round the libraries of the town; and in one discovered this treatise of Lupold, which pleased him greatly. As he was to be off again next morning, there was no time to have it copied, at least by one hand: so the manuscript was cut up and distributed among a number of scribes, and in the space of a night the desired copy was ready. Subsequently Wimpfeling heard of the incident from one of the brethren in the monastery, and obtained the original manuscript to publish. When such things could happen, no wonder that some manuscripts are imperfect and others have disappeared.

Wimpfeling's next endeavour to assert the glories of Germany was completed in 1502; but did not appear till 1505. It was based upon the work of a friend, Sebastian Murrho of Colmar (died 1494). The title, *Defensio Germaniae* or *Epithoma Germanorum*, sufficiently explains its purpose. After a brief account of Germany in Roman times—his hero being not Arminius, but 'the first German king, Arioviscus, who fought with Julius Caesar',—and fuller records of the Germanic Emperors since Charlemagne, Wimpfeling comes to the praise of his own days; the men of learning, the famous soldiers, the architects who could build the great tower of Strasburg, the painters, the inventors of printing and of that terrible engine the bombard. But nearest to his heart lay a question debated then as now: to whom should rightfully belong the western part of the Rhine valley, between the river and the Vosges? It was there that his home lay, Schlettstadt, one of the fairest cities of the plain. With all the 'zeal and fervour of the ancient German princes' he sets out to prove that it must be German: 'where are there any traces' he cries 'of the French language? There are no books in French, no monuments, no letters, no epitaphs, no deeds or documents. For seven or eight centuries there is nothing but Latin or German.' The cathedral of Spires, the fine monastery of St. Fides in his native town, supply him with a further argument: would the good Dukes of Swabia have lavished so much money, the substance of their fathers, upon Gallic soil, to pour it out among the French? With such arguments he convinced himself and others. Almost at the same time Peutinger put out a little volume of 'Conversations about the wonderful antiquities of Germany'; supporting Wimpfeling with further evidence and concluding satisfactorily that French had never ruled over Germans.

A work of very different calibre which appeared about this time was the *Germaniae Exegesis* of Francis Fritz, who Latinized his name into Irenicus. Wimpfeling was growing grey when he had made his defence of Germany: the new champion was a young man of 23, who had scarcely emerged from his degree. The book was published in 1518; printed at Hagenau by Anshelm at the cost of John Koberger, the great Nuremberg printer, and fostered by Pirckheimer. In his later years Irenicus became a Lutheran and displayed some dignity in refusing to sacrifice his convictions to worldly interests; but at this time he was enthusiastic and heady, and as a result his work is an uncritical jumble. 'Puerile and silly' Erasmus called it, when he saw some of the proof-sheets at Spires in 1518. 'A most unfortunate book', wrote Beatus Rhenanus in 1525, 'without style and without judgement.' To Aventinus in 1531 it was 'an impudent compilation from Stabius and Trithemius, by a poor creature of the most despicable intelligence'. But even a bad book can be a measure of the time, showing the ideas current and the catchwords that were thought likely to attract the reading public. It is much larger than Wimpfeling's *Defence*, and even more miscellaneous; ranging over many aspects of Germany ancient and modern. To us in the present inquiry its interest lies in the frequency with which the excellence of Germany is asserted against Italian sneers. The following specimen will illustrate this point, and also explain Erasmus' epithets. In the chapter on the German language (ii. 30) Irenicus is throughout engaged in refuting the charge of German barbarism. 'It may be true', he says, 'that German is not so much declined as Latin: but complexity does not necessarily bring refinement. Germany is as rich in dialects as Italy, and to speak German well merits high praise. Italian may be directly descended from Latin; but German too has a considerable element of Latin and Greek words. Guarino and Petrarch have written poetry in their vernaculars, and so the Italians boast that their language is more suited to poetry. But more than 1000 years ago Ovid wrote a book of German poetry; and Trebeta, son of Semiramis, is known to have been the first person to compose in German.'

In spite of such stuff, Pirckheimer, who saw the book in manuscript, was delighted with it. 'You have achieved what many have wished but few could have carried out. Every German must be obliged to you for the lustre you have brought to the Fatherland.' After stating that he had arranged with Koberger for the printing, he points out details which might be improved: more stress might be laid on the connexion of the Germans with the Goths, 'which the dregs of the Goths and Lombards—by which I mean the Italians—try to snatch from us'; and the universal conquests of the Goths might be more fully treated. Finally he suggests that before publication the work should be submitted to Stabius: 'the book deserves learned readers, and I should wish it to be as perfect as possible.'

This brief survey may close with a far more considerable work, the *Res Germanicae* of Beatus Rhenanus, published in 1531; from which we have made some extracts above. The book is sober and serious, and the subject-matter is handled scientifically; but in his preface Beatus is careful to point out that German history is as important as Roman, modern as much worth studying as ancient.

Such was the soil into which fell the seed that Luther went forth to sow. When Tetzel came marching into German towns, with the Pope's Bull borne before him on a cushion, and brandishing indulgences for the living and the dead, when the coins were tinkling in the box, and the souls, released by contract, were flying off out of purgatory, the religious sense of thinking men was outraged by this travesty of the Day of Judgement: but scarcely less were they angered to see the tinkling coins, honest German money, flying off as rapidly as the souls, to build palaces for the supercilious Italians. In the great struggle of the Reformation the main issue was of course religious; but even its leader could feel added bitterness in the knowledge that this shocking traffic was ordained from Italy to benefit an Italian Pope. If the sympathies of educated Germany had not already been strongly moved in the same direction, it is conceivable that Luther's intrepid protest might have lacked the support which carried it to success.

J. HUIZINGA

Erasmus's Mind †

[Part I]

Erasmus's mind: Ethical and aesthetic tendencies, aversion to all that is unreasonable, silly and cumbrous—His vision of antiquity pervaded by Christian faith—Renascence of good learning—The ideal life of serene harmony and happy wisdom—Love of the decorous and smooth—His mind neither philosophic nor historical, but strongly philological and moralistic—Freedom, clearness, purity, simplicity—Faith in nature—Educational and social ideas

What made Erasmus the man from whom his contemporaries expected their salvation, on whose lips they hung to catch the word of deliverance? He seemed to them the bearer of a new liberty of the mind, a new clearness, purity and simplicity of knowledge, a new harmony of healthy and right living. He was to them as the possessor of newly discovered, untold wealth which he had only to distribute.

What was there in the mind of the great Rotterdamer which promised so much to the world?

The negative aspect of Erasmus's mind may be defined as a heartfelt aversion to everything unreasonable, insipid, purely formal, with which the undisturbed growth of medieval culture had overburdened and overcrowded the world of thought. As often as he thinks of the ridiculous text-books out of which Latin was taught in his youth, disgust rises in his mind, and he execrates them—Mammatrectus, Brachylogus, Ebrardus and all the rest—as a heap of rubbish which ought to be cleared away. But his aversion to the superannuated which had become useless and soulless extended much farther. He found society, and especially religious life, full of practices, ceremonies, traditions and conceptions, from which the spirit seemed to have departed. He does not reject them offhand and altogether: what revolts him is that they are so often performed without understanding and right feeling. But to his mind, highly susceptible to the foolish and ridiculous things, and with a delicate need

† From *Erasmus of Rotterdam* (New York, 1924; London: Phaidon Press, 1952) 101–116.

of high decorum and inward dignity, all that sphere of ceremony and tradition displays itself as a useless, nay, a hurtful scene of human stupidity and selfishness. And, intellectualist as he is, with his contempt for ignorance, he seems unaware that those religious observances, after all, may contain valuable sentiments of unexpressed and unformulated piety.

Through his treatises, his letters, his *Colloquies* especially, there always passes—as if one was looking at a gallery of Brueghel's pictures—a procession of ignorant and covetous monks who by their sanctimony and humbug impose upon the trustful multitude and fare sumptuously themselves. As a fixed motif (such motifs are numerous with Erasmus) there always recurs his gibe about the superstition that a person was saved by dying in the gown of a Franciscan or a Dominican.

Fasting, prescribed prayers, the observance of holy days, should not be altogether neglected, but they become displeasing to God when we repose our trust in them and forget charity. The same holds good of confession, indulgence, all sorts of blessings. Pilgrimages are worthless. The veneration of the saints and of their relics is full of superstition and foolishness. The people think they will be preserved from disasters during the day if only they have looked at the painted image of Saint Christopher in the morning. 'We kiss the shoes of the saints and their dirty handkerchiefs and we leave their books, their most holy and efficacious relics, neglected.'

Erasmus's dislike of what seemed antiquated and worn out in his days, went farther still. It comprised the whole intellectual scheme of medieval theology and philosophy. In the syllogistic system he found only subtlety and arid ingenuity. All symbolism and allegory were fundamentally alien to him and indifferent, though he occasionally tried his hand at an allegory; and he never was mystically inclined.

Now here it is just as much the deficiencies of his own mind as the qualities of the system which made him unable to appreciate it. While he struck at the abuse of ceremonies and of Church practices both with noble indignation and well-aimed mockery, a proud irony to which he was not fully entitled preponderates in his condemnation of scholastic theology which he could not quite understand. It was easy always to talk with a sneer of the conservative divines of his time as *magistri nostri*.[1]

His noble indignation hurt only those who deserved castigation and strengthened what was valuable, but his mockery hurt the good as well as the bad in spite of him, assailed both the institution and persons, and injured without elevating them. The individualist Erasmus never understood what it meant to offend the honour of an office, an order, or an establishment, especially when that institution is the most sacred of all, the Church itself.

Erasmus's conception of the Church was no longer purely Catholic. Of that glorious structure of medieval-Christian civilization with its mystic foundation, its strict hierarchic construction, its splendidly fitting

1. Our masters *[Editor]*.

symmetry he saw hardly anything but its load of outward details and ornament. Instead of the world which Thomas Aquinas and Dante had described, according to their vision, Erasmus saw another world, full of charm and elevated feeling, and this he held up before his compatriots.

It was the world of Antiquity, but illuminated throughout by Christian faith. It was a world that had never existed as such. For with the historical reality which the times of Constantine and the great fathers of the Church had manifested—that of declining Latinity and deteriorating Hellenism, the oncoming barbarism and the oncoming Byzantinism—it had nothing in common. Erasmus's imagined world was an amalgamation of pure classicism (this meant for him Cicero, Horace, Plutarch; for to the flourishing period of the Greek mind he remained after all a stranger) and pure, biblical Christianity. Could it be a union? Not really. In Erasmus's mind the light falls, just as we saw in the history of his career, alternately on the pagan antique and on the Christian. But the warp of his mind is Christian; his classicism only serves him as a form, and from Antiquity he only chooses those elements which in ethical tendency are in conformity with his Christian ideal.

And because of this, Erasmus, although he appeared after a century of earlier Humanism, is yet new to his time. The union of Antiquity and the Christian spirit which had haunted the mind of Petrarch, the father of Humanism, which was lost sight of by his disciples, enchanted as they were by the irresistible brilliance of the antique beauty of form, this union was brought about by Erasmus.

What pure Latinity and the classic spirit meant to Erasmus we cannot feel as he did because its realization does not mean to us, as to him, a difficult conquest and a glorious triumph. To feel it thus one must have acquired, in a hard school, the hatred of barbarism, which already during his first years of authorship had suggested the composition of the *Antibarbari*.[2] The abusive term for all that is old and rude is already Gothic, Goths. The term barbarism as used by Erasmus comprised much of what we value most in the medieval spirit. Erasmus's conception of the great intellectual crisis of his day was distinctly dualistic. He saw it as a struggle between old and new, which, to him, meant evil and good. In the advocates of tradition he saw only obscurantism, conservatism, and ignorant opposition to *bonae literae*,[3] that is, the good cause for which he and his partisans battled. Of the rise of that higher culture Erasmus had already formed the conception which has since dominated the history of the Renaissance. It was a revival, begun two or three hundred years before his time, in which, besides literature, all the plastic arts shared. Side by side with the terms restitution and reflorescence the word renascence crops up repeatedly in his writings. 'The world is coming to its senses as if awaking out of a deep sleep. Still there are some left who recalcitrate pertinaciously, clinging convulsively with hands and feet to their old ignorance. They fear that if *bonae literae* are reborn and

---

2. Anti-barbarians [Editor].   3. Good letters [Editor].

the world grows wise, it will come to light that they have nothing.' They do not know how pious the Ancients could be, what sanctity characterizes Socrates, Virgil, and Horace, or Plutarch's *Moralia*,[4] how rich the history of Antiquity is in examples of forgiveness and true virtue. We should call nothing profane that is pious and conduces to good morals. No more dignified view of life was ever found than that which Cicero propounds in *De Senectute*.[5]

In order to understand Erasmus's mind and the charm which it had for his contemporaries, one must begin with the ideal of life that was present before his inward eye as a splendid dream. It is not his own in particular. The whole Renaissance cherished that wish of reposeful, blithe, and yet serious intercourse of good and wise friends in the cool shade of a house under trees, where serenity and harmony would dwell. The age yearned for the realization of simplicity, sincerity, truth and nature. Their imagination was always steeped in the essence of Antiquity, though, at heart, it is more nearly connected with medieval ideals than they themselves were aware. In the circle of the Medici it is the idyll of Careggi, in Rabelais it embodies itself in the fancy of the abbey of Thélème; it finds voice in More's *Utopia* and in the work of Montaigne. In Erasmus's writings that ideal wish ever recurs in the shape of a friendly walk, followed by a meal in a garden-house. It is found as an opening scene of the *Antibarbari*, in the numerous descriptions of meals with Colet, and the numerous *Convivia* of the *Colloquies*. Especially in the *Convivium religiosum*[6] Erasmus has elaborately pictured his dream, and it would be worth while to compare it, on the one hand with Thélème, and on the other with the fantastic design of a pleasure garden which Bernard Palissy describes.[7] The little Dutch eighteenth-century country-seats and garden-houses in which the national spirit took great delight are the fulfilment of a purely Erasmian ideal. The host of the *Convivium religiosum* says: 'To me a simple country-house, a nest, is pleasanter than any palace, and, if he be king who lives in freedom and according to his wishes, surely I am king here'.

Life's true joy is in virtue and piety. If they are Epicureans who live pleasantly, then none are more truly Epicureans than they who live in holiness and piety.

The ideal joy of life is also perfectly idyllic in so far that it requires an aloofness from earthly concerns and contempt for all that is sordid. It is foolish to be interested in all that happens in the world; to pride oneself on one's knowledge of the market, of the King of England's plans, the news from Rome, conditions in Denmark. The sensible old man of the *Colloquium Senile*[8] has an easy post of honour, a safe mediocrity, he judges no one and nothing and smiles upon all the world. Quiet for oneself, surrounded by books—that is of all things most desirable.

4. Moral Essays [Editor].
5. His essay "On Old Age" [Editor].
6. The Religious Feast [Editor].
7. The Abbey of Thélème is Rabelais's fantasy of a libertarian monastery; Bernard Palissy, better known as a potter, wrote on gardening in the latter part of the sixteenth century [Editor].
8. The Old Man's Conversation [Editor].

On the outskirts of this ideal of serenity and harmony numerous flowers of aesthetic value blow, such as Erasmus's sense of decorum, his great need of kindly courtesy, his pleasure in gentle and obliging treatment, in cultured and easy manners. Close by are some of his intellectual peculiarities. He hates the violent and extravagant. Therefore the choruses of the Greek drama displease him. The merit of his own poems he sees in the fact that they pass passion by, they abstain from pathos altogether—'there is not a single storm in them, no mountain torrent overflowing its banks, no exaggeration whatever. There is great frugality in words. My poetry would rather keep within bounds than exceed them, rather hug the shore than cleave the high seas.' In another place he says: 'I am always most pleased by a poem that does not differ too much from prose, but prose of the best sort, be it understood. As Philoxenus accounted those the most palatable fishes that are no true fishes and the most savoury meat what is no meat, the most pleasant voyage that along the shores, and the most agreeable walk that along the water's edge; so I take especial pleasure in a rhetorical poem and a poetical oration, so that poetry is tasted in prose and the reverse.' That is the man of half-tones, of fine shadings, of the thought that is never completely expressed. But he adds: 'Farfetched conceits may please others; to me the chief concern seems to be that we draw our speech from the matter itself and apply ourselves less to showing off our invention than to present the thing.' That is the realist.

From this conception results his admirable, simple clarity, the excellent division and presentation of his argument. But it also causes his lack of depth and the prolixity by which he is characterized. His machine runs too smoothly. In the endless *apologiae* of his later years, ever new arguments occur to him; new passages to point, or quotations to support, his idea. He praises laconism, but never practises it. Erasmus never coins a sentence which, rounded off and pithy, becomes a proverb and in this manner lives. There are no current quotations from Erasmus. The collector of the *Adagia* has created no new ones of his own.

The true occupation for a mind like his was paraphrasing, in which, indeed, he amply indulged. Soothing down and unfolding was just the work he liked. It is characteristic that he paraphrased the whole New Testament except the Apocalypse.

Erasmus's mind was neither philosophic nor historic. His was neither the work of exact, logical discrimination, nor of grasping the deep sense of the way of the world in broad historical visions in which the particulars themselves, in their multiplicity and variegation, form the image. His mind is philological in the fullest sense of the word. But by that alone he would not have conquered and captivated the world. His mind was at the same time of a deeply ethical and rather strong aesthetic trend and those three together have made him great.

The foundation of Erasmus's mind is his fervent desire of freedom, clearness, purity, simplicity and rest. It is an old ideal of life to which he gave new substance by the wealth of his mind. Without liberty, life is no life; and there is no liberty without repose. The fact that he never took sides definitely resulted from an urgent need of perfect independence. Each engagement, even a temporary one, was felt as a fetter by Erasmus. An interlocutor in the *Colloquies*, in which he so often, spontaneously, reveals his own ideals of life, declares himself determined neither to marry, nor to take holy orders, nor to enter a monastery, not enter any connection from which he will afterwards be unable to free himself—at least not before he knows himself completely. 'When will that be? Never, perhaps.' 'On no other account do I congratulate myself more than on the fact that I have never attached myself to any party,' Erasmus says towards the end of his life.

Liberty should be spiritual liberty in the first place. 'But he that is spiritual judgeth all things, yet he himself is judged of no man,' is the word of Saint Paul. To what purpose should he require prescriptions who, of his own accord, does better things than human laws require? What arrogance it is to bind by institutions a man who is clearly led by the inspirations of the divine spirit!

In Erasmus we already find the beginning of that optimism which judges upright man good enough to dispense with fixed forms and rules. As More, in *Utopia*, and Rabelais, Erasmus relies already on the dictates of nature, which produces man as inclined to good and which we may follow, provided we are imbued with faith and piety.

In this line of confidence in what is natural and desire of the simple and reasonable, Erasmus's educational and social ideas lie. Here he is far ahead of his times. It would be an attractive undertaking to discuss Erasmus's educational ideals more fully. They foreshadow exactly those of the eighteenth century. The child should learn in playing, by means of things that are agreeable to its mind, from pictures. Its faults should be gently corrected. The flogging and abusive schoolmaster is Erasmus's abomination; the office itself is holy and venerable to him. Education should begin from the moment of birth. Probably Erasmus attached too much value to classicism, here as elsewhere: his friend Peter Gilles should implant the rudiments of the ancient languages in this two-year-old son, that he may greet his father with endearing stammerings in Greek and Latin. But what gentleness and clear good sense shines from all Erasmus says about instruction and education!

The same holds good of his views about marriage and woman. In the problem of sexual relations he distinctly sides with the woman from deep conviction. There is a great deal of tenderness and delicate feeling in his conception of the position of the girl and the woman. Few characters of the *Colloquies* have been drawn with so much sympathy as the girl with the lover and the cultured woman in the witty conversation with the abbot. Erasmus's ideal of marriage is truly social and hygienic. Let us beget children for the State and for Christ, says the lover, children endowed by their upright parents with a good disposition, children who see the good example at home which is to guide them. Again and again he reverts to the mother's duty to suckle the child herself. He indicates how the house should be arranged, in a simple and cleanly manner; he occupies himself with the problem of useful children's dress. Who stood up at that time, as he did, for the fallen girl, and for the prostitute compelled by necessity? Who saw so clearly the social danger of marriages of persons infected with the new scourge of Europe, so violently abhorred by Erasmus? He would wish that such a marriage should at once be declared null and void by the Pope. Erasmus does not hold with the easy social theory, still quite current in the literature of his time, which casts upon women all the blame of adultery and lewdness. With the savages who live in a state of nature, he says, the adultery of men is punished, but that of women is forgiven.

Here it appears, at the same time, that Erasmus knew, be it half in jest, the conception of natural virtue and happiness of naked islanders in a savage state. It soon crops up again in Montaigne and the following centuries develop it into a literary dogma.

[Part II]

Erasmus's mind: Intellectual tendencies—The world encumbered by beliefs and forms—Truth must be simple—Back to the pure sources—Holy Scripture in the original languages—Biblical humanism—Critical work on the texts of Scripture—Practice better than dogma—Erasmus's talent and wit—Delight in words and things—Prolixity—Observation of details—A veiled realism—Ambiguousness—The 'Nuance'—Inscrutability of the ultimate ground of all things

Simplicity, naturalness, purity, and reasonableness, those are to Erasmus the dominant requirements, also when we pass from his ethical and aesthetic concepts to his intellectual point of view; indeed, the two can hardly be kept apart.

The world, says Erasmus, is overloaded with human constitutions and opinions and scholastic dogmas, and overburdened with the tyrannical authority of orders, and because of all this the strength of gospel doctrine is flagging. Faith requires simplification, he argued. What would the Turks say of our scholasticism? Colet wrote to him one day: 'There is no end to books and science. Let us, therefore, leave all roundabout roads and go by a short cut to the truth.'

Truth must be simple. 'The language of truth is simple, says Seneca; well then, nothing is simpler nor truer than Christ.' 'I should wish', Erasmus says elsewhere, 'that this simple and pure Christ might be deeply impressed upon the mind of men, and that I deem best attainable in this way, that we, supported by our knowledge of the original languages, should philosophize *at the sources* themselves.'

Here a new watchword comes to the fore: back to the sources! It is not merely an intellectual, philological requirement; it is equally an ethical and aesthetic necessity of life. The original and pure, all that is not yet overgrown or has not passed through many hands, has such a potent charm. Erasmus compared it to an apple which we ourselves pick off the tree. To recall the world to the ancient simplicity of science, to lead it back from the now turbid pools to those living and most pure fountain-heads, those most limpid sources of gospel doctrine—thus he saw the task of divinity. The metaphor of the limpid water is not without meaning here; it reveals the psychological quality of Erasmus's fervent principle.

'How is it', he exclaims, 'that people give themselves so much trouble about the details of all sorts of remote philosophical systems and neglect to go to the sources of Christianity itself?' 'Although this wisdom, which is so excellent that once for all it put the wisdom of all the world to shame, may be drawn from these few books, as from a crystalline source, with far less trouble than is the wisdom of Aristotle from so many thorny books and with much more fruit . . . the equipment for that journey is simple and at everyone's immediate disposal. This philosophy is accessible to everybody. Christ desires that his mysteries shall be spread as widely as possible. I should wish that all good wives read the Gospel and Paul's Epistles; that they were translated into all languages; that out of these the husbandman sang while ploughing, the weaver at his loom; that with such stories the traveller should beguile his wayfaring. . . . This sort of philosophy is rather a matter of disposition than of syllogism, rather of life than of disputation, rather of inspiration than of erudition, rather of transformation than of logic. . . . What is the philosophy of Christ, which he himself calls *Renascentia*, but the restoration of Nature created good?—moreover, though no one has taught us this so absolutely and effectively as Christ, yet also in pagan books much may be found that is in accordance with it.'

Such was the view of life of this biblical humanist. As often as Erasmus reverts to these matters, his voice sounds clearest. 'Let no one', he says in the preface to the notes to the New Testament, 'take up this work, as he takes up Gellius's *Noctes atticae* or Poliziano's Miscellanies[9] . . . We are in the presence of holy things; here it is no question of eloquence, these matters are best recommended to the world by simplicity and purity; it would be ridiculous to display human erudition here, impious to pride onself on human eloquence.' But Erasmus never was so eloquent himself as just then.

What here raises him above his usual level of force and fervour is the fact that he fights a battle, the battle for the right of biblical criticism. It revolts him that people should study Holy Scripture in the Vulgate when they know that the texts show differences and are corrupt, although we have the Greek text by which to go back to the original form and primary meaning.

He is now reproached because he dares, as a mere grammarian, to assail the text of Holy Scripture on the score of futile mistakes or irregularities. 'Details they are, yes, but because of these details we some-

9. I.e., for light entertainment [Editor].

times see even great divines stumble and rave.' Philological trifling is
necessary. 'Why are we so precise as to our food, our clothes, our money-
matters and why does this accuracy displease us in divine literature alone?
He crawls along the ground, they say, he wearies himself out about
words and syllables! Why do we slight any word of Him whom we venerate and worship under the name of the Word? But, be it so! Let whoever
wishes imagine that I have not been able to achieve anything better, and
out of sluggishness of mind and coldness of heart or lack of erudition
have taken this lowest task upon myself; it is still a Christian idea to
think all work good that is done with pious zeal. We bring along the
bricks, but to build the temple of God.'

He does not want to be intractable. Let the Vulgate be kept for use in
the liturgy, for sermons, in schools, but he who, at home, reads our
edition, will understand his own the better in consequence. He, Erasmus, is prepared to render account and acknowledge himself to have
been wrong when convicted of error.

Erasmus perhaps never quite realized how much his philological-crit-
ical method must shake the foundations of the Church. He was surprised at his adversaries 'who could not but believe that all their authority
would perish at once when the sacred books might be read in a purified
form, and when people tried to understand them in the original'. He did
not feel what the unassailable authority of a sacred book meant. He
rejoices because Holy Scripture is approached so much more closely,
because all sorts of shadings are brought to light by considering not only
what is said but also by whom, for whom, at what time, on what occasion, what precedes and what follows, in short, by the method of historical philological criticism. To him it seemed so especially pious when
reading Scripture and coming across a place which seemed contrary to
the doctrine of Christ or the divinity of his nature, to believe rather that
one did not understand the phrase *or that the text might be corrupt.*
Unperceived he passed from emendation of the different versions to the
correction of the contents. The epistles were not all written by the apostles to whom they are attributed. The apostles themselves made mistakes, at times.

The foundation of his spiritual life was no longer a unity to Erasmus.
It was, on the one hand, a strong desire for an upright, simple, pure and
homely belief, the earnest wish to be a good Christian. But it was also
the irresistible intellectual and aesthetic need of the good taste, the harmony, the clear and exact expression of the Ancients, the dislike of what
was cumbrous and involved. Erasmus thought that good learning might
render good service for the necessary purification of the faith and its
forms. The measure of church hymns should be corrected. That Christian expression and classicism were incompatible, he never believed.
The man who in the sphere of sacred studies asked every author for his
credentials remained unconscious of the fact that he acknowledged the
authority of the Ancients without any evidence. How naïvely he appeals
to Antiquity, again and again, to justify some bold feat! He is critical,

they say? Were not the Ancients critical? He permits himself to insert
digressions? So did the Ancients, etc.

Erasmus is in profound sympathy with that revered Antiquity by his
fundamental conviction that it is the practice of life which matters. Not
he is the great philosopher who knows the tenets of the Stoics or Peripatetics by rote—but he who expresses the meaning of philosophy by his
life and his morals, for that is its purpose. He is truly a divine who
teaches, not by artful syllogisms, but by his disposition, by his face and
his eyes, by his life itself, that wealth should be despised. To live up to
that standard is what Christ himself calls *Renascentia*. Erasmus uses the
word in the Christian sense only. But in that sense it is closely allied to
the idea of the Renaissance as a historical phenomenon. The worldly
and pagan sides of the Renaissance have nearly always been overrated.
Erasmus is, much more than Aretino or Castiglione, the representative
of the spirit of his age, one over whose Christian sentiment the sweet
gale of Antiquity had passed. And that very union of strong Christian
endeavour and the spirit of Antiquity is the explanation of Erasmus's
wonderful success.

The mere intention and the contents of the mind do not influence
the world, if the form of expression does not cooperate. In Erasmus the
quality of his talent is a very important factor. His perfect clearness and
ease of expression, his liveliness, wit, imagination, gusto and humour
have lent a charm to all he wrote which to his contemporaries was irresistible and captivates even us, as soon as we read him. In all that constitutes his talent, Erasmus is perfectly and altogether a representative of
the Renaissance. There is, in the first place, his eternal *à propos*. What
he writes is never vague, never dark—it is always plausible. Everything
seemingly flows of itself like a fountain. It always rings true as to tone,
turn of phrase and accent. It has almost the light harmony of Ariosto.
And it is, like Ariosto, never tragic, never truly heroic. It carries us away,
indeed, but it is never itself truly enraptured.

The more artistic aspects of Erasmus's talent come out most clearly—
though they are everywhere in evidence—in those two recreations after
more serious labour, the *Moriae Encomium* and the *Colloquia*. But just
those two have been of enormous importance for his influence upon his
times. For while Jerome reached tens of readers and the New Testament
hundreds, the *Moria* and *Colloquies* went out to thousands. And their
importance is heightened in that Erasmus has nowhere else expressed
himself so spontaneously.

In each of the Colloquies, even in the first purely formulary ones,
there is the sketch for a comedy, a novelette or a satire. There is hardly
a sentence without its 'point', an expression without a vivid fancy. There
are unrivalled niceties. The abbot of the *Abbatis et eruditae colloquium*[1]
is a Molière character. It should be noticed how well Erasmus always

1. "The Abbot and the Learned Lady" *[Editor]*.

sustains his characters and his scenes, because he *sees* them. In 'The woman in childbed' he never forgets for a moment that Eutrapelus is an artist. At the end of 'The game of knuckle-bones', when the interlocutors, after having elucidated the whole nomenclature of the Latin game of knuckle-bones, are going to play themselves, Carolus says: 'but shut the door first, lest the cook should see us playing like two boys'.

As Holbein illustrated the *Moria*, we should wish to possess the *Colloquia* with illustrations by Brueghel, so closely allied is Erasmus's witty clear vision of incidents to that of this great master. The procession of drunkards on Palm Sunday, the saving of the shipwrecked crew, the old men waiting for the travelling cart while the drivers are still drinking, all these are Dutch genre pieces of the best sort.

We like to speak of the realism of the Renaissance. Erasmus is certainly a realist in the sense of having an insatiable hunger for knowledge of the tangible world. He wants to know things and their names: the particulars of each thing, be it never so remote, such as those terms of games and rules of games of the Romans. Read carefully the description of the decorative painting on the garden-house of the *Convivium religiosum:* it is nothing but an object lesson, a graphic representation of the forms of reality.

In its joy over the material universe and the supple, pliant word, the Renaissance revels in a profusion of imagery and expressions. The resounding enumerations of names and things, which Rabelais always gives, are not unknown to Erasmus, but he uses them for intellectual and useful purposes. In *De copia verborum ac rerum*[2] one feat of varied power of expression succeeds another—he gives fifty ways of saying: 'Your letter has given me much pleasure,' or, 'I think that it is going to rain'. The aesthetic impulse is here that of a theme and variations: to display all the wealth and mutations of the logic of language. Elsewhere, too, Erasmus indulges this proclivity for accumulating the treasures of his genius; he and his contemporaries can never restrain themselves from giving all the instances instead of one: in *Ratio verae theologiae,* in *De pronuntiatione,* in *Lingua,* in *Ecclesiastes.*[3] The collections of *Adagia, Parabolae,* and *Apophthegmata*[4] are altogether based on this eagerness of the Renaissance (which, by the way, was an inheritance of the Middle Ages themselves) to luxuriate in the wealth of the tangible world, to revel in words and things.

The senses are open for the nice observation of the curious. Though Erasmus does not know the need of proving the secrets of nature, which inspired a Leonardo da Vinci, a Paracelsus, a Vesalius, he is also, by keen observation, a child of his time. For peculiarities in the habits and customs of nations he has an open eye. He notices the gait of Swiss soldiers, how dandies sit, how Picards pronounce French. He notices

2. "The Fullness of Words and Things" *[Editor].*
3. "The Reason of True Theology," in "On Pronunciation," "On Speech," "On Language," in

"The preacher" *[Editor].*
4. "Adages," "Parables," and "Proverbs" *[Editor].*

that in old pictures the sitters are always represented with half-closed
eyes and tightly shut lips, as signs of modesty, and how some Spaniards
still honour this expression in life, while German art prefers lips pouting
as for a kiss. His lively sense of anecdote, to which he gives the rein in
all his writings, belongs here.

And, in spite of all his realism, the world which Erasmus sees and
renders, is not altogether that of the sixteenth century. Everything is
veiled by Latin. Between the author's mind and reality intervenes his
antique diction. At bottom the world of his mind is imaginary. It is a
subdued and limited sixteenth-century reality which he reflects. Together
with its coarseness he lacks all that is violent and direct in his times.
Compared with the artists, with Luther and Calvin, with the statesmen,
the navigators, the soldiers and the scientists, Erasmus confronts the
world as a recluse. It is only the influence of Latin. In spite of all his
receptiveness and sensitiveness, Erasmus is never fully in contact with
life. All through his work not a bird sings, not a wind rustles.

But that reserve or fear of directness is not merely a negative quality.
It also results from a consciousness of the indefiniteness of the ground
of all things, from the awe of the ambiguity of all that is. If Erasmus so
often hovers over the borderline between earnestness and mockery, if he
hardly ever gives an incisive conclusion, it is not only due to cautious-
ness, and fear to commit himself. Everywhere he sees the shadings, the
blending of the meaning of words. The terms of things are no longer to
him, as to the man of the Middle Ages, as crystals mounted in gold, or
as stars in the firmament. 'I like assertions so little that I would easily
take sides with the sceptics wherever it is allowed by the inviolable
authority of Holy Scripture and the decrees of the Church.' 'What is
exempt from error?' All subtle contentions of theological speculation
arise from a dangerous curiosity and lead to impious audacity. What
have all the great controversies about the Trinity and the Virgin Mary
profited? 'We have defined so much that without danger to our salvation
might have remained unknown or undecided. . . . The essentials of our
religion are peace and unanimity. These can hardly exist unless we make
definitions about as few points as possible and leave many questions to
individual judgement. Numerous problems are now postponed till the
oecumenical Council. It would be much better to put off such questions
till the time when the glass shall be removed and the darkness cleared
away, and we shall see God face to face.'

'There are sanctuaries in the sacred studies which God has not willed
that we should probe, and if we try to penetrate there, we grope in ever
deeper darkness the farther we proceed, so that we recognize, in this
manner, too, the inscrutable majesty of divine wisdom and the imbecility of human understanding.'

MIKHAIL BAKHTIN

[Medieval and Renaissance Folk Humor] †

[As its title clearly indicates, Bakhtin's *Rabelais and His World* is not directly concerned with Erasmus. But by emphasizing a major tradition in medieval and Renaissance thinking, it illuminates a great many areas other than its primary subject.

Bakhtin, who was born in 1895 and died in 1975, wrote his book in 1930 but could publish it only thirty-five years later; it was translated into English in 1968 and promptly achieved international success.

The tradition that Bakhtin explores has its origins in the serio-comic writers of antiquity like Lucian and Apuleius, but also in the mock-orations of medieval universities, and in the rough, colloquial semi-sacred jocosities of fair and marketplace. Stylistically, these various elements do not so much combine as jostle together in the mixed, incongruous mode sometimes referred to as a gallimaufry. Of the three elements that Bakhtin distinguishes in Rabelais—ritual spectacle, parody, and billingsgate—only the latter is not conspicuously present in *The Praise of Folly*. A section of Bakhtin's introduction is reprinted here as a preliminary sample of his approach. He was primarily a critical theorist, and the amplifications of his theory are of intense contemporary interest. But much that he says about Rabelais will be of direct interest to a student of Erasmus—as he himself points out.]

The aim of the present introduction is to pose the problem presented by the culture of folk humor in the Middle Ages and the Renaissance and to offer a description of its original traits.

Laughter and its forms represent, as we have said, the least scrutinized sphere of the people's creation. The narrow concept of popular character and of folklore was born in the pre-Romantic period and was basically completed by von Herder and the Romantics. There was no room in this concept for the peculiar culture of the marketplace and of folk laughter with all its wealth of manifestations. Nor did the generations that succeeded each other in that marketplace become the object of historic, literary, or folkloristic scrutiny as the study of early cultures continued. The element of laughter was accorded the least place of all in the vast literature devoted to myth, to folk lyrics, and to epics. Even more unfortunate was the fact that the peculiar nature of the people's laughter was completely distorted; entirely alien notions and concepts of humor, formed within the framework of bourgeois modern culture and aesthetics, were applied to this interpretation. We may therefore say without exaggeration that the profound originality expressed by the culture of folk humor in the past has remained unexplored until now.

And yet, the scope and the importance of this culture were immense in the Renaissance and the Middle Ages. A boundless world of humorous forms and manifestations opposed the official and serious tone of

† Translated by Hélène Iswolsky (Bloomington: Indiana UP, 1984) 4–15.

medieval ecclesiastical and feudal culture. In spite of their variety, folk
festivities of the carnival type, the comic rites and cults, the clowns and
fools, giants, dwarfs, and jugglers, the vast and manifold literature of
parody—all these forms have one style in common: they belong to one
culture of folk carnival humor.

The manifestations of this folk culture can be divided into three distinct forms.

1. *Ritual spectacles:* carnival pageants, comic shows of the marketplace.
2. *Comic verbal compositions:* parodies both oral and written, in
   Latin and in the vernacular.
3. *Various genres of billingsgate:* curses, oaths, popular blazons.

These three forms of folk humor, reflecting in spite of their variety a
single humorous aspect of the world, are closely linked and interwoven
in many ways.

Let us begin by describing each of these forms.

Carnival festivities and the comic spectacles and ritual connected with
them had an important place in the life of medieval man. Besides carnivals proper, with their long and complex pageants and processions,
there was the "feast of fools" *(festa stultorum)* and the "feast of the ass";
there was a special free "Easter laughter" *(risus paschalis)*, consecrated
by tradition. Moreover, nearly every Church feast had its comic folk
aspect, which was also traditionally recognized. Such, for instance, were
the parish feasts, usually marked by fairs and varied open-air amusements, with the participation of giants, dwarfs, monsters, and trained
animals. A carnival atmosphere reigned on days when mysteries and
soties were produced. This atmosphere also pervaded such agricultural
feasts as the harvesting of grapes *(vendange)* which was celebrated also
in the city. Civil and social ceremonies and rituals took on a comic
aspect as clowns and fools, constant participants in these festivals, mim-
icked serious rituals such as the tribute rendered to the victors at tour-
naments, the transfer of feudal rights, or the initiation of a knight. Minor
occasions were also marked by comic protocol, as for instance the election of a king and queen to preside at a banquet "for laughter's sake" *(roi
pour rire)*.

All these forms of protocol and ritual based on laughter and consecrated by tradition existed in all the countries of medieval Europe; they
were sharply distinct from the serious official, ecclesiastical, feudal, and
political cult forms and ceremonials. They offered a completely different, nonofficial, extraecclesiastical and extrapolitical aspect of the world,
of man, and of human relations; they built a second world and a second
life outside officialdom, a world in which all medieval people participated more or less, in which they lived during a given time of the year.
If we fail to take into consideration this two-world condition, neither
medieval cultural consciousness nor the culture of the Renaissance can

be understood. To ignore or to underestimate the laughing people of the Middle Ages also distorts the picture of European culture's historic development.

This double aspect of the world and of human life existed even at the earliest stages of cultural development. In the folklore of primitive peoples, coupled with the cults which were serious in tone and organization were other, comic cults which laughed and scoffed at the deity ("ritual laughter"); coupled with serious myths were comic and abusive ones; coupled with heroes were their parodies and doublets. These comic rituals and myths have attracted the attention of folklorists.

But at the early stages of preclass and prepolitical social order it seems that the serious and the comic aspects of the world and of the deity were equally sacred, equally "official." This similarity was preserved in rituals of a later period of history. For instance, in the early period of the Roman state the ceremonial of the triumphal procession included on almost equal terms the glorifying and the deriding of the victor. The funeral ritual was also composed of lamenting (glorifying) and deriding the deceased. But in the definitely consolidated state and class structure such an equality of the two aspects became impossible. All the comic forms were transferred, some earlier and others later, to a nonofficial level. There they acquired a new meaning, were deepened and rendered more complex, until they became the expression of folk consciousness, of folk culture. Such were the carnival festivities of the ancient world, especially the Roman Saturnalias, and such were medieval carnivals. They were, of course, far removed from the primitive community's ritual laughter.

What are the peculiar traits of the comic rituals and spectacles of the Middle Ages? Of course, these are not religious rituals like, for instance, the Christian liturgy to which they are linked by distant genetic ties. The basis of laughter which gives form to carnival rituals frees them completely from all religious and ecclesiastic dogmatism, from all mysticism and piety. They are also completely deprived of the character of magic and prayer; they do not command nor do they ask for anything. Even more, certain carnival forms parody the Church's cult. All these forms are systematically placed outside the Church and religiosity. They belong to an entirely different sphere.

Because of their obvious sensuous character and their strong element of play, carnival images closely resemble certain artistic forms, namely the spectacle. In turn, medieval spectacles often tended toward carnival folk culture, the culture of the marketplace, and to a certain extent became one of its components. But the basic carnival nucleus of this culture is by no means a purely artistic form nor a spectacle and does not, generally speaking, belong to the sphere of art. It belongs to the borderline between art and life. In reality, it is life itself, but shaped according to a certain pattern of play.

In fact, carnival does not know footlights, in the sense that it does not acknowledge any distinction between actors and spectators. Footlights would destroy a carnival, as the absence of footlights would destroy a theatrical performance. Carnival is not a spectacle seen by the people; they live in it, and everyone participates because its very idea embraces all the people. While carnival lasts, there is no other life outside it. During carnival time life is subject only to its laws, that is, the laws of its own freedom. It has a universal spirit; it is a special condition of the entire world, of the world's revival and renewal, in which all take part. Such is the essence of carnival, vividly felt by all its participants. It was most clearly expressed and experienced in the Roman Saturnalias, perceived as a true and full, though temporary, return of Saturn's golden age upon earth. The tradition of the Saturnalias remained unbroken and alive in the medieval carnival, which expressed this universal renewal and was vividly felt as an escape from the usual official way of life.

Clowns and fools, which often figure in Rabelais' novel, are characteristic of the medieval culture of humor. They were the constant, accredited representatives of the carnival spirit in everyday life out of carnival season. Like Triboulet[1] at the time of Francis I, they were not actors playing their parts on a stage, as did the comic actors of a later period, impersonating Harlequin, Hanswurst, etc., but remained fools and clowns always and wherever they made their appearance. As such they represented a certain form of life, which was real and ideal at the same time. They stood on the borderline between life and art, in a peculiar midzone as it were; they were neither eccentrics nor dolts, neither were they comic actors.

Thus carnival is the people's second life, organized on the basis of laughter. It is a festive life. Festivity is a peculiar quality of all comic rituals and spectacles of the Middle Ages.

All these forms of carnival were also linked externally to the feasts of the Church. (One carnival did not coincide with any commemoration of sacred history or of a saint but marked the last days before Lent, and for this reason was called *Mardi gras* or *carême-prenant* in France and *Fastnacht* in Germany.) Even more significant is the genetic link of these carnivals with ancient pagan festivities, agrarian in nature, which included the comic element in their rituals.

The feast (every feast) is an important primary form of human culture. It cannot be explained merely by the practical conditions of the community's work, and it would be even more superficial to attribute it to the physiological demand for periodic rest. The feast had always an essential, meaningful philosophical content. No rest period or breathing spell can be rendered festive per se; something must be added from the spiritual and ideological dimension. They must be sanctioned not by the world of practical conditions but by the highest aims of human existence, that is, by the world of ideals. Without this sanction there can be no festivity.

---

1. Fevrial, or Le Feurial, was the court fool of Francis I and of Louis XII. He appears repeatedly in Rabelais under the name of Triboulet (Translator's note.)

The feast is always essentially related to time, either to the recurrence of an event in the natural (cosmic) cycle, or to biological or historic timeliness. Moreover, through all the stages of historic development feasts were linked to moments of crisis, of breaking points in the cycle of nature or in the life of society and man. Moments of death and revival, of change and renewal always led to a festive perception of the world. These moments, expressed in concrete form, created the peculiar character of the feasts.

In the framework of class and feudal political structure this specific character could be realized without distortion only in the carnival and in similar marketplace festivals. They were the second life of the people, who for a time entered the utopian realm of community, freedom, equality, and abundance.

On the other hand, the official feasts of the Middle Ages, whether ecclesiastic, feudal, or sponsored by the state, did not lead the people out of the existing world order and created no second life. On the contrary, they sanctioned the existing pattern of things and reinforced it. The link with time became formal; changes and moments of crisis were relegated to the past. Actually, the official feast looked back at the past and used the past to consecrate the present. Unlike the earlier and purer feast, the official feast asserted all that was stable, unchanging, perennial: the existing hierarchy, the existing religious, political, and moral values, norms, and prohibitions. It was the triumph of a truth already established, the predominant truth that was put forward as eternal and indisputable. This is why the tone of the official feast was monolithically serious and why the element of laughter was alien to it. The true nature of human festivity was betrayed and distorted. But this true festive character was indestructible; it had to be tolerated and even legalized outside the official sphere and had to be turned over to the popular sphere of the marketplace.

As opposed to the official feast, one might say that carnival celebrated temporary liberation from the prevailing truth and from the established order; it marked the suspension of all hierarchical rank, privileges, norms, and prohibitions. Carnival was the true feast of time, the feast of becoming, change, and renewal. It was hostile to all that was immortalized and completed.

The suspension of all hierarchical precedence during carnival time was of particular significance. Rank was especially evident during official feasts; everyone was expected to appear in the full regalia of his calling, rank, and merits and to take the place corresponding to his position. It was a consecration of inequality. On the contrary, all were considered equal during carnival. Here, in the town square, a special form of free and familiar contact reigned among people who were usually divided by the barriers of caste, property, profession, and age. The hierarchical background and the extreme corporative and caste divisions of the medieval social order were exceptionally strong. Therefore such free, familiar contacts were deeply felt and formed an essential element of the carnival spirit. People were, so to speak, reborn for new, purely human relations. These truly human relations were not only a fruit of imagination or abstract thought; they were experienced. The utopian ideal and the realistic merged in this carnival experience, unique of its kind.

This temporary suspension, both ideal and real, of hierarchical rank created during carnival time a special type of communication impossible in everyday life. This led to the creation of special forms of marketplace speech and gesture, frank and free, permitting no distance between those who came in contact with each other and liberating from norms of etiquette and decency imposed at other times. A special carnivalesque, marketplace style of expression was formed which we find abundantly represented in Rabelais' novel.

During the century-long development of the medieval carnival, prepared by thousands of years of ancient comic ritual, including the primitive Saturnalias, a special idiom of forms and symbols was evolved—an extremely rich idiom that expressed the unique yet complex carnival experience of the people. This experience, opposed to all that was readymade and completed, to all pretense at immutability, sought a dynamic expression; it demanded ever changing, playful, undefined forms. All the symbols of the carnival idiom are filled with this pathos of change and renewal, with the sense of the gay relativity of prevailing truths and authorities. We find here a characteristic logic, the peculiar logic of the "inside out" (à l'evers), of the "turnabout," of a continual shifting from top to bottom, from front to rear, of numerous parodies and travesties, humiliations, profanations, comic crownings and uncrownings. A second life, a second world of folk culture is thus constructed; it is to a certain extent a parody of the extracarnival life, a "world inside out." We must stress, however, that the carnival is far distant from the negative and formal parody of modern times. Folk humor denies, but it revives and renews at the same time. Bare negation is completely alien to folk culture.

Our introduction has merely touched upon the exceptionally rich and original idiom of carnival forms and symbols. The principal aim of the present work is to understand this half-forgotten idiom, in so many ways obscure to us. For it is precisely this idiom which was used by Rabelais, and without it we would fail to understand Rabelais' system of images. This carnival imagery was also used, although differently and to a different degree, by Erasmus, Shakespeare, Lope de Vega, Guevara, and Quevedo, by the German "literature of fools" (Narren-literatur), and by Hans Sachs, Fischart, Grimmelshausen, and others. Without an understanding of it, therefore, a full appreciation of Renaissance and grostesque literature is impossible. Not only belles lettres but the utopias of the Renaissance and its conception of the universe itself were deeply penetrated by the carnival spirit and often adopted its forms and symbols.

Let us say a few initial words about the complex nature of carnival laughter. It is, first of all, a festive laughter. Therefore it is not an individual reaction to some isolated "comic" event. Carnival laughter is the laughter of all the people. Second, it is universal in scope; it is directed at all and everyone, including the carnival's participants. The entire world is seen in its droll aspect, in its gay relativity. Third, this laughter is ambivalent: it is gay, triumphant, and at the same time mocking, deriding. It asserts and denies, it buries and revives. Such is the laughter of carnival.

Let us enlarge upon the second important trait of the people's festive laughter: that it is also directed at those who laugh. The people do not exclude themselves from the wholeness of the world. They, too, are incomplete, they also die and are revived and renewed. This is one of the essential differences of the people's festive laughter from the pure satire of modern times. The satirist whose laughter is negative places himself above the object of his mockery, he is opposed to it. The whole ness of the world's comic aspect is destroyed, and that which appears comic becomes a private reaction. The people's ambivalent laughter, on the other hand, expresses the point of view of the whole world; he who is laughing also belongs to it.

Let us here stress the special philosophical and utopian character of festive laughter and its orientation toward the highest spheres. The most ancient rituals of mocking at the deity have here survived, acquiring a new essential meaning. All that was purely cultic and limited has faded away, but the all-human, universal, and utopian element has been retained.

The greatest writer to complete the cycle of the people's carnival laughter and bring it into world literature was Rabelais. His work will permit us to enter into the complex and deep nature of this phenomenon.

The problem of folk humor must be correctly posed. Current litera-ture concerning this subject presents merely gross modernizations. The present-day analysis of laughter explains it either as purely negative satire (and Rabelais is described as a pure satirist), or else as gay, fanciful, recreational drollery deprived of philosophic content. The important point made previously, that folk humor is ambivalent, is usually ignored.

We shall now turn to the second form of the culture of folk humor in the Middle Ages: the comic verbal compositions, in Latin or in the ver-nacular.

This, of course, is not folklore proper although some of these com-positions in the vernacular could be placed in that category. But comic literature was infused with the carnival spirit and made wide use of car-nival forms and images. It developed in the disguise of legalized carnival licentiousness and in most cases was systematically linked with such cel-ebrations.[2] Its laughter was both ambivalent and festive. It was the entire recreational literature of the Middle Ages.

Celebrations of a carnival type represented a considerable part of the

---

2. A similar situation existed in ancient Rome where comic literature reflected the licentiousness of the Saturnalias, to which it was closely linked.

life of medieval men, even in the time given over to them. Large medieval cities devoted an average of three months a year to these festivities. The influence of the carnival spirit was irresistible: it made a man renounce his official state as monk, cleric, scholar, and perceive the world in its laughing aspect. Not only schoolmen and minor clerics but hierarchs and learned theologians indulged in gay recreation as relaxation from pious seriousness. "Monkish pranks" *(Joca monacorum)* was the title of one of the most popular medieval comic pieces. Confined to their cells, monks produced parodies or semiparodies of learned treatises and other droll Latin compositions.

The comic literature of the Middle Ages developed throughout a thousand years or even more, since its origin goes back to Christian antiquity. During this long life it underwent, of course, considerable transformation, the Latin compositions being altered least. A variety of genres and styles were elaborated. But in spite of all these variations this literature remained more or less the expression of the popular carnival spirit, using the latter's forms and symbols.

The Latin parody or semiparody was widespread. The number of manuscripts belonging to this category is immense. The entire official ideology and ritual are here shown in their comic aspect. Laughter penetrates the highest forms of religious cult and thought.

One of the oldest and most popular examples of this literature, "Cyprian's supper" *(coena Cypriani)* offers a peculiar festive and carnivalesque travesty of the entire Scriptures. This work was consecrated by the tradition of "Paschal laughter" *(risus paschalis)*; the faraway echoes of the Roman Saturnalia can be heard in it. Another ancient parody is the "Grammatical Virgil Maro" *(Vergilius Maro Grammaticus)*, a semiparodical learned treatise on Latin grammar which is at the same time a parody of the scholarly wisdom and of the scientific methods of the early Middle Ages. Both works, composed at the very borderline between the antique world and the Middle Ages, inaugurated this humorous genre and had a decisive influence on its later forms. Their vogue lasted almost up to the Renaissance.

In the further development of humorous Latin literature, parodical doublets of every ecclesiastical cult and teaching were created—the so-called *parodia sacra*, "sacred parody," one of the most peculiar and least understood manifestations of medieval literature. There is a considerable number of parodical liturgies ("The Liturgy of the Drunkards," "The Liturgy of the Gamblers"), parodies of Gospel readings, of the most sacred prayers (the Lords' Prayer, the Ave Maria), of litanies, hymns, psalms, and even Gospel sayings. There were parodies of wills ("The Pig's Will," "The Will of the Ass"), parodies of epitaphs, council decrees, etc. The scope of this literature is almost limitless. All of it was consecrated by tradition and, to a certain extent, tolerated by the Church. It was created and preserved under the auspices of the "Paschal laughter," or of the "Christmas laughter"; it was in part directly linked, as in the parodies of liturgies and prayers, with the "feast of fools" and may have been performed during this celebration.

There were other parodies in Latin: parodies of debates, dialogues, chronicles, and so forth. All these forms demanded from their authors a certain degree of learning, sometimes at a high level. All of them brought the echoes of carnival laughter within the walls of monasteries, universities, and schools.

Medieval Latin humor found its final and complete expression at the highest level of the Renaissance in Erasmus's "In Praise of Folly," one of the greatest creations of carnival laughter in world literature, and in von Hutten's "Letters of Obscure People."

No less rich and even more varied is medieval humorous literature composed in the vernacular. Here, too, we find forms similar to the *parodia sacra*: parodies of prayers, of sermons (the *sermons joyeux* in France), of Christmas carols, and legends of the saints. But the prevailing forms are the secular parody and travesty, which present the droll aspect of the feudal system and of feudal heroics. The medieval epic parodies are animal, jesting, roguish, foolish; they deal with heroic deeds, epic heroes (the comic Roland), and knightly tales ("The Mule without a Bridle," "Aucassin and Nicolette"). There are various genres of mock rhetoric: carnivalesque debates, comic dialogues, and *euloges*. Carnivalesque humor is also reflected in the *fabliaux* and in the peculiar comic lyrics of vagrant scholars.

All these genres are linked to carnivalesque forms and symbols more closely than the Latin parodies. But it is the medieval comic theater which is most intimately related to carnival. The first medieval comic play that has been preserved, *The Play in the Bower* by Adam de la Halle, is a remarkable example of a purely carnivalesque vision and conception of the world. De la Halle's play contains in embryonic form many aspects of Rabelais' own world. The miracle and morality plays acquired to a certain extent a carnivalesque nature. Laughter penetrated the mystery plays; the diableries which are part of these performances have an obvious carnivalesque character, as do also the *soties* produced during the late Middle Ages.

We have here described only a few better known manifestations of humorous literature, which will suffice for the posing of our problem. As we advance in our analysis of Rabelais' work we shall examine in detail these genres, as well as many less known examples of medieval humorous writings.

PAUL OSKAR KRISTELLER

Erasmus from an Italian Perspective †

Erasmus' attitudes towards Italy and the Italians and the extent of his dependence on Italian sources have been the subject of several compe-

† *Renaissance Quarterly* (1970): 1–14. Most footnotes have been omitted.

tent studies. The prevalent view, however, tends to minimize Erasmus' debt to Italy. The great representative of Northern humanism, it is argued, surpassed in scholarly stature his Italian contemporaries and hence had nothing to learn from them. As a moral and religious thinker deeply rooted in the traditions of the *Devotio Moderna*, he was far removed from the secular and even pagan tendencies of Italian humanism. He spent most of his life, apart from his native Holland, in Paris and Louvain, London, Oxford and Cambridge, Basel and Freiburg, all of them important intellectual centers in their own right and with their own traditions. The three years of his Italian journey, undertaken when he was around forty years of age, do not seem to occupy a very large place in his intellectual biography. Yet to say that the work of Erasmus cannot be derived from Italian influences (as I should be ready to concede) is not the same thing as to say that this work may be completely understood apart from any Italian influences or precedents (something I am inclined to deny). The Italian journey may have had a more lasting impact on Erasmus than many scholars, or even Erasmus himself, were willing to admit. Moreover, the Italian influences on Erasmus must not be attributed only to his stay in Italy from 1506 to 1509, significant as that stay may have been. Long before he saw Italy, and long after he returned to the North, Erasmus was exposed to indirect Italian influences in the very Northern centers where he lived, especially in the Low Countries and in England, in Paris and in Basel, a point that has rightly been stressed by several scholars. Finally, we should not underestimate the impact that the reading of the works of the Italian humanists had on Erasmus, from his youth on throughout the remainder of his life. The whole subject of Erasmus' relations with Italy definitely needs much further study. I could not hope to do it justice in a short paper, but I should like to review some of its aspects, summing up the results of previous studies, and indicating a few points that may be further pursued by Erasmus specialists. They concern especially his relation to early Italian humanism, which has often been discussed, and his relation to Florentine Platonism, which has usually been overlooked.

The story of Erasmus' Italian journey has been told by several scholars and can be followed with the help of his correspondence, although few letters have survived from his Italian period and their testimony must be supplemented by later letters and writings. He passed through Turin and obtained a doctorate in theology at its university. He stayed for some time at Bologna and made from there an excursion to Florence. He lived in Venice in the circle of Aldus Manutius and came to know rather closely a number of Italian and Greek scholars. He made friends in Padua and Ferrara where he stayed for shorter periods, visited Siena and Naples, and finally spent several months in Rome where he met many scholars and was introduced to several cardinals. After his departure from Italy, and throughout the rest of his life, Erasmus maintained an active correspondence with Italy. His friends and correspondents included important scholars such as Bembo, Sadoleto, and Calcagnini. He also became involved in several literary and religious controversies with Italians. His numerous statements about Italy, the Italians, and Italian scholarship have been collected and quoted more than once. Some of them are warm and favorable, others are colored by his controversies and hence should not be taken at their face value.

Yet in dealing with Erasmus and Italy, I should like to focus on literary rather than on personal or biographical evidence. First of all, as I have said, Erasmus was well-acquainted with the writings of many Italian humanists. In his letters, and especially in his *Ciceronianus*, he mentions numerous Italian humanists and passes judgments on their writings, suggesting that he had actually read at least some of them. It appears that he admired especially the Italian humanists of the fifteenth-century, and he states emphatically that at that time Italy was ahead of the North in literary scholarship. In his later life, he kept stressing that many of the greatest Italian scholars were dead at the time when he visited Italy and that some of the best Italian scholars whom he met during his visit had died by the time he was commenting on the state of learning in Italy. In our estimate of these judgments, we must remember that Erasmus was ignorant of the Italian language and hence in no position to appreciate the contributions in Italian that were made in increasing numbers to literature and to scholarship.

It is obvious from Erasmus' letters and other writings that he had a special admiration for Lorenzo Valla, especially for his *Elegantiae* which he praised more than once and for his *Annotations on the New Testament* which he discovered in Louvain and edited in Paris some time before his Italian journey. He also praised Ermolao Barbaro (who had visited the Low Countries), Angelo Poliziano, and Giovanni Pico. He has less to say about Marsilio Ficino, but he seems to have respected him, and he probably used his Latin translation of Plato that was printed many years earlier than the Greek text. The writings of all these Italian scholars were available in the North and especially in the Low Countries. At present, we cannot be sufficiently specific on this matter, for the Italian influences in the Low Countries may be documented by a few manuscripts and printed editions but have not yet been studied in a comprehensive way as they have been for France, England, or Basel.

Apart from Erasmus' explicit references to Italian scholars, we have other indications of his familiarity with their works. We have reason to believe that his Latin style owes something to them, and we gladly accept the opinion of a very competent judge who claims that Erasmus' style notably improved after his Italian journey. For we know that he spoke nothing but Latin with his Italian friends. We also know that Erasmus hoped to improve his knowledge of Greek and to enlarge his acquaintance with Greek literature when he went to Italy, and we have ample reason to believe that this hope was fulfilled, especially in Venice where he belonged to the circle of Aldus and met with several native Greek scholars and Italian Hellenists. Erasmus repeats and endorses the view that Latin learning and letters were reborn, after a long sleep, with Petrarch and his disciples, and he shares with his Italian predecessors their aversion to scholastic philosophy and theology. Moreover, we notice a clear affinity between Erasmus and the earlier Italian humanists when we look at the pattern of his work, at the literary genres he cultivated, and at the scholarly topics and disciplines to which he contributed, or failed to contribute. Like the Italian humanists, Erasmus was an editor and commentator of Greek and Latin classical texts, a Latin translator from the Greek, and a prolific author of treatises, dialogues, declamations, and invectives, and, above all, of letters. All these genres, and the specific way in which they are handled by him, fall into the pattern of early Italian humanism. The same is true of the range of their content: Greek and Latin grammar and scholarship, Latin rhetoric, questions of ethics and politics, of education and religion. On the other hand, Erasmus shows no significant interest in logic or metaphysics, in mathematics or in natural philosophy. I am afraid we cannot assign to him an important place in the history of science, and if we considered only the contributions made to the sciences as significant facts of intellectual history, Erasmus might not fare too well. We need at least two cultures if we want to do him justice.

We have not yet spoken of one facet of Erasmus' work that was very important to his contemporaries, especially during the later part of his life, and that has attracted most of the attention of later historians: his contribution to religious thought and scholarship. There is throughout his work, even where we might least expect it, a pervasive strand of Christian piety. Erasmus admires the ancients, to be sure, but he warns his readers against their morals and religion. He rejects the scholastic theology of the Middle Ages, including Thomas and Scotus, to which he had been exposed at Paris, and it is a matter of debate how much of it he absorbed or understood. Yet he insists on the Bible and the Church Fathers as the main sources of religion. He accepts the ritual practice of the Catholic Church as symbols but considers the spiritual attitude of the worshipper as the real substance of religion. He preaches throughout a simple piety which for him is compatible or even identical with simple philosophical morality. Finally, he devotes a very large share of his enormous capacity for work to the editing, translating, and annotating of the New Testament and of the Greek and Latin Fathers, applying to these religious texts the same historical and philological methods which the Italian humanists had developed for the study of the Greek and Latin classics. Erasmus' work on the Bible and on the Fathers was an immense contribution to religious scholarship that exercised a great influence on later scholars and theologians both Protestant and Catholic and that must still be further studied and evaluated in greater detail. Erasmus, like Valla, Poliziano, and Budé, had a high conception of grammar and philology and placed it above dialectic. His peculiar combination of piety and learning surely followed the traditions of the *Devotio Moderna*, but he went much further. His works, and sometimes his words and those of his admirers, suggest that he meant to replace the traditional scholastic theology with a new historical and humanistic theology. He probably obtained his theological degree at Turin in order to have greater authority in his controversies with the professional theologians of the Northern universities. It is this combination of simple piety and religious scholarship that has prompted recent historians to label the attitude of Erasmus and of his friends as Christian humanism. This term has some merit, provided that we emphasize the scholarly component of Renaissance humanism, and do not smuggle in some of the connotations and implications that the term 'humanism' has acquired in modern times and that are largely alien to Erasmus and his age.

There is no doubt that this Christian humanism, as we have described it, is in many ways peculiar to Erasmus, that it was rooted in the tradition of the *Devotio Moderna*, and that it exercised a greater influence in the North than it did in Italy (although Erasmus' influence in Italy is a broad subject that seems to be in need of further study). Yet I should like to qualify the statement frequently made that the Christian humanism of Erasmus and other Northern scholars must be contrasted with the pagan or secular humanism of the Italians. First of all, there were many Northern humanists before and after Erasmus that were as pagan or secular as any of the Italians had been. On the other hand, it is easy to show that Erasmus' Christian humanism, however defined, had its Italian precedents, some of them well known to himself. Erasmus' insistence on a simple piety strengthened by classical learning but devoid of scholastic theology had its counterpart in Petrarch, in Salutati, and in many Italian humanists of the fifteenth century, many of them still unexplored. Erasmus' scholarly work on the Bible and on the Church Fathers was also preceded by similar efforts made by Italian scholars, although they were surely less extensive and less influential. In the case of biblical studies, Valla's *Annotations* on the New Testament were not only known to Erasmus, but were actually edited by him many years before he published his own edition of the New Testament. Naturally Erasmus improved on the work of Valla and added much to it, as he had to say in reply to his critics, but there seems to be no doubt that he was indebted to Valla for a number of details, for his method, and, above all, for the very idea of applying humanistic scholarship to the Greek text of the New Testament and to the Latin Vulgate. An actual comparison between the work of Valla and of Erasmus on the New Testament has not yet been attempted so far as I know. It is true that Valla's annotations did not circulate very widely before Erasmus' edition, but there are other manuscripts besides the one found by Erasmus in the Low Countries, and we know that Valla's *Annotations* were seen and approved by Cusanus. Another important predecessor of Erasmus in biblical scholarship has been recently mentioned who was probably not known to Erasmus: Giannozzo Manetti. He made a new translation of the New Testament and of the Psalms, and this translation, though never printed or adequately studied, survives in several manuscripts, including one that reached the Low Countries during the first half of the sixteenth century. Pico's studies on the Hebrew text of the Psalms have but recently been discovered in a number of manuscripts and were probably unknown to Erasmus and his contemporaries.

More numerous were Erasmus' predecessors in the field of patristic scholarship, although none of them can measure up to his massive achievement as an editor and translator of the Fathers. The Latin Fathers, and especially Augustine and Jerome, were amply represented in all major libraries of the fifteenth century, they were read and cited by many humanists and were occasionally used as texts in humanist courses on Latin prose literature. Moreover, many writings of the Latin Fathers were copied and later edited in print by humanist scholars in Italy and elsewhere, and we may safely assume, although this point has not yet been studied in detail, that these copies and editions reflect the same standards of textual criticism that were customarily applied to the writings of the Latin authors of pagan antiquity.

However, we know a little more about the study of the Greek Fathers. The Italian humanists of the fifteenth century translated into Latin a very large body of Greek patristic literature, including many works that had not been known in the West during the preceding centuries. Numerous Italian humanists, laymen as well as priests and monks, participated in this work, and we find among them such important figures as Ambrogio Traversari, General of the Camaldulensians, and Pietro Balbo of Pisa, Bishop of Tropea, the friend and scholarly assistant of Cusanus. That some of these works were known in the Low Countries can be shown through manuscript and other evidence. Erasmus appears to know some of these translators, not Traversari or Balbo, but Franciscus Aretinus and George of Trebisond, and it seems safe to infer that he was familiar with the precedent they had established as translators of Greek patristic writings, even if he may not have used their translations in his actual work. The question whether he did use their translations is of course in need of further study.

Having surveyed Erasmus' relations with Italian humanism, I should like to mention another aspect of his work and thought that seems to have been largely neglected by his interpreters although it is deserving of some attention: there is a distinctly Platonist strand in Erasmus, and much of it may be traced to the influence of Florentine Platonism. Apart from a few letters, I find the chief evidence in the *Enchiridion* and in the *Praise of Folly*. I am inclined to think that this Platonist orientation goes back to Erasmus' earlier years, although it may have received some further impulse during his Italian period. Plato's works in Ficino's Latin translation, with his introductions and commentaries, were available in print from 1484, whereas the Greek text of Plato was printed only in 1513 and hardly accessible to Erasmus in manuscript before he reached Venice. Moreover, Erasmus knew Pico's works, and among the Northern scholars who had some influence on Erasmus there were at least two who had direct connections with the Florentine Academy: Robert Gaguin in Paris and John Colet in London and Oxford. In the case of Colet, there are several important references to Ficino and Pico in his lectures, and we have recently learned that he was in correspondence with Ficino although he did not meet him when he was in Italy. In view of these circumstances, we should not be surprised to find Platonist elements in some of Erasmus' writings.

I should like to begin with the *Enchiridion militis Christiani* [1] which was first published in 1503. In this book Erasmus is not 'giving advice to illiterate soldiers,' as Bertrand Russell more wittily than correctly asserts, but supplies a handbook for a Christian soldier allegorically understood, that is, for a Christian fighting for Christ against the devil. In defending the study of the ancients, Erasmus recommends the Platonists above other ancient philosophers because they are nearest in style and content to the Bible. Speaking in his own name, Erasmus stresses that man is composed of a soul and a body. The body is akin to the animals, is pleased with visible objects, and has a downward tendency. The soul, on the other hand, is akin to the divine and has an upward tendency. 'It despises things that can be seen; for it knows that they are perishable, it seeks things which truly are, which always are. Being immortal, it loves things immortal.' In discussing the contrast between reason and the passions, Erasmus cites Plato's *Timaeus* and *Phaedo* and tries to harmonize Plato's distinctions with those of St. Paul, the inner and the outer man, the spirit and the flesh. Perfect piety consists in the effort to proceed from visible to invisible things. Between the intelligible and the visible world, man is, as it were, a third world that shares in both. There are several more references to Plato and the Platonists in the *Enchiridion*, together with a persistent tendency to identify a simplified Platonic philosophy and a simplified Christian religion. I do not wish to maintain that Erasmus' position is historically accurate, philosophically defensible, or theologically desirable. I merely wish to point out that there is an aspect and an element of Platonist philosophy that Erasmus consciously endorses and that he believes to be compatible with the religious and theological position he is trying to present and to defend.

Even more striking and surprising are the Platonist elements in the *Praise of Folly*, a work he composed shortly after his return from Italy and published in 1511. It is well known, or it should be well known, that Erasmus followed the pattern of certain ironical eulogies composed by Isocrates, Lucian, and Seneca. The larger part of the work is a satire and consists of a criticism of all human states and professions including not only the monks and theologians, but also the grammarians, poets, and rhetoricians with whom Erasmus might have identified himself. In the last part of his work, Erasmus collects statements from ancient and especially from Christian writers that seem to contain a praise of folly, and here it appears that the entire work is based on a 'deliberate ambiguity,' to use a fashionable phrase. For the fools are ridiculous in the eyes of the wise, whereas the wise in turn are foolish in the eyes of the

---

1. "Handbook of the Christian Soldier" [Editor].

fools. The truly wise are here persistently described as pious Christians and also as Platonic philosophers, and in this context Plato's simile of the cave is explicitly referred to, just as the genealogy of Folly at the beginning of the work is clearly patterned after the genealogy of love in Plato's *Symposium*. The Christians, we are told, agree with the Platonists that the soul, while imprisoned in the body, is unable to contemplate or to enjoy true being. Philosophy is a meditation on death, for it takes the soul away from visible and corporeal things. The vulgar are concerned only with the visible and the corporeal, whereas the pious are directed towards the intelligible and invisible. Thus each of them appears foolish in the eyes of the other. Plato is right in praising love as a kind of divine madness. For he who ardently loves lives no longer in himself but lives in the person who is the object of his love (here we note a clear echo of Ficino's commentary on the *Symposium*). The work concludes with a description of the ecstasy which is experienced by a few pious persons during the present life and must be interpreted as a foretaste of the future life as it will be experienced by the blessed souls.

The work thus maintains some of its ironic tone to the very end, especially through the recurrent references to madness and folly. Yet the last chapters culminate in an enthusiastic description of contemplation as a supreme experience which the truly pious may attain for a limited time. The tone and terminology are distinctly Platonist, and the wording and doctrine are reminiscent of Marsilio Ficino rather than of Plato and Plotinus.

Our interpretation may seem somewhat strained to the casual reader of the *Praise of Folly*, but it is confirmed by some of Erasmus' letters. These letters contain repeated references to Platonic passages, especially in the *Republic*, and Erasmus seems to mention them with approval. In a letter to Agostino Steuco (who happened to be a Platonist), Erasmus rejects a plan to write against Platonic philosophy: 'If you condemn both Platonic and Aristotelian philosophy, you leave us none.'[2] It is evident from other passages that he prefers the Platonic to the Aristotelian doctrine. In a letter of 1516, he recommends to a friend the frequent reading of Plato and Seneca 'who will not let your soul remain on the ground.'[3] However, more important for our purpose are two letters in which Erasmus defends and explains his *Praise of Folly* and at the same time explicitly stresses its Platonist orientation.

The first of these is a long letter written in 1515 to Martin Dorp. Referring to the last part of the *Praise of Folly*, Erasmus writes as follows: 'I first mention three madnesses of Plato among which the happiest is that of the lovers which is nothing but a kind of ecstasy. But the ecstasy of the pious is nothing else but a foretaste of the future happiness through which we shall be absorbed into God, being in Him rather than in ourselves. But Plato calls this madness when a person is driven out of him-

2. *Opus epistolarum* 9 (1938), 208.   3. *Ibid.*, 2 (1910), 358.

self and lives in that which he loves and enjoys it.'[4] Erasmus returns to the same theme in a letter of 1520 to George Halewin, who translated the *Praise of Folly* into French. Here he is even more explicit.

> The passage in the *Praise of Folly* that troubles you, namely in which sense I say that some things truly are, will be clear to you when you remember Plato's fable of the cave and of those born in it, who admire the shadow of things as if they were true things. Things that are grasped by the senses cannot be said to exist in a true sense since they are not eternal and do not always remain in the same way. Only those things truly are that are grasped by the contemplation of the mind. Plato stresses this in many passages, and so does Aristotle in his *Metaphysics* and St. Paul in the second Epistle to the Corinthians chapter 4: 'not when we contemplate the things which are seen, but those which are not seen. For the things which are seen are temporal, but those which are not seen are eternal.' Just as God exists among all things in the most perfect way because he exists in the simplest way and is farthest removed from the grossness of perceptible things, thus the things that come closest to Him are said to exist most truly. Thus the soul exists more truly than does the body. Although the philosopher removes himself from the perceptible things and practices the contemplation of things intelligible he does not completely enjoy them except when the soul, fully freed from the material organs through which it now operates, exercises its full force. For although there are some forces which the soul exercises through less material organs, as when it thinks or remembers, yet the philosophers doubt whether the mind which the Greeks call Nous does anything in this body without a corporeal organ. . . .[5]

If my interpretation of the *Praise of Folly* may have seemed at first a bit pedantic, it can now be affirmed that Erasmus himself was no less pedantic in his outlook. For in trying to explain and defend the passages in the *Praise of Folly* which we have singled out as Platonic, Erasmus does not hesitate to give us a whole treatise on Platonic metaphysics as he understands it. It is a simplified account, to be sure, and it is carefully worded in such a way that it will appear compatible with the doctrine of St. Paul. Yet it retains some of the authentic ring of Platonism, and when we examine its emphasis and its wording more closely, we recognize as its source the Florentine Platonism of Marsilio Ficino.

I realize that the passages which I have chosen and quoted constitute but a very small part of the huge written work of Erasmus, and hence I can understand why they have been neglected and almost entirely overlooked. I do not wish to maintain that Platonism constitutes the dominant element in Erasmus' thought or writing. I merely wish to note that there is at least a Platonist element in Erasmus and that he occupies a

4. *Ibid.*, 2, 90–114, at 103.   5. *Ibid.*, 4 (1922), 289.

place in the history of Platonism. I am glad to add that this Platonism shows some clear traces of Italian influence, and that it is after all conspicuous in two of Erasmus' major writings, the *Enchiridion* and the *Praise of Folly*.

I hope I have been able to show that Erasmus was, to a much greater extent than is usually realized, a student and disciple of the Italian Renaissance, of its humanism as well as of its Platonism. When we pay tribute to him and admire him as a guide in religious and political problems, and as a model of humanistic scholarship, we should not overlook the fact that he was, among many other things, also a continuator and transmitter and even a part and parcel of the great scholarly, literary, and moral tradition embodied in the Italian humanism of the fifteenth and also of the sixteenth century, and of the great metaphysical and theological tradition represented by Renaissance Platonism.

ROBERT M. ADAMS

Draining and Filling: A Few Benchmarks in the History of Humanism

Humanism, which under a large perspective is not to be defined as a body of tenets or doctrines, is not to be identified, either, with a particular subject matter or area of interest. Its basic concern is several potentials of the human mind—to learn and communicate approximate truths, to govern some part of itself and the world outside it, to reach agreement on the rudiments of civilized existence. That seems relatively clear and simple as a preliminary premise; but it is so inclusive that it leaves hardly anything outside the area of humanistic concern. Even supernatural religion, originally and repeatedly invoked to contrast with the humanist approach (either as antithesis or supplement) depends in many particulars on human arguments and judgments. The Christian scripture cannot authenticate itself as the word of God; it must be judged by comparison with other claimants, of whom Mohammed and Buddha are only two obvious examples. Its text must be constructed by rational deduction and philological analysis from a variety of more or less probable manuscript sources. Most of us must read it in fallible translations which repeatedly differ from one another, and which in important details have been a matter of dispute for centuries. Churches which offer authoritative interpretive guidance in matters of belief have repeatedly been mistaken in the past and give no evidence of being incapable of error in the future. If the logical powers of the human mind must be invoked to assess and discriminate among the mysteries of faith, there can be hardly anything in the cosmos that does not come under the rubric of "humanism."

A *priori* definition, however, is only one, and the least interesting, of the ways to come at humanism; a more fruitful approach is historical. As it has existed, primarily in the western world over the last half a millennium and more, humanism has proved a remarkably elastic attitude. It has a political, a theological, a literary and stylistic, an art-historical, and an educational application—to mention no others. At different times and under different circumstances it has meant more or less. The term may expand to fill up the space left by more rigid and demanding interests, or shrink before them. It may amount to as little as a concern with Greek or Roman literature and the values associated with them; or else, it may be as much as an explanation of the entire cosmos. It is surpassingly receptive of coloration from the intellectual and social currents within which particular humanists (never more than a tiny, mostly uncoordinated minority) exist at a given moment. Like the concept of "toleration," with which it has interesting affinities, humanism is a receptacle for left-over concepts and values, a "reservoir" term in the sense that how much it contains depends not only on how much is put into it, but how much is drained off and assigned to other categories. A great deal of behavior that used to be called "toleration" is now better described as "indifference" or "insensibility"; a great deal of what once passed under the generic name of humanism is now known as medicine, linguistics, archaeology, or anthropology—to name only a few of the descendant disciplines.

Long before the term "humanism" came into being (it was popularized in the nineteenth century to describe a cultural change that had occurred half a millennium before), the same process of change and adaptation was under way. The ideal of *paideia* as it developed among the Greek city-states combined literary culture, piety, and social discipline in a program aiming ultimately at effective civic participation. Under the Hellenistic and Roman empires, civic participation became, for most men, less of an immediate possibility; thus the Latin equivalent of *paideia, humanitas*, added elements more appropriate to its circumstances—ideas of self-correction and self-cultivation implying an inner center of gravity rendering the cultured individual independent of circumstances yet exemplary for other men. A capacious mind, a balanced judgment, the capacity to fulfill with propriety all the offices of private and public life, these constituted the classic ideal of *humanitas*. Yet in different contexts the implications of the word could change entirely. When the middle ages contrasted mere *humanitas* with the angelic purity of a divine existence, the word carried overtones of sin, weakness, imperfection. It had been drained of several previous contents and refilled with another; that is the constant shape taken by its history.

The kernel of what would become "the humanities" and then "humanism" bore in the early Renaissance the name of *studia humanitatis*; it comprised the study of humane letters, i.e., the classic civilizations of Greece and Rome, defining itself (by implied contrast with the great theocentric structures of scholasticism) as the study of human interests and values by means other than formal logic and for purposes other than theological argumentation. The contrast was developed through arguments over prose style, over the accurate interpretation of ancient documents, over the concept of historic time. Medieval philosophers had tended to think of the world's body, its history, and the sacred scriptures as three complementary if not quite identical texts written by the hand of God, which it was the business of human thought to interpret into a single ideal timeless harmony directing man to his salvation. The Old Testament was sometimes figured as mill for grinding the rough corn of Jewish life into the fine flour of the Christian dispensation; the pelican, the unicorn, and the basilisk, as they appeared in popular bestiaries, were animated moral lessons contrived to guide the conduct of men; the heavenly bodies in their divinely appointed courses sang a majestic hymn of praise to the Lord. Virgil in his fourth eclogue had prophesied the birth of Christ because, though a pagan, he enjoyed obscure intimations of Christian truth; the wanderings of Ulysses on his way home from Troy were an allegory of the Christian soul on its pilgrimage to heaven. The early humanists, though they did not set out directly to shatter this imaginative harmony—rather, in many instances, clung to it as long as possible—encouraged a sense of the pastness of the past and the meaning of texts in their own historic contexts that gradually dissolved, piece by piece, the universal scholastic systems.[1]

As the phantoms of allegorical correspondence had to be cleared off ancient texts, so a good deal of traditional lore and superstitious practice came under question within the church; and finally, where they were corrupt, the texts of the church fathers and of the sacred scripture itself had to be looked at critically. As in these matters they were disturbing old and very comfortable habits, not to speak of vested interests, the humanists came under heavy attack; and, not unnaturally, they seemed at first to be defined almost entirely by their opposition to settled tradition and established hierarchy.

Nowadays, it goes without saying, humanists don't define themselves against elaborate moral allegories, superstitious practices, or corrupt translations of the Bible; most of these battles have long been fought out. Like the world as a whole, humanists have largely forgotten about the universal moral synthesis. These days, they are more likely to define themselves with relation to the sciences and perhaps the teeming, amoral marketplace than with an eye to theologians of any persuasion. But in fact definition is no longer really a practical concern. Humanism has been defined so many times over, against so many different antithetical concepts, that the word has largely lost currency. Most people drift into and out of activities and attitudes that used to be called "humanist"

1. An important historical question was whether the history of the Jews alone, or the history of the several gentile cultures as well, formed a seamless web with Christian history. It is hard to tell whether the different allegorical, analogical, and typological bridges thrown up to tie the different ages of the world together are evidence that it was seen as a unity or rather that it was recognized as a disunity which desperate human ingenuity had, imaginatively, to unite. Similar questions have been mooted regarding the English metaphysical poets and the continental wit-writers, such as Gongora and Marino.

without any sense of passing a boundary. Like the word "renaissance," the word "humanism," when it requires too much preliminary definition, ceases to be worth the trouble.

The vicissitudes of the term over recent centuries are too many and too intricate to describe in detail, but a few of the high and low points may convey the range of its transformations. Mr. Trevor-Roper in his valuable essay (above, pp. 267–85) has well described how during the dark ages of religious warfare in the sixteenth and seventeenth centuries, Catholic militants put Erasmus's books on the Index Expurgatorius, and the few lingering Erasmians took essentially to the closet. Though few of them were martyred, the humanist ideas and values they had espoused went into eclipse. But in the eighteenth century, the skies cleared. Starting in 1703, Jean LeClerc issued a splendid new edition of the works of Erasmus, and later in the century, kind if a bit perfunctory sentiments appeared in the great *Encyclopédie* edited by Diderot. Erasmus (though listed oddly under the heading "Rotterdam") was called "un des plus grands hommes de la republique des lettres," and "un des premiers qui ait traité les matiéres de la religion avec la noblesse et la dignité qui conviennent à nos mystéres de la religion avec la noblesse et la dignité qui conviennent à nos mystéres." In summary, he was "le plus bel ésprit de son temps."[2] This generous appraisal is not too surprising; the established mode of eighteenth-century neo-classicism in literature, art, and architecture built directly on foundations laid by the early humanists; the deism dominant in France, and present in England as well, agreed in its feeling for clarity, simplicity, and individual responsibility with the *philosophia Christi* of Erasmus. After its long winter, humanism seemed to be resurrected, vindicated, given a new lease on life. And yet there was one conspicuous element that had all but disappeared—the word itself. Boileau and Pope used the classics, as had the humanists, in a rich variety of ways—to mirror, ridicule, compliment, teach, and tease their contemporaries; but the word "humanist" never occurred to either man as a word of self-description, nor did other people commonly apply it to them. Like Erasmus, the *philosophes* of the eighteenth century boldly satirized clerics, especially theologians and recluses. But the name "humanist" and the idea of humanism in the programmatic and reformist sense were stuck back in the sixteenth century; nobody laid claim to them any more.

As a matter of fact, the *Encyclopédie* treated "humanism" in minimal terms, defining it through "the humanities" as simply part of the academic curriculum. In the broader sense of the word, "humanism" was assumed to have predeceased Erasmus himself; a later nineteenth-century encyclopedia would make that judgment perfectly explicit: "Erasmus lived to see the death of humanism." And yet not only the root idea of humanism but the application of classic texts to modern experience

2. "One of the greatest men in the republic of letters . . . one of the first men who treated matters of religion with the nobility and dignity appropriate to our mysteries . . . the finest spirit of his day."

returned from time to time to vivid life. Following the English revolution of 1640, both the French and the American revolutions of the late eighteenth century drew spiritual sustenance from classic precedents. The society of the Cincinnati in America, the title of First Consul in France, though but verbal tags, indicate the trend in men's thinking. Figures as diverse as Shelley the English poet, Jefferson the gentleman planter turned populist politician, and David the painter-laureate of the French Revolution drew on the classics for their visions of the good society—or was it rather that they infused the semblance of classic form with a new and revolutionary content? Humanism in a sixteenth-century sense this insurrectionary classicism certainly wasn't; yet its claim to be a legitimate descendant of humanist principles was just as good as any advanced by the cold and somewhat bloodless classicism of the academies.

For through the eighteenth and well into the nineteenth century, and especially in England's caste-bound society, study of the classics retained, if only vestigially, some of the social prestige it used to have in the Renaissance. Latin, when the vernacular tongues were still in process of formation, had been the international language of both church and state. In popular reputation at least, if not in reality, it had borne the cachet of a "permanent" tongue, more substantial and enduring than the fly-by-night modern idioms. The classic style was rooted in the solid soil of general human nature purified of idiosyncrasies and eccentricities, endorsed by the verdict of history and the consensus of the learned. Before the seventeenth century, the modern world really had very little to set against the overpowering presence of the classics; and in the word-wars between "ancients and moderns" that enlivened the later seventeenth century, the ancients could at least hold their own so long as the debate was confined to literary and artistic matters. (Science was a very different thing; there the moderns triumphed easily, at least when they knew enough about scientific matters to use the weapons available to them.)

But by the eighteenth century many of the old rationales for study of the classics had faded. As far as everyday life was concerned, Latin and Greek were unequivocally dead languages, while the modern dialects had developed "classics" of their own. Thus, though various ostensible reasons might be advanced for making the classics the center of an academic curriculum, the major force sustaining that arrangement slowly degenerated into simple social prestige. No less than the old school tie, knowledge of the classics (or at least of a few classical tags) became a badge of gentility. Its advantages were many, if paradoxical. For practical purposes like making money or swaying an electorate, a classical education was useless or worse than useless; as a rule it was painful—actually physically painful—to acquire; it was very expensive; it was a hallmark recognized by only a few, but a very exclusive few. Acquaintance with Horace or Propertius was like a warranty of cosmopolitan urbanity, untarnished by the least stain of puritanical earnestness. No doubt this was a monstrous distortion of the values of humanism as evidenced by Erasmus or More, yet in a highly stratified class society with a strongly held hierarchy of social values, the pre-eminence of the dead languages, often euphemized as "a good sound English classical education" lasted a surprisingly long time.

Indeed, for insiders, playing the classical game was not only good fun but good for the self-esteem. One was enrolled in an élite, intimate but international and omni-secular, whose members could respond to the hint of an allusion, the shadow of a remote parallel, witty variations on a recognized theme. The mode reaches back in the history of humanism to Petrarch, who addressed imaginary letters to the great figures of antiquity. It was revived in the nineteenth century by Walter Savage Landor, whose *Imaginary Conversations*, very largely between figures of the classical era, presuppose in the reader not only a good classical education but a feeling for the severe, restrained classic temper. Appearing as they did against a literary background dominated by Walter Scott and Lord Byron, Landor's *Imaginary Conversations* were bound to appear thin, almost precious. Yet they too were a fulfillment of the humanist concern with that stereoscopic vision which holds both past and present in a single double focus.

Because of its emphasis on formal style, discriminating criticism, and a hierarchy of social values, humanism has always had the dangerous potential for slipping into stuffed-shirtery. Such self- or mutual-admiration often takes the not-very-devious form of proposing, if not one's self, then one's clique (an ill-defined "we") or one's special wisdom as a pattern for society at large. It's hard not to take a jaundiced view of such pretensions, nowadays; but in the past things were not always so. Liberal and fair-minded as he was, Matthew Arnold was able, barely a hundred years ago, to formulate and popularize a phrase based on the humanist value scale that rings particularly hollow without a ripe imperial enterprise to support and justify it. "Learning and propagating the best that has been said and thought in the world" was his program for literary, social, and, by implication, spiritual criticism. From a modern perspective, its most striking aspect is the tacit assumption that there is one "best" for all the various peoples, classes, and cultural groupings of humanity—one ideal of excellence possessed by the arbiters of taste for the ruling class of the ruling nation of the ruling race. Nothing to do then but queue up in the imitation line. The concept is easy to parody, and parody is partly justified because humanism so far as it is committed to the classic ideal really is based on imitation and convention. But parody lags far behind events. Arnold's formula was quickly shattered by events of which its maker, in his worse nightmares, could barely dream. In less than half a century, the decay of empire, the agitation of women, socialists, and other minorities, culminating in the crashing, prolonged savageries of the First World War, left in shambles the assurance underlying a single "classic" standard of taste. Indeed, even before liberal England died its own strange death, and before the strident, barbaric voices of modernism were heard in the land, stirrings had been felt at the very heart of the classic value system, in a revaluation and reinterpretation of the classics themselves. And with the classics being transformed, from the inside out as it were, how could classic standards of taste—and humanism itself, that "reservoir" concept—fail to be drained and filled anew?

The major agent of change was a small group of scholars in the relatively new field of comparative anthropology; they were known, inaccurately but conveniently, as the "Cambridge School," and their analysis of classic texts as familiar as those of Virgil, Sophocles, Ovid, and Homer revealed them to be full of survivals from primitive and frequently animistic rites. Behind their ideal images, the lofty Olympians were found to conceal survivals from the days of fertility rituals, magic spells, fetishism, superstition, and human sacrifice. Under the painstaking analyses of Sir James Frazer, Miss Jane Harrison, Gilbert Murray, F. M. Cornford, and some irregular volunteers from the ranks of the Jungian psychologists, the classic ideal revealed an inner character far different from its traditional "correct" exterior.[3] The meaning of convention and imitation might seem to have changed completely when the conventional thing to imitate became the fracturing of convention; yet the new format of nonconformity, shocking at first to people who had grown up amid the more placatory forms of nineteenth-century idealism, soon established itself as a convention of its own. What the Cambridge anthropologists had done for the Olympic deities, *Ulysses* did for the Dickensian novel, and *The Waste Land* for the Tennysonian poem—taking Dickens and Tennyson simply as emblems of a certain attitude toward literary surfaces. For some, no doubt, the old humanism seemed to have been betrayed by the very texts on which it had relied for most of Western history. Perhaps, on the other hand, the change was simply a matter of new meanings being generated out of the classic texts, as previously new social meanings had been infused into them. In any event, one of the consequences was the swift erosion of a long-established, long-unquestioned structure of literary judgments—one based ultimately on humanist and classical precedents. Milton's reputation was subject to sometimes strident challenge, Dostoevsky replaced Turgenev among the great Russian novelists, metaphysical poets were reanimated as romantic reputations collapsed, words like "irony" and "ambiguity" took on a new and previously unrecognized resonance. Not all these changes were directly connected with the altered image of the classic world and classic values,

---

3. Cracking surfaces and probing underneath them was a characteristic activity of the early twentieth century. In painting, the illusions of three-dimensional representation were shattered by Cubist angularities; attempts at verisimilitude in dramatic staging were supplanted by schematic or symbolic sets; the social pretences of eminent Victorians were gleefully lacerated; melody gave way in music to systematic dissonance; the curtain of a Newtonian universe dissolved into dynamic, abstract patterns of space and energy; the social codes of accommodation and deference gave way to brutal frankness and sometimes exultant violence. The list could be expanded manyfold. In all these changes the influence of Freud and Marx is more easily suggested than demonstrated—which is not to say it wasn't important.

but they are evidence of a sweeping change in the temper of humanism from a vision of gentle uniformities to one of harsh contrasts. (The difference can be capsulized by contrasting Robert Bridges' early poems on classical themes, such as "Demeter" and "Prometheus," with Pound's "Homage to Sextus Propertius"—or the paintings of Frederick Lord Leighton with "Three Dancers" [1925] by Picasso.) It is surely suggestive, if not demonstrably significant, that the first stirrings of this mighty change made themselves felt within the apparently somnolent field of classical studies, the seedbed of *humanitas*.

Amid this sweeping transvaluation of values, which began about 1890, erupted into international prominence in 1910, and continued for some two or three decades after that, a widespread impression grew up that cultural values were disappearing altogether; and in reaction to this threatened chaos, a movement arose, centered in American academic circles though not entirely confined to them, under the significant name of the New Humanism. Like many other American windstorms, the New Humanism was intense but very temporary. It differed from the old humanism mainly in its corrective and polemical stance. Sixteenth-century humanists had brought light and liberty from a tradition-ridden, caste-dominated tyranny; twentieth-century humanists found society, already too liberated, suffering from a pandemonium of chaotic and destructive feelings. Without actually saying so, they coopted for much of their emotional drive widespread horror at the collapse of civilized values evident in the First World War. Two overlapping groups in particular had reason to feel guilty over the disaster of Europe: the socialists, who in the hour of crisis had abandoned their international principles and supported, on both sides, the imperialist war; and the intellectuals, who under pressure of war hysteria, had abandoned their responsibility to think and criticize. What M. Julien Benda denounced as "the treason of the clerks" was very much in the post-war atmosphere; it provided substance to refill once again the often-drained, often-refilled word "humanism."[4] In the climate of rather sour anti-romanticism characteristic of the 'twenties, astringent correctives actually seemed to have a chance; and Professor Irving Babbitt, a co-founder of the New Humanism, applied his styptic pen to the root of the problem with his attack on the sentimental primitivism first popularized by Jean-Jacques Rousseau, starting back in 1750. From Rousseau's cult of the liberated emotions, disparagement of the arts and sciences, and enthusiasm for "nature," it was not difficult to trace the growth of that all-indulgent irrationalism, the horrible consequences of which were to be seen in the world around us.

But though diagnosis was relatively easy, finding something to do about

---

4. Many of its critics saw the New Humanism as an offshoot of old-fashioned American puritanism; it also had affinities with the "Action Française" movement of Charles Maurras, an incipient fascist organization. From Thomas More to Ezra Pound, authoritarianism has had a consistent appeal for intellectuals impatient with the common political process—their imagination transports them more easily to the position of dominance than to that of subjection.

an evil (permissive and therefore agreeable) which had sunk so deeply and widely into the body of contemporary civilization was a good deal harder. After two hundred years and more, romanticism continues to exfoliate and renew itself—often taking, as has been provokingly remarked, the form of anti-romanticism. (Admiration for the middle ages as an era of "unified sensibility" is the most popular of the anti-romantic romanticisms, but there are dozens of others.) What sort of humanism can be invoked to bring under control a climate of feeling, a definition of self, that was itself rooted in humanism? The New Humanists had to import so many elements of thought and feeling that were antithetical to humanism in its traditional senses, that their critics had a field day. There was also the hard problem of deciding how much of contemporary culture was so contaminated by romanticism, so corrupt, that it had better be thrown away. One might have thought writers like Eliot, Pound, and Joyce likely to appeal to the New Humanists; but no, they too had been contaminated by the omnipresent romanticism, an unconcern for form, a vulgar and sensational subject matter. Thus, after discarding the hard-surface modernists and rejecting the soft-surface romantics, the New Humanism was left with almost no *locus standi*. Just then the great depression came along, putting a whole new set of urgent problems on the international agenda, and the entire furore over humanism vanished like a puff of smoke. It had tried to accommodate too many incompatible and transitory attitudes, and had aimed at too radical a social as well as an intellectual reform. It collapsed, not from shock, but from inherent instability. But the aptitude of humanism to accept, if only for a moment, even elements contrary to its own original nature had been curiously demonstrated.

Nowadays, humanism is heard of mainly in two contexts, apart from the routine, self-perpetuating business of "humanities" courses in colleges and universities. On a fairly primitive level, it is invoked in protests by fundamentalist television preachers as a catchall appendage to the main object of their attack, the "secularism" which is itself a code word for mechanical materialism. What is implied is an unholy alliance between the practical materialism of the marketplace and the agnosticism or silent indifference to religious values of the academy. The not-very-covert aim of those who denounce "secular humanism" is to introduce religious teachings (tacitly understood to be Christian fundamentalist teachings) into the system of elementary education. Humanism comes into the terminology partly because the word is vague, partly because it is understood to imply, through commitment to reason, that much of the world, its working, and its history can be understood without the hypothesis of God. (The formula, it will be noted, says "much" of the world, not "all"; and by the "hypothesis of God" it means direct divine intervention in natural phenomena, not the unquestionable fact that men have believed in God and been strongly influenced by their beliefs.)

But of course if one brings the matter down to specifics, there is no reason why the teaching of algebra, the anatomy of the frog, or the principles of electricity should involve a discussion of the deity. Where such a discussion is appropriate, as in teaching the poetry of Milton, the settlement of New England, or the thinking of Tolstoi, it comes up spontaneously and relevantly. It doesn't of course take the form of indoctrination, which is what the fundamentalist preachers want; but opportunities for indoctrination are plentiful outside the classroom. And if there is such a thing as negative indoctrination, its aim is to leave the student unprejudiced—in religion as in politics—until he is mature enough to find his own way through a large and extremely complicated field.

More adult and more interesting critics of humanism are the critical deconstructionists who over the last couple of decades have steadily attacked humanist assumptions from within what seemed to be the last citadel of a forlorn cause, the field of *belles lettres*. Quite explicit in their opposition to humanism, the deconstructionists base their critiques partly on a social but mainly on a linguistic analysis. The importance that humanists attach to man and distinctively human concerns has been invalidated, they suppose, by the accumulating crises of our time, to which the poor featherless biped is obviously unequal. It is a set of profound crises to which Nietzsche began calling attention more than a century ago, and which has been rendered more urgent, not only by world events and the explosive expansion of scientific technology, but by the pervasive influence of existentialist philosophy. Declaring themselves not only free from, but compelled to escape, the cagework categories of previous thinkers (including, as particular friends of convention, the humanists), the existentialists undertook to recover their free individual essence through an act of commitment to the entire self. To the extent possible, they tried to cut off history and live in the new.

This glorification of unconditioned and arbitrary choice led into a different and later argument, to dissolve the bonds of linguistic communication altogether. For if language is a network to control, direct, and repress thoughts quite as much as to express them, critical analysis of language is a necessary preliminary to freeing the potentially self-creative self from the prison-cell of nothingness. Thus, more gradually than suddenly, a denial that any interpretation of a text was privileged from criticism led to a broader assertion that no text under any circumstances could convey an unequivocal meaning. This conclusion, literally accepted, would wipe out all humanist discourse, along with a great deal more; among other consequences, it opened the way for free creative misinterpretation as an ultimate mode of discourse. And since one man's misinterpretation (authenticated by an authenticity of which he is the only judge) is as good as any other man's or child's, it converted texts automatically into pretexts for word play—self-creation or self-indulgence, whichever. So here once again humanism, with its pathetic effort at communication between human beings, was triumphantly slain—its best if not its only weapon, language, shown to be useless for those ends to which humanists would turn it.

It's not clear that getting rid of the unchallengeable "privileged inter-pretation" of a text wasn't and isn't a pretty good thing. No interpretation deserves the easy application of excluding qualifiers like "privileged" and "authoritative." In everyday conversation interpretations make their slow way by a process of probing and self-correction with which everyone is familiar: "Did you mean . . . ?" "No, what I meant was. . . ." "But then how do you account for . . . ?" and so forth and so on. Implicit in all such questioning is an attitude of antagonism and challenge. When such a conversation concerns a silent third party, that is, a text, the two interlocutors speak for different parts of the author's mind, each aiming to show that his theme has greater valency than the other. A good deal of waste motion enters into the process; sometimes convincing resolu-tions can't be found, now and then they can. By a slow process of grop-ing and probing, disturbed by continual distractions and irrelevancies, backtrackings and revaluations, we sometimes edge a little closer to someone else's thinking. And though "very close indeed" still falls short of utter comprehension, one interpretation can sometimes establish itself as superior to another—not absolutely or irrevocably superior, but pro-visionally superior, till countered by a stronger force or exposed under a different light.

People who argue that this is impossible, that a text can never have a single determinate meaning, even a provisional one, come very close to the sterile paradox of the Cretan liar. (The Cretan liar says that all Cre-tans are liars. If he is telling the truth, then his statement is a lie because he is an exception. If he is lying, it must be because some Cretans tell the truth.) If their argument convinces, then it's an exception to the rule it propounds; if it doesn't, then a distinction can be made between inter-pretations, and, if it can be made, the better one is for the moment definitive. (All truth, human or divine, is provisional in the sense that a blinding universal revelation may at any moment obliterate everything we think we know; but that doesn't keep us from getting out of bed in the morning.) And here humanism, so often laid to rest, raises its head once more from the grave and encourages us to make variant interpre-tations of texts, to compare them, to discard the worse and improve the better, to integrate them with each other and with some other things we know—to join, in a word, in conversation about them. Indeed, absolute scepticism about the possibility of a single textual interpretation—like utter ignorance of the world around us—may open our blinkered eyes to things previously overlooked. But it also clutters the experience of a text with an infinitude of useless and distracting anti-structures. The innocent eye passes over everything and discriminates nothing. Under-standing is a process of shuffling particulars by a process of trial and error that is potentially infinite; to shorten it, we make and criticize hypotheses. Nothing could be more old-fashioned than the procedure, whether one wants to call it dialogic or dialectic; but it resembles also a program that revolutionaries have advocated under the formula "three steps forward, two steps back." He who proposes to command language can hardly be too cautious.

Commanding language or being commanded by it, the question comes curiously close to the old conflict between Erasmus and Luther over the freedom or enslavement of the will. Humanists have a natural bias toward asserting the freedom of the human mind to impose meaning on language, to extract meaning from it, and to make those meanings more or less correspond. No part of the process is perfect. Language is the creation, not of philosophers and linguists, but of those myriad jostling forces we can call, in a single term, the marketplace. Still, the more we are aware of its given oddities, the better we can make it obey our desires. There is an African dialect, I recall, in which the word for head, soccerball, orange, and coconut is all one and the same. Most inconvenient, one would think. Yet it's not to be doubted that the natives find ways to use the word in most of the practical affairs of life without fear of misunderstanding. Our own modern English is riddled with similar oddities and anomalies; like every other language in the world, it offers to the artist in words no gleaming panoply of sterile scalpels, but only bent and rusty edges, blunt with long use and encrusted with extraneous connotations. Still, it's the work of an artist in words to use gross materials and clumsy tools to make something precise and delicate. In the history of the culture, it has consistently been accepted as a challenge.

Though never unconditioned by our social and linguistic existence, no one need be buried underneath it unless he chooses to be. One can recognize a number of possible reasons for such choice, of which a good many boil down to the rune of Friedrich Engels: *Freedom is the recognition of necessity.* An obvious point of prudence in recognizing necessity is to distinguish carefully—far more carefully than a man like Engels was equipped to do—a genuine, diamond-hard necessity from a merely paste or plastic one. A strong contemporary argument for maintaining command of our language—imperfect as our minds are, imperfect as language is—must be the very shabby record of technology in trying to substitute electronically for the working of the human brain. Indeed, within the strict parameters of their original programming, when given problems of a particular order (if this, then what?) machines can muster up a lot of alternatives very fast. For purposes of counting, keeping records, displaying a range of information, they are admirable, if not flawless. (If given seven slightly differing forms of a name, even though all are listed at the same address, the machine will be incapable of surmising, as any sensible person would do, that they are all the same person.) Getting misinformation or obsolete information out of an electronic memory is another matter; it is dangerously difficult, in fact. And when the machine is asked to simulate the processes of human judgment—to recognize the duplicities of irony or the reverberations of a remote biblical parallel, for example—I do not believe we have begun to realize the frightful difficulties and dangers that lie ahead.

Thus it's to be expected the future of humanism will be largely determined by the predetermined role of the human mind as the maker and controller of its own technology. One early task will be to keep the concept of "intelligence" from degenerating into the two dismaying uses of the word now current in the phrases "artificial intelligence" and "the intelligence community." It's to be hoped that we've got rid (so far as one can ever exterminate from the human ego) the snob aspects of humanism. The problems confronting humane discourse and those committed to using it are as serious as they ever were, or more so; the word "conversation," with its overtone of light chitchat, may seem a trifling device for confronting major issues of vital interest, amounting to nothing less than survival. Yet, in the context of nuclear disarmament, for example, what means is there, other than exchange of views, for narrowing differences and managing crises? The difficulties are innumerable, but the alternatives are inconceivable. Humanists by themselves cannot solve problems of this order, but to the extent they are ever solved, it's predictable that humanist attitudes will be recognized as a component of the solution. That alone would fill some cups to overflowing.

Starting in high places, the stream of humanist thought has been diverted to serve many men's extraneous purposes; at times it has seemed to stagnate or disappear altogether (but it was just taking a new form or flowing for the moment inside other currents). Nowadays it continues to take new forms in response to new circumstances. For that reason alone, it's worth going back to the source or near it—to the work of Erasmus—in order to savor its fresh and scarcely diminished vitality.

Erasmus: A Chronology†

1466   Born, perhaps at Gouda, perhaps at Rotterdam, the illegitimate son of Roger Gerard, a cleric, and a widow named Margaret.

1475 84   With his older brother Peter (also illegitimate) at a school in Deventer run by the Brothers of the Common Life.

1484   Father dies; guardians send him to a school at 's-Hertogenbosch.

1492   After service in an Augustinian monastery, and prolonged resistance to the final step of ordination, is made a priest.

1495–96   Attends, but with many interruptions because of ill health, the University of Paris, i.e., the Sorbonne; writes a manual of correspondence and the first *Colloquies*, as means of teaching conversational Latin.

1499–1500   At the invitation of a titled pupil, William Blount baron Mountjoy, visits England.

1500   Publishes the first brief collection of *Adages* assembled from classical authors.

1500–1504   Wanders from university to university, teaching mostly private pupils, working on his Greek, and studying texts of the church fathers.

1504   Publishes at Antwerp the *Handbook of the Christian Soldier*, a tract urging return to sincere, simple Christianity.

1505   Having discovered the manuscript of Lorenzo Valla's annotations on the New Testament, publishes it. (Valla had died in 1457.)

1505–6   Second trip to England, again at the invitation of Mountjoy.

1506–8   Visits Italy, takes a doctorate at Turin, and prints with Aldus Manutius a much enlarged version of the *Adages*.

†This outline has neglected perforce the great mass of Erasmus's "minor" writings, which constitute most of the eleven folio volumes of LeClerc's 1703 edition; it has passed over the correspondence, which by itself fills the twelve volumes of Allen's 1906–58 edition. (Someone has estimated that Erasmus occasionally wrote as many as forty letters in a day.) The quarrels of Erasmus with his contemporaries constitute another enormous subject, which had to be overlooked here. Erasmus was always under attack from one quarter or another, and he was too touchy to let anyone else have the last word. On the positive side, he was often flooded with presents from admiring and grateful readers, humble as well as distinguished, from every corner of Europe. Restless as quicksilver, he was also tenacious of mind, and utterly honest intellectually. Europe would not know for many generations how much she owed to him.

1508   Returns to England, and while staying with Thomas More writes the *Praise of Folly*; teaches Greek at Cambridge and works on the letters of Jerome, the writings of Seneca, and the New Testament translation.

1513   *Julius Exclusus* published, though without Erasmus's name to it.

1514   Moves to Basle and establishes connection with printing house of John Froben.

1516   Publishes the New Testament edition with a dedication to Pope Leo X. Publishes also the Saint Jerome (in four volumes), the first in a series that grew to include Cyprian (1520), Arnobius (1522), Hilarius (1523), Irenaeus (1526), Ambrose (1527), Augustine (1528), Chrysostom (1530), Basil (1532), and Origen (1536). Though much of the copying and correcting was done by assistants, Erasmus devoted long hours and incredible energy to collecting manuscripts, supervising texts, and solving problems of disputed readings.

1521   Rejecting a multiplicity of generous offers from all over Europe, settles in Basle.

1522   The second augmented edition of the *Colloquies*; a third will follow in 1526.

1524   After much persuasion, and going against the grain of his temper, writes a book *On Free Will* against the teaching of Luther; *On the Enslaved Will* is Luther's bitter reply. About the same time, Erasmus draws up a short account of his own life.

1527   Froben dies, and some months later the reform party triumphs in Basle; both events make life in the Swiss city unpleasant for Erasmus.

1529   Moves to Freiburg in Breisgau, where he is made welcome by the local prince, and where he is still safe under the protection of the Emperor. Remains at Freiburg for six years, pursuing his scholarly work in semi-retirement.

1535   Returns to Basle to work on his commentary on Ecclesiastes, as well as on many other chores. The city is calmer now, and he feels easy there. From Pope Paul III come intimations that he might receive a cardinal's hat, and income sufficient for a prince of the church. He declines, and writes at Basle one of his last works, *On the Purity of the Church*.

1536   Aged seventy, more or less, Erasmus dies on July 11. Much of his estate is left to a friend, Boniface Amerbach, for distribution to promising young scholars and to provide dowries for penniless girls. He dies without priest or confessor, and leaves no money to have masses said for his soul.

Selected Bibliography

Bainton, Roland H. *Erasmus of Christendom*. New York, 1969.
Gilmore, Myron P. *The World of Humanism*. London, 1952.
Harbison, E. H. *The Christian Scholar in the Age of the Reformation*. New York, 1956.
Kaiser, Walter. *Praisers of Folly*. London, 1964.
Markish, Shimon. *Erasmus and the Jews*. Tr. Anthony Olcott. Chicago, 1986.
Phillips, M. M., *Erasmus and the Northern Renaissance*. New York, 1949.
Post, R. R. *The Modern Devotion*. Leyden, 1968.
Rummel, Erika. *Erasmus as a Translator of the Classics*. Toronto, 1985.
Screech, M. A. *Ecstasy and* The Praise of Folly. London, 1980.
Smith, P. S. *Erasmus: A Study of His Life, Ideals, and Place in History*. New York, 1923 and 1962.
Swain, Barbara. *Fools and Folly during the Middle Ages and the Renaissance*. New York, 1932.
Thompson, Craig R. *The Colloquies of Erasmus*. Chicago, 1965.
Williams, Kathleen, ed. *Twentieth-Century Interpretations of* The Praise of Folly. Englewood Cliffs, N.J., 1969.

Starting in 1969 a freshly edited *Opera Omnia* of Erasmus has been appearing in Amsterdam. The second edition of *The Praise of Folly* (Basle, 1515) contained copious annotations by an admirer of Erasmus, Gerardus Listrius. Erasmus was not satisfied with them and refused to let Listrius annotate any of his other writings; but the annotations, frequently reprinted, are often useful. LeClerc's 1703 edition includes not only Lister's annotations but a set of amusing drawings by Hans Holbein the Younger, illustrating the various types of folly discussed in the text. They were drawn in the margins of a copy of the 1515 edition shortly after that date, but not reproduced until 1676.

NORTON CRITICAL EDITIONS

DOUGLASS *Narrative of the Life of Frederick Douglass, an American Slave, Written by Himself* edited by William L. Andrews and William S. McFeely

DREISER *Sister Carrie* edited by Donald Pizer Second Edition

Eight Modern Plays edited by Anthony Caputi

ELIOT *Middlemarch* edited by Bert G. Hornback

ELIOT *The Mill on the Floss* edited by Carol T. Christ

ERASMUS *The Praise of Folly and Other Writings* translated and edited by Robert M. Adams

FAULKNER *The Sound and the Fury* edited by David Minter Second Edition

FIELDING *Joseph Andrews with Shamela and Related Writings* edited by Homer Goldberg

FIELDING *Tom Jones* edited by Sheridan Baker Second Edition

FLAUBERT *Madame Bovary* edited with a substantially new translation by Paul de Man

FORD *The Good Soldier* edited by Martin Stannard

FORSTER *Howards End* edited by Paul B. Armstrong

FRANKLIN *Benjamin Franklin's Autobiography* edited by J. A. Leo Lemay and P. M. Zall

FULLER *Woman in the Nineteenth Century* edited by Larry J. Reynolds

GOETHE *Faust* translated by Walter Arndt, edited by Cyrus Hamlin

GOGOL *Dead Souls* (the Reavey translation) edited by George Gibian

HARDY *Far from the Madding Crowd* edited by Robert C. Schweik

HARDY *Jude the Obscure* edited by Norman Page

HARDY *The Mayor of Casterbridge* edited by James K. Robinson

HARDY *The Return of the Native* edited by James Gindin

HARDY *Tess of the d'Urbervilles* edited by Scott Elledge Third Edition

HAWTHORNE *The Blithedale Romance* edited by Seymour Gross and Rosalie Murphy

HAWTHORNE *The House of the Seven Gables* edited by Seymour Gross

HAWTHORNE *Nathaniel Hawthorne's Tales* edited by James McIntosh

HAWTHORNE *The Scarlet Letter* edited by Seymour Gross, Sculley Bradley, Richmond Croom Beatty, and E. Hudson Long Third Edition

HERBERT *George Herbert and the Seventeenth-Century Religious Poets* selected and edited by Mario A. DiCesare

HERODOTUS *The Histories* translated and selected by Walter E. Blanco, edited by Walter E. Blanco and Jennifer Roberts

HOBBES *Leviathan* edited by Richard E. Flathman and David Johnston

HOMER *The Odyssey* translated and edited by Albert Cook Second Edition

HOWELLS *The Rise of Silas Lapham* edited by Don L. Cook

IBSEN *The Wild Duck* translated and edited by Dounia B. Christiani

JAMES *The Ambassadors* edited by S. P. Rosenbaum Second Edition

JAMES *The American* edited by James W. Tuttleton

JAMES *The Portrait of a Lady* edited by Robert D. Bamberg Second Edition

JAMES *Tales of Henry James* edited by Christof Wegelin

JAMES *The Turn of the Screw* edited by Robert Kimbrough

JAMES *The Wings of the Dove* edited by J. Donald Crowley and Richard A. Hocks

JONSON *Ben Jonson and the Cavalier Poets* selected and edited by Hugh Maclean

JONSON *Ben Jonson's Plays and Masques* selected and edited by Robert M. Adams

KAFKA *The Metamorphosis* translated and edited by Stanley Corngold

LAFAYETTE *The Princess of Clèves* edited and with a revised translation by John D. Lyons

MACHIAVELLI *The Prince* translated and edited by Robert M. Adams Second Edition

MALTHUS *An Essay on the Principle of Population* edited by Philip Appleman

MANN *Death in Venice* translated and edited by Clayton Koelb

MARX *The Communist Manifesto* edited by Frederic L. Bender

MELVILLE *The Confidence-Man* edited by Hershel Parker

MELVILLE *Moby-Dick* edited by Harrison Hayford and Hershel Parker

MEREDITH *The Egoist* edited by Robert M. Adams

Middle English Lyrics selected and edited by Maxwell S. Luria and Richard L. Hoffman

Middle English Romances selected and edited by Stephen H. A. Shepherd

MILL *Mill* selected and edited by Alan Ryan

MILL *On Liberty* edited by David Spitz
MILTON *Paradise Lost* edited by Scott Elledge Second Edition
Modern Irish Drama edited by John P. Harrington
MORE *Utopia* translated and edited by Robert M. Adams Second Edition
NEWMAN *Apologia Pro Vita Sua* edited by David J. DeLaura
NEWTON *Newton* edited by I. Bernard Cohen and Richard S. Westfall
NORRIS *McTeague* edited by Donald Pizer Second Edition
Restoration and Eighteenth-Century Comedy edited by Scott McMillin Second Edition
RICH *Adrienne Rich's Poetry and Prose* edited by Barbara Charlesworth Gelpi and
Albert Gelpi
ROUSSEAU *Rousseau's Political Writings* edited by Alan Ritter and translated by
Julia Conaway Bondanella
ST. PAUL *The Writings of St. Paul* edited by Wayne A. Meeks
SHAKESPEARE *Hamlet* edited by Cyrus Hoy Second Edition
SHAKESPEARE *Henry IV, Part I* edited by James L. Sanderson Second Edition
SHAW *Bernard Shaw's Plays* edited by Warren Sylvester Smith
SHELLEY *Frankenstein* edited by Paul Hunter
SHELLEY *Shelley's Poetry and Prose* selected and edited by Donald H. Reiman and
Sharon B. Powers
SMOLLETT *Humphry Clinker* edited by James L. Thorson
SOPHOCLES *Oedipus Tyrannus* translated and edited by Luci Berkowitz and
Theodore F. Brunner
SPENSER *Edmund Spenser's Poetry* selected and edited by Hugh Maclean and
Anne Lake Prescott Third Edition
STENDHAL *Red and Black* translated and edited by Robert M. Adams
STERNE *Tristram Shandy* edited by Howard Anderson
STOKER *Dracula* edited by Nina Auerbach and David Skal
STOWE *Uncle Tom's Cabin* edited by Elizabeth Ammons
SWIFT *Gulliver's Travels* edited by Robert A. Greenberg Second Edition
SWIFT *The Writings of Jonathan Swift* edited by Robert A. Greenberg and William B. Piper
TENNYSON *In Memoriam* edited by Robert H. Ross
TENNYSON *Tennyson's Poetry* selected and edited by Robert W. Hill, Jr.
THACKERAY *Vanity Fair* edited by Peter Shillingsburg
THOREAU *Walden and Resistance to Civil Government* edited by William Rossi
Second Edition
THUCYDIDES *The Peloponnesian War* translated by Walter Blanco edited by Walter Blanco
and Jennifer Tolbert Roberts
TOLSTOY *Anna Karenina* edited and with a revised translation by George Gibian
Second Edition
TOLSTOY *Tolstoy's Short Fiction* edited and with revised translations by Michael R. Katz
TOLSTOY *War and Peace* (the Maude translation) edited by George Gibian Second Edition
TOOMER *Cane* edited by Darwin T. Turner
TURGENEV *Fathers and Sons* translated and edited by Michael R. Katz
VOLTAIRE *Candide* translated and edited by Robert M. Adams Second Edition
WASHINGTON *Up from Slavery* edited by William L. Andrews
WATSON *The Double Helix: A Personal Account of the Discovery of the Structure of DNA*
edited by Gunther S. Stent
WHARTON *Ethan Frome* edited by Kristin O. Lauer and Cynthia Griffin Wolff
WHARTON *The House of Mirth* edited by Elizabeth Ammons
WHITMAN *Leaves of Grass* edited by Sculley Bradley and Harold W. Blodgett
WILDE *The Picture of Dorian Gray* edited by Donald L. Lawler
WOLLSTONECRAFT *A Vindication of the Rights of Woman* edited by Carol H. Poston
Second Edition
WORDSWORTH *The Prelude: 1799, 1805, 1850* edited by Jonathan Wordsworth,
M. H. Abrams, and Stephen Gill